The China–US Trade War and South Asian Economies

The USA and China, the world's largest economic powers, have been engaged in trade war since January 2018. The impact of this trade war is felt not only by the USA and China but also by other economies which are linked with them. This book provides insights into damage caused by this trade war. It also explores some opportunities arising for a few economies from this trade war.

The first section of the book looks at the impact of the trade war on the global economy. It goes deeper to examine the trade war impact on the South Asian region. It is well-known that any imposition of new tariffs or an increase in existing tariffs would make imports more costly and render the exported goods less competitive. Yet, the book posits that the trade war has provided a window of opportunity to other countries not caught in it. Countries like Bangladesh, India, and Sri Lanka have actually reaped benefits from the widening trade dispute between the world's two biggest economies.

This book will be a useful reference to help policymakers to undertake informed decisions and initiate programmes to minimise the trade war impact.

Rahul Nath Choudhury is a trade economist currently based in New Delhi. Earlier he was associated with the National University of Singapore, as a Visiting Research Fellow. His primary research interests include foreign direct investments, international trade, e-commerce, digital trade, and technology policy. Rahul has been a freelance consultant for organisations like ADB, IFC, AEPC, CII, and a few MNCs as well. Rahul has diverse experience of working in both the public and the private sector in academia and the industry. He has contributed to numerous book chapters and academic journals and commentaries.

Routledge Frontiers of Political Economy

Power and Influence of Economists
Contributions to the Social Studies of Economics
Edited by Jens Maesse, Stephan Pühringer, Thierry Rossier and Pierre Benz

Rent-Seeking and Human Capital
How the Hunt for Rents is Changing Our Economic and Political Landscape
Kurt von Seekamm Jr.

The Political Economy of State Intervention
Conserving Capital over the West's Long Depression
Gavin Poynter

Intangible Flow Theory in Economics
Human Participation in Economic and Societal Production
Tiago Cardao-Pito

Foundations of Post-Schumpeterian Economics
Innovation, Institutions and Finance
Beniamino Callegari

Distributive Justice and Taxation
Jørgen Pedersen

The China–US Trade War and South Asian Economies
Edited by Rahul Nath Choudhury

Politics and the Theory of Spontaneous Order
Piotr Szafruga

For more information about this series, please visit: www.routledge.com/books/series/SE0345

The China–US Trade War and South Asian Economies

Edited by
Rahul Nath Choudhury

Routledge
Taylor & Francis Group
LONDON AND NEW YORK

First published 2021
by Routledge
2 Park Square, Milton Park, Abingdon, Oxon OX14 4RN

and by Routledge
52 Vanderbilt Avenue, New York, NY 10017

Routledge is an imprint of the Taylor & Francis Group, an informa business

British Library Cataloguing-in-Publication Data
A catalogue record for this book is available from the British Library

Library of Congress Cataloging-in-Publication Data
A catalog record has been requested for this book

ISBN: 978-0-367-51381-8 (hbk)
ISBN: 978-1-003-05361-3 (ebk)

Typeset in Galliard
by Newgen Publishing UK

Contents

List of figures vii
List of tables x
List of contributors xii
Foreword xvii
Acknowledgements xix
List of abbreviations xxi

Introduction 1
RAHUL NATH CHOUDHURY

PART I
US–China trade war: assessing the global economic implications 9

1 Global economic impact of US–China trade tensions 11
BADRI NARAYANAN GOPALAKRISHNAN AND LEKSHMI NAIR

2 US–China trade war: a new order or a secular decline of economic outlook? 19
SAURABH BANDYOPADHYAY

3 US–China trade war: an analysis of trade relations 32
SUNANDAN GHOSH

4 Impact of US–China trade war on the global economy, free trade, and WTO 68
PRAVIN JADHAV AND RAHUL NATH CHOUDHURY

PART II
What is there for the regional economy? 79

5 US–China trade war: an opportunity for India 81
DINKAR NAYAK AND AKASH KUMRA

6 Implications of US–China trade war for India 97
SAON RAY AND SMITA MIGLANI

7 US–China trade war: the potential impact on Bangladesh 124
ANU ANWAR

8 US–China trade war: trade and investment implications for Sri Lanka 137
JANAKA WIJAYASIRI AND ANUSHKA WIJESINHA

PART III
Decoding the benefit of preferential trading partners 173

9 US–China trade war and the RCEP negotiations: an analysis 175
SANCHITA CHATTERJEE

10 US–China trade war: impact on potential trade of their FTA partners 201
SWATI SINGH AND SACHIN SISODIYA

PART IV
Is it for the establishment of technological supremacy? 215

11 The US–China technology conflict: the causes 217
DANIEL GROS

12 Technology rents and the new Great Game 229
DAN CIURIAK AND MARIA PTASHKINA

Conclusion 249
RAHUL NATH CHOUDHURY

Index 253

Figures

1.1	Changes to GDP if threatened tariffs are implemented	16
1.2a, b	Sectors most affected by implemented and threatened tariffs	17
2.1	US–China trade: a precipitous declining trend	21
2.2	Quarterly growth (%) of the US manufacturing employment (Q4: 2018–19 to Q4: 2019–20)	21
2.3	Quarterly export share of India with the US and China: 2016–17 to 2019–20	23
2.4	Quarterly import share of India with the US and China: 2016–17 to 2019–20	23
2.5	Quarterly export share of Rest of Asia (net of China) and the Rest of World (minus US China and the Rest of Asia) with India: 2016–17 to 2019–20	24
3.1	US trade balances with China, South and South-East Asia (1993–2018)	35
3.2	China's trade balances with USA, South and South-East Asia (1993–2018)	36
3.3	US imports from China and South and South-East Asian countries (1993–2018)	37
3.4	Country's share in South Asian exports to the US	37
3.5	US imports from India, Malaysia, Thailand, and Vietnam (1993–2018)	38
3.6	USA's imports from China – CUSUM and CUSUM of squares	39
3.7	USA's imports from South Asia and India	40
3.8	USA's imports from select South-East Asian countries – CUSUM tests	42
3.9	US exports to China, Thailand, South Asia, and South-East Asia 1993–2018	44
3.10	Share of South Asia's import from the US (1993–2018)	45
3.11	US exports to Hong Kong and select South and South-East Asian countries	45
3.12	USA's exports to China – CUSUM and CUSUM of squares	46
3.13	USA's exports to South Asia – CUSUM and CUSUM of squares	47

3.14	USA's exports to South-East Asia – CUSUM and CUSUM of squares	48
3.15	USA's exports to Hong Kong and select South and South-East Asian countries	49
3.16	Chinese imports from USA, South and South-East Asian countries (1993–2018)	51
3.17	Country's share in South Asian exports to China	52
3.18	Major South-East Asian exporters to China (1993–2018)	53
3.19	China's imports from USA and South-East Asia – CUSUM tests	54
3.20	China's imports from select South East Asian countries – CUSUM tests	55
3.21	China's exports to USA, Hong Kong, South and South-East Asia (1993–2018)	57
3.22	China's exports to South Asia (1993–2018)	58
3.23	China's exports to major South and South-East Asian countries (1993–2018)	59
3.24	China's exports to USA – CUSUM and CUSUM of squares	60
3.25	China's imports from India and South Asia – CUSUM	61
3.26	China's imports from SE Asia – CUSUM and CUSUM of squares	62
3.27	China's exports to Hong Kong and major South-East Asian countries – CUSUM tests	65
5.1	India's exports to USA and China (% share, 2009–2019)	87
5.2	India's imports from USA and China (% share, 2009–2019)	88
6.1	Share of classes of goods in total Indian exports (2008–2017) (%)	104
6.2	Share of classes of goods in total Indian imports (2008–2017) (%)	104
6.3	India's imports and exports of intermediate goods	105
6.4	India's imports and exports of final goods	107
6.5	India's imports and exports of capital goods	109
6.A1	Gross exports of India, sectors, 2007 (goods)	114
6.A2	Gross exports of India, 2017 (goods)	115
6.A3	Gross imports of India, 2007 (goods)	115
6.A4	Gross imports of India, 2017 (goods)	115
6.A5	Gross exports of India, countries, 2007	116
6.A6	Gross exports of India, countries, 2017	117
6.A7	Gross imports of India, countries, 2007	118
6.A8	Gross imports of India, countries, 2017	119
8.A1	Direction of trade – Sri Lanka, 2017	163
8.A2	Product composition of trade – Sri Lanka, 2017	164
8.A3	Composition of Sri Lanka's exports to the US, 2017	164
8.A4	Composition of Chinese exports to the US, 2017	165
8.A5	Changes in Sri Lanka's exports to the US of tariff-affected products on List 1 (One year)	165

8.A1 US tariffs imposed on China 151
8.A2 Foreign direct investments (FDI) in Sri Lanka, top ten country wise breakdown, US$ mn 152
8.A3 Foreign direct investment of BOI enterprises by sector, US$ mn 153
8.A4 Products in which Sri Lanka has a comparative advantage over China in US (HS6 level) 154
8.A5 Trade diversion to Sri Lanka due to US imposing additional tariffs on China (US$1000) 161
8.A6 Tariff lists under Section 301 and relevance to Sri Lanka's exports, 2019 162
8.A7 Where might production capacity in China move to? 163
9.1 Summary of substantive provisions of the US–China Agreement 177
9.2 Timeline and summary of provisions of the RCEP 179
9.3 Engagement of RCEP-I and the US with each other through FTAs 182
9.4 Comparing RCEP provisions with ASEAN+1 FTAs 183
9.5 Comparing RCEP provisions with non-ASEAN RCEP-I FTAs 185
9.6 Origin country of value-added as % of gross exports to the country in 2015 190
9.7 Origin of value-added from a country as % of gross imports from the country in 2015 191
9.8 Data on the top five patent offices 192
9.9 Global Innovation Index 2019 rankings 193
9.10 IPR provisions in different FTAs of RCEP-I and US–China Agreement 194
10.1 USA's and China's trade with the world (2013–18) in US$ billion 203
10.2 USA imports from China in three selected sectors (2013–18) in US$ billion 204
10.3 China imports from USA in three selected sectors (2013–18) in US$ billion 205
10.4 United States' exports, imports, and trade balance of automobile sector to FTA partners (2013–18) in US$ billion 207
10.5 United States' exports, imports and trade balance of electrical machinery sector to FTA partners (2013–18) in US$ billion 208
10.6 United States' exports, imports, and trade balance of iron and steel sector to FTA partners (2013–18) in US$ billion 209
10.7 China's exports, imports, and trade balance of automobile sector to FTA partners (2013–18) in US$ billion 211
10.8 China's exports, imports, and trade balance of electrical machinery sector to FTA partners (2013–18) in US$ billion 212
10.9 China's exports, imports, and trade balance of iron and steel sector to FTA partners (2013–18) in US$ billion 213
11.1 Trade and current account imbalances 219

Contributors

Anu Anwar

Anu Anwar is a Fellow at the Asia Center, Faculty of Arts and Sciences, Harvard University. He is also an Associate in Research at Fairbank Center for Chinese Studies, and a Visiting Fellow at the University of Tokyo's Institute for Advanced Studies on Asia. Before joining Harvard, Mr. Anwar worked as a Research Fellow at the US Department of Defense's Institute – Daniel K. Inouye Asia-Pacific Center for Security Studies. He was also an Affiliate Scholar at East-West Center, Hawaii. His area of research covers Chinese foreign policy, US–China strategic competition, and Asian geopolitics.

Saurabh Bandyopadhyay

Dr Saurabh Bandyopadhyay is presently working as a Fellow at the National Council of Applied Economic Research (NCAER), New Delhi. He obtained his Ph.D. in Economics from Jawaharlal Nehru University (JNU). He has a prominent carrier spanning over 20 years in the field of evidence-based research in development economics. He has published many papers, articles, and reports traversing a wide spectrum of issues linked to agriculture, trade, industry, banking, infrastructure, and institutions. His special interests include study on trade policy and its impact on industrial productivity at the sectoral level for India and the world.

Sanchita Chatterjee

Sanchita Chatterjee is a trade policy and development specialist, currently based in Thailand. She has also served managerial and research roles in her work with several organisations, including an intergovernmental organisation, an Indian conglomerate, diplomatic missions, and educational institutions. Ms. Chatterjee was also engaged in several collaborative projects with the Commonwealth Secretariat, London, the United Nations Conference on Trade & Development (UNCTAD), and the UK Department for International Development. She has extensive experience in strategy development for various sectors, including development professionals, trade negotiators, and non-government organisations.

Rahul Nath Choudhury (Editor)

Dr Rahul Nath Choudhury is a trade economist currently based in New Delhi. Earlier he was associated with the National University of Singapore, as a Visiting Research Fellow. His primary research interest includes foreign direct investments, international trade, e-commerce, digital economy, and technology policy.

Dan Ciuriak

Dan Ciuriak is Director at Ciuriak Consulting Inc. (Ottawa), Senior Fellow with the Centre for International Governance Innovation (Waterloo), Fellow-in-Residence with the C. D. Howe Institute (Toronto), Distinguished Fellow with the Asia Pacific Foundation of Canada (Vancouver), and Associate with BKP Development Research & Consulting GmbH (Munich). His areas of interest include international trade and finance, innovation and industrial policy, and economic development. Previously, he was Deputy Chief Economist at the Department of Foreign Affairs and International Trade (DFAIT, now Global Affairs Canada) with responsibility for economic analysis in support of trade negotiations and trade litigation, and served as contributing editor of DFAIT's Trade Policy Research series (2001–2007 and 2010 editions).

Sunandan Ghosh

Dr Ghosh is an Assistant Professor at the Department of Humanities and Social Sciences, Indian Institute of Technology, Kharagpur. Before Joining IIT- KGP, Dr Ghosh was teaching at the Centre for Development Studies, Thiruvananthapuram, Kerala, India. He obtained his Ph.D. in Economics from the Jadavpur University, Kolkata, India. His research interests include international economics, economics of regional integration, and applied game theory. He is credited with numerous national and international publications.

Badri Narayanan Gopalakrishnan

Badri Narayanan Gopalakrishnan is a senior economist with the University of Washington Seattle, non resident senior fellow with ECIPE Brussels and CSEP New Delhi. He has 16 years' experience and expertise in economic modelling/data science in many areas such as international trade, energy, agriculture, industry and health, the economic impact of new technologies. He has been a consultant with World Bank, FAO, UN, European Commission, the governments of India and the USA, WHO, PWC, McKinsey, KPMG, several academic and research institutions all over the world.

Daniel Gros

Daniel Gros has been Director at CEPS since 2000. Among other current activities, he serves as an adviser to the European Parliament and is a member of the Advisory Scientific Committee of the European Systemic Risk Board (ESRB) and the Euro 50 Group of eminent economists. Previously he has held positions at the IMF and the European Commission and served as an adviser to several governments, including those of the UK and the US at the highest level. He is an Editor of *Economie Internationale* and *International Finance*. Daniel holds a Ph.D. in Economics from the University of Chicago and has written several books and numerous articles in scientific journals. His main areas of expertise are the European Monetary Union, macroeconomic policy, public finance, banking, and financial markets as well as trade policy.

Pravin Jadhav

Dr Pravin Jadhav obtained his Ph.D. from the Indian Institute of Foreign Trade, New Delhi. At present, he is Assistant Professor in the Institute of Infrastructure, Technology, Research, and Management Ahmedabad, Gujarat, India. He has extensive research experience in both industry and academia. He has published and presented a good number of research papers in the field of business economics, international business, foreign direct investment (FDI), and international trade. He has served as a researcher in planning commission's working Sub Group on Technology Intensity in India's Manufacturing Exports, for 12th Five Year Plan (2012–2017).

Akash Kumra

Dr Kumra is an Associate Professor at the Department of Economics, Faculty of Arts, the Maharaja Sayajiroa University of Baroda, Gujarat, India. He holds a Ph.D. from the same university. His research interests include international trade, foreign direct investment, and trade integration.

Smita Miglani

Ms Smita Miglani is associated with ICRIER, New Delhi. She has over ten years of experience in policy-oriented research, working with key ministries of the central government in India. She has also been involved in important studies undertaken for international organisations such as the British High Commission, European Commission, the American Chamber of Commerce, and domestic industry associations. Smita holds an M.Phil. (Economics) degree from Jawaharlal Nehru University, Delhi and is experienced in the use of econometrics and advanced economic analysis. Her broad areas of research interest are international trade and investment, industry analysis, finance, and infrastructure development. She has published work in reports, working papers, books, and refereed journals. Her research work has contributed to India's negotiating strategies for bilateral trade and investment agreements and policy reforms decisions at the domestic level.

Lekshmi Nair

Dr Lekshmi Nair is Assistant vice president at Citi, Texas, USA. She holds a Ph.D. in economics with over a decade of experience in research and consultancy. Her skills include frontier research problems in investment, portfolio analysis, and asset pricing. Before this, she was a data science consultant at Toyota Motors North America and was a research fellow at Infinite Sum Modeling Inc.

Dinkar Nayak

Dr Dinkar Nayak is an RBI chair professor at the RBI Endowment Unit, Faculty of Commerce, the Maharaja Sayajirao University of Baroda, Vadodara, Gujarat, India. Dr Nayak has teaching experience of more than 30 years, and his research interests include international trade, regional economics, and financial economics. A long list of research articles published by various national and international journals and as book chapters go to his credit. He is also an author of several books. He is a key resource person for many Indian universities.

Maria Ptashkina

Maria Ptashkina is an economics Ph.D. candidate at University Pompeu Fabra, Barcelona, Spain. Her main research interests include macroeconomics, international economics, and trade policy. She is a former fellow at the International Center for Trade and Sustainable Development and former delegate from the Russian Federation to the Asia-Pacific Economic Cooperation Forum. Maria is a former member of intergovernmental policy research groups on issues related to international trade and investment (the Group of Twenty, BRICS (Brazil, Russia, India, China, and South Africa) and the One Belt, One Road initiative.

Saon Ray

Saon Ray is Senior Fellow, Indian Council for Research on International Economic Relations (ICRIER), New Delhi. An economist specialising in industry and international trade issues, her areas of interest include global value chains, technological upgrading of Indian industries, free trade agreements and trade creation effects, technology transfer, foreign direct investment, efficiency and productivity of firms, energy, and climate change-related issues. She has published widely on these issues in books and journal articles. Her latest book, *Global Value Chains and the Missing Links: Cases from Indian Industry* was published by Taylor & Francis in 2018. Her Ph.D. in Economics from Jawaharlal Nehru University examined the role of intellectual property rights in transferring technology to developing countries.

Swati Shukla Singh

Dr Swati Shukla Singh is currently employed at the Centre for Research on International Trade, IIFT, Department of Commerce, Ministry of Commerce and Industry, Government of India Assistant Professor. Swati did her Ph.D. on 'Regional trading arrangements – A study of ASEAN and India', from Symbiosis International University. She has research and teaching experience of more than ten years and has published her works widely in several peer-reviewed journals. her field of research interest includes regional economic integration, intra-industry trade, non-tariff measures, and trade facilitation: global value chains, international trade operations, and logistics.

Sachin Sisodiya

He has obtained MA Economics from Delhi School of Economics. He is an awardee of the prestigious Krishna Raj Travel Fellowship for conducting an independent research project. Previously, he worked with the Centre for Regional Trade (CRT), a think tank of the Ministry of Commerce and Industries, Government of India.

Janaka Wijayasiri

Dr Janaka Wijayasiri is a Research Fellow and Head of International Economic Policy Research at the Institute of Policy Studies of Sri Lanka, an economic think tank. His areas of research interest have been primarily related to trade issues at the bilateral, regional, and multilateral levels. These include issues of policy significance to Sri Lanka in areas covering bilateral and regional preferential trade initiatives, multilateral negotiations under the World Trade Organisation (WTO), and issues related to the export industries in Sri Lanka. He has been part of Sri Lanka's official delegation representing the academia at regional forums such as Bay of Bengal Initiative for Multi-Sectoral Technical and Economic Cooperation (BIMSTEC) and the Indian Ocean Rim Association for Regional Cooperation (IOR-ARC). He has also participated in various bilateral trade negotiations with other countries, including China with which Sri Lanka is currently seeking agreements.

Anushka Wijesinha

Anushka Studied in Economics, University of Leeds Business School and University College London; alumnus, Harvard Kennedy School Executive Education. Formerly: Chief Economist, Ceylon Chamber of Commerce; Head of Industry and Competitiveness, Institute of Policy Studies; Special Adviser on Industrial Policy and Youth Entrepreneurship to the UK Minister of Industry and Commerce; consultant to multilateral like World Bank and ADB. Currently, Adviser to the UK Minister of Development Strategies and International Trade and leads the work on the innovation and entrepreneurship strategy.

Foreword

In the last three decades, the idea of globalisation and free trade has gained prominence in the world. Despite some drawbacks, globalisation and the free trade regime have been beneficial for economic development, poverty reduction, and enhanced integration among countries. However, in recent years a trade war has started between the USA and its leading trading partners, in particular between the USA and China. The question is whether with this trade war globalisation has started walking in the opposite direction. No one had indeed expected such an extraordinary event until quite recently. With the establishment of the GATT in 1948, and finally, with the advent of the WTO in 1995, trade agreements and rules prevented such a trade war. It is also worth mentioning that WTO rules have compelled even powerful countries to respect international agreements on trade rules. Needless to say that a trade war does not align with global development initiatives such as the 2030 Agenda of Sustainable Development Goals (SDGs).

What will be the impact of the trade war on the global economy? The effect will depend on how long this war endures and how intense it gets. It can have short-term, medium-term, and even long-term impacts. In the short term, the USA's introduction of substantial additional tariffs on imports from its leading trading partners, especially China, and vice versa will have a large effect on the volume of bilateral trade between them. That could lead to an increase in exports to the US from certain countries, as the US would then search for cheaper imports from those countries. If the trade war persists in the medium to long term and intensifies with more countries participating, there is a high risk of a global economic recession. This trade war will hurt consumer demand in the world's major economies, especially in North America and the European Union.

Studies found that all of the world's major economies would suffer as a result of this trade war. Countries in South Asia, too, will see a decline in exports. As more countries participate in the trade war, the scale of the damage will rise. As the duration and scope of the trade war are not yet visible, it creates a lot of uncertainty around the global trade system. An uncertain trade regime is not conducive to developing countries and to South Asian countries in particular, which over the years have become increasingly trade dependent. When the global trade regime is guided by some rules and principles, like those established through the GATT and WTO processes over the last six decades, these rules and principles benefit all countries in general, and developing countries in particular. Nonetheless, the effectiveness of those rules and principles is at stake with the worsening of the ongoing trade war. The WTO's position, in particular, is greatly weakened, which could lead to an uncertain global trade regime. If the USA pulls out of the WTO, the global trade regime will probably face the biggest challenge since the Second World War.

Many other parallel scenarios may arise during the trade war. For example, given that Chinese exports to the USA market face escalating tariffs, Chinese firms may consider relocating their factories to other countries to avoid the additional tariff burden. This scenario might contribute to soaring foreign direct investment (FDI) in other developing countries by China. South Asian and Southeast Asian countries will be the primary beneficiaries of this FDI. Nevertheless, much of the success in attracting this Chinese FDIs will depend on the status of the domestic business environment, infrastructural constraints, and political economy issues such as the quality of institutions in the host country and geopolitical relations the host country has with China and other neighbouring countries.

The world cannot afford a full-scale trade war. Re-emphasising the importance of a rules-based global trade regime is now essential. Given the evolving threats and uncertainties in the global trade regime, the need to re-energise the WTO is being increasingly felt.

In this context, the publication of this book *The China–US Trade War and South Asian Economies* is timely. This book very rightly analyses the major issues related to trade war and their implications for the South Asian countries. I wish the book a wider circulation among the academics and policymakers in South Asia.

Professor Selim Raihan
Department of Economics, University of Dhaka, Bangladesh
Executive Director, South Asian Network on Economic Modeling (SANEM)

Acknowledgements

The journey of editing this volume started in mid-2019 when I was working with the National University of Singapore. Since then, this journey has been exciting, enlightening, and wonderful in several expects. As this is my first edited book, I was delighted when I got the final approval from the publisher. However, this exercise could not have completed without help and support of many friends, colleagues, and well-wishers. Now that I have accomplished my goal, I would like to take this opportunity to convey my sincere gratitude to all those who have contributed in numerous ways and helping me to give a final shape to my book.

First and foremost, I would like to express my sincere gratitude to the Institute of South Asian Studies (ISAS) at the National University of Singapore for giving me all the necessary support and resources to work on this project.

I would like to express my deep gratitude to Dr Amitendu Palit, Senior Research Fellow; and Research Lead at ISAS, for his encouragement and intellectual support in conceptualising the volume. Dr Palit generously guided me in developing my book proposal and taking it forward.

Dr Amit Ranjan, of ISAS, was another big support. I am indebted to his encouragement, support, and help in resolving infinite small issues that emerged during the edit. He was a constant motivation and a guide during the journey.

My good friend Dr Chulanee Attanayake, at ISAS, has always been a rescuer and great resource person for me. I am thankful to her for generous help and support.

I have rarely done any academic exercise where my friend Rijesh from ISID New Delhi, has not had some input. I always find him during any academic crisis. This volume was no different. I am grateful to him. Thanks Anna!

I am also thankful to all the authors for their contributions to this edited volume. I am grateful to them for having faith in me to undertake this task. I have learned a lot of things working with all the scholars who are authorities in their respective areas. Thank you all!

I am sincerely thankful to Ms Lam Yongling, editor at Taylor & Francis, Singapore, and the anonymous reviewers for keeping their faith on me since the proposal stage and pushing me to complete the task.

Last but not least, I would also like to thank the Almighty or the unknown super power for His blessings not only to undertake this journey, but also to complete it.

Rahul Nath Choudhury

Abbreviations

ADB	Asian Development Bank
AI	Artificial Intelligence
AIIB	Asian Infrastructure Investment Bank
ASEAN	Association of Southeast Asian Nations
BAT	Baidu, Alibaba, and Tencent
BEC	Broad Economic Categories
BOI	Board of Investment
BRI	Belt and Road Initiative
CAGR	Compound Annual Growth Rate
CEPS	Centre for European Policy Studies
CFIUS	Committee on Foreign Investment in the United States
CGE	Computable General Equilibrium
CIIE	China International Import Expo
CIS	Commonwealth of Independent States
CEPII	Centre d'Études Prospectives et d'Informations Internationales
CPTPP	Comprehensive and Progressive Agreement for Trans-Pacific Partnership
CU	Custom Union
CUSUM	Cumulative Sum
DARPA	Defence Advanced Research Projects Agency
DDE	Data-Driven Economy
DEPA	Digital Economic Partnership Agreement
ECRA	Export Control Reform Act
EIU	Economic Intelligence Unit
EPZ	Export Processing Zone
EU	European Union
FAANG	Facebook, Apple, Amazon, Netflix, and Google
FAO	Food and Agriculture Organisation
FIA	Foreign Investment Agency
FIE	Foreign Invested Enterprises
FIRRMA	Foreign Investment Risk Review Modernisation Act
FTA	Free Trade Agreements
FTAAP	Free Trade Agreement of the Asia-Pacific

GATS	General Agreement on Trade in Services
GATT	The General Agreement on Tariffs and Trade
GCC	Gulf Cooperation Council
GDP	Gross Domestic Product
GDPR	General Data Protection Regulation
GSP	Generalised System of Preferences
GTAP	Global Trade Analysis Project
GVC	Global Value Chain
HS	Harmonised System
HSBC	Hong Kong and Shanghai Banking Corporation
IBM	International Business Machine
IP	Intellectual Property
IPR	Intellectual Property Rights
IT	Information Technology
ITC	International Trade Centre
JAAF	Sri Lanka's Joint Apparel Association
KORUS	Korea-US Free Trade Agreement
LDCs	Least Developed Economies
MERCOSUR	Southern Common Market (MERCOSUR for its Spanish initials)
MFN	Most Favoured Nation
ML	Machine Learning
MNC	Multinational Corporations
MRIOT	Multiregional Input-Output Table
NAFTA	North American Free Trade Agreement
NDB	New Development Bank
NSC	National Security Council
NSIB	National Security Innovation Base
NSS	National Security Strategy
ODA	Official Development Assistance
OECD	Organisation for Economic Cooperation and Development
PNTR	Permanent Normal Trade Relations
PPE	Personal Protective Equipment
R&D	Research and Development
RCA	Revealed Comparative Advantage
RMG	Ready-Made Garments
RVC	Regional Value Chain
SITC	Standard International Trade Classification
SLAEA	Sri Lanka Apparel Exporters Association
SOE	State-Owned Enterprises
STEM	Science, Technology, Engineering, and Mathematics
TIFA	Trade and Investment Framework Agreement
TPP	Trans-Pacific Partnership
TRIMS	Agreement on Trade-Related Investment Measures
TRIPS	Trade-Related Intellectual Property Rights

UAE	United Arab Emirates
UK	United Kingdom
UNCTAD	United Nations Conference on Trade and Development
UNFPA	United Nations Population Fund
USA	United States of America
USITC	United States International Trade Commission
USMCA	United States–Mexico–Canada Agreement
USTR	United States Trade Representative
VAT	Value Added Tax
WITS	World Integrated Trade Solution
WTO	World Trade Organisation

Introduction

Rahul Nath Choudhury

1 The background

Since the mid-2018s, the US and China, the world's two largest economies, have been locked in a trade confrontation that has resulted in several rounds of retaliatory tariffs. The popular media, as well as the academic jargon, refer to it as the Trade War. The trouble started on 8 March 2018, when the US President Donald Trump announced a proclamation imposing additional tariffs on steel (25%) and aluminium (10%), based on Section 232 national security justifications. Throughout 2018, the US administration implemented a series of trade measures to curtail imports, first targeting specific products (solar panels and washing machines) from all countries, and then explicitly targeting imports from China. One of the prime reasons why the US decided to impose tariffs on Chinese goods was to reduce the US trade deficit with China. It was one of the main points of US President Donald Trump's new trade policy, which he announced in March 2018. By June 2020, the US tariffs applied exclusively to Chinese goods were US$550 billion, while Chinese tariffs solely applied to US goods were US$185 billion. On several occasions, the USA has accused China of misusing trade policies and adopting malpractices while flooding the US market with cheap products and thereby hurting the US business interests.

2 The timeline of the trade war so far

To take corrective measures and to reduce a mounting trade deficit against China, in March 2018, the US raised tariffs on Chinese imports for US$50 billion worth of goods – first applying 25% tariffs on US$34 billion and then an additional US$16 billion.[1] In May 2018, the US increased tariffs further from 10% to 25%. China responded by raising the tariffs on a subset of products that were already subject to tariffs. China imposed 15–25% tariff on 128 product categories, including wine, steel, pork, fruit, wine, and recycled aluminium, on US imports. China took advantage of antidumping duties described under WTO rules and placed 178.6% anti-dumping duties on sorghum imported from the US. In August 2018, China filed complaints against the US in WTO. In the same month, the US imposed 25% tariff on 279 goods worth $16 billion: electric scooters, semiconductors, plastics, motorbikes, chemicals, plastics. In response, China also levied 25% tariff on 333 goods worth $16 billion, on products like medical equipment, coal, fuel, buses and copper scrap. In September 2018, China terminated trade talks with the US and released an official statement on opposition against the US.

In September 2018 US imposed a 10% tariff on $200 billion worth of imports from China, which will be subject to further increase up to 25%. At the same time, China imposed 5% and 10% tariffs on $60 billion worth of US imports. In December 2018, the G-20 summit was held in Buenos Aires, where the US and China both decided that they would not increase tariffs for ninety days, and the US declared that they would delay the new list of goods on which they would levy higher tariffs. In response to the same, China increased the import of agriculture and energy products and lowered tariffs on cars and auto products from 25% to 15%.

In September 2019, the US imposed 15% tariffs on a large subset of the remaining US$300 billion worth of imports from China not yet subject to tariffs (see Chapter 8 for details) while China retaliated on some US products (a subset of US$75 billion). Chinese tariffs of 15% on approximately US$160 billion worth of goods were scheduled to take effect from December 2019, but these were postponed indefinitely. Instead, the two economies entered into a trade agreement formally known as the 'Economic and Trade Agreement between the United States of America and China' (enforced from February 2020) and the US announced a decrease in the 15% tariff on $120 billion worth of goods from China to 7.5%. China took corresponding measures and cancelled its schedule tariff increase. Under this agreement, China has agreed to purchase about $200 billion worth of US goods and services in 2020 and 2021 ($78 billion in additional manufactured goods, $54 billion in additional energy purchases; $32 billion in additional farm products purchases; and $38 billion worth of services), on top of the amounts imported in 2017. This import commitment does not cover all US exports to China but applies to select agriculture, energy, manufacturing, and services imports. In 2017, the US exported about $170 billion to China, so the deal would require China to more than double its purchases of US products in the next two years (USTR, 2020). The US agreed to remove Chinese tech giant Huawei from its entity list (list of entities prohibited from trading with the US). Huawei is a downstream user of almost 17% of the semiconductors and microchips exported from the US. The trade agreement (Chapter on Intellectual Property Protection) mandates China to respect trade secrets, confidential business information, patents, and prohibits piracy and counterfeiting on e-commerce platforms (USTR, 2020).

3 Assessing the impact of the conflict

It is evident that the ongoing trade war has impacted the economies significantly. The subject has also got serious attention from scholars and practitioners of international trade and political economy analysts all over the world. All theories of trade advocated free trade among the economies to gain both absolute and relative advantage (Smith, 1776; Ricardo, 1817). Trade theories confirm some of the possible consequences of a trade war or tariff war (Freund et al., 2020). The trade war may also bring the deadweight loss or the loss of economic efficiency that occurs when equilibrium for goods and services consumption is not achieved due to the imposition of tax. It reduces welfare for both consumers and producers and, in turn, the social or economic surplus.

A large body of literature has tried to assess the impact of the tariffs raised by China and the USA. The empirical studies conducted in this area suggest US exports have been steadily decreasing since the beginning of the trade war. Paterson (2020) finds total US export to China declined by 22%. Similar results were also reported by Robinson and Thierfelder (2019). The study reveals that both the United States and China lose significantly from the trade war. However, for China, the volume is lesser than for the US. Further, China can successfully divert its exports away from the United States, expanding in other potential markets while increasing total export volume. The United States is less able to divert its exports and change sources of imports, many of which are part of supply chains that are difficult to relocate. Another study conducted by UNCTAD in 2019 shows that US tariffs caused a 25% export loss, inflicting a US$35 billion blow to Chinese exports in the US market for tariffed goods in the first half of 2019.

The effect of the trade war is not limited to the US and China. It has impacted many other trading nations that are closely integrated with these two economies through the global production network and supply chain. This impact is felt across the region. The global economy is in a gloomy state. IMF predicts global economic growth to fall to a 3% in 2020, the slowest pace since the 2008 financial crisis. The World Trade Organisation forecasted a cut from 3% to 2.7% during the same time period. Similarly, all other major agencies have slashed their predictions for global economic growth.[2] The Baltic Dry Index, a composite index calculated by the London stock exchange, which tracks bulk commodities shipping and serves as a credible indicator of future trade activity, has fallen sharply since August 2018. And the common reason cited by all of them is the ongoing trade war. In this context, this book evaluates the impact of the trade war on the global economy with a special focus on the South Asian region. The study also examines the role of technology companies in this struggle.

Although there is a growing body of literature in the form of commentary and other short articles, no systematic and comparative empirical analyses have been carried out so far, to the best of our knowledge, covering so many aspects of the trade war, published in a book or any other comprehensive form. It is important to systematically estimate the possible impact of the war on the global economy. This is the lacuna the current book will try to fulfil. An overall estimation is required if we are to understand the damage caused by the war. This will help policymakers to take informed decisions and initiate programmes to minimise its impact.

Along with the global economic impact, scholars have also looked for the effects of the trade war in the case of individual countries. The analysts found mixed results. Some countries have emerged as beneficiaries of the trade war, while some have been negatively impacted. Furthermore, some sectors in an economy have been benefited and others have been hurt. Calculating data from the International Monetary Fund, Huang and Smith (2020) reported that US imports from the European Union and Mexico increased by $31.2 billion and $11.6 billion in 2018. Among the ASEAN group, countries like Vietnam, Taiwan, and Thailand have emerged as big beneficiaries (Witada and Lobo, 2019; Huang and Smith 2020).

Among the South Asian countries, India and Bangladesh have been the biggest beneficiaries of the war. The positive impact of the war has also been experienced in the island nation, Sri Lanka. A significant increase in garment exports from Bangladesh to the US has been noticed. Sri Lanka has been able to divert some of its exports from China to other economies. India has been able to attract many investors who were looking to relocate their manufacturing base from China. The current study has analysed the impact of the trade war in these three countries. A country-wise analysis of the impact of the trade war is presented in Part II of the book. Two chapters explore the issue in the Indian context while a chapter each for Sri Lanka and Bangladesh investigate the topic.

The trade war has also impacted various ongoing regional trading agreements. The Regional Comprehensive Economic Partnership (RCEP) is expected to be impacted significantly. RCEP, considered to be one of the biggest FTA in the world, represents 50% of the global population and 32% of worldwide GDP. Trade among the current members accounts for 28% of world trade. Importantly China is a member of this agreement and also shares a close economic tie with most of the negotiating members who are affected by the trade war. Many experts believe that, due to the trade war, China wanted to accelerate the negotiation process of the RCEP, primarily to gain broader market access to the ASEAN region and India. This would potentially help China to reduce the losses made in the US market. The complexities of the RCEP with regards to the trade war are scrutinised in Part III of the book. The same section also reveals the potential trade diversion from the USA and China to their FTA partners. It has been argued that due to tariff escalation both China and the USA will try to penetrate further in those markets where they have bigger market access and the advantage of preferential tariff rates.

Besides some of these economies, the trade conflict has also impacted several sectors. The technology or ICT industry is one of them. Eventually, it became clear that the technology sector was going to play a major role in the tussle between these two economic rivals. US President Trump signed an executive order to restrict Chinese telecommunications companies Huawei and ZTE Corporation from selling their equipment and services in the United States (Demetri, Stacey, & Liu, 2019). In addition, the Department of Commerce put Huawei on an export control blacklist that forbids the US individuals and businesses from selling goods to these companies without a license from the US government. Such a license can be denied 'if the sale or transfer would harm US national security or foreign policy interests'.[3]

Apparently, the USA's dominance in the technology industry was challenged by China. As new technologies seek to realign the global balance of power in favour of those countries which possess them, the two countries are in a race to gain an edge. China has swiftly moved up in the global technological value chain, creating world-class industries in the ICT sector, from 5G and artificial intelligence to biotechnology and quantum computing. China considers technology as the medium through which it can establish its supremacy in the global digital market. Pursuant to this, its 'Digital Silk Road' policy announced in a white paper published in 2015 attempts to expand its digital dominance to 65 countries. Chinese policy apparently urges home-grown companies like Baidu, Alibaba, and Tencent (BAT) to push their products and services to international markets. Several experts are of the opinion that China could replace the United States as the world leader in technological development. This issue is explored in Part IV of this book.

4 Prelude to the chapters

The book starts by discussing how the trade war between the two largest economies is affecting other countries. The chapter is articulated jointly by Dr Badri Gopalakrishnan and Dr Nair. The authors hypothesised that the net economic effect of the trade war might be positive or negative, depending on the combination of adverse global supply shocks and trade diversions. The chapter explores the effects of all policy measures in global trade wars, in a combined way using the GTAP model. Their result confirms the ambiguity: an overall positive effect on countries other than those that have increased tariffs, and a negative effect that is negligible for some and prominent for others. The study forecasts global GDP to fall by 0.16%, or nearly $150 billion. In Asia and the Pacific alone, the decline is 0.12% of GDP, or $43 billion. The United States experiences the largest decline, with an estimated decline of 0.65% of GDP, at more than $120 billion.

Taking the discussion forward in the next chapter, Dr Saurabh Bandyopadhyay analysed the effect of the trade tussle on the emerging economies from Asia. The author suggests the US–China trade war is having a far-reaching impact on the emerging economies, which were theorised to take advantage of the scenario. Instead of any benefit, the escalation of the stringent measures both ways would cause a lasting global recession and new geopolitical confrontation. This chapter evaluates in turn the scenario based on the available trade balance data for India–China trade, India–US trade and India–ROA (Rest of Asia without China), and India–ROW (without ROA, China, and the US). The author suggests that what Asia needs is not new geopolitical splits, but a sustainable, long-term plan for faster economic integration and development, indicated by the overwhelming consensus among Asian countries on working to reach a Free Trade Agreement of the Asia-Pacific (FTAAP) that also includes the US.

In Chapter 3, Dr Sunandan Ghosh tries to understand the impact of the trade war on US–China bilateral trade and their trade with South and South-East Asian economies. He analyses the existence of structural changes in the trading relations. The chapter finds that trade between the USA and South/South-East Asian economies and trade between China and South/South-East Asian economies show structural changes that predate the trade war. These results are not unexpected as we still don't have data points after the onset of the trade war. However, the analysis doesn't find any significant impact of the trade war on US–China bilateral trade or trade with South and South-East Asian nations. In the last chapter in the section Dr Pravin and I examine the various reasons for the trade war between the US and China and illustrate the impact of recent hostility on bilateral trade between these two countries. Further, Chapter 4 evaluates the effect of the trade war on bilateral trade and the functions and basic principles of the World Trade Organisation (WTO).

Part II inquires about the impact of the trade war on the individual South Asian economies. In Chapter 5, Dr Nayak and Dr Kumra evaluate the revealed comparative advantage (RCA) for India, China, and the USA in the world market. The chapter identifies the pattern of RCA using the Balassa (1965) index of the export data of these three countries. The authors calculated an index at the sector as well as at the product level of the HS classification. Based on the calculated RCA, the authors investigate the possibility of trade diversion benefits to India on account of the USA tariff on Chinese goods. Their findings indicate that the trade diversion effects in favour of India have taken place in chemicals, metal ore, and a few other products. It is also revealed that India has the opportunity to export products like vehicles, fiber optical cables, and soybean to China and commodities like electrical machinery, solar panels, and toys to the USA.

Chapter 6, contributed by Dr Ray and Smita Miglani, ponders a critical area of global supply chain and how it is affected by the trade war with reference to India. Using the BEC classification to characterise India's exports and imports, and particularly the importance of intermediate goods in its trade basket with China and USA, they find India's imports of intermediate goods accounted for 83% of its total merchandise imports in 2017, while imports of final and capital goods made up 6% and 11% respectively in 2017. Also, in 2017, 60% of export value was in exports of intermediate goods. By comparison, the share of final and capital goods reached 33% and 6% respectively in 2017. The authors record India has consistently been a net importer of intermediate goods over the period 2008–17. Further, it is a net exporter of final goods and a net importer of capital goods for the period of 2008–17.

As the trade war now extends beyond the trade and has brought changes in the geopolitical relationship between the United States and China, this has alarmed many countries who have trade stakes with these two nations. The impending effect of the trade war on supply chain dynamics and investment patterns could help Bangladesh to emerge as a potential winner from the conflict. The US and China have been stable trading partners in Bangladesh for decades. Bangladesh could gain benefit from both countries but in different ways. This is elaborated by Anu Anwar in Chapter 7. Anwar warns that Bangladesh needs to adroitly craft its policy to seize new opportunities as they come, and to provide enabling conditions for more foreign direct investment – all by avoiding unintended risks and consequences.

Sri Lanka has long been in the limelight due to its strategic geopolitical location and its close economic ties with China. It is obviously affected by the trade war to a certain extent. Chapter 8 by Janaka Wijayasiri and Anushka Wijesinha investigates the impact of the trade war on Sri Lanka's trade and investment flows and the prospects for the country to gain from the ensuing shifts. The authors argue that for Sri Lanka to reap the benefits of the trade war, it will have to step up trade and investment reforms to boost exports and create a favourable business environment to attract investment. At the same time, a prolonged trade war could dampen world trade and economic growth, reducing any gains.

Part III identifies the relationship between the trade war and the RCEP. Chapter 9, written by Sanchita Chatterjee, investigates the link between two significant issues in the contemporary study of trade economics. What are the implications of the trade war for the RCEP negotiations, particularly through the lens of regional value chains and intellectual property rights in the region? A qualitative analysis of the importance of the trade war compared with other global events and the internal pulls and pushes of the RCEP is presented tactfully by the author. She also analyses the provisions which have been agreed upon so far and possible provisions that might help companies which are either taking advantage of or are adversely affected by the trade war.

Chapter 10, contributed by Swati Singh and Sachin Sisodiya, aims to explore the impact of the US–China trade war on its FTA partners. They investigated whether the trade war has affected the FTA partners of the USA and China positively or adversely. The analysis is done for three important sectors: automobiles, electrical machinery, and iron and steel. These three sectors were among those who faced the higher tariffs at the very beginning of the trade war between the two super economies.

In the final section of the book, we attempt to understand the role of the technological sector in escalating the trade war. The first chapter in Part IV, articulated by Daniel Gros, throws light on how the technological dominance of the USA firms has been challenged by emerging Chinese giants. This chapter investigates how, within a short span of time, Chinese firms have grown so large and disrupted the global technology sector. The author discusses how China discriminates in favour of its domestic firms and against foreign-owned firms. Daniel also features growing concerns about forged technology, violation of patents, and intellectual property rights by Chinese tech giants.

In the final chapter of this book, Dan Ciuriak and Maria Ptashkina argue that only technological developments are sufficiently important to explain the scale, the timing, and the contours of the conflict. The issues run deep and are pervasive, reflecting the transition to a data-driven economy built on the nexus of artificial intelligence, machine learning, and big data. This chapter also analyses how the technology war unfolded, intending to dominate the data-driven economy.

The book ends with an editorial summary and conclusion.

Notes

1 The information used in this section is available at the USTR website. Readers may see www.ustr.gov for detailed information. Further, we have also consulted various online portals of newspapers for gathering the information. The information is updated till the May 2020 since the beginning of the trade war.

2 The predictions were made before the outbreak of the coronavirus (COVID-19). Hence, they do not cover the economic impact of COVID-19.

3 See details at www.commerce.gov/news/press-releases/2019/05/department-commerce-announces-addition-huawei-technologies-co-ltd

References

Demetri, S., Stacy. K, & Liu, B. (2019). Donald Trump issues executive order laying ground for Huawei ban. *Financial Times,* 16 May. Retrieved from www.ft.com/content/c8d6ca6a-76ab-11e9-be7d-6d846537acab

Freund, C., Maliszewska, M., Mattoo, A., & Ruta, M. (2020). When elephants make peace. The impact of the China-U.S. trade agreement on developing countries. *Policy Research Working Paper 9173.* Washington, DC: World Bank.

Huang, Y., & Smith, J. (2020). In U.S.-China trade war, new supply chains rattle markets. Washington, DC: Carnegie Endowment for International Peace. Retrieved from https://carnegieendowment.org/2020/06/24/in-u.s.-china-trade-war-new-supply-chains-rattle-markets-pub-82145

Paterson, S. (2020). Trade war impacts and why a US-China trade deal won't boost the economy. Hinrich Foundation. Retrieved from www.hinrichfoundation.com/research/article/us-china-trade/trade-war-impacts-on-economy/

Ricardo, D. (1817). *Principles of Political Economy and Taxation.* London: G. Bell & sons.

Robinson, S., &Thierfelder, K. (2019). *US-China Trade War: Both Countries Lose, World Markets Adjust, Others Gain.* Policy Brief 19–17. Washington, DC: Peterson Institute for International Economics.

Smith, A. (1776). *An Inquiry into the Nature and Causes of The Wealth of Nations* (book V, chapter II). London: printed for W Strahan and T Cadell in The Strand.

UNCTAD (2019). *Trade and Trade Diversion Effects of United States Tariffs on China.*

Retrieved from https://unctad.org/en/pages/newsdetails.aspx?OriginalVersionID=2226

USTR (2020). *Economic and Trade Agreement between the Government of the United States of America and the Government of the People's Republic of China.* Retrieved from https://ustr.gov/countries-regions/china-mongolia-taiwan/peoples-republic-china/phase-one-trade-agreement/text

Witada, A. & Lobo, Richard. S. (2019). Trade wars: Risks and opportunities for Asia-Pacific economies from US tariffs. *Trade, Investment and Innovation Working Paper* (01). Bangkok: UN ESCAP.

Part I

US–China trade war

Assessing the global economic implications

1 Global economic impact of US–China trade tensions

Badri Narayanan Gopalakrishnan and Lekshmi Nair

1 Introduction

Since early March 2018, the trade war between the USA and China has been through two rounds. In the first round, the US President Trump signed the order levying tariffs on Chinese steel and aluminum imports on 8 March, using Section 232 of a 1962 US law that allows safeguards based on 'national security'. As a countermeasure, on 24 March 2018, the spokesperson of the Ministry of Commerce commented on China's release of a list of discontinuation concessions against the US steel and aluminum imports under section 232. In the second round, on 4 April 2018, United States Trade Representative (USTR) published a proposed list of products in industries such as aerospace, information and communication technology, robotics, and machinery imported from China that could be subject to additional tariffs. As retaliation, China imposed tariffs on products such as soybeans and other agricultural products, automobiles, chemicals, and airplanes originating in the US at the rate of 25%, involving about $50 billion worth of China's imports from the US in 2017. The trade changes between the two biggest economies in the world concern not only these two countries but also countries in other parts of the world. Countries that are interlinked with these large trading nations have significantly been affected. Although there exists a large set of studies in this area, most of these studies are about the economic impact of global trade tensions, and further focus on the impact of these tensions on government tax revenue from various sources, for different countries, while there is a lack of studies that tie these two strands together. In this chapter Section 2 reviews the literature; Section 3 explains the methodology, while Section 4 shows the results and concludes.

2 Literature review

In the literature review of the public finance implications of global trade tensions discussed below, we focus on studies that addressed the government revenue impacts of tariffs in different countries, experiences of other customs unions, and the legal aspects of customs unions.

Kowalski (2005) has addressed the tariff revenue concerns that some developing countries have been expressing in the context of the multilateral trade negotiations under the Doha Development Agenda. In the paper, the author discussed the methodological issues associated with estimating revenue impact and provided the impact estimates for a sample of developing countries. Kowalski found that the differences in impact are linked to cross-country differences in existing tariff regimes as well as the formulas for tariff cuts. Efficient tax replacement policies and past experiences are discussed in this study.

Vaillant and Lalanne (2007), in their study on tariff revenue-sharing rules in the customs unions, have presented two mechanisms that are prevalent in the existing customs unions. One is to share the revenue based on the size of some important measures of the country, like imports, consumption, population, etc., and the other is to source a common fund to carry out financing of common policies.

Vaillant (2008) has studied the possible changes in terms of movement of goods, the customs revenue collection, and sharing mechanisms that should be brought about to enhance the functionality of the customs union, MERCOSUR, which has Argentina, Brazil, Paraguay, Uruguay, and Venezuela as member nations. He has also analysed the implications of the above, given the asymmetries and disparities among the member nations. The study reveals the gradual evolution of the customs union and that, in the initial stages, only goods whose inclusion will have no fiscal effect were chosen. Focused on imparting a fiscal neutrality, the paper reveals three possible alternative routes to allocate the common revenue – an exact fiscal offset in which a charge is made in accordance with destinations of extra-regional imports; distribution in accordance with some general rule that approximates the scale of the countries and/or any other objective; capitalisation of a common fund to finance shared policies and integration institutions.

Cirera, Willenbockel, and Lakshman (2011) have examined the empirical evidence of the impact of reductions in tariffs on employment and fiscal revenue in developing countries, based on the review of quantitative studies that controlled for other factors affecting employment and tax revenue in these countries. Computable General Equilibrium studies are included and compared with the results of the econometric evidence. The results from the synthesis based on the clustering method show that the majority of CGE simulation studies that address the fiscal effects of trade reforms involving tariff reductions report negative total tax revenue impacts or the need for increases in other tax rates to compensate for lost tariff revenue. According to the results, CGE results allow us to look at the isolated impact on tax revenue from reducing tariffs selectively, while econometric evidence is likely to select the impact of simultaneous interventions affecting tax revenue. However, the assumption of a frictionless reallocation of labour and other factors across sectors is an oversimplification not always supported by the econometric evidence, and hence the CGE results need to be interpreted with caution.

Busser (2014), in his study, examines the tax policy of Arab countries, concludes that it is important for governments to build a fiscal space to promote social security. There is a huge diversity in the contribution of tax revenues to the total government revenues, varying from 1% in Kuwait to 89% in Palestine. GCC countries derive a significant share of their income from the export of oil-related products, and tax revenues contribute only a minuscule portion. Gradeva (2014) has studied VAT fraud in intra-EU trade, especially after the introduction of the EU single market in 1993. The single market has abolished all the customs procedures at the borders of member nations, and so VAT cannot be collected at the borders before goods enter the destination country. The study presents possible VAT fraud in the transitional VAT system that is in practice, and such evasions can be in any of the following forms: underreported sales, not registering the firm with the tax authorities, misclassification of products by firms that sell several products, and false claims for credit based on overstated VAT paid on inputs and imported products which are not brought into tax. It also reveals that there is a positive correlation between the level of VAT rate and trade gap, which is calculated as the difference between the value of the goods declared while exporting and the reported import value of the same set of products in the importing country.

ESCWA (2017) in its study on the impacts of the introduction of value-added tax in GCC countries has reported the fiscal implications of VAT. It reveals that, though VAT introduction in GCC has raised several questions on the cost of doing business, the fact that countries with VAT have lower variance in GDP favours the GCC countries, who are struggling with instabilities from fluctuating oil prices. The study reveals that the introduction of VAT will have no significant impact on the economy and that its implications on trade, sectoral production, and growth will depend on the government's approach towards the collected revenue.

According to the estimates of York, Pomerleau, and Bellafiore (2019), the tariffs imposed by the Trump administration on imported solar panels, washing machines, steel, aluminum, and various products imported from China will amount to a total tax increase of $86.13 billion. At the same time, their estimates also show that the total revenue generated by the federal government will be lower than this. The reason is that tariffs function like an excise tax and reduce real income, which in turn offsets some of the tariffs' generated revenue. Consequently, wages are reduced, which leads to less individual income, payroll tax revenue, and lower profits for businesses. This reduces corporate income tax revenues, as well as revenues from pass-through businesses under individual income tax. However, the effects of tariffs on government revenue need to be examined in detail based on economic modelling of such mechanisms.

Ovádek and Willemyns (2019) have examined the critical aspects of the WTO laws of customs union (CU), the issues inherent in the design of CUs around the world, and how they are being solved practically. By analysing the historical, economic, and current international legal scenarios, the study reveals that the elements vary between different CUs. The study points out how Article XXIV of GATT lacks clarity on joint negotiation of PTAs, customs revenue apportionment, and legal arrangements such as trade remedies and rules of origin. This lack of clarity has resulted in ambiguities and hence the diversity that is prevalent among the customs union designs today. Custom unions in existence are far from 'Perfect CUs', and this asynchronisation between the external and internal aspects has led to underperformance. To protect the customs unions from negatively impacting non-members, WTO should enforce Article XXIV more seriously, especially in dispute-settling proceedings.

The preliminary literature review found that, currently, the literature deals with general revenue implications of international trade policies or trade tensions and also with custom administration. Meanwhile, modelling of the economic welfare impacts of custom revenue collection mechanisms has been barely addressed in empirical studies. Therefore, the economic modelling features of the current study, which will add new variables and equations, to understand the allocation of tariff revenues and compensation mechanisms, are new contributions to the literature of customs unions.

3 Methodology

To assess the economic impact of tariffs, we employ the Global Trade Analysis Project (GTAP) CGE model that has been used extensively for the global-scale policy impact analysis since the early 1990s by governments, research institutes, and economists around the world. GTAP combines economic theory and empirical data to account for all trade flow interactions among industries, consumers, and countries globally. The model estimates total economic impacts from a specific set of policy changes. The economic losses or benefits estimated may not happen instantaneously. It may take some time for them to materialise, with the ultimate outcome influenced in practice by other policies and mitigation measures that affected economies may put in place. The model simulates the effects of trade policy changes on the endogenous variables – those whose values are allowed for by the model: prices, production, consumption, imports, exports, investment, and welfare. The baseline year is 2017, and the difference in the values of the endogenous variables between the projected baseline scenario and the simulated scenario represents the effects of the policy changes.

The policy changes are modelled as the following scenario: all tariffs implemented up to date as well as all 'threatened tariffs'. The 'implemented tariffs' include current tariff hikes by the United States and retaliation that has either already occurred or been notified to WTO in 2018. In this scenario, Canada, China, the European Union, India, Indonesia, Japan, Mexico, the Republic of Korea, Turkey, and the United States raise their tariffs as per their official notifications to WTO. The additional tariff rates range from 10% to 140%. The threatened tariffs are those mentioned in the economies' official communiqués, news, etc. but not yet notified to WTO or implemented. These include potential tariffs on cars and car parts (as a consequence of the United States Section 232 Auto Investigation – discussed earlier), as well as further escalating retaliatory tariffs between China and the United States.

4 Results and conclusions

As a result of the implemented tariffs so far, global GDP is estimated to fall by 0.16%, or nearly $150 billion. This is just $10 billion short of the total official development assistance (ODA) given by the developed economies in 2016. In Asia and the Pacific alone, the decline is 0.12% of GDP, or $43 billion. The United States experiences the largest decline, with an estimated decline of 0.65% of GDP, at more than $120 billion. The United States loses the most because it has engaged in trade conflicts not only with China but also with other significant trade partners, most of whom retaliated.

Figure 1.1 shows that global GDP losses reach $214 billion if all the tariff hikes threatened but not yet undertaken in 2018 are indeed implemented. Most of these losses are accounted for by economic losses in China and the United States, while all other economies in the Asia-Pacific region see a rise in GDP, with the exception of Turkey, which records a slight decline. Vietnam, Kyrgyzstan, and Mongolia are all expected to benefit from the trade war to the tune of more than 0.5% of their respective GDPs.

There are wide regional variations in the sector-level impacts of the trade tensions, which are shown in Figure 1.2.

Figure 1.2 shows the top five growing and top five declining sectors in the region, excluding China, when both 'implemented' and 'threatened' tariffs are applied (scenario 2). Figure 1.2 also shows the same for Asia-Pacific least developed economies (LDCs). Construction is expected to be the big winner in LDCs and the Asia-Pacific region, whereas potential motor-vehicle tariffs are expected to affect the automotive and parts sectors the most in the region as a whole. Since LDCs are not large automotive or parts producers, sectors experiencing the most declines there are textiles, wearing apparel, and plant fibres. Although the sectoral declines observed in LDCs are small, it may be noted that the sectors concerned are labour-intensive sectors characterised by a particularly high proportion of female workers.

In terms of tax revenue, we find from our analysis[1] that the increased tariffs do not necessarily get translated into greater revenue, because the fall in imports far outweighs the rise in tariff rates, in both the US and China. However, in many other countries, we observe some increase in tariff revenue, due to greater imports and exports.

Broadly, we may conclude from our analysis that the USA and China are both going to lose economically due to the ongoing trade war, while some other countries in Asia and the Pacific may gain due to the trade diverting away from the two giants to these countries. Revenue implications also may favour these other countries and not the imposers of tariffs. It is in the interest of both these countries to reduce their focus on trade wars, and instead, work on positive ways to reduce dependence on each other, by increasing trade with others through greater trade integration.

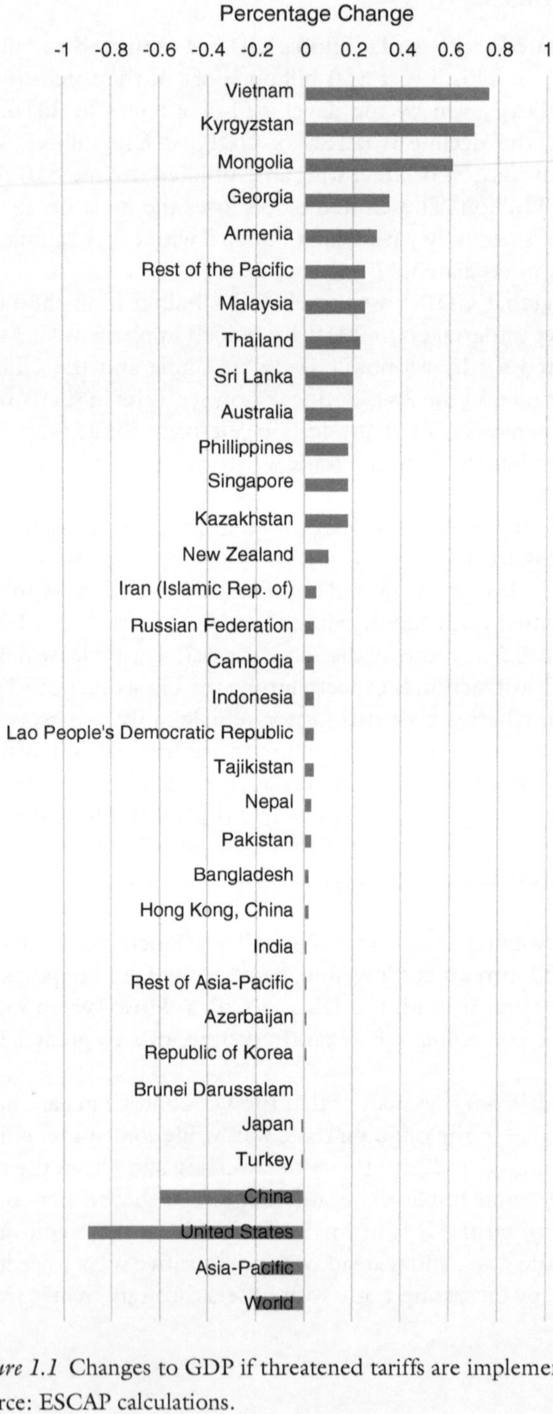

Figure 1.1 Changes to GDP if threatened tariffs are implemented.
Source: ESCAP calculations.

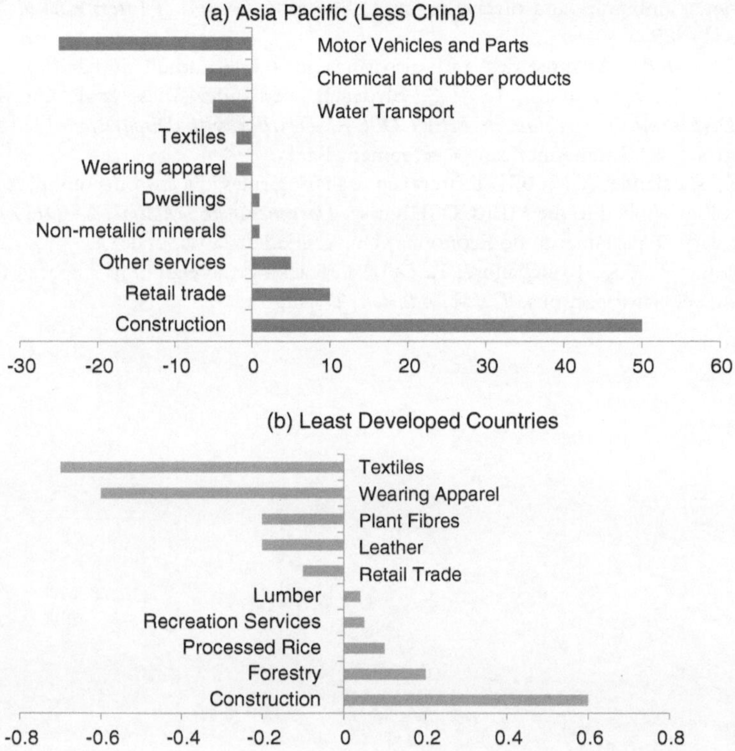

Figure 1.2 Sectors most affected by implemented and threatened tariffs.
Source: UN ESCAP.

Note

1 These detailed results are available on request.

References

Busser, M. (2014). *Tax Policy in Arab Countries.* E/ESCWA/SDD/2014/Technical Paper.3. New York: ESCWA.

Cirera, X., Willenbockel, D., & Lakshman, R. (2011). What is the evidence of the impact of tariff reductions on employment and fiscal revenue in developing countries: A systematic review. *EPPI-Centre Technical Report*, 1907.

ESCWA (2017). *The Impacts of the Introduction of Value Added Tax in Gulf Cooperation Council Countries.* E/ESCWA/EDID/2017/Technical Paper, 3. New York: ESCWA.

Gradeva, K. (2014). VAT fraud in intra-EU trade. Goethe University Frankfurt, 7 August. Retrieved from www.etsg.org/ETSG2014/Papers/378.pdf

Kowalski, P. (2005). *Impact of Changes in Tariffs on Developing Countries' Government Revenue.* OECD Trade Policy Papers, 18. Paris: OECD Publishing.

Ovádek, M., & Willemyns, I. (2019). International law of customs unions: Conceptual variety, legal ambiguity and diverse practice. *European Journal of International Law*, *30*(2), 361–389.

Vaillant, M. (2008). Asymmetries and disparities in the economic integration of a south-south customs union. In J. S. Blyde, E. Fernández-Arias, & P. Giordano (eds), *Deepening Integration in MERCOSUR: Dealing with Disparities*. 115–148. Washington, DC: Inter-American Development Bank.

Vaillant, M., & Lalanne, A. (2007). Tariff revenue sharing rules in a customs union: A new methodology applied to the MERCOSUR case. *Documento de Trabajo/FCS-DE*, 7/07. Montevideo: Departamento de Economía, Universidad de la República.

York, E., Pomerleau, K., & Bellafiore, R. (2019). Tracking the economic impact of US tariffs and retaliatory actions. *Tax Foundation*, 27 August.

2 US–China trade war

A new order or a secular decline of economic outlook?

Saurabh Bandyopadhyay

1 Introduction

At the time of accession to the World Trade Organisation (WTO) in 2001, China's economy had already grown to become second only to the United States (US) in purchasing power parity (Morrison, 2019). Meanwhile, China's global trade influence had also expanded and gradually outshone the US as the major supplier of goods to the countries of Europe, Asia, Africa, and South America. As long as it functioned as a cheap factory, China's growth was welcomed by the US, and its appearance as a new market for consumer goods was readily foreseen. However, from the mid-2010s, triggered by China's military expansion into the South China Sea and its sprawling Belt and Road Initiative (BRI) as well as its ambitious plans to move up the value chain in 2015, the relationship between China and the US became more aggressive.

The 'America First' platform gained currency with the election of Donald Trump as the US president in 2016. Unhappy with the trade imbalance with China, the Trump administration kicked off a trade war in 2018, imposing tariffs in two waves to around $400 billion worth of goods shipped between the US and China (Colback, 2020). The fallout for companies related to both countries has been extensive. This confrontational relationship led to disruption in the bilateral trade in goods and services and, ultimately, to the global supply chains. The disruption has specifically affected nations who are in the global network of production and are closely linked with these two big markets. It has perhaps accelerated a trend that was already under way, giving China an incentive to develop its own standards and achieve self-reliance in critical strategic sectors, including the high technology sector. The most significant consequence of this is the potential for a longer term decoupling of China and the US, and the emergence of two rival and separate spheres of influence, in both trade and services.

This chapter attempts to bring out continuous evaluation of the present conflicting scenario based on the available trade balance data for India-China Trade, India-US Trade and India-ROA (Rest of Asia without China), and India-ROW (without ROA, China, and the US). One of the objectives of this chapter, thus, would be to partially capture the positional transition in terms of the flows of commodities and services. This would, in a way, reflect the fact that there is not much gain emanating from a conflict scenario. Another objective of this chapter is to bring out the geopolitical splits in Asia due to this conflict, which is sidestepping their interests. Asian countries need a sustainable and long-term plan for faster economic integration and development, indicated by the overwhelming consensus by them on working to reach a Free Trade Agreement of the Asia-Pacific (FTAAP) that also includes the US. The chapter suggests that these conflicts may escalate into a 'decoupling' of both economies, which poses significant risks not only to US–China bilateral relations but also to the US system and the existing world economic order. In this scenario, the chapter argues, the developing countries still could reap the benefit by getting more engaged in the global value chains (GVCs) by adapting their trade and industrial policies. The chapter discusses in detail the trade scenario of the US, China, and some major economies.

The chapter is organised as follows. Section 2 outlines the position of China and the USA in the global trade scenario. This section also analyses the impact of the trade war on other countries. Section 3 describes Chinese emergence as the global economy and a leader in the global production network. Section 4 explores China's growing trade surplus with the USA while the next section comments on the implications of US trade policy for China and other affected economies. Section 6 summarises the opportunities in the global value chain for the emerging economies. The final views of repositioning and convergence are noted as a concluding reflection.

2 US–China and the share of global trade

With growth rates above the average trend during the past two decades and the largest trade surplus with the US, China is the primary target of the trade war unleashed by the US. Steep tariffs are the first weapon in bilateral tensions damaging global economic integration tied to ever more intense technology competition. This move by the US is alarming. In the worst-case scenario, these conflicts may dissociate both economies, cause lasting global recession, and usher in new geopolitical confrontation. The Trump administration, in particular, relies on an emergency status quo, new campaign finance, and 'big money', which poses significant risks not only to US–China relations but also to internal democratic norms and the existing international order. As a consequence, US–China trade has shown a precipitously downward trend. Estimates based on the quarterly growth of exports to China and imports from China to the US have noted a steep decline over the years, as noted in Figure 2.1.

The declining growth of US–China trade is reflected through various indicators in the US, the crucial one being employment. The quarterly growth rate of employment in manufacturing also declined continuously, as may be noted from Figure 2.2.

It may be noted from the figure that in Q4 (January–March) of 2018–19, employment growth was almost 2%, which came down successively, quarter after

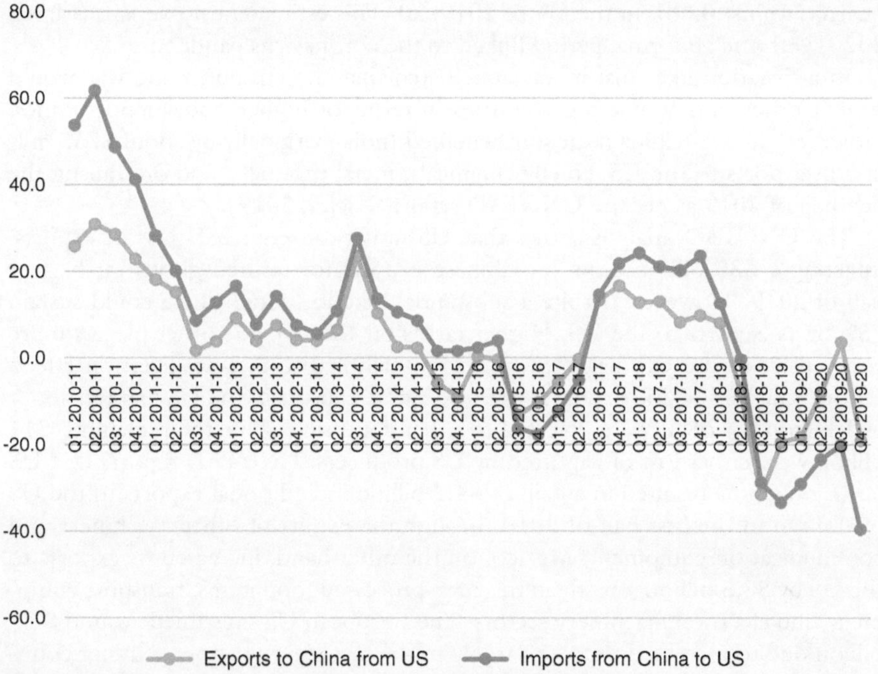

Figure 2.1 US–China trade: a precipitous declining trend.

Source: www.census.gov/foreign-trade/balance/c5700.html: Note: Quarters are calculated on the Financial Year basis, i.e. Q1: April–June, Q2: July–September, etc.

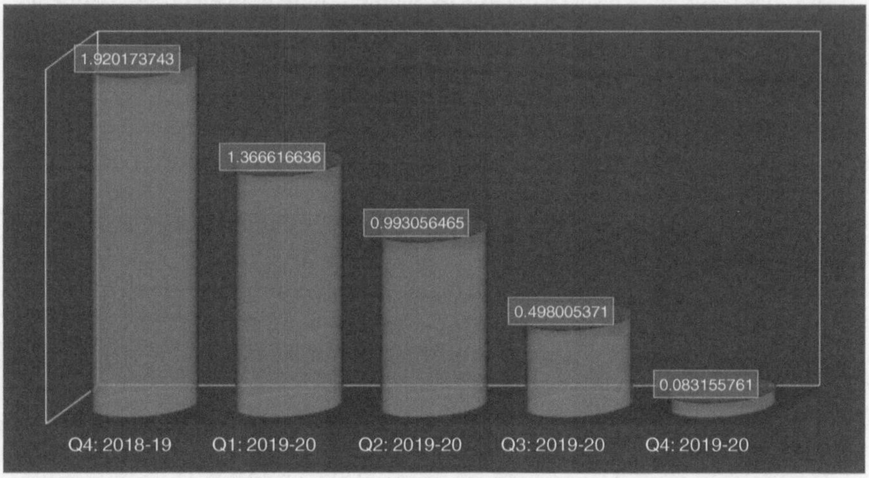

Figure 2.2 Quarterly growth (%) of the US manufacturing employment (Q4: 2018–19 to Q4: 2019–20).

Source: US Bureau of Labor Statistics.

quarter, to just 0.08% in the Q4 of 2019–20. This estimate just overlaps (March 2020) with the abnormal period linked to the coronavirus pandemic.

In a situation like this, it was anticipated that the ensuing trade war would benefit other non-conflicting countries in terms of higher trade opportunities. However, the US–China trade war benefited India marginally by about $755 million in exports to the US, chiefly chemicals, metal products, and ore during the first half of 2019 as per the UNCTAD report (Nicita, 2019).

The UNCTAD analysis shows that US tariffs caused a 25% loss of exports, inflicting a $35 billion blow on Chinese exports for tariffed goods in the first half of 2019. However, despite a substantial hike in tariffs, China could sustain 75% of its exports to the US. Higher tariffs on China made other players more competitive in the US market, which eventually led to a trade diversion effect. Of the total $35 billion export losses of Chinese exports in the US market, about $21 billion (or 63%) were diverted to other countries, while the remaining $14 billion were either lost or captured by US producers. UNCTAD reports that US tariffs on China resulted in a gain of $4.2 billion in additional exports to the US by Taiwan in the first half of 2019 through the export of office machinery and communication equipment. Mexico, on the other hand, increased its exports to the US by $3.5 billion, mostly in the agro-processed food items, transport equipment, and electrical machinery sectors. The European Union gained around $2.7 billion due to increased exports, largely in the machinery sectors. Among countries benefiting from trade diversions, Vietnam's exports to the US augmented by $2.6 billion, driven by export of communication equipment and furniture. The benefits for Korea, Canada, and India were smaller but still considerable and ranged from $0.9 billion to $1.5 billion. The rest of the benefits were largely to the advantage of other South-East Asian countries. Thus, the ongoing US–China trade war has resulted in a sharp decline in bilateral trade between these countries, higher prices for consumers, and increased imports from countries not directly involved in the trade war.

The trade war unleashed by the US ultimately hurt both countries and consumers in the US bore the fullest burden of tariffs as their associated costs have largely been passed down to them in the form of higher prices. However, Chinese firms have also absorbed part of the costs by reducing the prices of their exports. The trade conflict could eventually compromise the stability of the international economic order and the future growth of the world economy. Moreover, the share of exports of countries like India and others gaining from trade diversion may be a temporary phenomenon. In fact, if we combine exports to the US and exports to China, then the trend of the share of exports of India to the US showed little variation, whereas for China it has rather increased, though by a small proportion. This fact may be observed from the Figure 2.3.

India's import share shows that the imports from the US have gone up while the value share of those from China has reduced (Figure 2.4). This could reflect the geopolitical scenario predominant during this period.

The trade conflict of the US and China has brought a newer form of realignment. The export share of the rest of Asia (without China) with India has gone

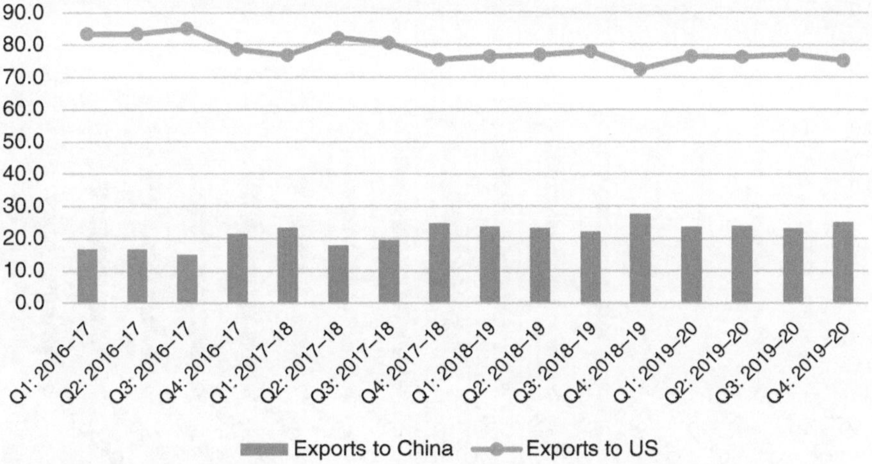

Figure 2.3 Quarterly export share of India with the US and China: 2016–17 to 2019–20.
Source: Trade Map.

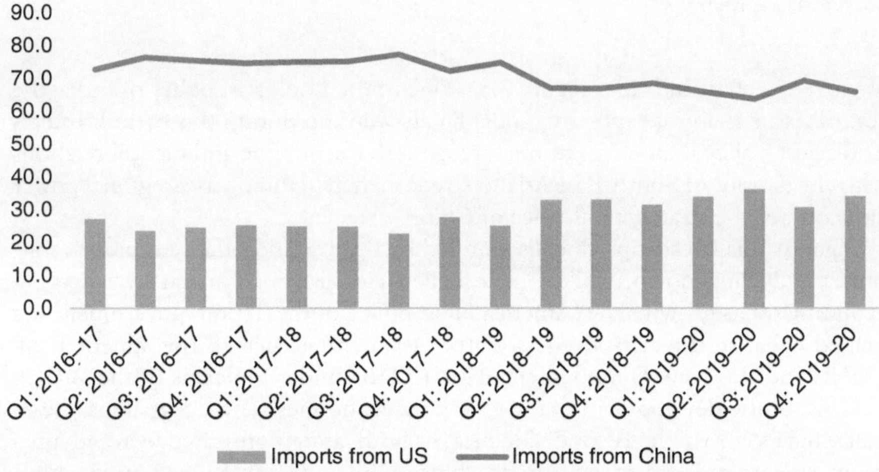

Figure 2.4 Quarterly import share of India with the US and China: 2016–17 to 2019–20.
Source: Trade Map.

up precipitously while the export share of the Rest of the World (without US, China, and the Rest of Asia) has shown a declining trend, reflecting the fact that the US–China trade conflict might have benefited the European and the Latin American countries more by raising their share of exports to the US through a trade diversion effect (as mentioned in the UNCTAD report) which finally

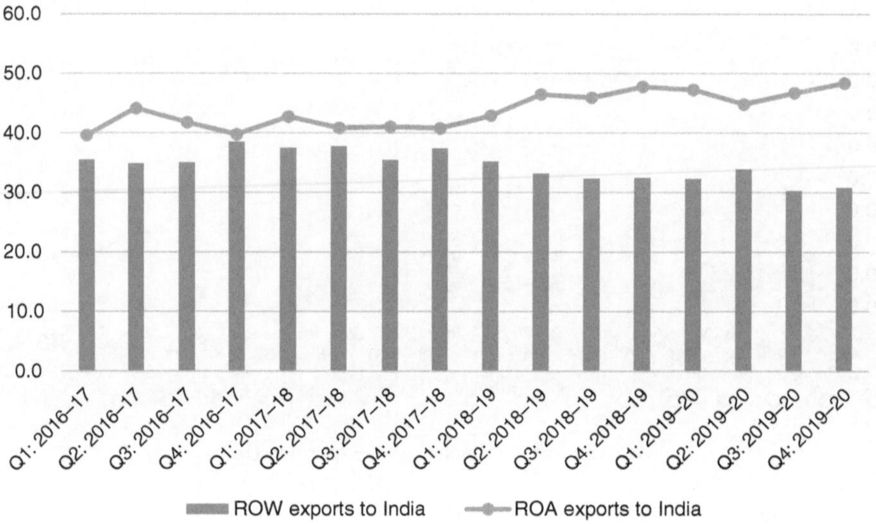

Figure 2.5 Quarterly export share of Rest of Asia (net of China) and the Rest of World (minus US China and the Rest of Asia) with India: 2016–17 to 2019–20.

Source: Trade Map.

impacted its share in India (Figure 2.5). Due to the Look East policy of India, the rest of Asia's share of exports to India finally went up during this period. India's Look East policy is an effort to nurture extensive economic and tactical relations with the nations of South-East Asia to strengthen its standing as a regional power and counter the strategic influence of China.

Against this backdrop, globalisation led by the US and other advanced economies is dialling down, while China-fuelled globalisation, driven by emerging economies, has grown. The 'America First' policy of the Trump government has helped enhance the attractiveness of the Asian Infrastructure Investment Bank (AIIB) and the New Development Bank (NDB) under the aegis of the BRICS nations for the development of the emerging economies. The US goal may be to halt China's economic rise or divide Asia, or both, as demonstrated by tough pronouncements and efforts to pressure China on its trade, investment, and technological policies, along with captivating many a deal for the Asia-Pacific and Asian countries (Steinbock, 2018). These deals, however, need a sustainable, long-term plan for accelerated economic integration and development, indicated by the consensus among Asian countries on working to reach a Free Trade Agreement of the Asia-Pacific (FTAAP) that includes the US as well. However, that may not be what the Trump administration desires. In terms of the size of their economies, defence budgets, and greenhouse gas emissions, both the US and China are the leading powers of the world. Both nations are permanent members of the United Nations Security Council. Even in 2017, they were each other's largest trading partners (Schwarzenberg Andres, 2018). This bilateral relationship is perceived by many to be the most consequential in the world.

3 The upsurge of China: the sequential context

Since the late 1970s, China has emerged as one of the fastest-growing economies in the world. From 1979 to 2000, China's Gross Domestic Product (GDP) in real terms grew more than sixfold (Morrison, 2019). Per capita income, however, remained low, but China's massive population in aggregate terms enabled it to be one of the larger economies of the world, much larger than Russia or India, or even both. At the same time, the growth in China's international trade has been impressive, such that the country's share of world trade increased fivefold, to about 4% at present (Morrison, 2019). No other country has experienced so rapid an increase in its share of world trade. Since 1995, China has been one of the world's top ten trading economies. The opening of its domestic markets for imports, foreign services, and foreign investment also implied increased local competition that the leadership expects to leverage into accelerated internal economic restructuring. The goal was basically to improve the quality of growth and enhance its level of sustainability.

China has seen exponential growth over the past few decades, breaking the barriers of a centrally planned closed economy to grow into a manufacturing and exporting hub of the world. China is referred to as the world's factory, given its huge manufacturing and export base, placing herself at the top of the global value chains. Over the years, the role of services has gradually increased, and manufacturing as a contributor to GDP has declined comparatively. Back in the 1980s, China was the seventh-largest economy, with a GDP of around $305 billion, while the size of the US then was then $2.86 trillion. After China initiated market reforms in 1978, it experienced economic growth averaging 10% of GDP annually (Morrison, 2019). In recent years, the pace of growth of China has slackened but still remains high in comparison to its peer nations.

4 US trade deficit with China: a billion-plus growing market

The bilateral agreement between China and the US, being a part of multilateral commitments, agreed on increased market opening at the outset. China's trade in merchandise is, on average, far more open than is usually known. By early 2001 China's average tariff rate had been cut to around 15%, almost half the level prevailing in India and roughly corresponding to tariffs in Brazil and Mexico. In addition, 60% of all imports entered in China under one or many import duty exemption programmes (Sub-Committee on East Asia and the Pacific, 2001). As a result, the actual tariff charged in China was exceedingly modest, within 5% of the value of imports. Similarly, China's import quotas and licensing requirements have been steadily reduced, and by 2000, they covered only 4% of all the imported commodities (Sub-Committee, 2001). Despite lower tariff and non-tariff barriers, the rate of expansion of US exports to China in the aggregate did not reveal any dramatic change.

Second, the conditions applied to China's WTO entry do nothing to reduce the US overall trade deficit, which is impacted by other macroeconomic factors such as the rates of national savings and investment. Americans turned out to be spenders rather than savers, whether US households or US businesses. Reducing the trade deficit requires Americans to save more or invest less. On their own, policies that open other countries' markets to US products, or close US markets to foreign products, do not alter the overall trade balance. Circumstances suggest that a sizeable fraction of investment in the US is financed by foreign capital, including capital from China. Third, with liberalisation in the textile and apparel trade, China gained most due to the use of advanced technology and low-cost workers. Apart from the bilateral trade deficit issues between the US and China, it is important to note that the US has also derived substantial non-trade benefits from greater participation in domestic distribution and service industries in China that WTO membership made possible.

China could not fulfil all of its WTO restrictions but still took early steps to meet some of its commitments to open foreign participation in audiovisual services, construction, retailing, legal services, and distribution services, along with accommodating many rules pertaining to the fiscal, financial, and regulatory regime. National People's Congress amended 177 domestic laws covering patents, copyrights, trademarks, and foreign investment in line with WTO commitments (Sub-Committee, 2001). The trade and investment liberalisation that China undertook under WTO has also increased the potential for US access to this market with a strong economic relationship. Increased access for agricultural products and automobiles became particularly important for the US entities.

Successful integration with the global economy also ensured China's constructive participation in a new multilateral round of trade openness, including the formation of a free trade area (FTA) with countries of the Association of Southeast Asian Nations (ASEAN). The deeper integration and the related speeding up of domestic economic reform helped to achieve an improved standard of living for China's billion-plus population, associated with an increasingly marketised economy.

5 Implications for the US policy

Following the Tiananmen Square crisis of 1989, a number of financial and technical cooperation programmes with China faced selective withholding by the US for several years. However, China still provides an opportunity for a unique experiment for the US in framing a coherent and effective policy as it has interlaced with the global economic and trading system but with large gaps in its adherence to global rules. There were three broad options for the US to respond:

- principle of accommodation;
- unrestricted strategic rivalry; and
- worldwide cooperation.

The third option could have been ideal in sorting out the array of conflicting interests between the US and China linked to climate change, P5+1 negotiation to roll back Iran's nuclear weapons programme, and foreign aid, etc. The US envisaged a larger role for a constructive China while simultaneously building barriers and coalitions against pressure in China's neighbourhood countries. On global issues, a workable approach should look for issues on which China, because of its own evolving interests, can and should play a greater role in supporting the global system. Examples include cybersecurity and cyber innovation, protecting the rights of foreign investors, central bank coordination, and protection of intellectual property rights. This intermediate policy framework may not brace the shock linked to accommodation or unrestrained rivalry, but it all needs an appropriate explanation how a radical roll in either direction would secure the complex range of US interests in its relationship with China. Moreover, China is ruled by the Communist Party, resistant to political liberalisation at home and employing nationalist rhetoric and behaviour in dealing with its neighbourhood, enhancing the chances for rivalry with the US.

6 Global value chains (GVCs): transition from crisis to opportunity

With the US–China trade conflict reaching to its zenith, the earlier value chain lead by China may not last. In August 2019, US announced an increase from 25 to 30% for the existing tariffs on US$250 billion of Chinese imports from October 2019 and new 15% tariffs on US$300 billion of Chinese imports from September 2019 (Jayant, 2019).[1] The impact of the trade war in the medium to longer term seems irreversible as it is clear that the dispute is not transitory in nature.

Using various datasets, Yi Huang, Chen Lin, Sibo Liu, and Heiwai Tang (2019) documented that firms' stock market responses are determined by the degree of their direct exposure to US–China trade and their indirect exposure through the GVCs. In particular, US firms that are more dependent on exports to and imports from China have lower stock returns and higher default risk, whereas the reduced import competition from China has a limited effect. As a consequence, US investment is now being diverted away from China into nations of South-East Asia. Investments in and from the US have also been equally affected following China's reciprocal tariffs.

At this juncture, the international fragmentation of production can in fact lead to increased job creation and economic growth of the developing countries, contrary to the generalised belief that it would decline due to the trade conflict. To reap the gains from newer GVC participation, countries' trade and investment policies need a modified and receptive approach. Nowadays, a single finished product often results from manufacturing and assembly in multiple countries, with each step in the process adding value to the end product. In order to achieve this, the manufacturing sector needs to be strong enough in terms of integration with GVCs.

Through GVCs, countries trade in products, know-how, and assemble things together. Imports of goods and services matter as much as exports to successful GVCs, which also integrate the know-how of lead firms and suppliers of key components along with stages of production in multiple offshore locations. The inter-firm flow of know-how is the key characteristic of GVCs, which is a powerful driver of productivity growth, job creation, and helps increase living standards. Countries that embrace GVCs grow faster, import skills and technology, and boost employment. With GVC-driven development, countries generate growth by moving to higher-value-added tasks, and by embedding more technology and know-how in all their agriculture, manufacturing, and services production. GVCs provide countries the opportunity to leap-frog their development process. However, there are many practical difficulties that are looming large in this context. Take, for example, the case of India, which has officially declared the aim to be a $5 trillion economy by 2024, in which the manufacturing sector is anticipated to play a pivotal role (Sharma, 2019). However, the sector is decimated by its low integration in GVCs.

In their study, Soan and Miglani (2018) highlighted that India's GVC integration, measured as the foreign value-added to India's exports and domestic value-added to India's intermediate good exports, remains weak. The reason for this is traced back to India's historical inward-looking industrial policies, starting from import substitution, the licensing policy with major emphasis on state-led industrialisation. India overtly focused more on the large domestic market without considering the employment and technological benefits of being part of a higher value chain. Policies such as industrial corridors, de-licensing, and Make in India could be a step in the right direction but may not be sufficient. With some exceptions, there is a lack of leading firms in India, which are central to all aspects of a value chain, from sourcing supplies to the final product in GVCs. Firms like Tata Motors in the automobile sector and Ranbaxy in the pharmaceutical sector play key roles in transferring technology, forming supply chains, and attracting foreign investment. However, India has very few such sectoral lead firms. Skill mismatch and shortage, lack of access to finance, custom procedures, and high taxes are all the biggest constraints that prevent lead firms from developing in India. Manufacturing and trade policies thus need better coordination to focus on establishing stronger GVC linkages by attracting more global lead firms to India.

It may be noted that some of the developing countries have fully embarked on the GVC revolution, but they still face challenges in aligning GVCs with their national development strategies. The right strategies could help developing countries maximise their participation in GVCs. With the substantial repositioning of the GVCs, governments need to have a clear vision and mandate to improve coordination among players and ensure the greater involvement of the private sector. Opening borders and attracting investment can help jump-start entry in GVCs. Countries will derive the greatest benefit by maximising the absorption potential of the domestic economy and by strengthening its linkages with GVCs. Many diverse policy areas affect the success of GVCs. They include, among others, trade policy, logistics, and trade facilitation, regulation of business services, investment, business taxation, innovation, industrial development, conformity to international standards, and the wider business environment fostering entrepreneurship. Finally, countries should identify measures that will complement their GVC strategies. These include a large range of dimensions, from investment in education and vocational training to environment and urbanisation, from ICT and infrastructure building to labour market mobility.

7 Concluding reflections: new realignment and possible consequences

The decades of full-on engagement with China was anticipated by the strategic thinking of the West, especially by the US, that it would alter the grey nature of Chinese internal politics, making it more liberal and open. The free and open liberal world order has now run into severe difficulties in challenging the great political wall of China. The intense engagement with China failed to alter its politics, but conversely, many liberal democracies have praised and adopted Chinese-style industrial planning policies. Western taxpayers supported China's bid for global influence. Successive US administrations, with the typical urge to further enlarge their big sized business and finance, played a crucial role in bringing China into the global community, emboldened by Bill Clinton's decision to welcome China into the WTO system. Subsequently, the outsourcing of manufacturing capabilities from the West to China allowed China to purposefully build its influence through control over global supply chains. Due to enormous financial returns accruing from labour arbitrage, governments of the West turned a blind eye, as China used this economic dependence to flex its political influence, first in Asia and now, through the Belt and Road Initiative (BRI), into the very heart of the European Union (EU).

The current worldwide pause prompted by coronavirus pandemic offers a moment to reflect on the contours of the BRI. Chinese expansion through the construction of new supply chains and trade routes has been designed to serve its economic interests by capturing the flow of raw materials from Asia and Africa and, subsequently, supplying finished products back to the world. And just as the colonial British sweetened their imperial design as a show of generosity by laying the railways network in India, the same is repeated when China sells its political scheme as a new way for global growth, solidarity, and development.

The other aspect relates to technology and its intensive exertion to control and leverage the global data economy for its own advantage. By globalising its technological prowess through next-generation communications infrastructure and digital platforms as surveillance tools to support authoritarian governance, China is now well-positioned to script future administrations and regimes around development, finance, and even war and conflict. This has been carried outby isolating its own people from external flows of information and technology. The same, less emphatically, applies to the US policy as well. Like China, the US leveraged its military and industrial strengths and its technological supremacy to build a world order that responded to its interests and pole position. However, US society was largely open so individuals, communities, and nations from around the world could engage, convince, or petition its institutions, write in its media, and, often, participate in its politics. Its hegemony was constrained by a democratic society and conditioned by its electoral cycles.

It was these features of the US system of functioning that encouraged nations to place some degree of faith in multilateral institutions and encouraged countries to participate in the free flow of goods, finance, and labour; to move towards open borders, markets, and societies; and, indeed, to embrace US-led globalisation at the turn of the last century. On the contrary, very few would be able to navigate the dark labyrinth of Chinese politics. Even during the pandemic, the questions surround China's transparency on thousands of deaths caused by the virus within China, which ultimately impacted over 180 countries of the world, with over 48.6 million infections by July 2020. If phases of subsequent globalisation are controlled by China, they could be less free and less open than before. Countries may opt to trade with nations where political trust exists, thus disintegrating further the prevailing supply chains. Governments may restrict flows of goods, services, finance, and labour when national strategic interests are at stake. Countries could be ready for a new phase of compartmentalised globalisation in the post-pandemic world in which the flavour of multilateral relations may be replaced mostly by bilateral transactions. This will have severe implications for world GDP growth in which the poor nations will be poorer, while wealthier nations will face internal rifts due to heightened socio-economic disparity within the economy.

Note

1 United States Trade Representative (USTR) Statement on Section 301 Tariff Action Regarding China, 23 August 2019: 'Today, China announced it will impose unjustified tariffs targeting U.S. products. In response to China's decision, and in order to achieve the objectives of the China Section 301 investigation, President Trump has instructed the USTR to increase by 5% the tariffs on approximately $550 billion worth of Chinese imports. For the 25% tariffs on approximately $250 billion worth of Chinese imports, USTR will begin the process of increasing the tariff rate to 30%, effective October 1 following a notice and comment period. For the 10% tariffs on approximately $300 billion worth of Chinese imports that the President announced earlier this month, the tariffs will now be 15%, effective on the already scheduled dates for tariff increases on these imports.'

References

Boudreaux, D. J., and Ghei, N. (2018). The benefits of free trade: Addressing key myths. *Trade and Immigration| Policy Briefs,*|23 May 2018.

Colback, L. (2020). Global supply chains are at risk as the world's two biggest economies threaten to decouple. *Financial Times*, 28 February.

Huang, Y., Lin, C., Liu, S., & Tang, H. (2019). Trade networks and firm value: Evidence from the US–China trade war: Centre for Economic Policy Research (CEPR) Discussion Paper No. DP 14173.

Jayant, M. (2019). How the US–China trade war fractured global value chains, 9 September. https://theasiadialogue.com/2019/09/09/how-the-us-china-trade-war-has-fractured-global-value-chains/

Medhat, A. (2018). *Trade War between US and China*. Cairo: Faculty of Economics and Political Science, Cairo University. www.researchgate.net/publication/330500744_US-China_Trade_War_2018?channel=doi&linkId=5c4c162b458515a4c74137ca&showFulltext=true

Morrison, W. M. (2019). *China's Economic Rise: History, Trends, Challenges, and Implications for the United States*. 25 June. Washington, DC: Congressional Research Service.

Nicita, A. (2019). Trade and trade diversion effects of the United States tariff on China, *UNCTAD Research Paper*, 37, UNCTAD/SER.RP/2019/9, November.

Ray, S., & Miglani, S. (2018). *Global Value Chains and the Missing Links: Cases from Indian Industry*. New Delhi: Routledge, India.

Schwarzenberg Andres, B. (2018). *U.S. Trade with Major Trading Partners*. 18 December. Washington, DC: Congressional Research Service-R45434.

Sharma, M. (2019). Can India become a $5 trillion economy? *The Economic Times*, 20 June. https://economictimes.indiatimes.com/news/economy/indicators/can-india-become-a-5-trillion-economy/articleshow/69869145.cms

Steinbock, D. (2018). Will Trump push for an 'America First' trade agreement in Asia modelled on his new NAFTA deal? *South China Morning Post*, 5 October. www.scmp.com/comment/insight-opinion/united-states/article/2169950/will-trump-push-america-first-trade-agreement

Sub-Committee on East Asia and the Pacific (2001). *After Hainan: Next Steps for US-China Relations*. Washington, DC: 107th Congress, Serial No. 107–7, 25 April.

3 US–China trade war

An analysis of trade relations

Sunandan Ghosh

1 Introduction

The theory of protection postulates that a large country (one that can affect world prices) would impose tariffs on imports from its trade partner to maximise its national welfare.[1] The source of improvement in national welfare is the improvement of terms of trade for the tariff-imposing country. However, this gain in the national welfare of the tariff-imposing country comes with a more than offsetting reduction in the national welfare of its trading partner. As a result, the country on which export tariffs are being imposed would impose tariffs in turn to restore the terms of trade. In the process, the volume of trade between these countries would diminish.[2] This is what we call tariff/trade war.

A chain of reciprocal tariff impositions by the world's largest economies[3] started in January 2018 when on 22 January 2018, the US government under President Donald Trump imposed 30% tariff on imported solar panels and 20% tariff on the first 1.2 million units of washing machines imported from China. On 8 March 2018, the US imposed 25% tariffs on steel imports and 10% on aluminium from all suppliers. In retaliation China imposed tariffs, ranging 15–25%, on 128 products worth US$3 billion. This tussle between these economic giants has continued since. This process of tariff retaliation by the USA and China came to be known as the 'US–China Trade War' in the popular press. After more than a year, a 'trade deal' was signed by the two countries on 15 January 2020. The 'deal' proposed cuts in US tariffs on imports from China in return for assurance by China to reduce USA's trade deficit with China (import of more US farm products, energy, and manufacturing commodities) along with redress of US complaints against China on the grounds of intellectual property rights. However, the outbreak of SARS-CoV-2 (Covid-19) and President Trump's allegations (which have been vehemently denied by President Jinping) about the source of the virus, along with US sanctions on China (over Hong Kong), led to a complete stall in the US–China trade negotiations.

The impact of this trade war is far-reaching. Theoretically, it affects the USA and China. In reality, this trade war is likely to affect the entire world economy. Both the involved nations are not only economic giants, but, particularly China, major trading nations. In the present-day world, integrated by global value chains, the trade war between the USA and China might leave a permanent dent in the global economy.

The present study tries to understand the impact of the US–China trade war on the bilateral trade between the world's largest economies. The focus of the chapter lies in investigating the existence, if any, of structural change in US-China bilateral trade. Furthermore, we try to analyse the impact of the trade war on Chinese and US trade with the economies of South Asia. We also consider the South-East Asian economies for a comparative study. For the purpose, the study uses annual trade data (SITC 4) from the World Bank (WITS).[4]

The rest of the chapter is organised as follows. Section 2 tries to touch upon the probable reasons for the trade war. Section 3 provides a rudimentary analysis of trade between China, the USA, South Asia, and South-East Asia. Section 4 provides a detailed analysis of the USA's trade with China and South and South-East Asian economies, including the analyses of structural changes. Section 5 analyses the trade scenario for China. The final section summarises the findings and concludes.

2 US–China trade war: probable reasons

There are multiple reasons why President Trump may have initiated this trade war.[5] The reason put forward by the US government was the burgeoning *trade deficit* that the US had with China. However, the imposition of tariffs is not a unilateral strategy. In fact, most people without much understanding of economic theory can understand that China, being a large country itself, would retaliate if tariffs are imposed on its exports, resulting in Chinese goods becoming less competitive in the US market. Hence, imposing tariffs to reduce trade deficit does not seem to be a very convincing argument. It would only result in the Scitovszky type scenario explained above.

One plausible reason for this action on the part of President Trump lies in the analysis of *trade and wage gap* in the US by Krugman (2000, p. 52):

> *an expansion of world trade, and especially of manufactures' exports from low-wage countries, has coincided with a fall in the real wages of less-skilled American workers (and with rising unemployment in other advanced countries). It is natural to suspect a link between trade and declining wages; indeed, many commentators, including some economists, have not hesitated to assert flatly that growing trade is the principal cause of wage decline.*

If we assume that the US has a larger endowment of skilled labour (as compared to China), the US will end up importing unskilled intensive manufacturing goods from China. This would lead to a fall in the prices of unskilled intensive goods in the US market, leading to a fall in the real wages of American unskilled workers. Imposing tariffs on imports from China would reverse this process and protect the unskilled US labour force. This also satisfies President Trump's political agenda.

Along with ballooning imports from China, one more thing may have contributed to the widening skilled-unskilled wage gap in the US: skill-biased technological progress. However, the US government has made concerted efforts to favour skill-biased *technology* improvement in the US and not allow China to acquire improved technology.

> *President Trump plans to ratchet commercial tensions higher by barring many Chinese companies from investing in US technology firms, and by blocking additional technology exports to Beijing. ... The twin initiatives are designed to prevent Beijing from moving ahead with plans outlined in its 'Made in China 2025' report to become a global leader in 10 broad areas of technology, including information technology, aerospace, electric vehicles, and biotechnology. This is reflected in 90% plunge in Chinese investments in the US in the first five months of 2018 as compared to the previous year.*
>
> (*The Times of India*, 25 June 2018)

Thus a mix of economic and political motives may have led the US government to start this trade war.

3 Trade data: some preliminary analyses

This section provides a very brief analysis of aggregate annual trade data for the USA and China and both the countries' trade with South and South-East Asian economies. We start with the experience of the US for the period 1993–2018.[6] All data used in the study have been taken from WITS. Figure 3.1 clearly shows the whopping trade deficit the US experienced from its trade with China during this period. US had a deficit of US$11.6 billion in 1993, which ballooned to US$260 billion in 2018. In fact, this very preliminary result shows the inability of US tariffs on Chinese exports to curb the US trade deficit with China. However, the US trade surplus with South-East Asia more than compensates its deficit with China. In 1993 the US had a deficit of US$23.72 billion for its trade with South-East Asia. This deficit kept on reducing and turned to a surplus of US$4 billion in 2002. The surplus kept on increasing, and in 2018 the US trade surplus with South-East Asia stands at a whopping US$480 billion. Very similar is the story for US trade with South Asia. In 1993 the US had a deficit of US$4.98 billion for its trade with South Asia, which turned to a surplus, over time, of US$97.66 billion in 2018. However, India, the most significant trading partner for the US among the South Asian countries, shows a different picture. The US had a deficit with India in all the years from 1993 to 2018. The deficit stood at US$13.2 billion in 2018.

Next, we do similar analyses of China's trade. China, unlike the US, has trade surpluses with both South and South-East Asian countries. Figure 3.2 provides evidence.

In the following sections, we do detailed analyses for the USA and China and their trade with each other, South Asia, and South-East Asia. We have considered

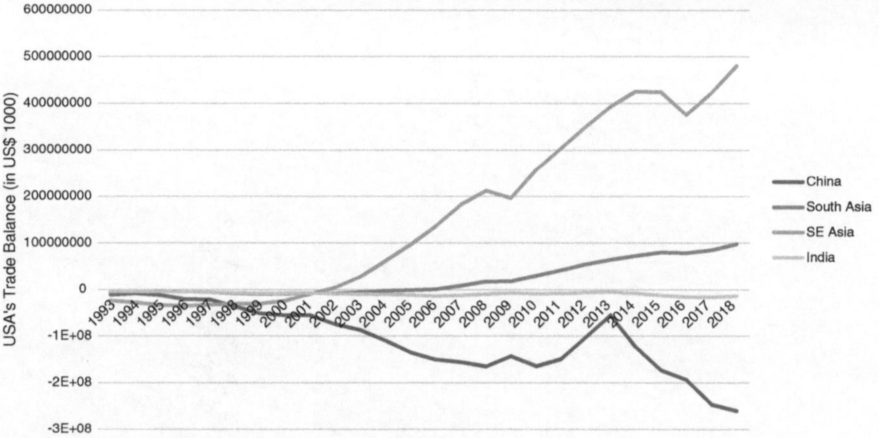

Figure 3.1 US trade balances with China, South and South-East Asia (1993–2018).
Source: Author's calculations using WITS Data.

all the eight South Asian and eight South-East Asian nations in this study (Cambodia, Lao PDR, and Timor-Leste have not been included).

4 USA's trade with China, South Asia, and South-East Asian countries

In this section, we will analyse the export and import patterns for the US. We focus our analyses on US trade with China, Hong Kong,[7] South Asian, and South-East Asian countries.

4.1 US imports from China, Hong Kong, South Asia, and South-East Asia

The USA's imports from China exceed US imports from any other South or South-East Asian country (Figure 3.3). US imports from China have increased 12.4% on average during 1993–2018. The only years in which US imports from China registered negative growth rates are 2009 (–13.13%) and 2016 (–4.51%). In fact, US imports from China have exceeded US imports from all South and South-East Asian nations since 1999. US imports from China were more than three times that of all the South and South-East Asian countries during 2009–15. This marginally slipped to about 2.8 times during 2016–18.

Now, we start decomposing this aggregate picture into some details. If we look at the South Asian economies, India is the only major exporter to the US, contributing more than 80% of US imports from South Asia in 2018. Not only that, but India's share is also increasing over time, while those of the rest are decreasing. This is captured in Figure 3.4.

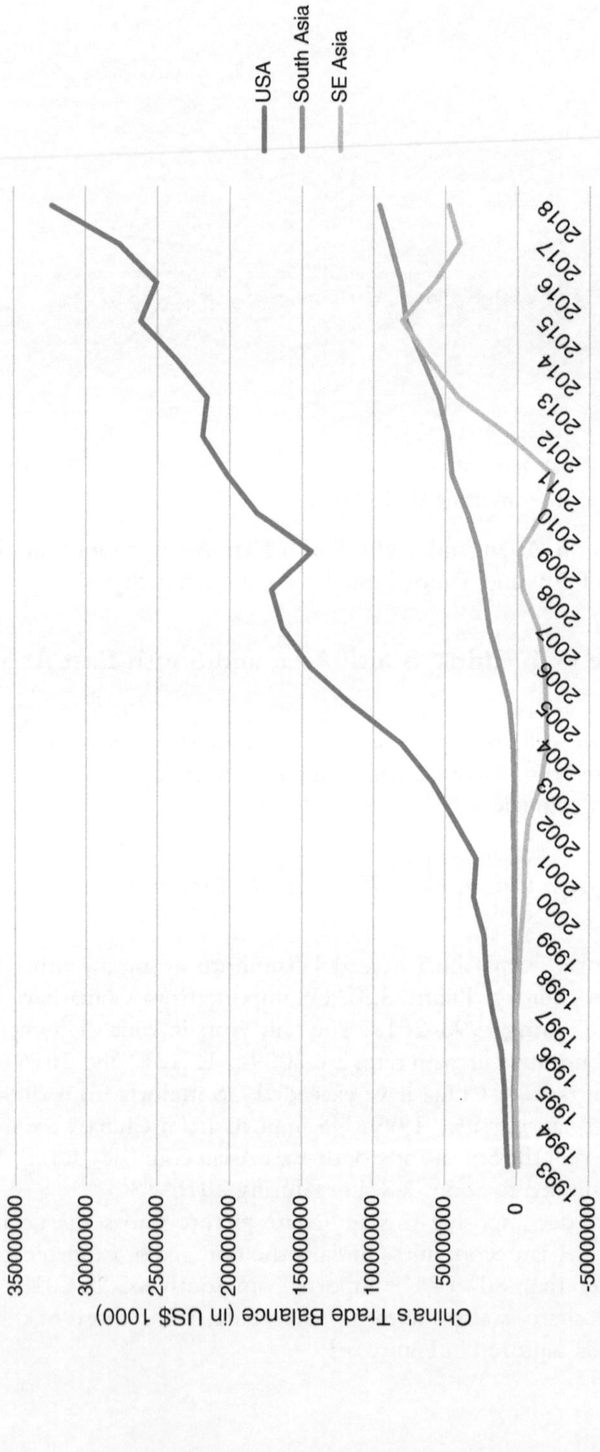

Figure 3.2 China's trade balances with USA, South and South-East Asia (1993–2018).

Source: Author's calculations using WITS Data.

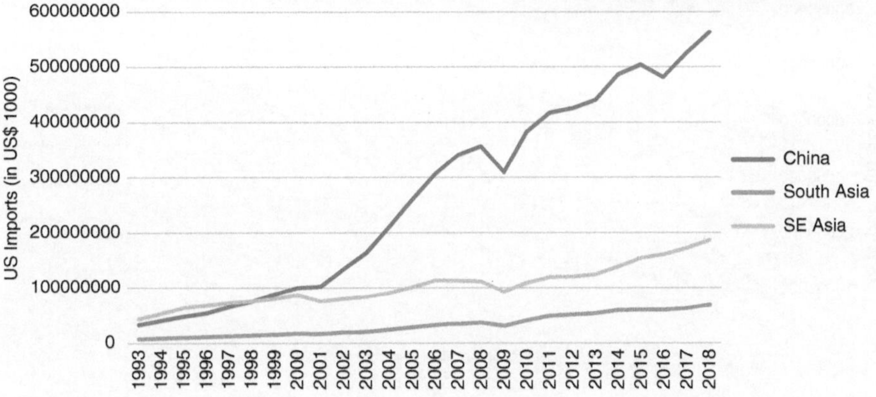

Figure 3.3 US imports from China and South and South-East Asian countries (1993–2018).
Source: Author's calculations using WITS data.

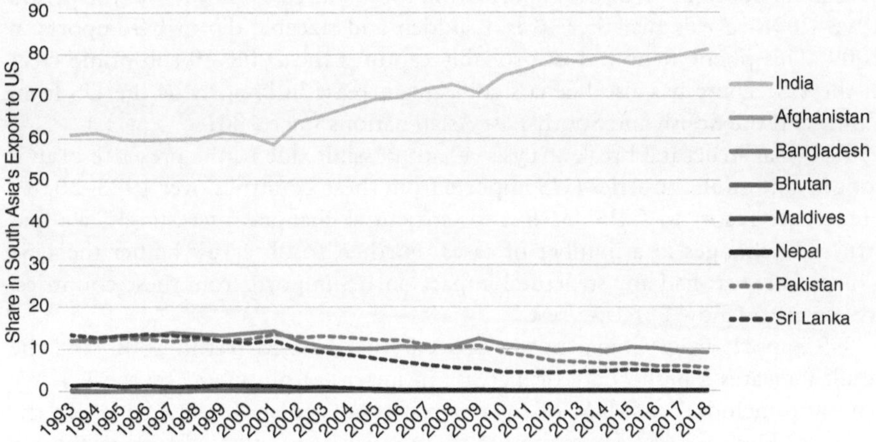

Figure 3.4 Country's share in South Asian exports to the US
Source: Author's calculations using WITS data

Malaysia, Thailand, and Vietnam are the major countries exporting to the USA from the South-East Asian group. The four countries India, Malaysia, Thailand, and Vietnam together make up more than 90% of total exports from South and South-East Asian countries to the US. At present, India tops the list, followed by Vietnam, Malaysia, and Thailand. US imports from India have surged since 2009, while Vietnam overtook Malaysia and Thailand from 2014 (Figure 3.5).

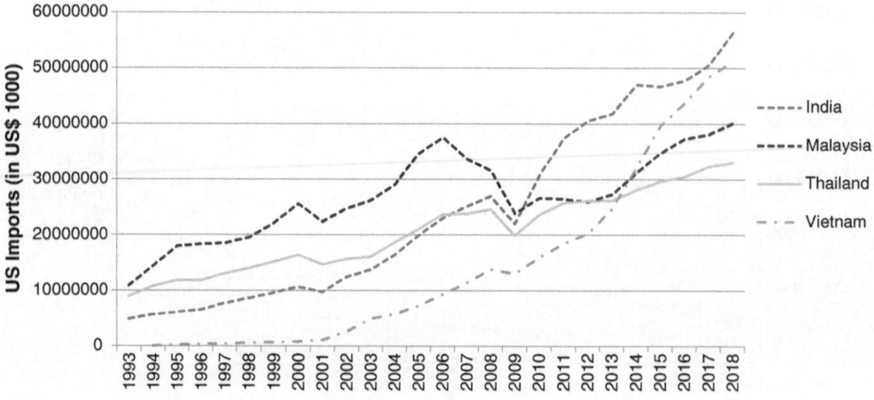

Figure 3.5 US imports from India, Malaysia, Thailand, and Vietnam (1993–2018).
Source: Author's calculations using WITS data.

Careful observation of US imports from these source countries over the period 1993–2008 reveals that there was a sudden and sizeable dip in US imports in 2009. This phenomenon most probably captures the 2008–10 sub-prime crisis in the US. There has also beena significant increase in imports by the US from China and the South and South-East Asian nations since 2001.

A formal structural break analysis[8] is not possible due to the presence of unit root in almost all the series (US imports from these countries over 1993–2018). Hence, we resort to CUSUM test for structural change. Interestingly, we find structural changes in a number of cases. Further, to observe whether the US–China trade war had any structural impact on US imports from these countries, we resort to Chow Forecast Test.

US imports from China show a break from CUSUM test in 2006, and the result indicates a higher rate of increase in imports from China by the US. We have also included CUSUM of squares test results to show the changes in the variance (Figure 3.6).[9] Thus, though there exists a structural change in the US imports from China series, statistically, there has still been no impact of the trade war on US imports.

US imports from South Asia show a structural change in 2012. This can be attributed to India (Figure 3.7). In fact, US imports from India exhibit a structural increase since 2012, long before the trade war started. So, statistically, we can say that the US began importing more from India from 2012, but such an increase is not related to the trade war.

If we consider the South-East Asian countries as a whole, there is no structural change at all. Now, if we look closer into the individual countries, we do find structural changes for US imports from the Philippines, Singapore, and Vietnam. US imports have decreased from the Philippines and Singapore since 2004. In contrast, US imports from Vietnam have increased since 2016 (see Figure 3.8).

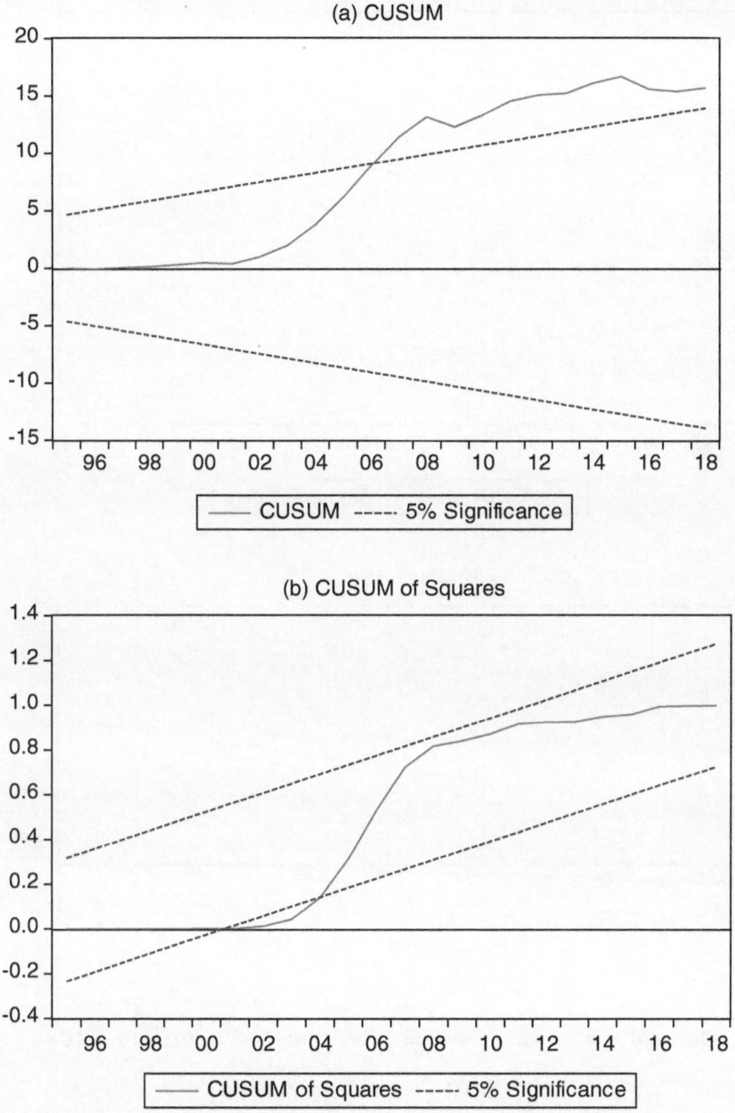

Figure 3.6 USA's imports from China – CUSUM and CUSUM of squares.
Source: Author's calculations.

This increase in US imports from Vietnam might be a result of the US–China trade war and requires further investigation. The other major players don't reveal any structural change.

We ran Chow Forecast Test to see whether there exists any break in the US imports from China, Hong Kong, and major South and South-East Asian trading

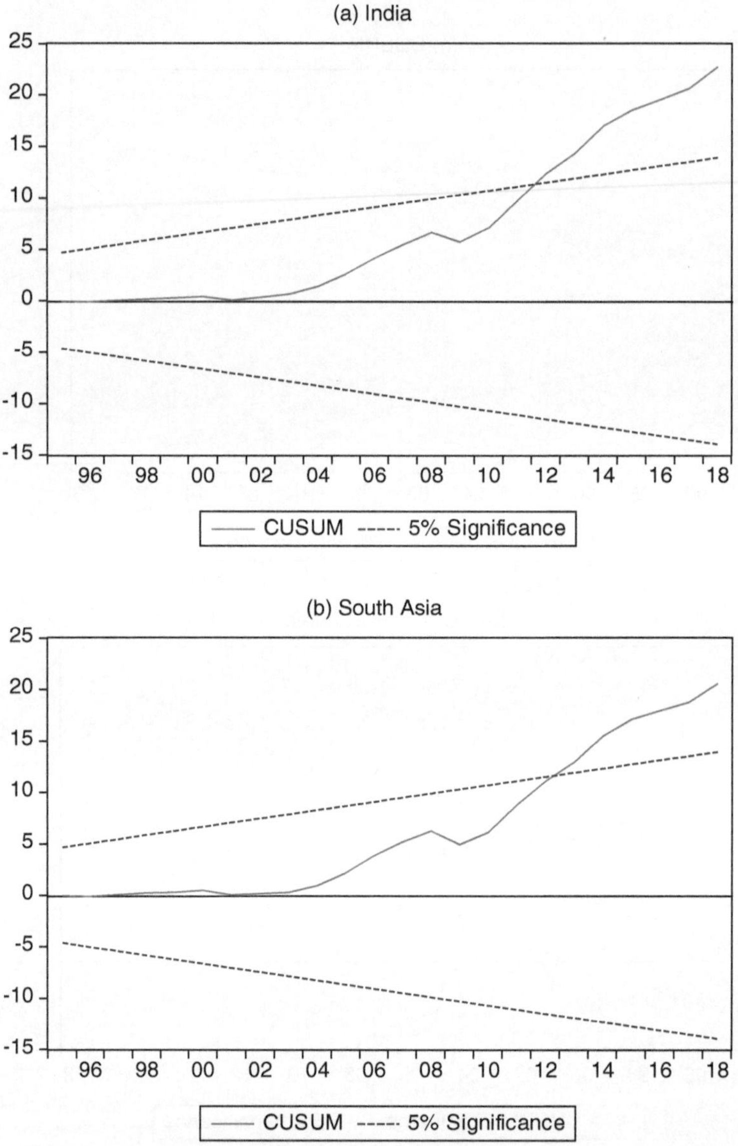

Figure 3.7 USA's imports from South Asia and India.
Source: Author's calculations.

partners. We find that US imports from China, India, and the Philippines do have structural breaks in 2002, and those from Vietnam and the entire South and South-East Asian countries in 2001, Malaysia in 2005, Hong Kong in 2009, Singapore in 2016. There is a second break for US imports from Vietnam in 2008. This result for Vietnam actually corroborates the fact of increasing US imports in 2001 and again in 2008, making Vietnam the top South-East Asian exporter to the US. US imports from Hong Kong declined till 2008 but again picked up from 2009. However, there are no breaks for US imports from Indonesia and Thailand. The results are summarised in Table 3.1.

4.2 US exports to China, Hong Kong, South Asia, and South-East Asia

Thailand is the biggest importer of US goods in this group of countries, closely followed by China. In fact, Thailand accounts for more than 70% of South-East Asian imports of US goods throughout the period 1993–2018. China's imports of US goods are far higher than the total South Asian imports of US goods. However, this gap has narrowed drastically over the period of this study. In 1993 China used to import seven times more than the South Asian countries. In 2018, this narrowed down to less than two times. Hence, unlike imports from China and South and South-East Asian countries, the picture is quite different when it comes to US exports to these countries (Figure 3.9).

Among the South Asian economies, India, Pakistan, and Sri Lanka are the major importers of US goods, followed by Nepal, Bangladesh, and Maldives (Figure 3.10). India's share of South Asian imports of US goods has fluctuated between 20 and 35%, with an average (over the period 1993–2018) of 28%. This is closely followed by Sri Lanka, with an average of 26% and then by Pakistan, with an average of 18%. However, Sri Lanka was the largest importer of US goods among the South Asian countries for a number of years (1993–5, 1998, 2006, 2015–17).

Apart from Thailand, the major South-East Asian importers from the US are Indonesia, the Philippines, and Vietnam. Since 2013, Vietnam has become the biggest importer of US goods among the South and South-East Asian nations closely followed by Hong Kong. Till 2009 Philippines was the top importer, but now it has slipped to the third position followed by Indonesia, Sri Lanka, India, and Pakistan. Pakistan's import of US goods has shown steady growth since 2009 (Figure 3.11).

As evident from Figures 3.9 and 3.11, US exports to these countries grew steadily from the start of the millennium, followed by two slight drops in 2009 and 2016. As analysed for US imports, we resort to CUSUM test for evidence(s) of structural changes in US exports to China and select South and South-East Asian countries. We find structural changes in US exports to China, South, and South-East Asian countries respectively in 2013, 2012, and 2008 (see Figures 3.12–3.14). Interestingly, all these structural changes indicate an increase of US exports to these destinations. US exports to all the South and South-East Asian countries show a sharp increase since 2009. This might signify the US's concerted effort to export more to come out of the sub-prime crises.

Now, we delve deeper into the picture and try to discover any structural change in US exports to individual countries. Interestingly, we find structural changes in US exports to almost all the South and South-East Asian countries

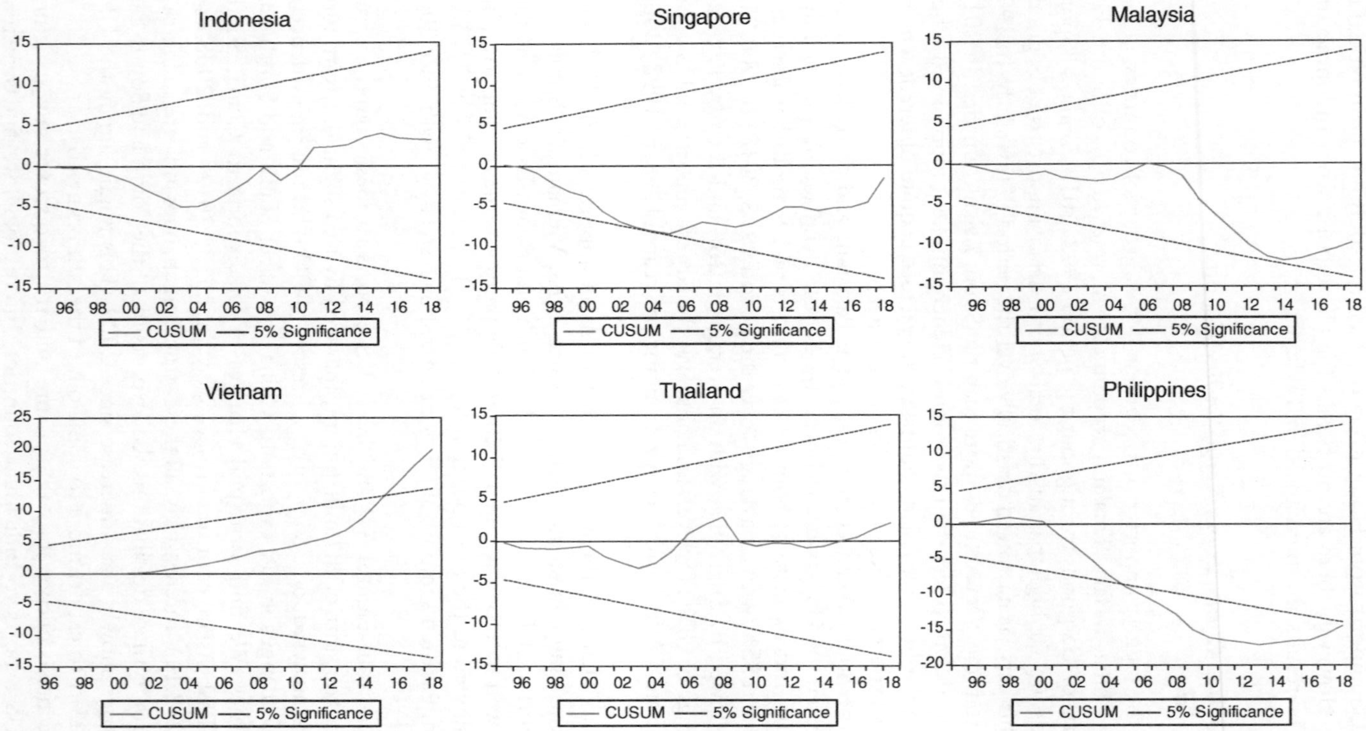

Figure 3.8 USA's imports from select South-East Asian countries – CUSUM tests.

Source: Author's calculations.

Table 3.1 Chow Forecast Test break dates for USA's imports (1993–2018)

Export Destination	*Year*	*F-statistic (Probability Value)*	*Likelihood Ratio (Probability Value)*
China	2002	157.5263 (0.0000)	154.6872 (0.0000)
South Asia	2000	158.5614 (0.0000)	166.4728 (0.0000)
SE Asia	2009	6.501083 (0.0009)	44.99372 (0.0000)
	2015	8.815436 (0.0003)	26.42506 (0.0000)
India	2002	89.28702 (0.0000)	139.9778 (0.0000)
Indonesia	No Break		
Malaysia	2005	12.75474 (0.0000)	76.35848 (0.0000)
Singapore	2016	5.154761 (0.0079)	14.34708 (0.0025)
Vietnam	2001	68303.09 (0.0000)	310.3162 (0.0000)
	2008	106.8501 (0.0000)	117.3997 (0.0000)
Hong Kong	2009	5.101502 (0.0031)	39.92458 (0.0000)
Philippines	2002	25.29265 (0.0003)	112.8977 (0.0000)
Thailand	No Break		

Source: Author's calculations.

(Figure 3.15). Apart from Thailand and Pakistan, US exports to these countries show a significant increase either during 2008–10 (Hong Kong, Philippines) or during 2012–14 (Indonesia, Maldives, Singapore, Sri Lanka, and Vietnam). US exports to Thailand started to increase significantly since 2007. US exports to Pakistan show structural change only in 2016. However, given Pakistan's much smaller economic size, it can't be a replacement of China as far as US exports are concerned.

We ran Chow Forecast Test to see whether there exists any break in the US exports to China, Hong Kong, and major South and South-East Asian trading partners. We find breaks in US exports to both China and South and South-East Asian countries in 2002. Among the South and South-East Asian countries, the breaks exist during the period 2002–4 for Hong Kong, India, Philippines, Singapore, Sri Lanka, Thailand, and Vietnam. US exports to Malaysia and Maldives exhibit a break in 2006 and that to Pakistan in 2009. During 2010–12 there are breaks for US exports to China, India, and Indonesia. US exports to Vietnam exhibit a second breakin 2008. These findings are reported in Table 3.2.

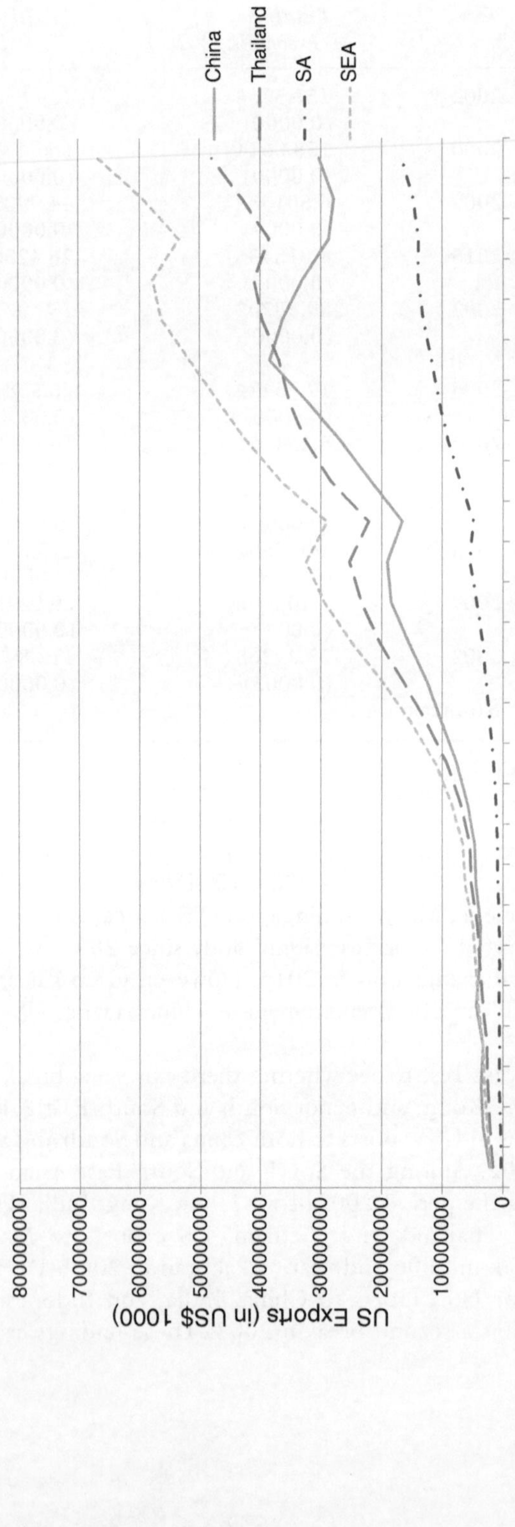

Figure 3.9 US exports to China, Thailand, South Asia, and South-East Asia 1993–2018.

Source: Author's calculations using WITS data.

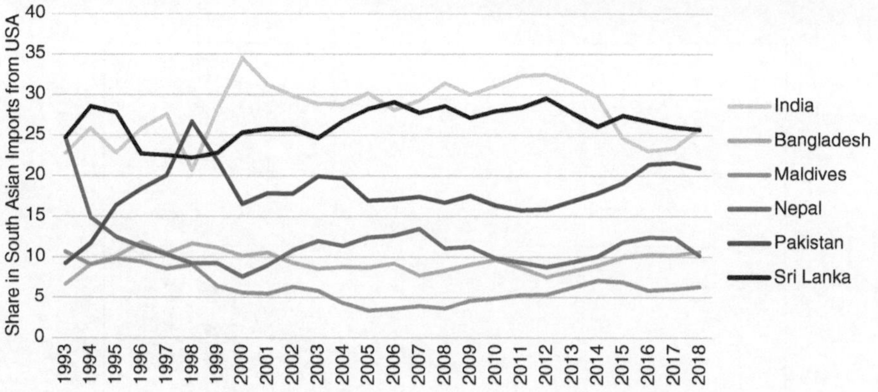

Figure 3.10 Share of South Asia's import from the US (1993–2018).
Source: Author's calculations using WITS data.

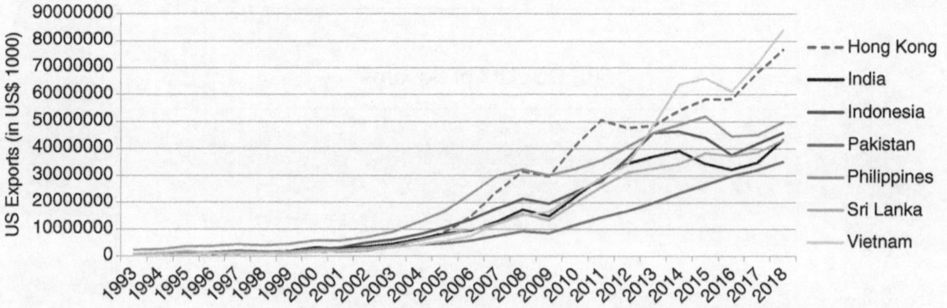

Figure 3.11 US exports to Hong Kong and select South and South-East Asian countries.
Source: Author's calculations using WITS data.

So, we find, at the aggregate level, the impact of the US–China trade war has so far had no significant impact on US trade with China, South Asia, or South-East Asia. Only US imports from Singapore and Vietnam need closer analyses as Singapore is a major trading country, and Vietnam has developed significant manufacturing capacity in the recent past.

5 China's trade with USA, South and South-East Asian countries

In this section, we will analyse the export and import patterns for China. Our analyses are focused on China's trade with the US, South Asian, and South-East Asian countries. The major aims of this section are to analyse the trends and growth patterns of China's trade with the US, South Asian, and South-East

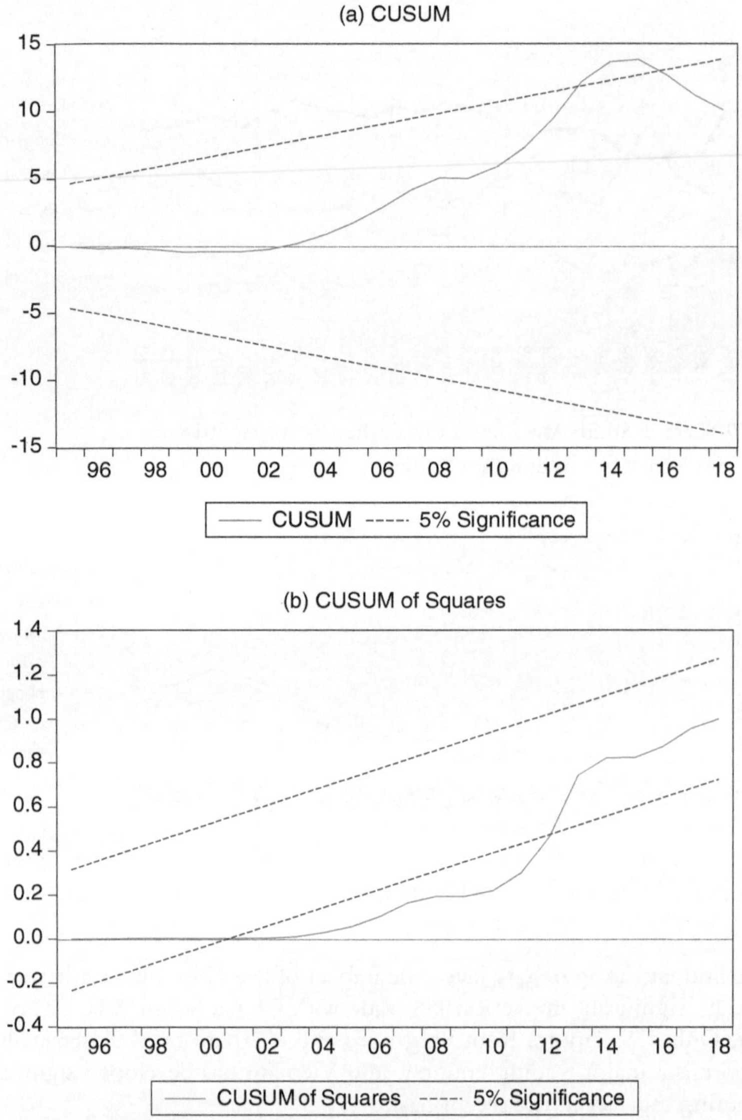

Figure 3.12 USA's exports to China – CUSUM and CUSUM of squares.
Source: Author's calculations.

Asian economies. We also try to find evidence of any structural change in Chinese exports and imports with the countries mentioned. Finally, we try to locate the changes that might have happened due to this very recent US–China trade war.

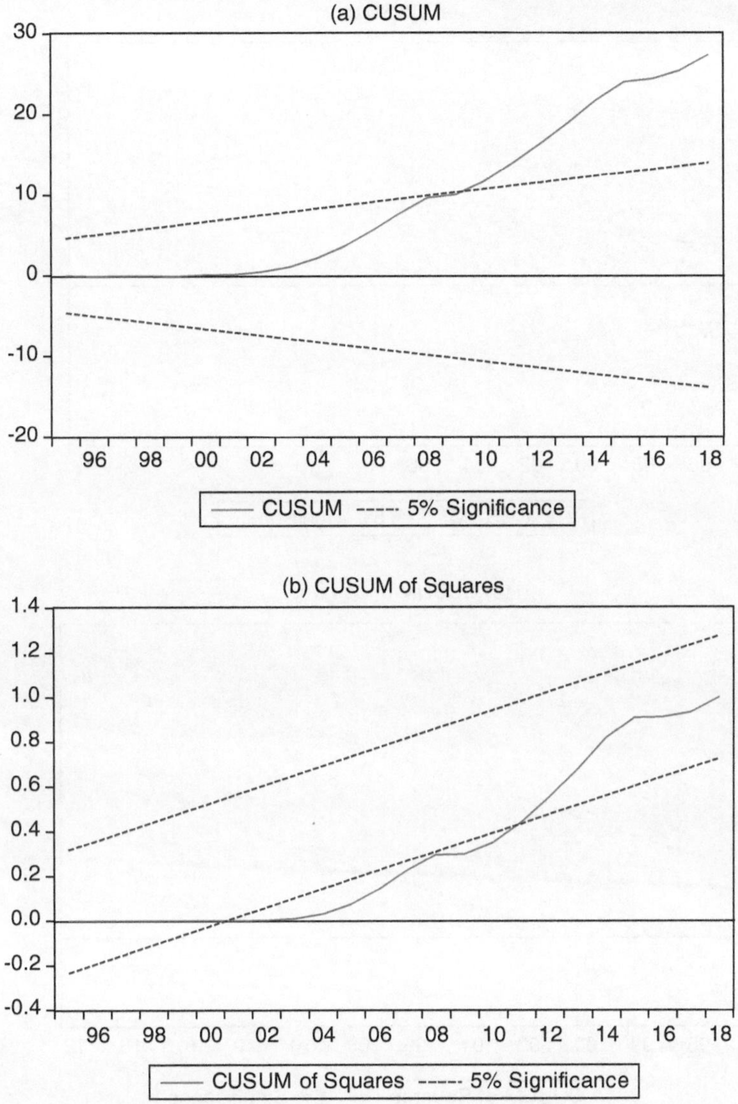

Figure 3.13 USA's exports to South Asia – CUSUM and CUSUM of squares.
Source: Author's calculations.

5.1 China's imports from USA, South and South-East Asian countries

China's imports from the US exceed that of entire South Asia by miles (Figure 3.16). During the early 1990s, China used to import from the US more than twenty times the imports from South Asia. Chinese imports from the US are still approximately

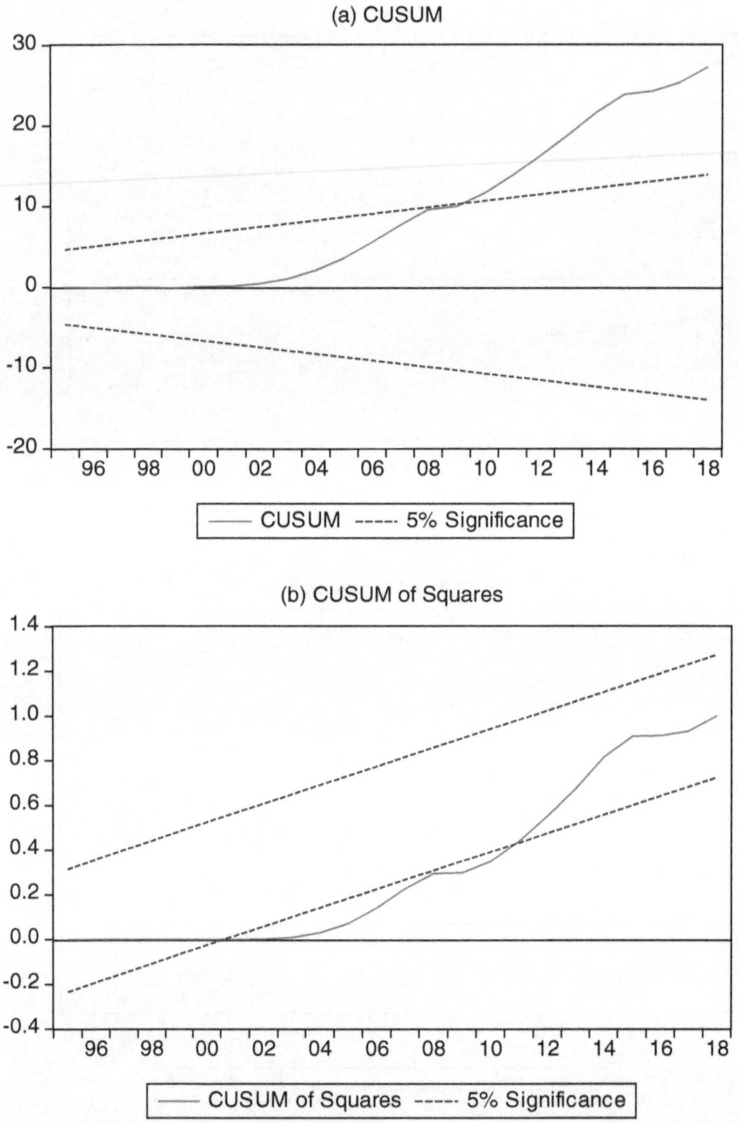

Figure 3.14 USA's exports to South-East Asia – CUSUM and CUSUM of squares.
Source: Author's calculations.

seven times Chinese imports from South Asia. Moreover, the rate of growth of Chinese imports from the US is almost 12% on average during 1993–2018 while that from South Asia is approximately 19%. Chinese imports from the US shrank by more than 9% in 2016. However, that was more than compensated immediately in

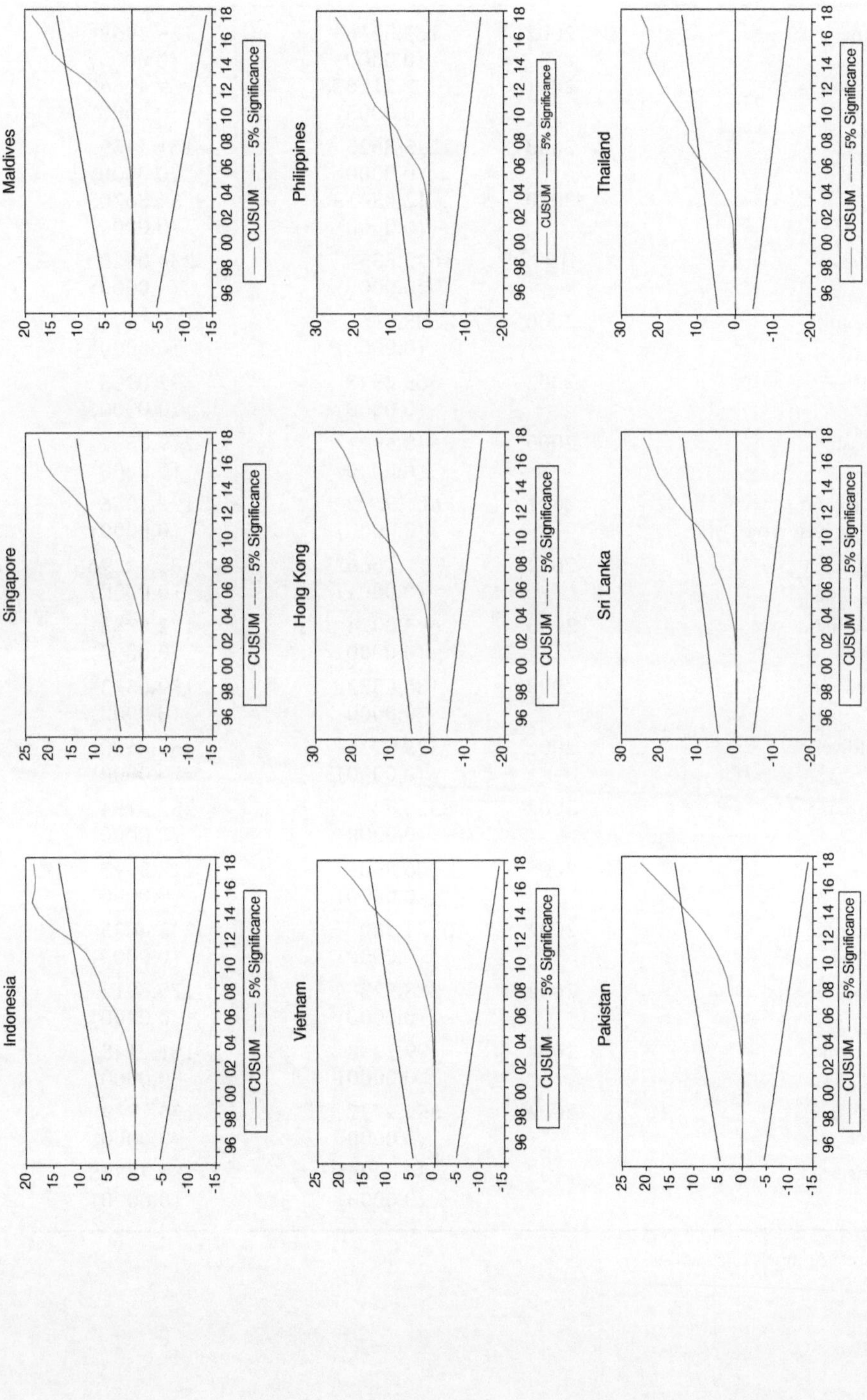

Figure 3.15 USA's exports to Hong Kong and select South and South-East Asian countries.

Source: Author's calculations.

Table 3.2 Chow Forecast Test break dates for USA's exports (1993–2018)

Export destination	*Year*	*F-statistic (Probability value)*	*Likelihood ratio (Probability value)*
China	2002	162.5216 (0.0000)	155.4968 (0.0000)
	2011	7.111678 (0.0005)	39.42665 (0.0000)
India	2003	245.3625 (0.0000)	161.1459 (0.0000)
	2010	12.08413 (0.0000)	54.86705 (0.0000)
Pakistan	.1999	1625.535 (0.0000)	234.0820 (0.0000)
Sri Lanka	2000	385.5552 (0.0000)	189.5496 (0.0000)
South Asia	2002	665.2528 (0.0000)	192.0903 (0.0000)
SE Asia	2000	3848.491 (0.0000)	249.3532 (0.0000)
South and South-East Asia	2002	806.9692 (0.0000)	197.1086 (0.0000)
Indonesia	2012	7.166629 (0.0004)	35.72296 (0.0000)
Malaysia	2006	645.0074 (0.0000)	172.5783 (0.0000)
Singapore	2002	186.4337 (0.0000)	159.0572 (0.0000)
Maldives	2006	325.8731 (0.0000)	154.8600 (0.0000)
Vietnam	2002	8370.52 (0.0000)	257.9154 (0.0000)
	2008	106.8501 (0.0000)	117.3997 (0.0000)
Hong Kong	2002	5184.980 (0.0000)	245.4635 (0.0000)
Philippines	2002	288.5238 (0.0000)	170.3912 (0.0000)
Sri Lanka	2004	199.2238 (0.0000)	151.0148 (0.0000)
Thailand	2002	359.9387 (0.0000)	176.1339 (0.0000)
Pakistan	2009	34.60051 (0.0000)	84.42358 (0.0000)

Source: Author's calculations.

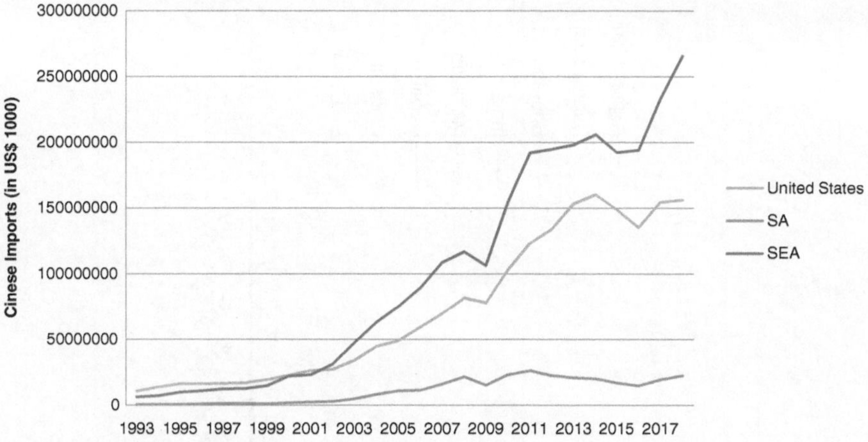

Figure 3.16 Chinese imports from USA, South and South-East Asian countries (1993–2018).
Source: Author's calculations using WITS data.

2017 by a growth of more than 14%. China's major imports are from South-East Asia. Chinese imports from South-East Asia are almost twelve times of those from South Asia and 1.5 times (on average) of those from the US.

If we look closer into Chinese imports from South Asia, India is the single major exporter (Figure 3.17). India's exports contribute about 80% of South Asian exports to China. A distant second is Pakistan. Pakistan's share dipped drastically from 31% in 1999 to 12% in 2003 to 5% in 2008, then reviving to about 10% at present. Since 2010, Bangladesh has been steadily increasing its share, though it is still less than 5%.

Among the South-East Asian economies, Indonesia, Malaysia, Philippines, Singapore, Thailand, and Vietnam are major exporters to China (Figure 3.18). Most interestingly, Vietnam has taken the leading position among the South-East Asian group in 2018, dethroning Malaysia. Vietnam's exports to China have grown at a whopping 33% on average over the period 1993–2018. Thailand comes in the third, followed by Singapore, Indonesia, Philippines.

Now, we perform CUSUM tests for evidence of structural changes in China's imports from the US, South Asia, and South-East Asia. We find that Chinese imports from the US have structurally increased since 2011. There is no such change as far as South Asia (and India) is concerned. China's imports from South-East Asia has increased significantly since 2010 (Figure 3.19). Thus, though there is a structural change in China's imports from the US, the change is positive and predates the US–China trade war. Moreover, such increased imports happened also from South-East Asia and at the same time. These findings suggest that the US–China trade war has so far had no effect on China's imports from the US at the aggregate level.

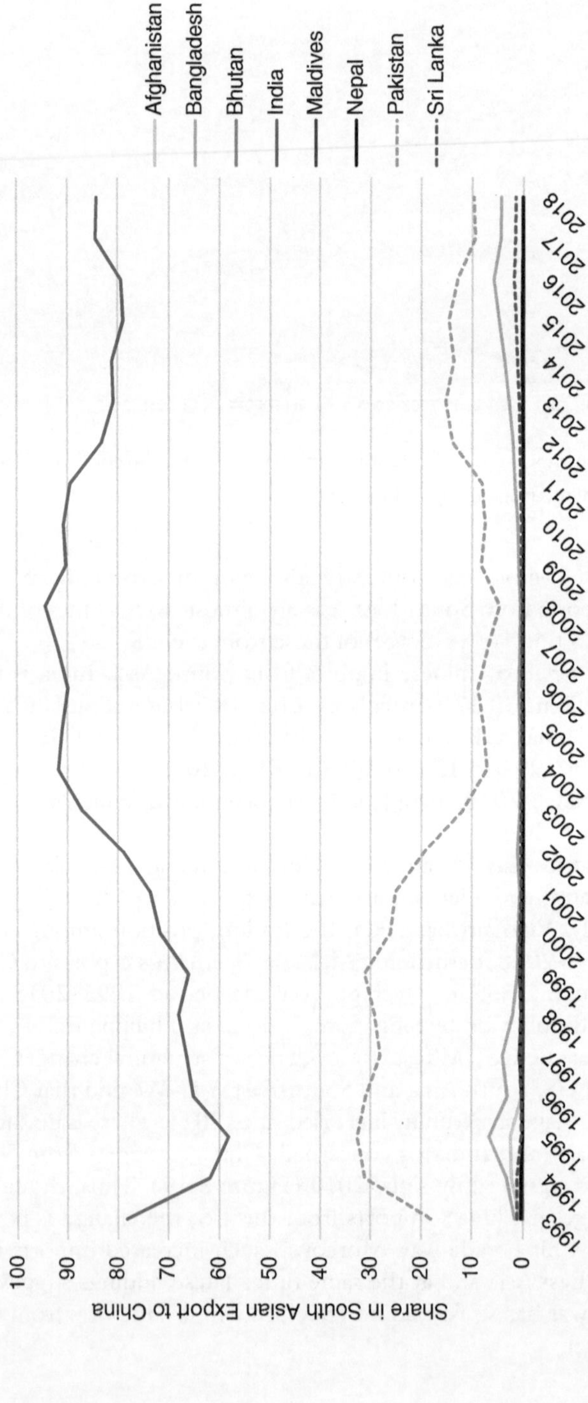

Figure 3.17 Country's share in South Asian exports to China.

Source: Author's calculations using WITS data.

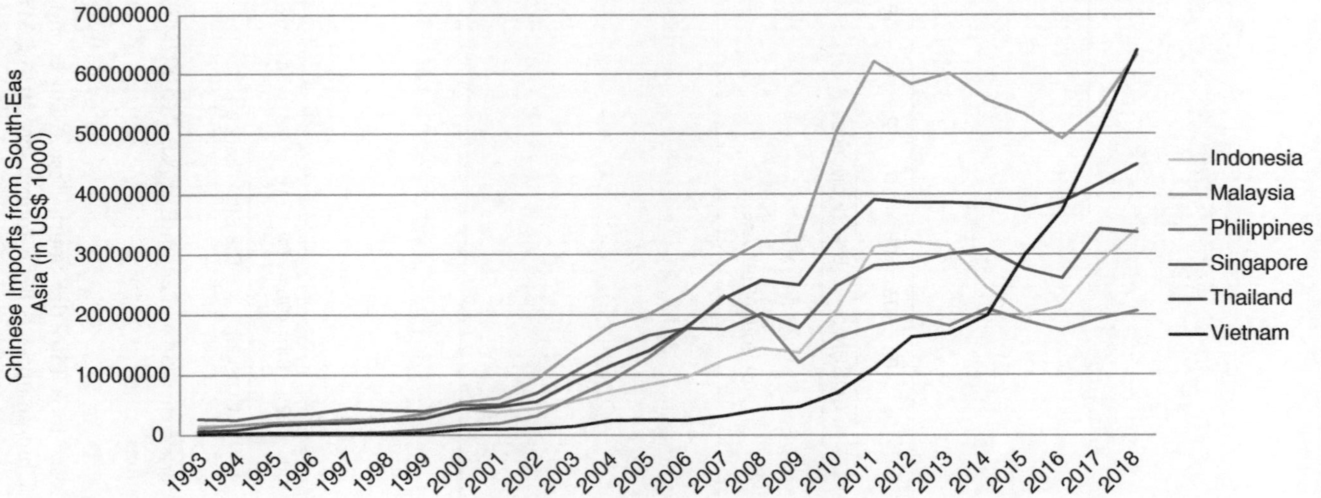

Figure 3.18 Major South-East Asian exporters to China (1993–2018).

Source: Author's calculations using WITS data.

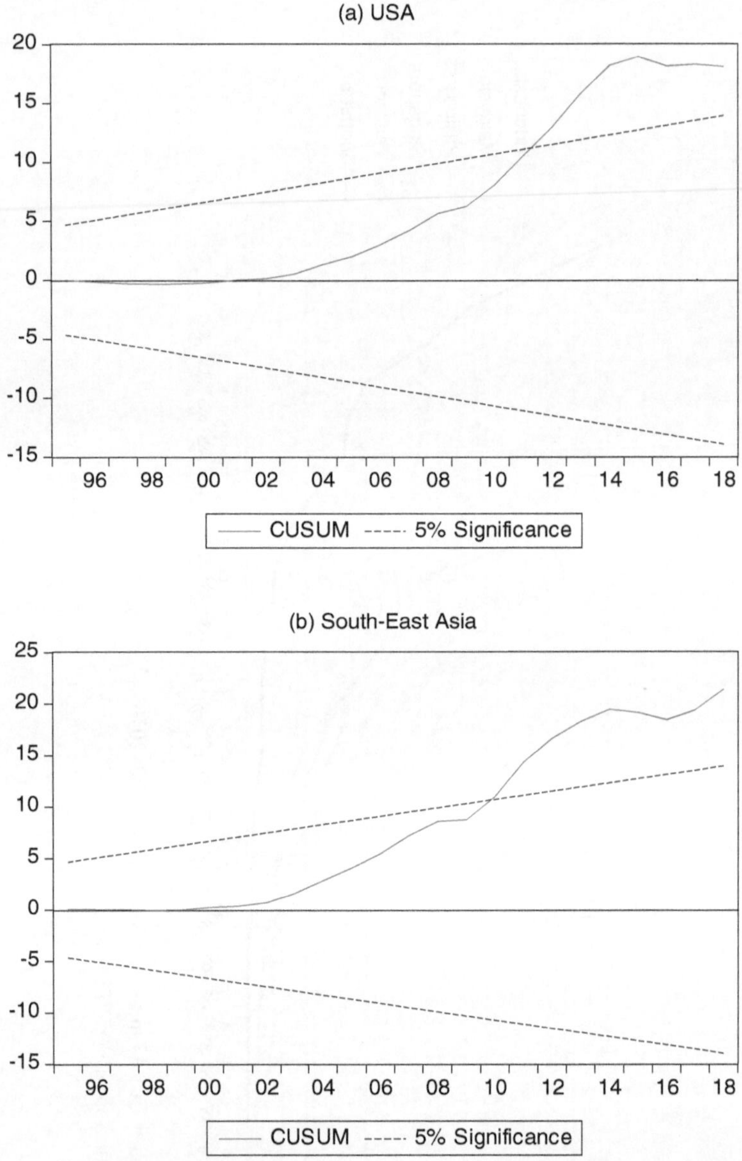

Figure 3.19 China's imports from USA and South-East Asia – CUSUM tests.
Source: Author's calculations.

We now take a closer look into the South-East Asian economies. We find structural changes in Chinese imports from Indonesia (2013), Malaysia (2011), Singapore (2011), Thailand (2009), and Vietnam (2018). The CUSUM test results are given in Figure 3.20. CUSUM test does not indicate any change for China's imports from the Philippines.

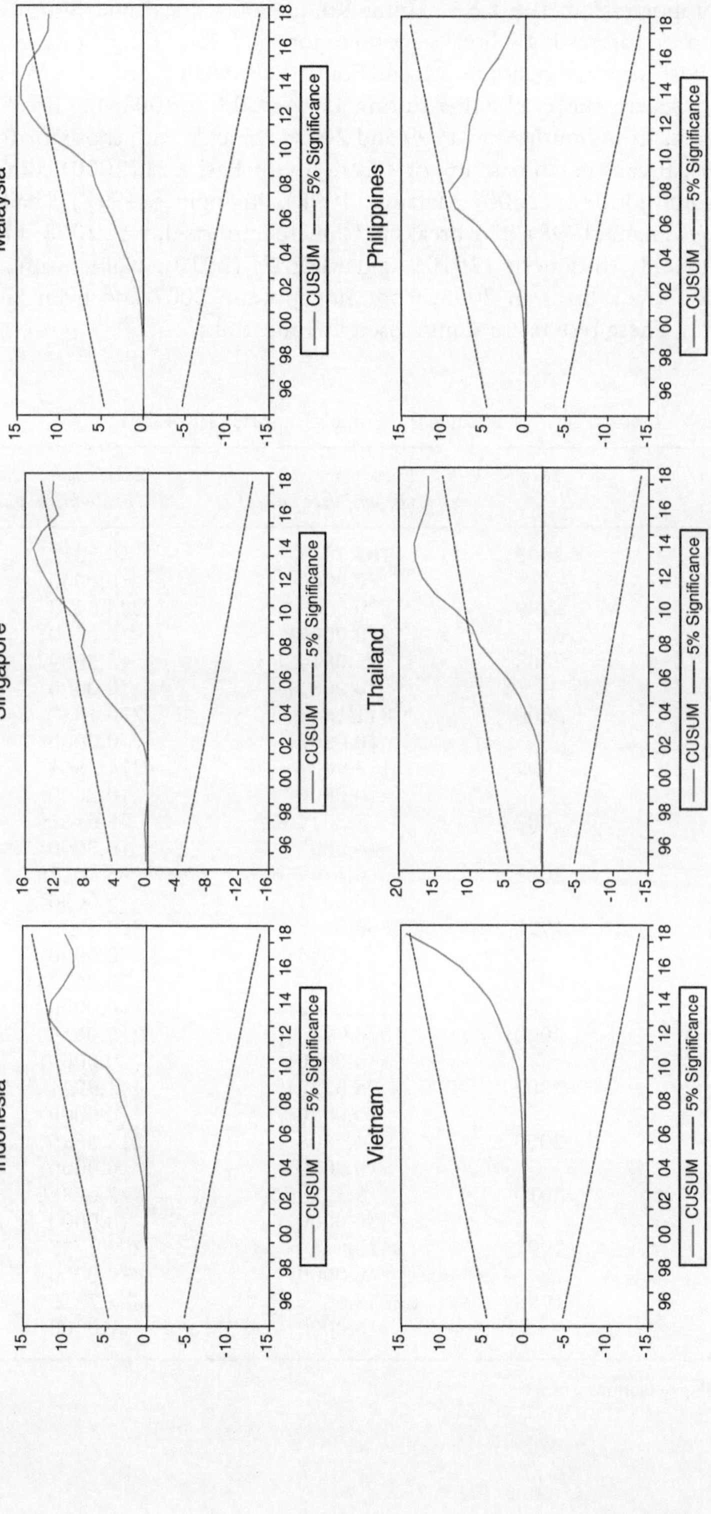

Figure 3.20 China's imports from select South-East Asian countries – CUSUM tests.

Source: Author's calculations.

Next, we apply Chow forecast test to find evidence(s) for a structural break(s) in Chinese imports from the USA, Hong Kong, South Asia, and South-East Asian economies. Interestingly breaks are there for the USA, Hong Kong, South Asia, South-East Asia, and major South and South-East Asian economies. We find that these breaks are clustered either during 1997–2003 or 2008–11. Breaks in Chinese imports from South Asia (1999 and 2007) coincide with those for India (1999, 2008). Breaks in Chinese imports from South-East Asia (2000) coincide with those from Indonesia (2000), Malaysia (1998), Philippines (1997), Thailand (2000), and Vietnam (1998). The breaks in Chinese imports during 2008–11 are from India (2008), Indonesia (2010), and Malaysia (2010). Chinese imports from the US show a break in 2003, from Singapore in 2002 and from Hong Kong in 2011. These results are summarised in Table 3.3.

Table 3.3 Chow Forecast Test break dates for China's imports (1993–2018)

Import destination	*Year*	*F-statistic (Probability value)*	*Likelihood ratio (Probability value)*
USA	2003	164.5334 (0.0000)	150.7817 (0.0000)
India	1999	1329.066 (0.0000)	228.8473 (0.0000)
	2008	5.081478 (0.0036)	43.35897 (0.0000)
SE Asia	2000	1841.164 (0.0000)	230.1857 (0.0000)
South Asia	1999	1113.907 (0.0000)	224.2564 (0.0000)
	2007	7.501462 (0.0007)	55.64619 (0.0000)
Hong Kong	2011	6.110956 (0.0011)	36.40178 (0.0000)
Philippines	1997	20558.36 (0.0003)	320.5520 (0.0000)
Indonesia	2010	23.87466 (0.0000)	70.96628 (0.0000)
	2000	1028.998 (0.0000)	215.0615 (0.0000)
Singapore	2002	96.51271 (0.0000)	141.9921 (0.0000)
Thailand	2000	974.9308 (0.0000)	213.6586 (0.0000)
Malaysia	2010	8.522852 (0.0000)	47.07388 (0.0000)
	1998	3420.846 (0.0000)	262.1735 (0.0000)
Vietnam	1998	62648.66 (0.0000)	337.7715 (0.0000)

Source: Author's calculations.

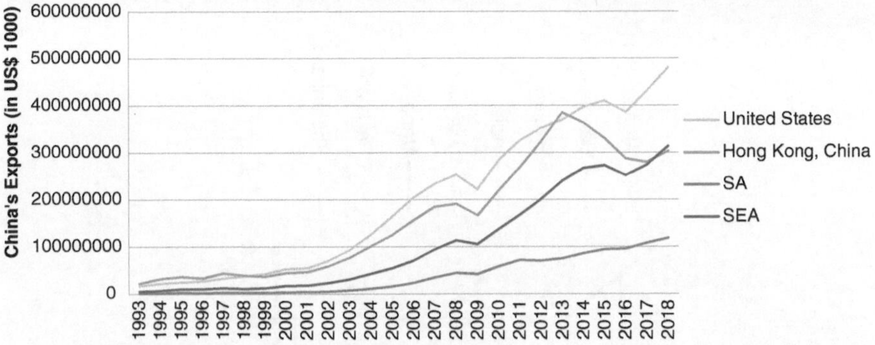

Figure 3.21 China's exports to USA, Hong Kong, South and South-East Asia (1993–2018).
Source: Author's calculations using WITS data.

5.2 China's exports to USA, South and South-East Asian countries

In this section, we try to analyse the Chinese exports to the US, South Asian, and South-East Asian destinations. Here, we also incorporate Hong Kong as it is a major gateway of Chinese exports to the rest of the world. China's exports to the US and Hong Kong exceed those to South or South-East Asia (Figure 3.21). China's exports to the US grew at an exponential rate of 14.2% per annum during 1993–2018, from US$17 billion in 1993 to US$480 billion in 2018. As mentioned earlier, this has led to a whopping trade deficit for the US and has been a major trigger for the US–China trade war. Hong Kong has remained another major export destination for China during this period. However, the average annual rate of growth of Chinese exports to Hong Kong has reduced to 5.67% during the last ten years (2008–2018) as compared to 17.63% during 1993–2007. South Asia's import of Chinese goods increased at an exponential rate of more than 20% per annum during this period, while Chinese exports to South-East Asia increased at a rate of 17.5%.

When we look at the disaggregated picture for South Asia, India is the major destination for Chinese exports to South Asia, making up more than two-thirds of Chinese exports to South Asia. A distant second is Pakistan, followed by Bangladesh and Sri Lanka (Figure 3.22). China's exports to India have increased by an exponential rate of 24% per annum over this period. China's exports to Pakistan have increased at a rate of 16.5%, while those to Bangladesh have increased at a rate of 17%. However, apart from India, the rest of South Asian countries are not significant export destinations for China.

When we look into the South-East Asian economies, the story is quite different. Indonesia, Malaysia, Philippines, Singapore, Thailand, and Vietnam all feature as important export destinations for Chinese exports (Figure 3.23). In fact, Vietnam has become the biggest importer of Chinese goods since 2013

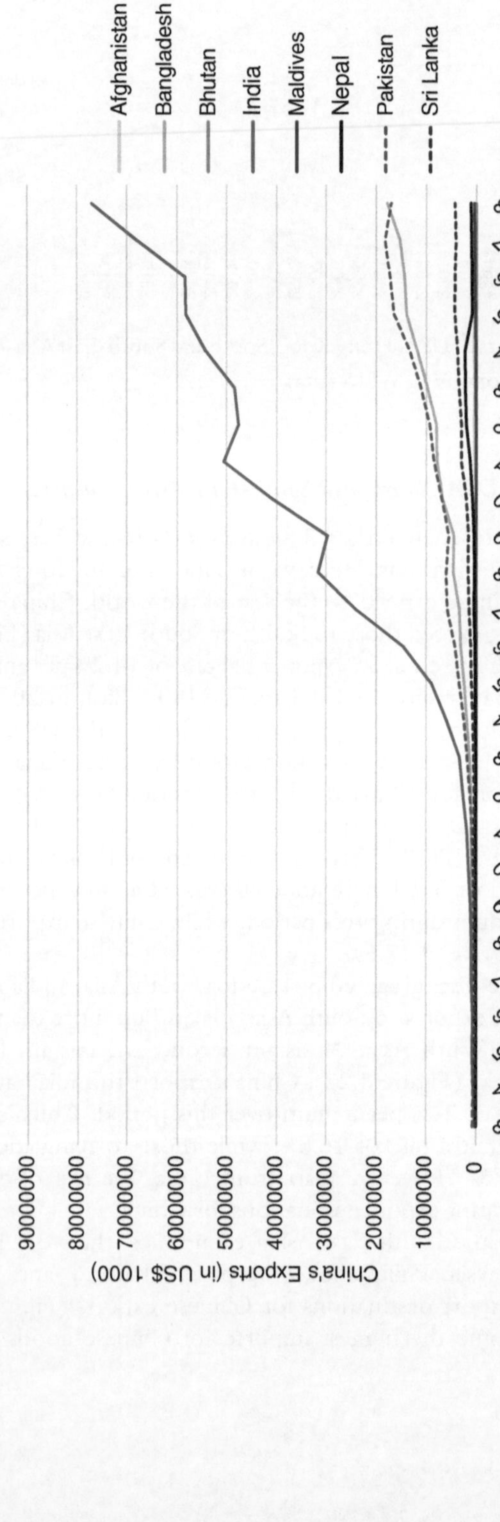

Figure 3.22 China's exports to South Asia (1993–2018).

Source: Author's calculations using WITS Data.

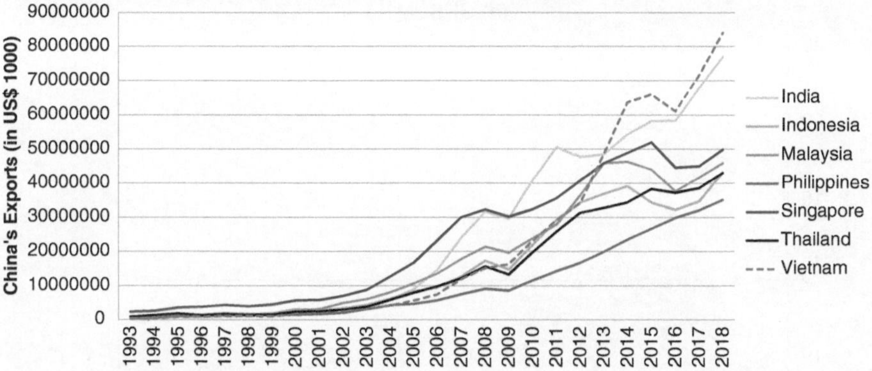

Figure 3.23 China's exports to major South and South-East Asian countries (1993–2018).
Source: Author's calculations using WITS Data.

followed by Singapore, Malaysia, Thailand, Indonesia, and the Philippines. Among the South and South-East Asian countries, India is the second biggest importer of Chinese goods.

Using CUSUM tests for evidence of structural changes, we find that Chinese exports to the US have structurally increased since 2007. Chinese exports have structurally changed, and increased, for South Asia (and India) in 2010. China's exports to South-East Asia have increased significantly since 2012 (Figures 3.24–3.26). Hence, all the structural changes happened during 2007–12, long before the US–China trade war started.

We now take a closer look at the South-East Asian economies. We find structural changes in Chinese exports to Indonesia (2012), Malaysia (2012), Philippines (2014), Singapore (2008), Thailand (2011), and Vietnam (2014). Structural change in Chinese exports to Hong Kong happened in 2013. Hence, China's exports surged during the period 2008–14.[10]

Next, we apply Chow forecast test to find evidence for structural break(s) in Chinese exports to the USA, Hong Kong, South Asian, and South-East Asian economies. Interestingly, those breaks are there and are clustered either during 1998–2002 or 2010–11. Breaks in Chinese exports to South Asia (2000) coincide with that for India (2000). Breaks in Chinese exports to South-East Asia (2000) can be attributed to those to Indonesia (2000), Malaysia (1998), Philippines (1998), Singapore (1998), Thailand (2000), and Vietnam (1998). The breaks in Chinese exports in 2010 are for Malaysia, the Philippines, and Thailand. Chinese exports to the US show a break in 1998, and to Hong Kong in 2002 and 2011. The results are provided in Table 3.4.

Thus, the only country for which we find any break for China's trade with the US, South Asia, and South-East Asia is Vietnam. As found from CUSUM test, China's imports from Vietnam have increased structurally in 2018. Other

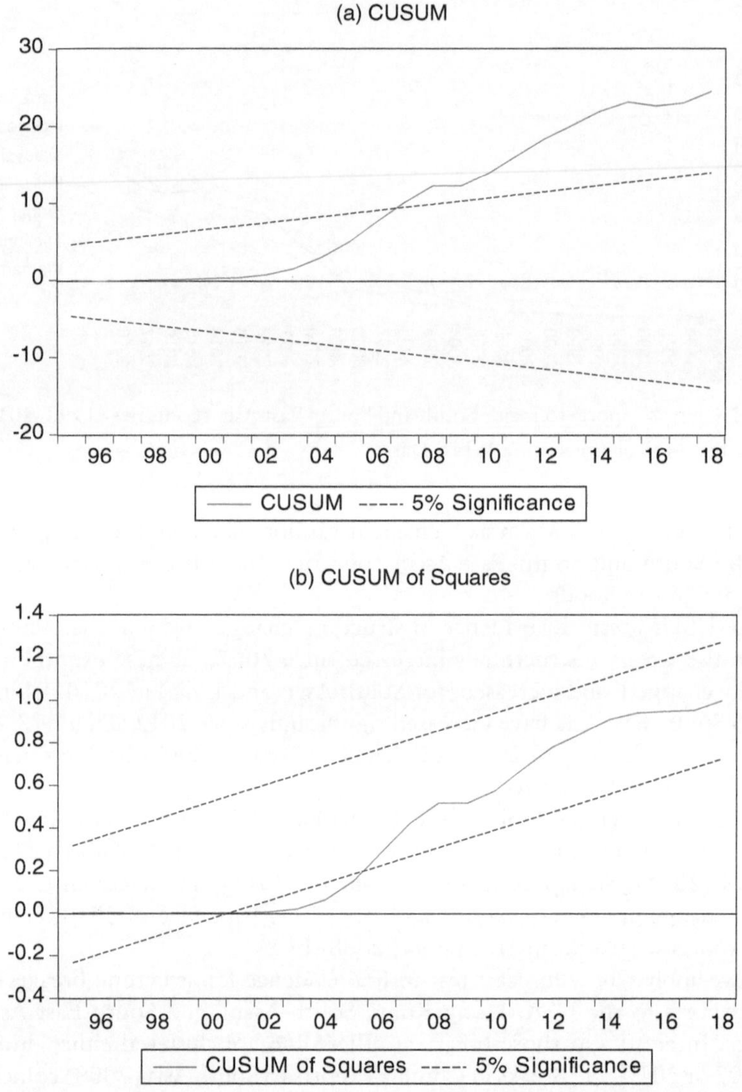

Figure 3.24 China's exports to USA – CUSUM and CUSUM of squares.
Source: Author's calculations.

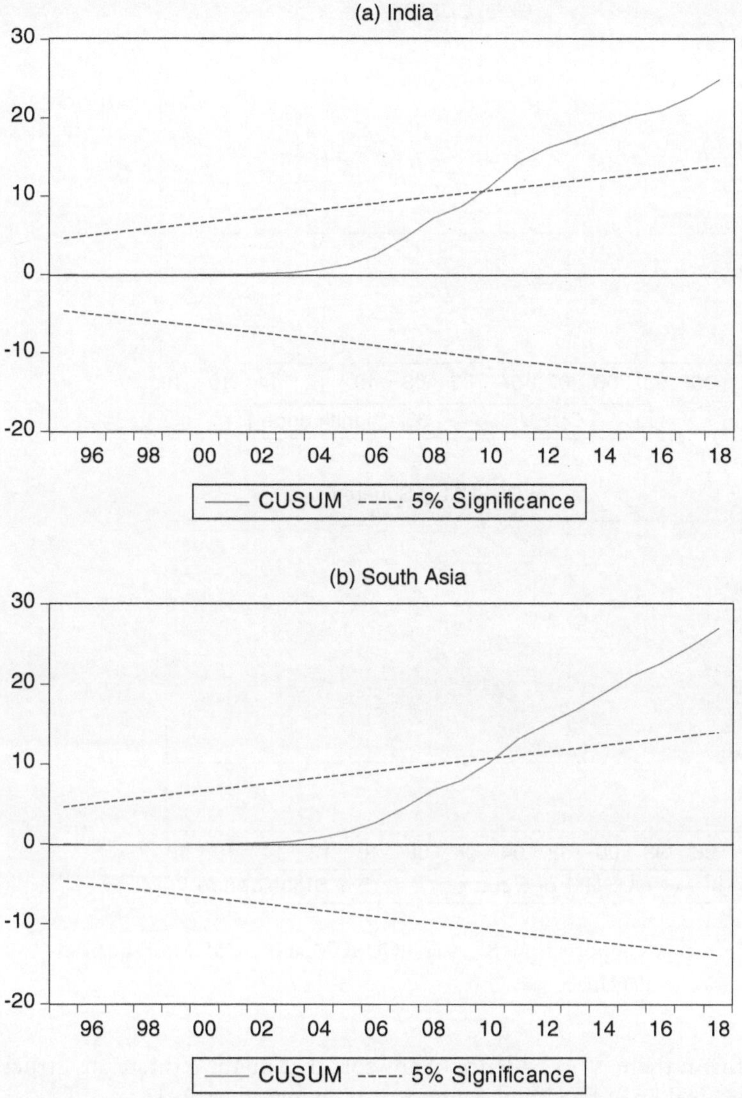

Figure 3.25 China's imports from India and South Asia – CUSUM.
Source: Author's calculations.

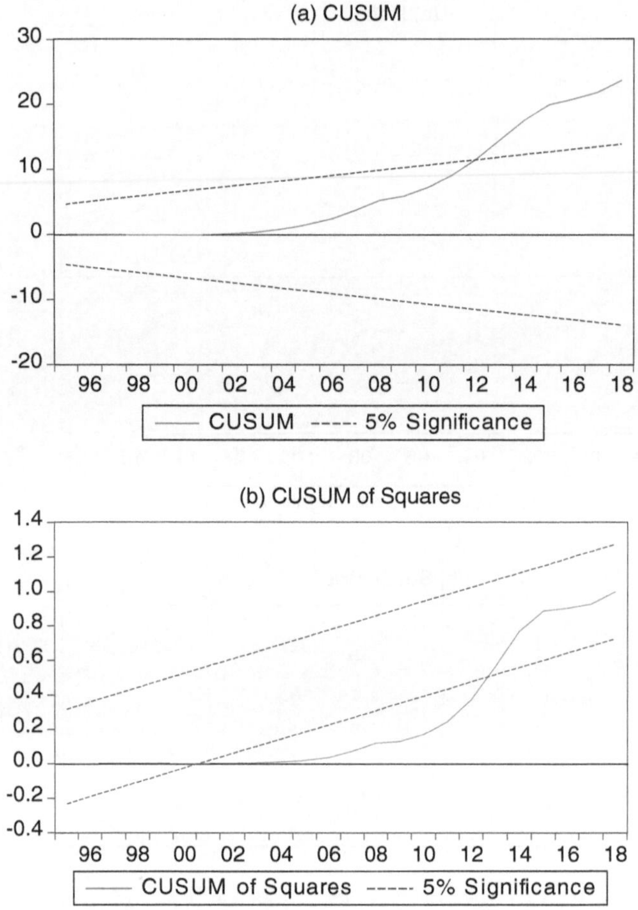

Figure 3.26 China's imports from SE Asia – CUSUM and CUSUM of squares.
Source: Author's calculations.

than Vietnam, there is no evidence of any sort that might indicate any structural change or break in either Chinese imports or exports post-2016.

6 Conclusion

This study made a modest attempt to analyse the trade patterns and dynamics of the US and China over the period 1993–2018. China's exports to the US exceed the total exports of South and South-East Asia to the US. China is also the second biggest importer of US goods after Thailand. However, the USA's trade deficit with China has been increasing at an exponential rate. Hence, the trade deficit might well be a major trigger for this trade war.

Table 3.4 Chow Forecast Test break dates for China's exports (1993–2018)

Export destination	*Year*	*F-statistic (Probability value)*	*Likelihood ratio (Probability value)*
USA	1998	1219.977 (0.0000)	235.3680 (0.0000)
India	2000	11468.49 (0.0000)	277.7419 (0.0000)
SE Asia	2000	892.0981 (0.0000)	211.3507 (0.0000)
South Asia	2000	3875.663 (0.0000)	249.5361 (0.0000)
Hong Kong	2002	162.5216 (0.0000)	155.4968 (0.0000)
	2011	7.111678 (0.0005)	39.42665 (0.0000)
Philippines	1998	1289.684 (0.0000)	236.8125 (0.0000)
	2010	37.94432 (0.0000)	82.37530 (0.0000)
Indonesia	2000	406.4321 (0.0000)	190.9197 (0.0000)
Singapore	1998	965.7965 (0.0000)	229.2943 (0.0000)
Thailand	2010	12.19835 (0.0000)	55.08213 (0.0000)
	2000	385.5552 (0.0000)	189.5496 (0.0000)
Malaysia	2010	7.869151 (0.0000)	45.34996 (0.0000)
	1998	2083.490 (0.0000)	249.2822 (0.0000)
Vietnam	1998	32587.37 (0.0000)	320.7775 (0.0000)

Source: Author's calculations.

In the USA's trade with South Asia India is the single major exporter from the group. In fact, there exists a structural increase in South Asia's export to the US in 2002, which coincides with a structural increase in India's exports to the USA. As far as South-East Asia is concerned; Malaysia, Thailand, Singapore, and Vietnam are the major exporters to the US. Sri Lanka, India, and Pakistan are the top importers of US goods. However, Thailand's imports from the US exceed those by China and any other South or South-East Asian country. Other than Thailand, Vietnam is a key importer from the South-East Asian bloc.

China's trade (sum of export and import) with South Asia and South-East Asia has increased during the period of the study, as mentioned in Section 4. The only difference is that there was a sudden dip in 2016 for the South-East Asian countries, which is not there for trade with South Asia. China's imports from India exceed that of any other South Asian country by miles. Vietnam and Malaysia are the two top exporters to China among the South-East Asian countries. India is also the major importer of Chinese goods in South Asia. Vietnam tops the list from the South-East Asian bloc.

We find structural changes in US and China trade (both export and import) with almost all the South Asian and South-East Asian countries. However, all the breaks predate the onset of the US-China trade war. Factually, almost all the break dates gather around two periods: 1998–2002 (a period just after the South-East Asian currency crisis) and 2008–12 (a period that covers the US sub-prime crisis). Thus, this finding might well indicate the concerted efforts of all the countries to recover from economic crises.

The study, however, does not find any strong evidence that the trade war has significantly impacted US–China bilateral trade. Trade between the USA and South/South-East Asian economies and trade between China and South/South-East Asian economies show structural changes that predate the trade war. However, these results are not unexpected as we still don't have data points after the onset of the trade war.

Singapore and Vietnam are the two South-East Asian nations for which further analysis is called for. Singapore's exports to the US and Vietnam's exports to both US and China show significant structural changes. Future research, including commodity-specific analyses, is also required to capture the complete essence of the trade war.

Appendix

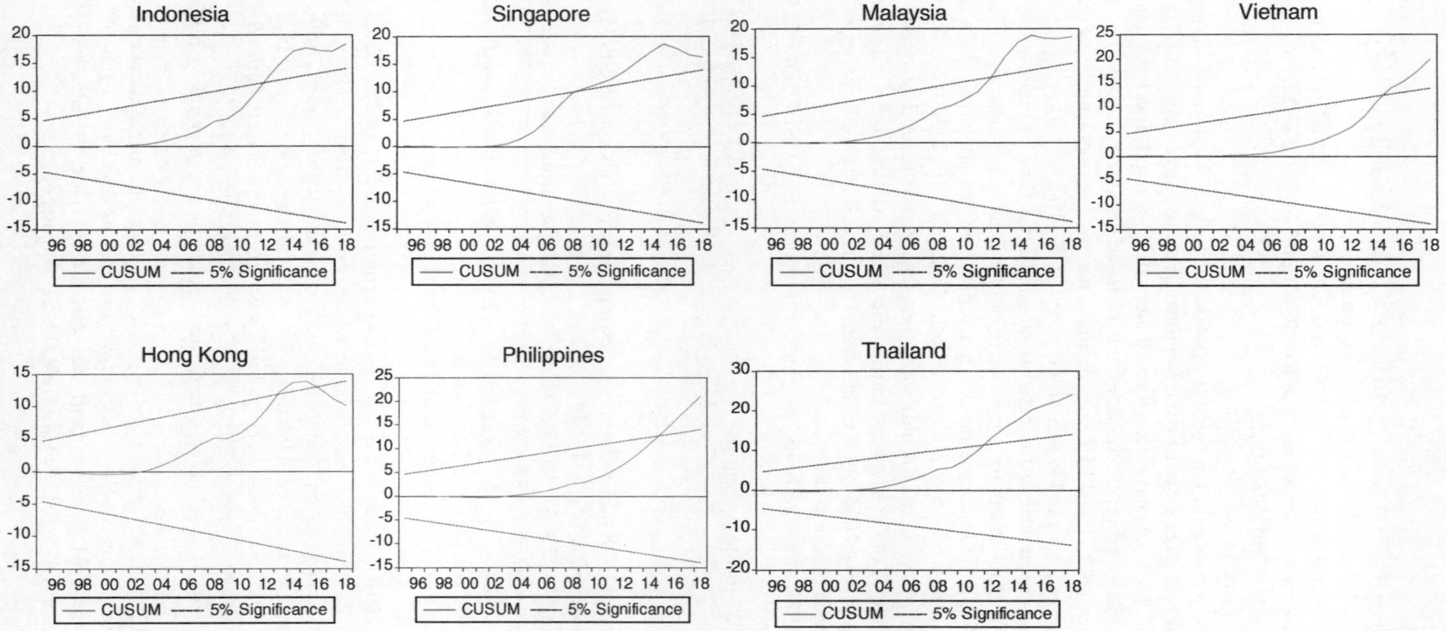

Figure 3.27 China's exports to Hong Kong and major South-East Asian countries – CUSUM tests.

Source: Author's calculations.

Notes

1 See, for instance, Caves, Frankel, & Jones (2002) for a detailed analysis.
2 See De Scitovszky (1942) for a detailed exposition.
3 According to World Bank (2018), USA and China rank first and second in terms of GDP and these two countries account for almost 40% of world GDP.
4 See https://wits.worldbank.org/
5 This section draws on Ghosh (2018).
6 There are three reasons for choosing the period for analysis. First, trade among nations is determined to a large extent by the Regional Trading Agreements (RTAs) and 90% of the present-day RTAs have been formed after 1990. Second, India is a major player in the South Asian group of countries and India adopted a managed float exchange rate regime in 1993. Third, the present study has tried to incorporate as many time points as possible after the US sub-prime crisis (2007–10).
7 Hong Kong has been included as it is a major gateway for Chinese exports and imports.
8 Testing for structural break for a given date can be done using the classic Chow break test. For multiple endogenous breaks in a series, one can apply the Bai and Perron (1998, 2003) methodology. However, both these tests not only fail to capture the breaks properly in presence of unit roots, but require adequate data points on both sides of the date(s) of the break(s). In this study, we are trying to find the existence of any such breaks post-2016 but data are available only till 2018. All the series involved exhibit existence of unit roots as well.
9 See Miller (1982) for a technical but lucid exposition on CUSUM and CUSUM of squares tests.
10 See Figure 3.27 in the Appendix.

References

Bai, J., & Perron, P. (1998). Estimating and testing linear models with multiple structural changes. *Econometrica*, *66*(1), 47–78.

Bai, J., & Perron, P. (2003). Critical values for multiple structural change tests. *The Econometrics Journal*, *6*(1), 72–78.

Caves, R. E., Frankel, J. A., & Jones, R. W. (2002). *World Trade and Payments: An Introduction*. 9th ed. London: Pearson Education

De Scitovszky, T. (1942). A reconsideration of the theory of tariffs. *Review of Economic Studies*, *9*(2), 89–110.

Economic Times (2018). Trade war is on! Donald Trump fires $34 bn tariff gun at China. 6 July. https://economictimes.indiatimes.com/news/international/business/trade-war-threat-gets-real-as-trump-confirms-china-tariffs/articleshow/64877569.cms

Ghosh, S. (2018). Protectionism: US tariff policy and India's response (part II).Centre for Development Studies Commentary on India's Economy and Society Series #4. http://cds.edu/wp-content/uploads/2019/02/CommentarySeries-4.pdf

Krugman, P. A. (2000). Technology, trade and factor prices. *Journal of International Economics*, *50*(1), 51–71.

Miller, S. E. (1982). The structural stability of the concentration-performance relationship in food manufacturing. *Southern Journal of Agricultural Economics*, 14(2), 43–49.

The Indian Express (2018). How tariff war can hit all trade. 9 July. http://epaper.indianexpress.com/1729011/Delhi/July-09,-2018#page/12/1

The Times of India (2018). US plans curbs on Chinese investment, citing security risks. 25 June. https://timesofindia.indiatimes.com/business/international-business/us-plans-curbs-on-chinese-investment-citing-security-risks/articleshow/64728845.cms
World Bank (2018). https://data.worldbank.org/i

4 Impact of US–China trade war on the global economy, free trade, and WTO

Pravin Jadhav and Rahul Nath Choudhury

1 Introduction

The world's two biggest economies, the United States of America (US) and China entered into a trade war in the year 2018. A trade war takes place when countries control and restrict each other's bilateral or multilateral trade by increasing tariff levels, non-tariff measures, or quotas on imports using domestic protectionism. These domestic protectionist policies restrict global trade and the idea of free trade, which is the basic principle of the World Trade Organisation (WTO). These protectionism measures also impact negatively on the trust over WTO and can lead to global distress.

International trade between the US and China increased significantly after the liberalisation of the trade regime by China in the late 1970s. As per the data of the United States International Trade Commission (USITC), the total volume of trade in 1979 was approximately $4 million, which increased to $659.8 billion in 2018. In 2018, China was the largest source of US total imports of $452.24 billion and making up around an 18.10% share in total imports by the US. Similarly, China is the third-largest destination of US exports. China makes around 6.5% of the total exports from the US (USITC) Production costs in China are lower due to economies of scale. China is the largest source of US imports, which benefits greatly US consumers as well as producers who use low-cost products and raw materials from China. US multinational enterprises (MNEs) established production of final products and assembly lines in China due to low production costs there.

Though the US–China commercial relationship is growing, the bilateral relationship between these two countries has become complicated. Recently, China has enforced several macroeconomic policies that appear to decrease trade and investment flows to the US. Some of the critical apprehension raised by the US legislators and investors relates to illegal cyber economic surveillance made by China against US firms. These are issues in intellectual property rights (IPR), violating WTO commitments by keeping incorrect records, favouritism given to government-known industries by providing subsidies and using industrial policy, and purposeful devaluation of the Chinese currency. All these issues have been raised by US policymakers who point to a negative impact on US-based industries and even job losses in some sectors in the US. The strain between the US and China not only increases the tension between both economies but also intimidates the entire world. The growth rate of the whole world was projected to drop by 0.5% in 2020 due to the US–China trade war (Freund et al., 2018). The Director-General of the WTO, Robert Azevedo, predicted that the trade war would pose excessive economic risks to world trade as a whole. This would also generate a negative impact on global growth, increase unemployment, and inflation worldwide (WTO, 2018).

Against this backdrop, this chapter attempts to examine the various reasons for the trade war between the US and China and illustrate the impact of the recent US–China trade war on bilateral trade between these two countries. Further, it evaluates its effect on the functions and basic principles of the World Trade Organisation (WTO).

2 Literature review

The literature on the recent US–China war is limited as it started mainly in the year 2018. But in the history of trade between the US and China, there are frequent examples of conflict. Chong and Li (2019) note that the US has raised five 'Section 301 investigations'[1] against China since 1991, in the areas of IPRs, discriminatory trade barriers, and clean energy. In these past examinations, both countries have threatened to use tariffs as a means of reprisal. Nevertheless, these conflicts were all ultimately resolved by negotiation, signing trade agreements, and taking the help of WTO under its dispute settlement mechanism.

A number of research papers evaluate the economic impact of the US–China trade war. These papers constitute the different simulations and situations which calculate the prices after raising tariffs by the US as well as China (Zhao and Sheng, 2018; Muro, 2018; Stiglitz, 2018; Carnegie, 2018). Guo et al. (2018) evaluate the impact of rising tariffs by 45% against China and the rest of the world. They find that the trade war led to a downturn in US-China bilateral trade and also illustrate that there will be social welfare losses to the US due to this war. Welfare losses to the US and China are also supported by the study of Carvalho, Azevedo, and Massuquetti (2019), which discussed that, due to protectionism, there would be a worse allocation of productive resources within the US and China. Guo et al. (2018) set out hypothetical situations to assess the impact of the US–China trade war. Li, He, and Lin (2018) constructed the framework of Nash bargaining and present different scenarios of the trade war and its impact on both countries. All these studies used hypothetical data. Chong and Li (2019) constructed a model using the real data of the ongoing trade war and performed simulation analysis; they concluded that, in the worst-case scenario, China will have a 1.1% decrease in employment and 1% decline in GDP.

Some of the studies (Ciuriak and Xiao, 2018; Bollen and Rojas-Romagosa, 2018) used a computable general equilibrium model and concluded that there would be a loss of competitiveness due to the increase in tariffs by countries. According to the results, there is a negative impact of the trade war on real GDP of the US, reducing it by 0.06, with overall economic welfare reduced by $6.3 billion and 22,700 jobs lost. An increase in the tariff will increase the price of goods imported from China. As per these studies, the rise in the prices of goods imported from China due to higher tariffs will also increase the price of final goods in the US. This will decrease the competitiveness of US products which use Chinese raw materials. These import restrictions decrease the welfare of the consumers and producers who need to pay higher prices due to higher tariffs on imported goods.

The impact of the US–China trade war is not limited to these two countries. Some of the studies focus on the impact of the US–China trade war on other countries like India and Vietnam. The effect of the US–China trade war on East Asia is evaluated by Calì (2018). This study used the partial equilibrium analysis and found that East Asian countries are the most exposed by the US–China trade war as these countries are integrated into Chinese-led supply chains. The trade war also impacts indirectly other countries and sectors. As there is a decrease in Chinese exports to the US, the East Asian countries that are the key suppliers of raw materials to China face a decline in their trade. Taiwan and Malaysia are pronounced the most vulnerable, with an evaluated loss in their gross domestic product of 0.24% and 0.20%. This study also estimated the impact of the trade war on investment and found that it leads to diversion of investment towards third countries as the cost of production increased in the US and China.

Abiad et al. (2018) evaluate the impact of trade conflict on developing Asia and found that it had an uneven impact. This study used the Multiregional Input-Output Table developed by the Asian Development Bank to evaluate the impact of the trade war, and under the worst-case scenario, the GDP of PRC declined by 1% and the US by 0.2%. This study also investigates whether the impact of a trade war on developing Asia is somewhat positive as some of the countries get benefits from trade diversion from China for electronics and textiles. The presence of tariffs on automobile parts and automobiles is more harmful to advanced countries like the European Union and Japan. This study also found that these conflicts created a large negative impact on employment in China and a small impact on improving the trade balance and the current account balance of China.

Some of the studies also explained the impact of the trade war on the functioning and violation of the WTO rules and regulations. As per the study of Lawrence (2018) and Rodrik (2017), trade war, particularly bilateral trade war, violates the foundations of WTO. Protection and restrictive policies also impact on trade relations between countries and create problems for free trade, which is the basic principle of WTO. As per the WTO commitments, no country can increase import duties or tariffs unilaterally and cannot discriminate between trading partners. Only on the grounds of national security higher tariffs are justified.

As discussed in the literature, most of the earlier studies explain the impacts of the US–China trade war on welfare, economic costs, international effects, political, international relations, and outcomes in a specific economy. But there are limited studies that explain the impact of the US–China trade war on their bilateral trade from 2018 to 2019. There is also some research on the impact of the trade war on an international organisation like WTO. This chapter attempts to bridge this gap in the literature.

3 Impact of US–China trade war on international trade

US–China trade relations started increasing after the signing of the bilateral trade agreement in July 1979. The economies gave each other the most favoured nation (MFN) treatment in 1980. (Morrison, 2018). The total volume of trade in 1979 was approximately $4 million, which increased to $659.8 billion in 2018. In 2019, as a result of the trade war, their trade declined to US$558.8 billion. In 2019 US exports to China were US$106.6 billion, down from US$120.1 billion in 2018; hence US exports to China declined by 11.25% between 2018 and 2019. The total imports of the US from China were $452.2 billion in 2019, which had been $539.7 billion in 2018; therefore, total US imports from China declined by 16.20%. Therefore, overall imports and export declined due to the trade war (Table 4.1).

Table 4.1 The bilateral trade relationship between US and China from 2010 to 2019

Year	*USA Export to China (US $ billion)*	*USA Import from China (US $ billion)*
2010	91.9	365.0
2011	104.1	399.4
2012	110.5	425.6
2013	121.7	440.4
2014	123.7	468.5
2015	115.9	483.2
2016	115.6	462.4
2017	129.8	505.2
2018	120.1	539.7
2019	106.6	452.2

Source: Calculations based on United States International Trade Commission (USITC).

Table 4.2 Top ten sources of US imports (US$ billion)

Sr.No	*Country*	*Year 2017*	*Year 2018*	*Year 2019*	*% Change 2018–2019*
1	China	505.2202	539.6756	452.2434	–16.20
2	Mexico	312.8088	346.1006	358.126	3.47
3	Canada	299.0902	318.8242	319.7357	0.29
4	Japan	136.4177	142.4251	143.6364	0.85
5	Germany	117.5479	125.8489	127.4621	1.28
6	South Korea	71.41641	74.26405	77.51113	4.37
7	Vietnam	46.47706	49.17361	66.68032	35.60
8	United Kingdom	53.28158	60.78309	63.18703	3.95
9	Ireland	48.86136	57.45449	61.76804	7.51
10	India	48.54975	54.34926	57.66548	6.10

Source: United States International Trade Commission (USITC).

Table 4.2 indicates the top ten sources of US imports, showing that China is the largest source of US imports. China is followed by Mexico, Canada, Japan, Germany, South Korea, Vietnam, the United Kingdom, Ireland, and India. Apart from China overall US imports increased between 2018 and 2019. Overall imports decreased by 16.20% due to the trade war from the year 2018 to 2019.

Table 4.3 explains the balance of trade between the US and China. It indicates that, from 2010 to 2018, there is a persistent rise in the trade deficit between the US and China. US imports from China were higher in this period. This is a key reason for the implementation of a tariff increment for some of the products imported from China. After the emergence of the trade war, a decline in the US trade deficit was noticed. The deficit reduced from US$41 in 2018 to US$34 billion in 2019. After the increase in the tariff for major commodities imported from China, overall imports from China declined, and this improved the trade balance of the US with China.

Table 4.4 illustrates the major commodities imported from China by the US at HS 2 digit level. Throughout 2010–19, nearly all US imports from China were labour-intensive products, such as furniture, bedding, toys, games, sports equipment, footwear, apparel and clothing accessories, plastics. However, over the past few years, an increasing proportion of US imports from China have been more technologically advanced products like nuclear reactors, boilers, electrical machinery. After the beginning of the trade war, the import from China for the most merchandise goods declined. The primary commodities imported in 2019 were electrical machinery, nuclear reactors, furniture, toys, footwear, apparel, plastics, iron, and steel. The import of iron and steel decreased by 16.35% from 2018 to 2019. Similarly, Table 4.4 explains that US merchandise imports of all top commodities from China declined from 2018 to 2019; therefore, we can conclude that, as a result of the US–China trade war, overall imports from China for all top commodities declined.

Table 4.5 illustrates US exports to China from 2010 to 2019, which indicates that the top ten commodities include nuclear reactors, aircraft, electrical

Table 4.3 The US merchandise trade deficit with China

Year	*Trade Balance*
2010	-27.30415527
2011	-29.5249709
2012	-31.5102467
2013	-31.8683831
2014	-34.48176915
2015	-36.73282901
2016	-34.68252071
2017	-37.54226462
2018	-41.95274497
2019	-34.56166654

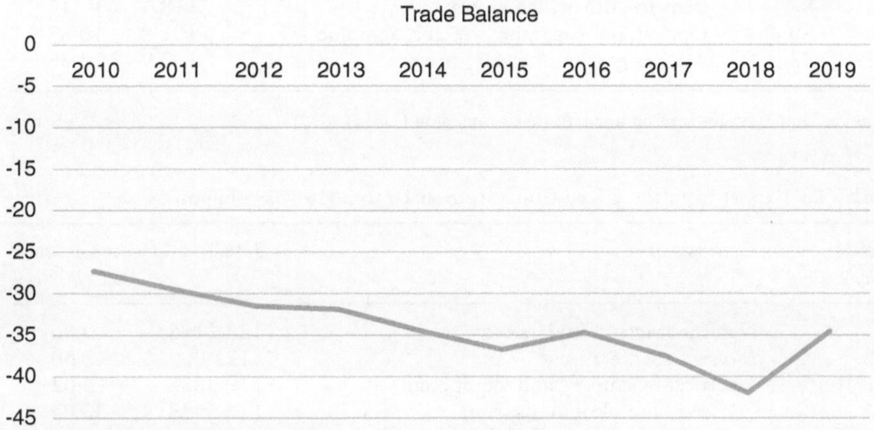

Source: Calculations based on United States International Trade Commission (USITC).

machinery, oil seeds, plastic articles, mineral fuel and mineral oil, organic chemicals. There is a significant decline in exports from the US to China between 2018 and 2019 of oil seeds and oleaginous fruits, electrical machinery, and equipment. Between 2018 and 2019 mineral fuel and aircraft/spacecraft exports from the US to China declined sharply by 55.44% and 42.60%, respectively.

In summary, there is a huge decline in international trade between the US and China after 2018. Table 4.6 summarises the percentage change in exports, imports, and trade balance between the US and China between 2018 and 2019.

Exports from the US to China decline by 11.25% while imports from China to the US decline by 16.2% between 2018 and 2019. There is an improvement in the trade balance between the US and China by 17.61%.

4 Impact of US–China trade war on free trade and WTO

The main objective of the WTO is to promote free trade and settle disputes between the trading partners. The recent US–China trade war poses a question

Table 4.4 Major US merchandise imports from China in 2010–2019: HS two digit level

Sr.No	*HS Code*	*Description*	*Import from China*	*% Change 2018–2019*
1	85	Electrical machinery etc.	1231.5	-17.49
2	84	Nuclear reactors, boilers etc.	1002.1	-20.99
3	94	Furniture; bedding, cushions etc.	262.9	-23.76
4	95	Toys, games and sports equipment	239.8	-4.64
5	64	Footwear, gaiters etc.	157.7	-4.3
6	61	Articles of apparel and clothing accessories	149.4	-7.7
7	39	Plastics and articles thereof	141.9	-6.51
8	62	Articles of apparel and clothing accessories, not knitted or crocheted	139.8	-9.03
9	87	Vehicles, other than railway	118.4	-19.13
10	90	Optical, photographic, cinematographic	101.8	-10.87
11	73	Articles of iron or steel	100.9	-16.35

Source: United States International Trade Commission (USITC).

Table 4.5 Export from the US to China from 2010 to 2019 (US$ billion)

HS Code	*Description*	*Total*	*% Change 2018–2019*
84	Nuclear reactors, boilers etc.	123.2158	-10.06
88	Aircraft, spacecraft etc.	122.009	-42.60
85	Electrical machinery and equipment	119.3337	12.02
12	Oil seeds and oleaginous fruits	116.5425	133.04
87	Vehicles, other than railway	95.19079	-2.63
90	Optical, photographic etc.	77.73907	-0.35
39	Plastics and articles	50.68314	-12.61
27	Mineral fuels, mineral oils etc.	35.88679	-55.44
47	Pulp of wood or other fibrous cellulosic material	33.19895	-20.61
29	Organic chemicals	28.10972	-19.24

Source: United States International Trade Commission (USITC).

Table 4.6 Summary of effects of trade war on international trade between US and China (% change 2018–19)

Export from the US to China	*Import from China to the US*	*Trade Balance*
-11.25	-16.2	17.61

Source: Authors' calculation based on USITC data.

about the basic principles of WTO. In 2018, the US government executed high tariffs on the import of steel, solar panels, washing machines, and aluminium from its trading partners at 25, 30, 50, and 10%, respectively (Schlesinger, 2018). To justify the above actions, the US government used Section 232 of its 1962 Trade Expansion Act. As per this act, if any imported goods constitute a threat to national security, then the president of the US can impose an additional tariff on such goods. Both China and the US have imposed higher tariffs on each other's goods. For example, US enforced tariffs on aircraft, weapons, medical equipment, and satellites worth $50–60 billion on 22 March 2018 and in response to this China enforced import tariffs on 128 US products, including cars, soybeans, aluminium (Caporal, 2018).

The tariff imposition by both countries was undertaken without consulting and following the multilateral trading system of WTO (Adekola, 2019). Though the US and China raised grievances with WTO, both the countries started protectionist measures before the hearings started. These two countries ignore the WTO rules, which throws doubt on the WTO's dispute settlement system. There is also a question over the influence on WTO by developed countries which mould WTO rules to their own requirements (Jones, 2018). As per the article of 23 of dispute settlement understanding, 'when Members seek the redress of a WTO violation, they shall do so only through the DSU'; article 23.2 refers to states that 'seek the redress of a violation of obligations or other nullification or impairment of benefits under the covered agreements or an impediment to the attainment of any objective of the covered agreements'. Therefore, as per WTO norms in the dispute settlement understanding, every country has a responsibility to approach the WTO when analysis identifies that a trading partner is following the WTO norms.

China defended the tariff imposition on the US by citing article 47 of its Foreign Trade Law 2014 in which China can request the trade partner to make changes in the trade treaties signed by China in the interests of the Republic of China. This clause also states that any trade treaty or agreement that might have an adverse impact on the Chinese economy can be suspended or their obligation can be terminated by requesting this to the trade partner. Though some of the provisions under article 47 are in line with the WTO framework, it has an adverse impact on the multilateral trading system.

As per provisions 23.1 and 23.2 of the dispute settlement understanding, countries can solve their trade dispute with the help of WTO, but the WTO dispute settlement bodies move at a slow pace. This creates a huge economic loss for countries; therefore, China used tariff barriers to restrict trade. In the case of the US–China trade war, both the countries did not follow the rules and obligations available under article 23.2. The US and China have not waited for the final decision of dispute settlement understanding of WTO. If all the WTO countries follow their own trade policies, then it will have an adverse impact on the working of multilateral bodies like WTO.

Therefore, questions are raised about loopholes in the different WTO agreements and dispute settlement system. Many countries use different tariff and non-tariff barriers clauses to put restrictions on the trade from their trading partners. According to Adekola (2019), unilateral and protectionist activities can be related to a loss of confidence in WTO functions and increase the risk of WTO being dysfunctional. If all the countries started using these tariff and non-tariff barriers clauses to put restrictions on imported goods, then the main principle of WTO to promote free trade is sidelined. Therefore, there is a need to reform the WTO dispute settlement system as well as different clauses under tariff and non-tariff measures, which restrict the free flow of goods and services (Schoenbaum, 1998). The question is to whether or not the existing rules and clauses of different tariff and non-tariff barriers are capable of preventing one-sided and protective trade policies. A review of all these clauses is needed to ensure better functioning of WTO. According to Adekola 2019, to curtail trade war between countries and build the confidence of members on the dispute settlement system, WTO should present retrospective monetary compensation, which can prevent the reoccurrence of a similar trade war and save the WTO from being dysfunctional.

Therefore, it is important to review the existing trade rules, different trade agreements, tariffs, and non-tariff measures carefully, and modify them so they do not create discrimination and obstacles to the basic principle of WTO, which is free trade. A developed country like the US has a major influence on WTO. It is important to have influential free trade rules under WTO to avoid the trade war.

5 Conclusion

The world's biggest economies entered into a trade war in the year 2018, which increased the uncertainty for business. Both the US and China slipped down in their world competitiveness rankings due to the trade war. This chapter has analysed the impact of the US–China trade war on bilateral trade between these two economies. Overall results indicate that imports and export both declined after the commencement of trade war between the US and China. US imports from China declined by 16.20%, and US exports to China declined by 11.21% between 2018 and 2019. The main reason for the recent trade war was the trade deficit of the US with China. After the commencement of trade war the trade deficit of the US with China improved by 8%, from −41 to −34% between 2018 and 2019. The top commodities exported and imported by the US to China also declined sharply from 2018 to 2019.

This study also indicates that the US used Section 232 of its 1962 Trade Expansion act to increase the tariff on Chinese products. This will negatively impact trust in WTO, and it will also decline the free trade between countries, which is the basic principle of WTO. This study suggests that WTO should review the existing safeguard measures and close the loopholes in the safeguard measures like a tariff, non-tariff measures, sanitary and phytosanitary measures, the technical barrier to trade, subsidies and countervailing measures, etc. Most of the developed countries are using these safeguard measures to restrict the imports from another country which is negatively impacting free trade. Improving the system will increase the trust in WTO, and it will support another principle of WTO, which is non-discrimination among countries.

Note

1 Section 301 of the U.S. Trade Act of 1974 (last edition 23 March 2018) authorises the President to take all appropriate action, including tariff-based and non-tariff-based retaliation, to obtain the removal of any act, policy, or practice of a foreign government that violates an international trade agreement or is unjustified, unreasonable, or discriminatory, and that burdens or restricts US commerce.

References

Abiad, A., Baris, K., Barnabe, J. A., Bertulfo, D. J., Camingue-Romance, S., Feliciano, P. N., Mariasingham, M. J., & Mercer-Blackman, V. (2018). The impact of trade conflict on developing Asia. *ADB Economics Working Paper Series*, 1–44. https://doi.org/10.22617/wps189770-2

Adekola, T. A. (2019). US–China trade war and the WTO dispute settlement mechanism. *Journal of International Trade Law and Policy*, *18*(3), 125–135. https://doi.org/10.1108/jitlp-02-2019-0011

Bollen, J., & Rojas-Romagosa, H. (2018). Trade wars: Economic impacts of US tariff increases and retaliations, an international perspective. CPB Background Document. The Hague: Centraal Planbureau (Netherlands Bureau for Economic Policy Analysis),

Calì, M. (2018). The impact of the US-China trade war on East Asia. *Vox*, CEPR Policy Portal, 16 October. https://voxeu.org/article/impact-us-china-trade-war-east-asia

Caporal, J. (2018). U.S., China tussle over Section 301's compatibility with WTO rules at DSB. 28 March. https://insidetrade.com/daily-news/us-china-tussle-over-section-301%E2%80%99s-compatibility-wto-rules-dsb

Carnegie, A. (2018). Trump's trade war escalates: History shows that threats won't work. *Foreign Affairs*, 25 June. www.foreignaffairs.com/articles/2018-06-25/trumps-trade-war-escalates

Carvalho, M., Azevedo, A., & Massuquetti, A. (2019). Emerging countries and the effects of the trade war between US and China. *Economies*, *7*(2), 45. https://doi.org/10.3390/economies7020045

Chong, T. T. L., & Li, X. (2019). Understanding the China–US trade war: Causes, economic impact, and the worst-case scenario. *Economic and Political Studies*, *7*(2), 185–202. https://doi.org/10.1080/20954816.2019.1595328

Ciuriak, D., & Xiao, J. (2018). Quantifying the impacts of the US Section 232 Steel and Aluminum Tariffs. C.D. Howe Institute Working Paper, 12 June 2018. SSRN: https://ssrn.com/abstract=3190699.

Dolgov, S. I., and Savinov, Y. A. (2018) International trade: USA on the warpath. *Russian Foreign Economic Bulletin*, *9*, 7–20.

Freund, C., Ferrantino, M., Maliszewska, M., & Ruta. M. (2018). Impacts on global trade and income of current trade disputes. *Macroeconomics, Trade Investment (MTI) Practice Notes*, *2*, 11. Washington, DC: World Bank.

Guo, M., Lu, L., Sheng, L., & Yu, M. (2018). The day after tomorrow: Evaluating the burden of Trump's trade war. *Asian Economic Papers*, *17*(1), 101–120. https://doi.org/10.1162/asep_a_00592

Jones, C. T. C. (2018). Trump cools China trade deal hopes. *The Times*, 24 May. www.thetimes.co.uk/article/trump-cools-china-trade-deal-hopes-sww83v70p

Kapustina, L., Lipková, Ľ., Silin, Y., & Drevalev, A. (2020). US-China trade war: Causes and outcomes. *SHS Web of Conferences*, *73*, 01012. https://doi.org/10.1051/shsconf/20207301012

Lawrence, R. Z. (2018). Can the trading system survive US-China trade friction? *China and World Economy*, *26*(5), 62–82. https://doi.org/10.1111/cwe.12256

Li, C., He, C., & Lin, C. (2018). Economic impacts of the possible China–US trade war. *Emerging Markets Finance and Trade*, *54*(7), 1557–1577. https://doi.org/10.1080/1540496x.2018.1446131

Morrison, W. (2018). China-U.S. Trade Issues. Washington, DC: Congressional Research Service. https://fas.org/sgp/crs/row/RL33536.pdf

Muro, M. (2018). How China's proposed tariffs could affect U.S. workers and industries. *Brookings,* 20 April. www.brookings.edu/blog/the-avenue/2018/04/09/how-chinas-tariffs-could-affect-u-s-workers-and-industries/

Rodrik, D. (2017). *Straight Talk on Trade: Ideas for a Sane World Economy.* Princeton, NJ: Princeton University Press.

Schlesinger, J. M. (2018). Trump to impose steep aluminum and steel tariffs. WSJ, 2 March. www.wsj.com/articles/trump-wont-quickly-announce-new-tariffs-on-aluminum-steel-1519921704

Schoenbaum, T. J. (1998). WTO dispute settlement: Praise and suggestions for reform. *International and Comparative Law Quarterly*, *47*(3), 647–658. https://doi.org/10.1017/s0020589300062217

Stiglitz, J. E. (2018). The US is at risk of losing a trade war with China. *Project Syndicate*, 5 August.

Vinogradov, A. O., Salitsky, A. I., & Semenova, N. K. (2019). US-China economic confrontation: Ideology, chronology, meaning. *Vestnik RUDN. International Relations*, *19*(1), 35–46. https://doi.org/10.22363/2313-0660-2019-19-1-35-46

WTO (2018). WTO report shows sharp rise in trade-restrictive measures from G20 economies. WTO, 22 November.

Yean Tham, S., Yi, A. K. J., & Ann, T. B. (2019). U.S.–China trade war: Potential trade and investment spillovers into Malaysia. *Asian Economic Papers*, *18*(3), 117–135. https://doi.org/10.1162/asep_a_00729

Zhang, Y. (2018). The US–China trade war: A political and economic analysis. *Indian Journal of Asian Affairs*, 31(1), 53–74.

Zhao, H., and Sheng, L. (2018). Quantitative analysis: How much is the impact of the U.S. tariffs on $200 billion Chinese imports? *Financial Times Chinese*, 1 August. www.ftchinese.com/story/001078732?full=y&archive

Part II

What is there for the regional economy?

5 US–China trade war

An opportunity for India

Dinkar Nayak and Akash Kumra

1 Introduction

The clash of two giant world economies, USA and China, began in 2018, when the Trump administration imposed an additional tariff of 30% on foreign solar panels. This affected China in particular as it was the largest exporter of this product. Further, in March 2018, the US administration imposed a 25% tariff on steel and 10% on aluminum on imports from a list of countries also including China. This was followed by a bilateral tariff of 25% by China on US soybeans and automobiles. The trade confrontation escalated further, not only because of several rounds of retaliatory tariffs but also due to the announcement by the USA of higher tariffs on a wide range of Chinese goods, from January 2019. The end result has been the disruption of trade not only between these two countries but also in other countries of the world.

With the surge in protectionism between the two largest global economies, it is natural to think that it will not only have negative consequences for world trade, but at the same time, the emerging economies not directly involved in the trade war might benefit from the shift in demand to sectors where they have comparative advantages. Therefore, even if the trade dispute generates losses, in terms of welfare and trade, for the US and China and for the world as a whole, certain sectors of emerging countries might benefit as a result of trade diversion. It is a known fact that any imposition of new tariffs or the increase in existing tariffs makes imports costlier in the destined market by making the exported goods uncompetitive. It has been contended that any increase in tariffs will raise the prices of foreign goods, resulting in reduced demand for imports.[1] Further, if the tariff is applicable only to specific countries, as in the United States–China trade war, it can lead to trade diversion effects as importers can avoid the tariffs by sourcing the goods from elsewhere. Trade diversion effects do not necessarily happen and generally are not complete, meanings that third countries are generally able to capture only part of the trade, with the rest being lost or internalized by the country imposing the tariff. But still, bilateral tariffs lead to higher prices for consumers, lower profits for exporting firms, and are accompanied by trade diversion effects that favour third countries (Nicita, 2019). It is in this context that the present chapter focuses on the opportunity for India's trade as a result of the USA–China trade war. More specifically, the chapter examines the revealed comparative advantage (RCA) enjoyed by India in the goods that are traded between the USA and China. Thus, the main objective of the chapter is to analyse the possible trade diversion from China and the USA to India on the basis of comparative advantage. The rest of the chapter is organized as follows: Section 2 presents the literature review. Section 3 describes the data source and methodology. Section 4 analyses the results. Finally, the fifth section concludes the study.

2 Review of literature

Revealed comparative advantage is one of the most widely used indicators for measuring a country's international trade performance. A country is considered to have a comparative advantage in the production of certain goods if it has a low relative cost in the production of that good compared to other countries. The use of both "relative" and "compared" means that there are two comparisons to be made. Relative cost means the production cost compared to the cost of other goods produced within the same country. The cost ratio is then compared across trading partner countries (Deardorff, 1998). Numerous studies have been conducted which have used the concept of revealed comparative advantage by mainly using data on export shares (Batra and Khan, 2005). Balassa (1977) developed the concept of RCA for analysing the pattern of comparative advantage of advanced western countries for the period between 1953 and 1971. The result supported the then-existing proof on trade-in technological intensive goods, evidencing the continuous improvement of the product cycle, with the USA keeping its ever enhancing technological lead. Balassa's results also showed that while the degree of technological advancement and the extent of export diversification go hand in hand, at a higher level, a reversal occurs. Leu's study (1998) examined the systematic shift of comparative advantage in East Asian countries by calculating and comparing RCA indices for ten selected countries in this region in the USA market. As per this study, the shifting comparative advantage is in accordance with the level of economic development of these countries. Richardson and Zhang (1999), by using the Balassa index of RCA for the USA, have analysed the patterns of export variation over time, regions, and sectors. It was found by them that the patterns differ across different regions of the world because of factors like geographical proximity of trading countries and the level of the per capita income (PCI). Bender and Li (2002) had examined the shift and structural performances of exports and RCA of East Asian and Latin American countries during the period between 1981 and 1997. They found that the changes in export patterns among different regions and shifts in RCA between regions are closely related.

Several studies are available which have analysed the dynamics of comparative advantage of China. The study by Hinloopen and Marrewijk (2004) is one of prominent among these studies. They have used the Balassa index of comparative advantage to highlight the dynamics. The pattern of China's RCA and its consequence has been studied using the market share changes in export. China's trade relations with South East and East Asian countries in the context of threat or opportunity have been analysed by Lall and Weiss (2004). Acharya (2008) computed the RCA for seven major economies, including China. As per the results of this study, during the period from 1996 to 2007, Canada, the USA, and Japan have lost their share of global exports, while China increased its share by three-fold mainly in non- RCA based medium and high-tech products. Research studies pertaining to India-China trade and their economic performances have also been conducted over the years. Batra and Khan (2005) have found that the pattern of comparative advantage differs at different levels of commodity disaggregation. In the case of India except for cotton, no other sector that ranks among the top ten as per the value of the RCA index maintains its comparing rank at the disaggregated level. For China, textiles, sets, worn clothing is so positioned. Boillot and Labouz (2006) tested two scenarios: the continuation of the bilateral trade expansion between the two economies ("Chindia"), or the end of the catching-up process and the emergence of a joint "India and China" upsurge at the world level. They found that the latter hypothesis appears more probable considering the models of specialization and industrial transformation followed by the two countries at both the micro and macroeconomic level. A quantitative assessment for 2015 shows China still largely ahead of India (services are not covered in the study) and a somewhat insignificant India-China bilateral flow at the world level. Another study by Tyagi (2014) has measured the comparative advantage among others in the bilateral context of India and China using aggregated trade data. As per this study, it is found that there is potential for bilateral trade, and there is a need to take advantage of the comparative advantage of commodities in the trade basket. Bagaria et al. (2014) have investigated the comparative advantage of India & China and how this has changed over the period of 2002–2012. It has been found that in some commodities, RCA remained stable throughout the study period, whereas in some commodities, there has been large variation. In some commodity groups India and China complement each other, whereas in some commodities they are competing with each other in the world market. In a similar study, Ahmad, Hussain and Sofi (2018) discussed the short- and long-run trade patterns of India and China. Applying revealed comparative advantage (RCA) and bilateral RCA, this study specifically tries to find out the pattern of exports and areas of specialization for India and China. Major findings suggest that both the countries have been performing well, in terms of merchandise trade exports, over the past few decades, especially since 2000. However, once we go from Standard International Trade Classification (SITC) two-digit to SITC four-digit level of analysis, the sample economies reveal their specialized products. At the disaggregated level, India's export basket is void of food products and raw materials, and it generally contains engineering goods and technologically driven products as advantageous products. The study finds that the areas of specialization are much wider, and the technology-embedded products are larger for China as compared to India.

Few studies are available which have examined the impact of the trade war on India's trade. Nag and Ayyub (2018) asserted that the USA's import of metal is moderately diversified and does not dependent on single or few suppliers. This is one of the sectors where emerging economies like India have an opportunity to tap the USA market. But at the same time, there is also a possibility that is facing market access restrictions in the traditional markets; the Chinese exporters may turn towards other destinations to dump their surplus metals. India being an emerging economy with a lot of metal consumption and one of the top producers of metals like Iron ore, Steel and Aluminium have both to fear and opportunity in China–USA trade war; it has the opportunity to tap American market by negotiating lower tariffs and has the fear that China may dump their surplus metal in India. This dumping may damage Indian metal manufacturing and exports as it would be faced with a very cheap metal export from China. Pencea (2019), in his study, focusing on the expected consequences of the trade war for the economies, companies, and population the USA, China, EU, and Asian countries, including India. According to him, the South-East Asian countries are, in their great majority, developing and emerging economies, whose companies are involved in the regional supply and production chains built around China. Thanks to their cost advantages. At the same time, other numerous companies headquartered in the highly developed economies of Asia (Japan, South Korea, Singapore, Honk Kong, Taiwan), Europe (the EU Member States) and the US, are also integral to the Asian regional value chains (RVCs), mainly due to their technological superiority and outstanding Research and Development and Innovation capabilities. In the second half of 2018, Asian companies have come to experience the consequences of the trade war and, consequently, to adopt different strategies of response. First, an increasingly consistent trend among the exporters to the US located in China is represented by the relocations of their production facilities to the neighbouring Southeast Asian countries, with a view to capitalizing on both their cost advantages or technological prowess, and on their lack of obstructions to the US market access. With development, China ceased to be a cheap production place. Depending on the complexity of the work involved, countries like India, Bangladesh, Pakistan, the Philippines, and even some Eastern European countries have become the favourite destinations of these companies for the relocation of labour-intensive activities. Further, among the Chinese exporters to the large American consumer goods trading networks (such as Wal-Mart, Macy's, etc.), which used to have their suppliers located mostly in China, the acquisitions from China are now drastically declining while new suppliers of garments are searched for in Bangladesh, Vietnam, India, Pakistan. Nicita (2019) has examined the trade and trade diversion effects of US tariffs on China. He is of the opinion that one consequence of the USA tariff in China is to increase the USA imports from elsewhere. Trade diversion effects show considerable variance both across countries and across sectors. Apart from existing trade agreements and geography, large countries with spare capacity and available trade infrastructure will be the ones to replace China in the USA market. It appears that Taiwan was the largest beneficiary. Trade diversion effects in favour of the Republic of Korea, Canada, and India were smaller but still significant (between the US $0.9 and 1.5 billion).

Thus from the foregone discussion, it is clear that while several studies have measured the comparative advantage, with respect to selected regions in general and China–India in particular, there is a dearth of literature which have examined the possibilities of trade diversion from China and USA to India in terms of comparative advantage against the background of the recent trade war between USA and China. The present study is an attempt to fill up the gap of literature in this regard.

In this study, an attempt has been made to evaluate the revealed comparative advantage (RCA) for India, China, and the USA in the world market. The paper identifies the pattern of RCA using the index of the export data of these three countries. Based on the calculated RCA, the paper will investigate the possibility of trade diversion benefits to India on account of USA tariff on Chinese goods and tariff by China on USA's goods.

3 Data source and methodology

The study is based on the secondary data for various variables such as export, imports, and others, which are collected from the RBI Publications and the official site of the United Nations Conference on Trade and Development (UNTCAD). A ten-year study period between 2009 and 2019 has been considered.

A two-part analysis has been carried out. In the first part, the trend analysis of exports and imports has been undertaken. For examining the trend, the various statistical tools such as line graph, bar graph, simple average, and standard deviation are used. This will throw some light and indicate India's trade position with respect to the USA and China. The trend is also examined by using the following simple linear equation as well as by the semi-log model.

$$\text{A. } Y = \beta_1 + \beta_2 t + \upsilon_t \quad (1)$$

$$\text{B. } Lny = \beta_1 + \beta_2 t + \upsilon_t \quad (2)$$

Where, Lny, shows the log of the variable under consideration, and 't' indicates the time element. The coefficient of the trend variable in the growth model (2), β_2, gives the instantaneous (at a point in the) rate of growth and not the compound (over a period of time) rate of growth. But the latter can be easily found by taking the antilog of the estimated from β_2 and subtracting 1 from it and multiplying the difference by 100.[2]

In the second part, the commodities in which India has a comparative advantage on the basis of RCA will be identified. This is done to find out in which commodities India can substitute the USA's export to China and China's export to the USA.

Revealed comparative advantage (RCA) is based on the Ricardian trade theory, which posits that patterns of trade among countries are governed by their relative differences in productivity. Although such productivity differences are difficult to observe, an RCA metric can be readily calculated using trade data to "reveal" such differences.[3] While the metric can be used to provide a general indication and first approximation of a country's competitive export strengths, it should be noted that applied national measures that affect competitiveness such as tariffs, non-tariff measures, subsidies, and others are not taken into account in the RCA metric. Trade data used are based on the three-digit level of the SITC commodity classification, Revision 3.

Country A is said to have a revealed comparative advantage in a given product i when its ratio of exports of product i to its total exports of all goods (products) exceeds the same ratio for the world as a whole:

$$RCA_{Ai} = \frac{\dfrac{X_{Ai}}{\sum_{j\in P} X_{Aj}}}{\dfrac{X_{wj}}{\sum_{j\in P} X_{wj}}} \geq 1$$

Where: *P* is the set of all products (with $i \in P$), X_{Ai} is the country A's exports of, product *i*, X_{wi} is the world's exports of the product *I*, $\Sigma_{j\in P}X_{Aj}$ is the country A's total exports (of all products *j* in *P*), and $\Sigma_{j\in P}X_{wj}$ is the world's total exports (of all products *j* in *P*).

When a country has a revealed comparative advantage for a given product (RCA >1), it is inferred to be a competitive producer and exporter of that product relative to a country producing and exporting that good at or below the world average. Thus, the country with a revealed comparative advantage in the product *i* is considered to have an export-strength in that product. The higher the value of a country's RCA for product *i*, the higher its export strength in the product *i*.[4]

3 Results

3.1 Trends in India's exports and imports

India's exports to the USA in absolute value indicate a rising trend; it continuously increased from Rs. 9241651 lacs in 2009–10 to Rs. 36648040 lacs in 2018–19. On the other hand, exports to China have witnessed a moderate increase over the same period it rose from Rs. 5471393 lacs in 2009–10 to Rs. 11728911 lacs in 2018–19. This indicates that the USA is playing a more important role in India's export basket as compared to China, thereby contributing more to India's export earnings. Similarly, trends are indicated when Indian exports to the USA and China are examined in terms of percent share.

The share of Indian exports to the US has grown on an average by 13.09% during the study period (2009–10 to 2018–19). The percentage share of India's exports to the USA increased from 10.93% in 2009–10 to 15.88% in 2018–19 (i.e. India's percentage share of exports to the USA grew by 45.29%). Whereas Indian exports to China grew on an average by 4.73% during the same period. The percentage share of India's exports to China also indicated a continuous

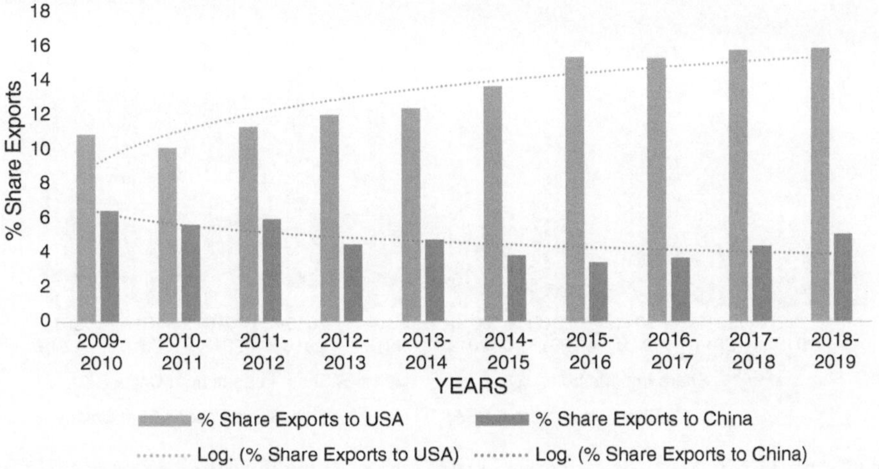

Figure 5.1 India's exports to USA and China (% share, 2009–2019).
Source: Authors calculations based on WITS data.

Table 5.1 Growth of India's exports to the USA and China (2009–10 to 2018–19)

India's exports	*Absolute value*	*Percentage share*
USA [CGR]	14.90*	5.47*
China [CGR]	4.19**	-4.36*
India's total exports [CGR]	8.95*	--------

Note: (*): significant at 1% level. (**): significant at 5% level. Trend is estimated by using semi-log model, lny=a+bt.

decline from 6.47% in 2009–10 to 5.08% in 2018–19 (i.e. India's percentage share of exports to China shrank by 21.45%). The same is also evident from the log-linear trend line (See Figure 5.1).

From the above we can conclude that the foreign demand for Indian goods is comparatively more in USA than in China. The data also show that Indian exports to the USA are more stable when compared to China. Regression estimates also confirm that India's exports to the USA have increased over a period of time and are statistically significant, both in terms of absolute value as well as in percentage share. (See Table 5.1.) In the case of China, although Indian exports have shown positive growth in absolute values, in terms of percentage share, they have registered significant negative growth of -4.36%. This leads to the conclusion that India should endeavour to enhance India's exports to China, thereby bringing stability in export earnings.

The situation with respect to India's imports from the USA and China indicates an opposite trend. India's imports from the USA increased from Rs.

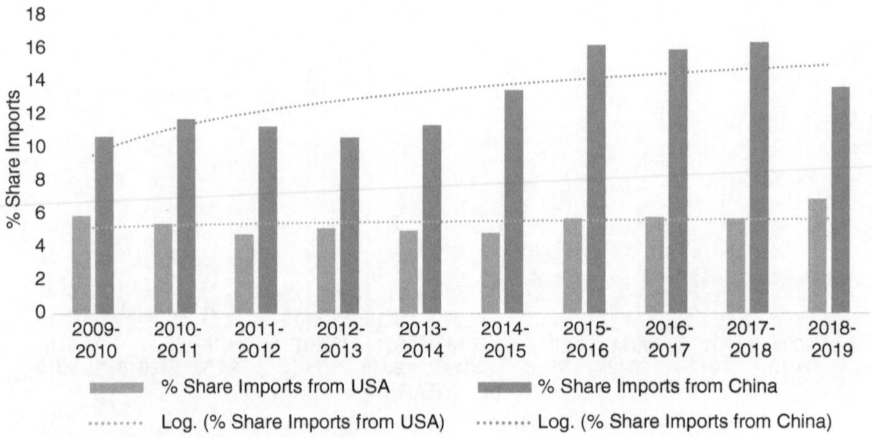

Figure 5.2 India's imports from USA and China (% share, 2009–2019).
Source: Authors calculations based on WITS data.

8058433 lacs in 2009–10 to Rs. 24855377 lacs in 2018–19. The imports from China have increased from Rs. 14604861 lacs in 2009–10 to Rs. 49207928 lacs in 2018–19. This shows that India depends more on China than on the USA for its imports.

In total Indian imports from the USA were 5.53%, and the share of imports from China was, on average, 13.16% during the period under consideration. Further, the share of Indian imports from China has shown an increasing trend from 10.71% in 2009–10 to 13.69% in 2018–19 (i.e. Indian imports grew by 27.82%). India's import share from the USA increased marginally from 5.91% in 2009–10 to 6.91% in 2018–19 (i.e. Indian imports grew by 17.00%). This trend is also indicated by the log-linear trend line (see Figure 5.2).

Regression estimates also confirm that India's imports from China have increased over a period of time and are statistically significant, both in terms of absolute value as well as in percentage share (see Table 5.2). Indian imports from the USA have indicated positive and significant growth in absolute value, but in terms of percentage share, it has registered a non-significant growth of 1.86%. Not only have imports from China shown positive and significant growth but they were also more unstable as compared to India's imports from the USA, in terms of percentage share. It shows that India's imports from China are more volatile, which has an adverse effect on India's foreign exchange reserves.

The above analysis shows that India is exporting more to the USA as compared to China, and is importing less from the USA as compared to China. Further, amongst the two exports and imports, India's exports to the USA are stable compared with India's exports to China. This ultimately indicates consistent export earnings from the USA as compared to China. Similarly, India's imports from

Table 5.2 Growth of India's imports from USA and China (2009–10 to 2018–19)

India's Imports	*Absolute value*	*Percent Share*
USA [CGR]	10.24*	1.86
China [CGR]	13.38*	4.77*
India's total Imports [CGR]	8.22*	....

Note: (*): significant at 1% level. (**): significant at 5% level. Trend is estimated by using semi-log model, lny=a+bt.

the USA are more stable as compared to imports from China. Although India enjoys a trade surplus with the USA, it is not sufficient to overcome the deficit in the balance of payments that India has with respect to China. This is where the current trade war between the USA and China is an opportunity for India to divert the USA's exports from China to India as well as China's exports from the USA to India. This requires the identification of products in which India exhibits a comparative advantage.

3.2 Revealed Comparative Advantage

Table 5.3 shows the top ten products in which India has registered a higher comparative advantage in the context of the USA and China. The table highlights that India enjoys RCA greater than one in the products such as rice (16.92), spices (12.38), pearls, precious and semi-precious stones (10.52), synthetic organic colouring matter and colouring lakes (10.51), during 2018.[5]

The table also shows the comparative performance of India in the production and exports of products on the basis of RCA during 2016 and 2018. India's revealed comparative advantage has increased in products such as spices (from 10.23 in 2016 to 12.38 in 2018), pearls, precious and semi-precious stones (from 9.98 in 2016 to 10.52 in 2018), synthetic organic colouring matter and colouring lakes (from 9.58 in 2016 to 10.51 in 2018), cotton (from 7.04 in 2016 to 7.82 in 2018).

It is clear from Table 5.4 that amongst the top 20 Indian products as per RCA rankings, there are ten commodities where India enjoys a comparative advantage against China, as the RCA of China is less than one. These commodities are rice (0.17), spices (0.45), pearls, precious and semi-precious stones (0.11), vegetable textile fibres, not spun; waste of them (0.04), cotton (0.02), stone, sand, and gravel (0.26), insecticides and similar products, for retail sale (0.98), meat of bovine animals, fresh, chilled, or frozen (0.01), pig iron & spiegeleisen, sponge iron, powder and granules (0.26), and petroleum oils or bituminous minerals > 70% oil (0.27), during 2018. But, in the case of America, there are 14 products where the value of the RCA index is less than one, such as rice (0.75), spices (0.21), synthetic organic colouring matter and colouring lakes (0.68), vegetable textile fibres, not spun; waste of them (0.04), crustaceans, molluscs, and aquatic invertebrates (0.17), textile yarn(0.71), floor coverings, etc. (0.67), jewellery

Table 5.3 India's Revealed Comparative Advantage in top ten products (2016 and 2018)

India	*Year*	*2018*	*2018*	*2018*
	RCA Index			
	ECONOMY [Top 10 products India]	China	India	USA
	PRODUCT			
1	[042] Rice	0.17	16.92	0.75
2	[075] Spices	0.45	12.38	0.21
3	[667] Pearls, precious & semi-precious stones	0.11	10.52	1.74
4	[531] Synth. organic colouring matter & colouring lakes	1.83	10.51	0.68
5	[265] Vegetable textile fibres, not spun; waste of them	0.04	9.97	0.04
6	[036] Crustaceans, molluscs, & aquatic invertebrates	1.17	8.43	0.17
7	[263] Cotton	0.02	7.92	4.35
8	[651] Textile yarn	1.76	6.66	0.71
9	[659] Floor coverings, etc.	1.33	6.16	0.67
10	[897] Jewellery & articles of precious material, n.e.s.	1.21	5.80	0.97
India	*Year*	*2016*	*2016*	*2016*
	RCA Index			
	ECONOMY [Top 10 products India]	China	India	U.S.A
	PRODUCT			
1	[883] Cinematograph films, exposed & developed	0.03	16.56	0.66
2	[042] Rice	0.14	15.87	0.96
3	[265] Vegetable textile fibres, not spun; waste of them	0.05	10.62	0.03
4	[075] Spices	0.70	10.23	0.17
5	[667] Pearls, precious & semi-precious stones	0.11	9.98	1.54
6	[531] Synth. organic colouring matter & colouring lakes	1.68	9.58	0.72
7	[263] Cotton	0.01	7.04	3.51
8	[659] Floor coverings, etc.	1.25	6.88	0.70
9	[036] Crustaceans, molluscs, & aquatic invertebrates	1.06	6.66	0.46
10	[897] Jewellery & articles of precious material, n.e.s.	1.05	6.45	0.97

Source: UNCTAD.

and articles of precious material, n.e.s (0.97), tea and mate (0.37), stone, sand, and gravel (0.73), made-up articles, of textile materials, n.e.s. (0.27), vapour-generating boilers, auxiliary plant, parts (0.54), pig iron and spiegeleisen, sponge iron, powder and granules (0.26), and cotton fabrics, woven (0.19), during 2018.

From Table 5.5, it is evident that, out of the top 20 products in terms of RCA, China has comparative advantage in ten products namely, pottery (5.13), lighting fixtures and fittings, n.e.s. (4.68), office machines (3.89), knitted or crocheted

Table 5.4 India's Revealed Comparative Advantage in top 20 products (2018)

India	*Year*	*2018*		
	RCA Index ECONOMY PRODUCT [Top 20]	China	India	USA
1	[042] Rice	0.17	16.92	0.75
2	[075] Spices	0.45	12.38	0.21
3	[667] Pearls, precious & semi-precious stones	0.11	10.52	1.74
4	[531] Synth. organic colouring matter & colouring lakes	1.83	10.51	0.68
5	[265] Vegetable textile fibres, not spun; waste of them	0.04	9.97	0.04
6	[036] Crustaceans, molluscs, & aquatic invertebrates	1.17	8.43	0.17
7	[263] Cotton	0.02	7.92	4.35
8	[651] Textile yarn	1.76	6.66	0.71
9	[659] Floor coverings, etc.	1.33	6.16	0.67
10	[897] Jewellery & articles of precious material, n.e.s.	1.21	5.80	0.97
11	[074] Tea & mate	1.34	5.19	0.37
12	[273] Stone, sand, & gravel	0.26	5.18	0.73
13	[591] Insecticides & similar products, for retail sale	0.98	4.92	1.35
14	[658] Made-up articles, of textile materials, n.e.s.	3.53	4.91	0.27
15	[011] Meat of bovine animals, fresh, chilled, or frozen	0.01	4.07	1.69
16	[711] Vapour-generating boilers, auxiliary plant; parts	2.33	3.99	0.54
17	[671] Pig iron & spiegeleisen, sponge iron, powder & granules	0.26	3.70	0.26
18	[334] Petroleum oils or bituminous minerals > 70% oil	0.27	3.50	1.38
19	[652] Cotton fabrics, woven	4.28	3.47	0.19
20	[267] Other man-made fibres suitable for spinning	1.44	3.25	2.54

Source: UNCTAD.

fabrics, n.e.s. (3.89) etc. with reference to both India and the USA because in the above-stated products, the value of the index for both the counties is less than one. On further examination of this table, China has a comparative advantage only in ten commodities where the RCA index for India is less than one. These products are, pottery (0.25), lighting fixtures and fittings, n.e.s. (0.15), office machines (0.30), knitted or crocheted fabrics, n.e.s. (0.65), baby carriages, toys, games, and sporting goods (0.20), cutlery (0.71), optical instruments and apparatus, n.e.s. (0.03), telecommunication equipment, n.e.s., and parts, n.e.s. (0.22), household type equipment, electrical or not, n.e.s. (0.14), and automatic data processing machines, n.e.s. (0.04). However, China has a comparative advantage in all the 20 commodities with respect to the USA, as the value of the index is

Table 5.5 China's Revealed Comparative Advantage in top 20 products (2018)

China	*Year*	*2018*		
	RCA Index ECONOMY **PRODUCT (Top 20)**	China	India	U.S.A
1	[261] Silk	5.72	1.77	0.01
2	[666] Pottery	5.13	0.25	0.14
3	[813] Lighting fixtures & fittings, n.e.s.	4.68	0.15	0.40
4	[652] Cotton fabrics, woven	4.28	3.47	0.19
5	[697] Household equipment of base metal, n.e.s.	4.12	1.11	0.34
6	[751] Office machines	3.89	0.30	0.29
7	[655] Knitted or crocheted fabrics, n.e.s.	3.89	0.65	0.26
8	[653] Fabrics, woven, of man-made fabrics	3.84	2.09	0.27
9	[894] Baby carriages, toys, games, & sporting goods	3.64	0.20	0.66
10	[658] Made-up articles, of textile materials, n.e.s.	3.53	4.91	0.27
11	[846] Clothing accessories, of textile fabrics	3.43	1.46	0.30
12	[696] Cutlery	3.26	0.71	0.49
13	[831] Travel goods, handbags, & similar containers	3.22	1.21	0.21
14	[871] Optical instruments & apparatus, n.e.s.	3.14	0.03	0.55
15	[844] Women's clothing, of textile, knitted or crocheted	3.12	1.33	0.11
16	[764] Telecommunication equipment, n.e.s., & parts, n.e.s.	3.10	0.22	0.77
17	[848] Articles of apparel, clothing access., excluding textile	3.05	1.55	0.25
18	[775] Household type equipment, electrical or not, n.e.s.	2.94	0.14	0.33
19	[752] Automatic data processing machines, n.e.s.	2.88	0.04	0.87
20	[842] Women's clothing, of textile fabrics	2.88	2.03	0.09

Source: UNCTAD.

less than one for the USA in all these commodities. Thus, it is advantageous for the USA to import all these products from China. In the event of the imposition higher import duties by the USA on these products, then out of selected 20 products in which China has greater revealed comparative advantage, USA can import from India commodities such as silk, cotton fabrics, woven, household equipment of base metal, n.e.s., fabrics, woven, of man-made fabrics, Made-up articles, of textile materials, n.e.s, clothing accessories, of textile fabrics, travel goods, handbags, and similar containers, women's clothing, of textile, knitted or crocheted, articles of apparel, clothing accessories, excluding textile, and women's clothing, of textile fabrics – in all these products India has RCA index of greater than one. Thus one consequence of US bilateral tariffs on China is to increase US imports from elsewhere.[6] It is in these products that there is a possibility of trade diversion from China to India.

Table 5.6 USA's Revealed Comparative Advantage in top 20 products (2018)

USA	*Year*	*2018*		
	RCA Index			
	ECONOMY	China	India	USA
	PRODUCT (Top 20)			
1	[896] Works of art, collectors' pieces, & antiques	0.08	0.25	5.09
2	[891] Arms & ammunition	0.08	0.41	4.66
3	[044] Maize (not including sweetcorn), unmilled	0.00	0.45	4.43
4	[263] Cotton	0.02	7.92	4.35
5	[223] Oil seeds & oleaginous fruits (incl. flour, n.e.s.)	0.33	0.82	3.54
6	[342] Liquefied propane and butane	0.11	0.00	3.36
7	[045] Cereals, unmilled (excluding wheat, rice, barley, maize)	0.13	1.33	3.35
8	[883] Cinematograph films, exposed & developed	0.10	0.24	2.99
9	[222] Oil seeds and oleaginous fruits (excluding flour)	0.09	0.85	2.67
10	[267] Other man-made fibres suitable for spinning	1.44	3.25	2.54
11	[289] Ores & concentrates of precious metals; waste, scrap	0.03	0.76	2.45
12	[774] Electro-diagnostic appa. for medical sciences, etc.	0.60	0.63	2.44
13	[872] Instruments & appliances, n.e.s., for medical, etc.	0.56	0.31	2.43
14	[597] Prepared addit. for miner. oils; lubricat., de-icing	0.12	0.39	2.30
15	[573] Polymers of vinyl chloride or halogenated olefins	0.65	0.43	2.21
16	[593] Explosives and pyrotechnic products	1.92	1.06	2.13
17	[251] Pulp and waste paper	0.02	0.00	2.01
18	[874] Measuring, analysing, & controlling apparatus, n.e.s.	0.60	0.33	1.79
19	[598] Miscellaneous chemical products, n.e.s.	0.58	0.43	1.75
20	[081] Feeding stuff for animals (no unmilled cereals)	0.29	1.20	1.74

Source: UNCTAD.

Table 5.6 reveals that out of the top 20 products, the USA has a comparative advantage in 15 products over both India and China. Some of these products include works of art, collectors' pieces, and antiques (5.09), arms and ammunition (4.66), maize unmilled (not including sweetcorn) (4.43), oil seeds and oleaginous fruits (including flour, n.e.s., 3.54), excluding flour, 2.67), liquefied propane and butane (3.36), cinematograph films, exposed and developed (2.99), ores and concentrates of precious metals; waste, scrap (2.45), electro-diagnostic appliances for medical sciences (2.44). Interestingly this table also indicates that amongst these products in only five products has India registered an index value of less than one. In the case of China, there were 18 commodities that have registered index values less than one. Table 5.6 gives evidence that it is worthwhile for China to import from India products such as cotton, oilseeds and oleaginous fruits (including flour, n.e.s.), and feeding stuff for animals (no unmilled cereals), if the USA puts a restriction on exports to China or if China increases its tariff on American imports. In these products, India has a comparative advantage over China.[7]

4 Conclusions

There is a generally held view that any increase in bilateral trade costs may lead to trade diversion. It is in this context that the present study attempts to find the opportunities available to India to increase its trade, especially its export to the USA and China, on account of the trade confrontation of the two giant economies of the world.

A two-part analysis was undertaken; in the first part, the trends of the imports and exports between India and the USA and China were examined. The trends indicated that, in value terms, India exported more to the USA than it imported. As a result, India has had a positive trade balance with America during the ten years between 2009 and 2019. At the same time, India has a negative trade balance with China, its imports being greater than its exports to China. It is in this context that, in the second part, the possibility of trade diversion from the USA and China to India was examined on the basis of comparative advantage in terms of the RCA index.

The analysis indicates that India can increase its exports to China of commodities such as ctton [code 263], cereals, unmilled (excluding wheat, rice, barley, maize) [045], other man-made fibres suitable for spinning [267], and feeding stuff for animals (no unmilled cereals) [081] which were earlier sourced from the USA and thereby can improve its trade balance with China.

Similarly, there is also a possibility of trade diversion from China to India with respect to the USA in commodities such as silk [261], cotton fabrics, woven [652], Household equipment of base metal, n.e.s. [697], fabrics, woven, of man-made fabrics [653], made-up articles, of textile materials, n.e.s. [658], clothing accessories, of textile fabrics [846], travel goods, handbags, and similar containers [831], women's clothing, of textile, knitted or crocheted [844], articles of apparel, clothing accessories, excluding textile [848], and women's clothing, of textile fabrics [842]. However, the trade diversion possibilities cited above will bear fruit only if appropriate and focused policy measures are adopted by the Indian government.

Notes

1 Amiti, Redding, and Weinstein (2019) provide a more exhaustive discussion of how tariffs affect demand and prices in the context of the United States–China trade war.
2 See Gujarati (2004).
3 In this study the concept of revealed comparative advantage as elucidated by Balassa (1965) has been used.
4 The advantage of using the comparative advantage index is that it takes into account the intrinsic advantage of a particular export product and is also consistent with the changes in an economy's relative factor endowment and productivity (Batra and Khan, 2005)

5 As the present study is undertaken at the backdrop the USA–China trade war which commenced from 2018, the RCA for the year 2018 is considered as point of reference.
6 A similar view has been expressed by Nicita (2019)
7 In all these products India's RCA index is greater than that of China.

References

Acharya, R. (2008). Analysing international trade patterns: Comparative advantage for the world's major economies. *Journal of Comparative International Management, 11*(2). Retrieved from https://journals.lib.unb.ca/index.php/JCIM/article/view/12446

Ahmad, I., Hussain, M., & Sofi, I (2018). An RCA analysis of India-China trade integration: Present, potential and prospects. *Foreign Trade Review, 53*(1), 49–58.

Amiti, M., Redding, S. J., & Weinstein, D. (2019). The impact of the 2018 trade war on U.S. prices and welfare. CEPR Discussion Papers, 13564.

Bagaria, N., Santra, S., & Kumar, R. (2014). A study on variation in comparative advantage in trade between China and India. *International Journal of Humanities and Social Studies, 2*(1), 101–107.

Balassa, B. (1965). Trade liberalization and revealed comparative advantage. *The Manchester School, 33*(2), 99–123.

Balassa, B. (1977). 'Revealed' comparative advantage revisited: A reappraisal. *The Manchester School of Economic and Social Studies, 45*(4), 327–344.

Batra, A., & Khan, Z. (2005). Revealed comparative advantage: An analysis for India and China. Retrieved from http://icrier.org/pdf/wp168.pdf

Bender, S., & Kui-Wai, L. (2002). The changing trade and revealed comparative advantages of Asian and Latin American manufacture exports. Yale University, Economic Growth Center Discussion Paper Series, 843.

Boillot, J.-J., & Labbouz, M. (2006). India-China trade: Lesson learned and projections for 2015. *Economic and Political Weekly, 41*(26), 2893–2901.

Deardorff, A. V. (1998). Benefits and costs of following comparative advantage. Discussion Paper, 423. University of Michigan.

Gujarati, D. N. (2004). *Basic Econometrics*, 2nd reprint. New Delhi: Tata McGraw-Hill.

Hinloopen, J., & Van Marrewijk, C. (2004). Dynamics of Chinese comparative advantage. Tinbergen Institute Discussion Paper No. 2004-034/2.

Kalirajan, K., Wang, Y., Yu, M., & Singh, K. (2016). China and India: A comparative analysis of trade and investment performance. Retrieved from http://mjyu.ccer.edu.cn/EABER_Routledge%20chapter_2.pdf.

Lall, S., & Weiss, J. (2004). People's Republic of China's competitive threat to Latin America: An analysis for 1990–2002, Asian Development Bank Institute, Discussion Paper, 14.

Lenti, R. T., & Beratta, S. (2012). India and China trading with the world and each other. *Economic and Political Weekly, 47*(44), 35–43.

Leu, M. G.-J. (1998). Changing comparative advantage in East Asian economies. School of Accountancy and Business Research Centre, Nanyang Technological University, Working Paper, 3-98.

Nag, B., & Ayyub, S. (2018). China-USA trade war; opportunities and challenges for India, *The Chartered Account Student, 22*(5), 34–35.

Nicita, A. (2019). *Trade and Trade Diversion Effects of United States Tariffs on China.* Geneva: UNCTAD. UNCTAD/SER.RP/2019/9.

Pencea, S. (2019). The looming USA-China trade war and its consequences. *Global Economic Observer* (Nicolae Titulescu University of Bucharest, Faculty of Economic Sciences; Institute for World Economy of the Romanian Academy), *1*, June.

Richardson, D. J., & Zhang, C. (1999). *Revealing Comparative Advantage: Chaotic or Coherent Patterns across Time and Sector and U.S. Trading Partner?* Cambridge, MA: National Bureau of Economic Research, Working Paper, 721.

Seshadri, V. S. (2009). The changing face of India's external trade. *Economic and Political Weekly*, *44*(35), 43–49.

Tyagi, S. (2014). *Composition, Intensity and Revealed Comparative Advantage in Sino-Indian Bilateral Trade: A Preliminary Study.* New Delhi: Institute of Chinese Studies, Occasional Paper, 8.

United Nations Conference on Trade and Development (UNCTAD) (n.d.). Data Center, unctad.org.

Weiss, J. (2004). People's Republic of China and its neighbours: Partners or competitors for trade and investment? Asian Development Bank Institute, Discussion Paper, 13.

6 Implications of US–China trade war for India

Saon Ray and Smita Miglani

1 Introduction

The trade war between the USA and China in 2018 has the potential to disrupt global value chains and production networks. Global trade is now organised through global value chains (GVCs) (OECD, 2012). Since the announcement in March 2018, of the imposition of Section 232 tariffs on steel and aluminium imports by the US, other countries have retaliated. The People's Republic of China and Mexico have announced similar import duties on US imports. Integrating into GVCs can be done in either of two ways: either through exporting or importing. Final goods can be exported through the value addition of intermediate goods. However, integration into GVCs is not an easy process since there is competition between several countries. Of the various factors that contribute to GVC integration, cost competitiveness remains critical. In this chapter, we examine the implications of the trade war for India.

In the next section, we briefly examine the timeline of the trade war, which helps to isolate the countries and products involved. In section 3, we consider the literature on global value chains and how production is organised via these production networks. Section 4 examines the trading pattern of India over the period 2008 to 2017, identifying key trading partners as well as products. The USA is the largest destination for Indian exports, while China is India's largest source of imports. We use Broad Economic Categories (BEC) classification to characterise Indian exports and imports. This classification helps to identify three categories of goods: intermediate goods, final goods, and capital goods in the system of national accounts. We observe the importance of intermediate goods in both India's exports and imports. Section 5 analyses the implications of the trade war between the US and China in India and asks if India can export more to the US. Section 6 concludes.

2 Brief background of the trade war

The soaring goods trade deficit of the US vis-à-vis China (US$419.2 billion in 2018, USTR) led to the trade war between these two countries. A brief timeline of the trade war is presented below, with the objective of drawing out the implications of the trade war for other countries like India. The trade war can be broken down into several battles in terms of the products involved:

Battle 1 – Solar panel and washing machines[1]

In 2017, the US International Trade Commission (USITC) found that imports of solar panels (31 October 2017) and washing machines (21 November 2017) had caused injury to the US solar panel and washing machine industries and recommended President Trump impose 'global safeguard' restrictions. On 22 January 2018, President Trump approved global safeguard tariffs on US$8.5 billion in imports of solar panels and US$1.8 billion of washing machines.

Battle 2 – Steel and aluminium

In 2017, President Trump instructed Commerce Secretary Wilbur Ross to self-initiate two investigations into whether steel (20 April) and aluminum (27 April 27) imports threaten US national security under Section 232 of the Trade Expansion Act of 1962. On 16 February 2018, the Department of Commerce releases the National Security Investigation report finding imports of steel and aluminum products threaten US national security under the rarely used Section 232 of the Trade Expansion Act of 1962. On 1 March 2018, President Trump announced forthcoming tariffs on all trading partners of 25% on steel and 10% on aluminum on national security grounds. These would go further than the Commerce Department recommendations, covering an estimated US$48 billion of imports, mostly from allies such as Canada, the European Union, Mexico, and South Korea. Only 6% of the imports covered are from China, due to prior US imposition of antidumping and countervailing duties. The Indian response to the above measures was to submit a list of 29 products to WTO to suspend concessions to counter the US decision.[2]. India retaliates after losing Special Trade Status and on 15 June 2019, India implements retaliatory tariffs against US exports in response to Trump's steel and aluminum tariffs of March 2018. India had announced the tariffs in mid-2018, as mentioned above. Reports tie India's action to the Trump administration's decision on 5 June 2019, to increase tariffs on India by removing the country from the US Generalised System of Preferences programme for developing countries.

Battle 3 – Unfair trade practices for technology, intellectual property

On 18 August 2017, US Trade Representative Robert E. Lighthizer self-initiates an investigation of China under Section 301 of the Trade Act of 1974, after President Trump's memorandum of 14 August 2017, instructing him to consider whether to investigate any of China's laws, policies, practices, or actions that may be unreasonable or discriminatory and that may be harming American intellectual property rights, innovation, or technology development. On 22 March 2018, the Trump administration released its report finding China is conducting unfair trade practices related to technology transfer, intellectual property, and innovation under Section 301 of the Trade Act of 1974. President Trump indicates forthcoming remedies of tariffs on Chinese products up to US$60 billion, a World Trade Organisation (WTO) dispute, and new rules on investment. On 3 April 2018, The Trump administration released its US$50 billion list of 1,333 Chinese products under consideration for 25% tariffs, which covers US$46.2 billion of US imports. The top sectors hit are machinery, mechanical appliances, and electrical equipment – roughly 85% of the imports targeted by the tariffs for other countries' retaliation is in intermediate inputs and capital goods, which would raise costs within American companies' supply chains.

Battle 4 – Autos as national security threat

The Commerce Department initiates the third national security investigation under President Trump into imported autos and parts, following the steel and aluminum cases. On 17 May 2019, President Trump delayed a decision on whether to impose auto tariffs after the US Department of Commerce report recommended: 'actions to adjust automotive imports' to protect national security.[3] On 27 August 2018, President Trump and President Enrique Peña Nieto of Mexico announced a preliminary US-Mexico trade agreement that would potentially replace the North American Free Trade Agreement (NAFTA). On 30 November 2018, all three countries signed the US–Mexico–Canada Agreement (USMCA) to replace NAFTA. Canada and Mexico signed side letters aimed at preventing threatened auto tariffs. The deal still needs to be ratified by legislators to take effect.[4] The auto tariffs would mainly target countries such as Japan, Germany, and South Korea.

Reaction to the auto tariffs includes exports of BMW and Daimler from the US to China, Harley Davidson decides to move to the EU, and Volvo decides to manufacture from South Carolina – all indicating the role of global value chains in trade.

The implications of the trade war for India can be understood by examining the goods that India is exporting to the US and importing from China. We turn to India's trade with these countries next.

3 Literature survey

A global value chain (GVC) refers to the international fragmentation of production and all the activities that firms engage in, at home or abroad, to bring a product to the market, from conception to final use (OECD, 2015). GVCs involve economies that are interconnected through different stages of a value chain. Trade in GVCs involves the flow of intermediate goods and services, which includes both imports and exports of intermediate inputs and finished products.[5]. Since parts and components cross borders many times, export restrictions such as tariffs and other barriers affect the efficient functioning of GVCs and raise costs. In contrast, trade facilitation measures such as efficient port and custom procedures and convergence of standards and certification requirements allow for the smooth operation of value chains.

Krugman (2008) looks into the case of computers, iPods, semiconductors, and auto-parts separately and finds that the input content of the outputs from these industries is quite high (especially for China). There is an implication that the developing nations have specialised in those portions of the production process of these seemingly sophisticated products that involved low-skilled labour (like assembly and testing in case of semiconductors). Hanson, Mataloni, and Slaughter (2005) analyse trends in international trade to observe that multinationals relocate their input processing in their foreign affiliates, thus creating a production sharing network.

A country's value addition in a GVC depends on its location in the value chain (OECD, 2015). Countries upstream produce raw materials or the knowledge (e.g. research and design) at the beginning of the process while countries downstream assemble processed products and specialise in customer services. Most upstream activities such as research and development (R&D) and design and certain services create more value than assembly functions.

Several elements of policy determine participation in GVCs: regional trade agreements; investment barriers to multinational corporations; infrastructure development; speed and flexibility of movement of physical goods and information; effectiveness of legal and regulatory systems; efficiency of services; developing a skilled workforce; friendliness of the business climate; and capacity of domestic firms (often SMEs) to contribute to the supply chain (OECD, 2015). Other factors include border administration, market access barriers, and transport logistics (UNCTAD, 2013). These issues have also been frequent targets of aid for trade.

Participation in GVCs helps enhance growth and productivity in a country due to international competition, access to foreign knowledge and technology, and increased scope for specialisation and economies of scale. Additionally, productivity is also enhanced through access to cheaper or higher quality intermediate inputs, which embody more productive technology and efficient allocation of resources. In addition to removing trade barriers, governments can increase their countries' competitiveness in a GVC by implementing structural policies, which strengthen factors of production that are 'sticky' and unlikely to cross national borders. These include investments in education, high-quality infrastructure, and encouragement of strong industry-university linkages.

Participation in GVCs requires a conducive business environment, which requires high-quality infrastructure, adherence to international standards, well-developed ICT networks, as well as soft infrastructure such as sound legal systems and good governance. Export processing zones (EPZs) can help emerging economies to attract foreign direct investment. Such zones are attractive for foreign investors because of the low costs and the ease of importing and exporting without tariff barriers and minimum administrative requirements. EPZs are estimated to account for almost half of China's exports and 40% of Mexico's.

Tariffs and protectionist policies can be detrimental to exports in a value chain due to the high costs imposed on exporters by tariffs in their target markets. Similarly, a tariff on imports of intermediate products increases the cost of production and serves as a tax on exports. In developing economies where export capacity is dependent on foreign investments, even small tariff costs can discourage firms from investing and may lead them to invest elsewhere. Other than removing trade barriers, trade can be facilitated by addressing bottlenecks such as instituting fast and efficient customs and port procedures, streamlining administrative procedures at the border, and converging standards and certification requirements. Investment promotion policies are also needed to promote both inward and outward investment and establish an environment conducive to receiving international investments linked to GVCs. While such measures can help facilitate a country's participation in a GVC, steps need to be taken to ensure that specialisation in specific production stages does not lead to isolated pockets of production with limited impact on the rest of the economy. Governments need to implement complementary policies to strengthen linkages with foreign firms and enhance the capability of domestic firms to ensure that the economy is benefiting from GVCs.

Once integrated into a GVC, emerging economies can upgrade their position in a value chain to higher-value-added activities to generate larger economic benefits in the form of high wage employment and higher incomes (Taglioni and Winkler, 2016). There are different approaches to upgrading: (i) *process upgrading*, when firms process tasks with greater efficiency and lower defect rates than their competitors; (ii) *product upgrading*, when firms supply higher value-added products than their rivals due to technological sophistication and quality; (iii) *functional upgrading*, which is essentially product upgrading but due to higher value-added products in new segments of the value chain, and (iv) *chain upgrading* when firms switch their locus of activities to new GVCs producing higher value-added goods or services (Gereffi, Humphrey, & Sturgeon, 2005).

Investments in knowledge-based capital (KBC) are important drivers for upgrading. This is useful for upstream activities such as new concept development, R&D, or the manufacturing of key parts and components. Investments in KBC not only drive productivity growth; they also determine the extent to which the final product can be differentiated in consumer markets, which in turn determines the total value the GVC can create. This can be done by supporting innovation and experimenting with new business models and organisational forms. Simultaneously, good intellectual property rights can help protect the KBC that firms acquire. Knowledge investment needs to be done in R&D, design, and data.

Participation in GVCs also entails a reallocation of resources to more productive activities and the displacement of workers. A country's adjustment to a GVC can be aided by sound social and labour market policies, such as re-employment services, training, and publicly subsidised work-experience programmes. Skill training can also help translate a country's involvement in GVCs into productivity growth.

4 India's trade story

India's export position was 27th in the world in 2007 (accounting for 0.96% of total world gross exports), while in 2017, it improved to 20th (accounting for 1.66% of total world gross exports). Can the trade war between the US and China prove to be beneficial for India and can it increase its share of world exports even further? This section analyses this question.

4.1 India's exports

Using Hausmann et al.'s Atlas of Complexity, we examine what India exported in 2007 and 2017.[6] Figure 6.A1 in the Appendix shows the exports of India in goods in 2007 (US$149 billion), and Figure 6.A2 shows its exports in 2017. Since 2007, India's exports have increased significantly in two categories: chemicals and vehicles.

4.2 India's imports

In imports, India has significantly increased its share of chemicals, stone, machinery, and electronics in 2017 compared to 2007 (Figure 6.A3 and 6.A4). The figures also report the total exports of goods, so gross exports of goods increased from US$216 billion in 2007 to US$407 billion in 2017. It is important to note that imports of goods exceed the exports of goods both in 2007 and 2017, thus reflecting the trade deficit of the country.

Figures 6.A5 and 6.A7 also reveal the destination and source (Figure 6.A6 and 6.A8) of India's exports and imports, respectively. Thus while the USA is the largest destination of goods exports in 2007 and 2017, China is the largest source both in 2007 and 2017. The share of these countries has risen in the exports from India and imports to India respectively over the above period.

4.3 Broad Economic Classification (BEC)

For this part, we use the trade data of classification by Broad Economic Categories (BEC). The BEC is a three-digit classification, which groups transportable goods according to their main end-use.[7] The BEC classification is consistent with the three classes of goods in the system of national accounts – intermediate goods, final goods, and capital goods. This allows for the analysis of trade patterns in these three classes of goods over the period 2008–17. The relationship between the three basic classes of goods in the SNA and the basic categories in BEC4 is shown in Table 6.A1. The top-level categories of the BEC are as shown in Table 6.1. Thus this classification lends itself easily to categorising goods in terms of consumer goods, final goods, and capital goods.

At the one-digit BEC categorisation, in the year 2018, India's top exported items to the world were industrial supplies (BEC 2) (about 32% of total exports to the world), consumption goods (BEC 6) (16% of total) and goods n.e.s. (BEC

Table 6.1 Categories of BEC classification

Code	*Category*
1	Food and beverages
2	Industrial supplies not elsewhere specified
3	Fuels and lubricants
4	Capital goods (except transport equipment), and parts and accessories thereof
5	Transport equipment and parts and accessories thereof
6	Consumer goods not elsewhere specified
7	Goods not elsewhere specified

Source: Authors' compilation using UN Comtrade.

7) (14% of total). At the two-digit level, the top categories were processed industrial goods (BEC 22), processed or refined fuels, and lubricants (BEC 32) and semi-durable consumer goods (BEC 62). India's top imported items from the world were industrial supplies n.e.s. (BEC 2) (39% of total imports from the world), fuels and lubricants (3) (32% of total), and capital goods (except transport equipment) (BEC 4) (17% of total). At the two-digit level, the top imported items were processed industrial goods (BEC 22), primary or unprocessed fuels and lubricants (BEC 31), and capital goods (except transport equipment) (BEC 41).

4.4 India's exports and imports

We examine the exports and imports of India using the BEC classification. Figure 6.1 displays the evolving shares of different classes of goods, i.e. intermediate, final, and capital goods and goods not elsewhere specified in total exports for India over the period of 2008–17. The export pattern displays a major fall in the trade value of exports of intermediate goods. In 2017, 60% of export value was in exports of intermediate goods compared to 69% in 2008. The share of final goods in total exports rose to 33% in 2017 from 25% in 2008. The share of capital goods remained constant if compared from 2008 to 2017. The share of goods not elsewhere specified in the total imports can be considered negligible (and hence will not be discussed here). By looking at the export patterns of India, it can be seen that the country has done quite well to improve the exports of final goods. The compound annual growth rate of total Indian exports is 1.93% over the period 2008–17.

Figure 6.2 shows shares of different classes of goods – intermediate goods, final goods, capital goods – in the total Indian imports over the period of 2008–17. Imports of intermediate goods account for 83% of total imports by India in 2017 compared to 82% in 2008. There is not much of a change in the import pattern of India as far as intermediate goods are concerned. Imports of final goods and capital goods made up 6% and 11% respectively in 2017, compared to 3% and 15% respectively in 2008. The compound annual growth rate of total Indian imports is 0.99% over the period 2008–17. If we look at the compound annual

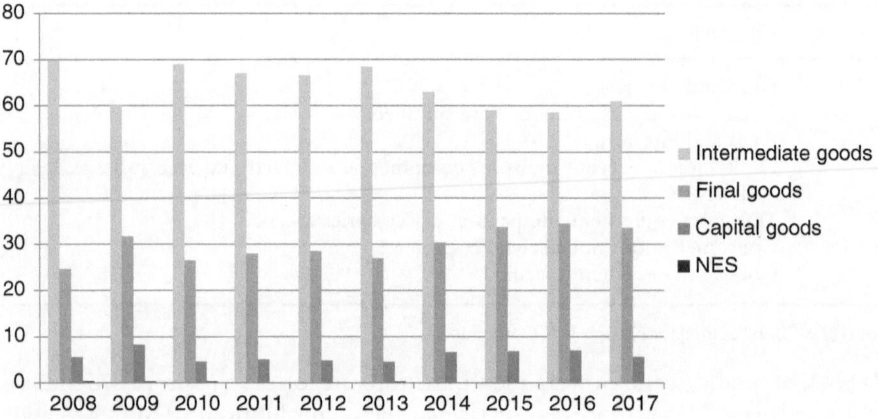

Figure 6.1 Share of classes of goods in total Indian exports (2008–2017) (%).
Source: Authors' illustration using UN Comtrade data.

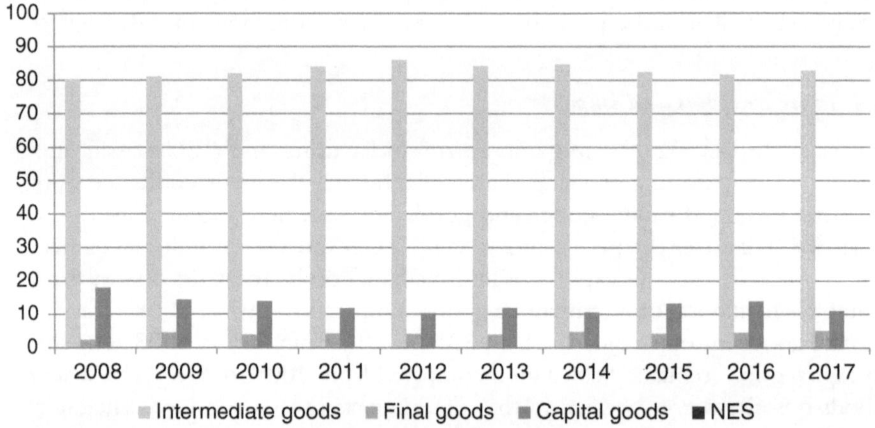

Figure 6.2 Share of classes of goods in total Indian imports (2008–2017) (%).
Source: Authors' illustration using UN Comtrade data.

growth rates of the different classes of goods, we see that there is a fall in the imports of capital good by 1.36% whereas the growth is positive for intermediate and final goods across time.

The trade patterns in intermediate goods, final goods, and capital goods imports and exports will be analysed in detail for India and the US and China in the rest of the chapter.

4.5 Indian trade patterns of intermediate goods

Intermediate goods occupy an important position in India's exports and imports (as shown in Figures 6.1 and 6.2). Figure 6.3 presents the Indian exports and imports of intermediate goods. Over the last ten years, India imported more intermediate goods than it exported. Thus, India is a net importer of intermediate goods. This highlights an important trend in Indian imports that India is mainly an assembler rather than a distributor. The compound annual growth rate (CAGR) for Indian imports of intermediate goods over a period of ten years is 1.05%, and for Indian exports of intermediate goods is 0.55%.

Table 6.2 shows the top ten exporting partners of India for intermediate goods for the years 2008, 2012, and 2017. In 2008, the United Arab Emirates, the United States, and China were the top three countries to which intermediate goods were exported, followed by Singapore, Hong Kong, and the Netherlands. In 2012 and 2017 the United States topped the list followed by the United Arab Emirates and China for both the years. In 2017, 13.6% of intermediate exports were exported to the United States. Table 6.3 shows the top ten importing partners of India for intermediate goods for the years 2008, 2012, and 2017.

Exports of intermediate goods to the UAE, China, Hong Kong, and Singapore represented 7.6%, 6.25%, 6.10%, and 4.76% of the total intermediate goods exports in 2017, respectively. We examine the categories that India exports to the USA below.

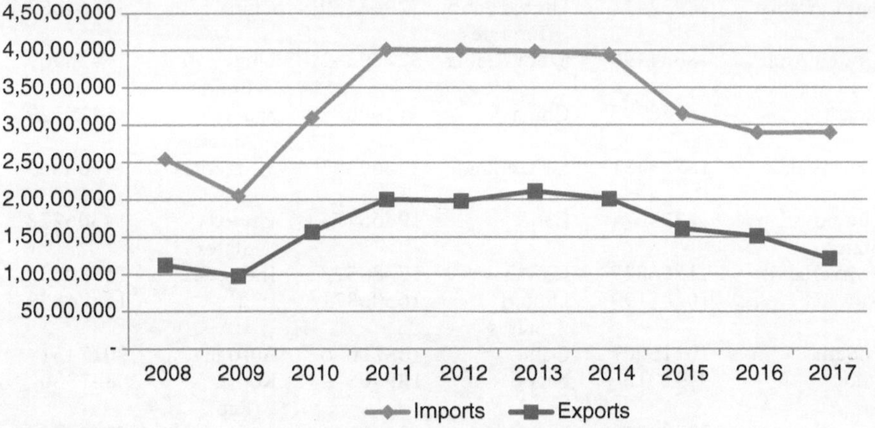

Figure 6.3 India's imports and exports of intermediate goods.
Source: Authors' illustration using UN Comtrade data.

Table 6.2 India's top ten exporting partners of intermediate goods

2008		*2012*		*2017*	
Country	*Trade Value (1000 US$)*	*Country*	*Trade Value (1000 US$)*	*Country*	*Trade Value (1000 US$)*
United Arab Emirates	12817174	United States	21920145	United States	17879604
United States	11372420	United Arab Emirates	15738403	United Arab Emirates	9999918
China	9416986	China	13833565	China	8196324
Singapore	6321908	Singapore	10532720	Hong Kong, China	8002094
Hong Kong, China	5871525	Hong Kong, China	9071422	Singapore	62447316
Netherlands	4870616	Netherlands	7454978	Bangladesh	3960758
Belgium	3871958	Saudi Arabia	6072828	Belgium	3669207
Korea, Rep.	3572320	Brazil	5373983	Germany	3523403
Saudi Arabia	3541178	Japan	5306106	Turkey	3136743
Germany	3231309	Indonesia	4758147	Italy	2966800

Source: Authors' calculation using UN Comtrade.

Table 6.3 India's top ten importing partners of intermediate goods

2008		*2012*		*2017*	
Country	*Trade Value (1000 US$)*	*Country*	*Trade Value (1000 US$)*	*Country*	*Trade Value (1000 US$)*
Saudi Arabia	22972471	United Arab Emirates	32943589	China	36464682
United Arab Emirates	18554490	Saudi Arabia	32779542	United Arab Emirates	16435969
China	18158707	China	31200082	Saudi Arabia	15429529
Iran, Islamic Rep.	13733351	Switzerland	27360465	Switzerland	14368065
United States	12273074	Iraq	19466774	United States	14306728
Switzerland	11806827	Kuwait	17780527	Indonesia	11780559
Kuwait	10741199	United States	16606871	Iraq	11476839
Nigeria	10110009	Qatar	16371076	Australia	9017431
Iraq	9492015	Nigeria	13930874	Korea, Rep.	8841380
Australia	9248982	Indonesia	13397164	Iran, Islamic Rep.	7560160

Source: Authors' calculation using UN Comtrade.

4.6 Indian trade pattern of final goods

Figure 6.4 presents the Indian exports and imports of consumption/final goods. Over the last ten years (2008–17), Indian exports are greater than Indian imports. Thus, India is a net exporter of final goods.

Table 6.4 shows the top ten exporting partners of India of final goods for the years 2008, 2012, and 2017. In 2008, the United States, United Arab Emirates, United Kingdom were the top three countries to which final goods were exported from India, followed by Germany, France, and Saudi Arabia. In 2012 and 2017, the United Arab Emirates and the United States were the top two exporting partners of India. In 2017, 21.1% of final exports were exported to the United States. Exports of final goods to the UAE, Vietnam, the United Kingdom, and Hong Kong represented 12.7%, 5.3%, 4.8%, and 3.6% of the total final goods exports in 2017, respectively.

Table 6.5 shows the top ten importing partners of final goods for the years 2008, 2012, and 2017, the United States having a maximum share of total imports in the year 2008. In 2017, 21.08% of final imports were sourced from China, followed by United States, Korea, Australia, and Canada with 10.2%, 8.3%, 5.17%, and 3.6% of the total final goods imports in 2017, respectively. The compound annual growth rate (CAGR) for Indian imports of final goods over a period of ten years is 6.88%, and for Indian exports of final goods is 5.1%.

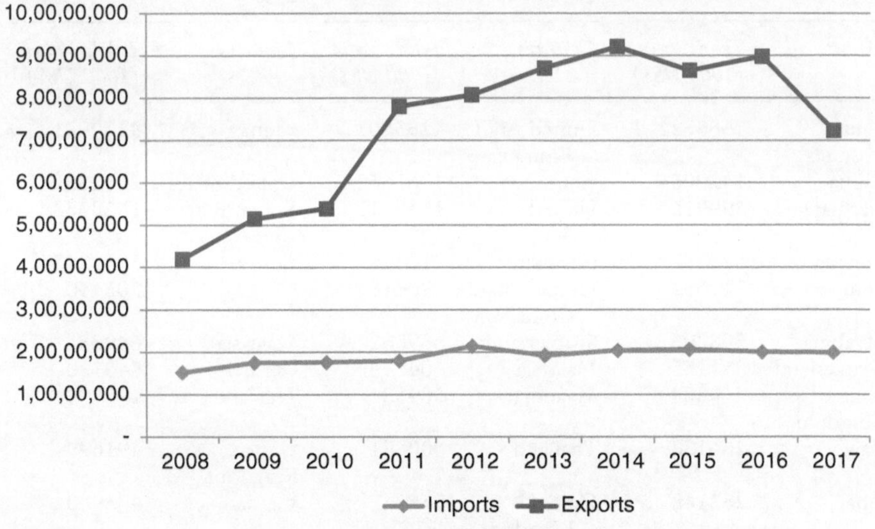

Figure 6.4 India's imports and exports of final goods.
Source: Authors' illustration using UN Comtrade data.

Table 6.4 India's top ten exporting partners of final goods

2008		*2012*		*2017*	
Country	*Trade Value (1000 US$)*	*Country*	*Trade Value (1000 US$)*	*Country*	*Trade Value (1000 US$)*
United States	8349660	United Arab Emirates	18143317	United States	15291044
United Arab Emirates	5119093	United States	13719328	United Arab Emirates	9225766
United Kingdom	3059363	United Kingdom	4480548	Vietnam	3826736
Germany	2363923	Germany	2729294	United Kingdom	3510361
France	1530416	Hong Kong, China	2718236	Hong Kong, China	2666015
Saudi Arabia	1494891	Saudi Arabia	1951749	Germany	2336130
Italy	1311165	France	1620898	Saudi Arabia	1632073
Netherlands	1216647	Vietnam	1617031	Mexico	1530000
Spain	1089146	Netherlands	1530779	France	1471193
Bangladesh	1001268	South Africa	1419424	Spain	1368068

Source: Authors' calculation using UN Comtrade.

Table 6.5 India's top ten importing partners of final goods

2008		*2012*		*2017*	
Country	*Trade Value (1000 US$)*	*Country*	*Trade Value (1000 US$)*	*Country*	*Trade Value (1000 US$)*
United States	1555722	United Arab Emirates	4255801	China	4120931
China	1429056	China	4061660	United States	2012330
Germany	599916	United States	1583112	Korea, Rep.	1623258
Canada	575937	Germany	911495	Australia	1012245
France	511632	Hong Kong, China	796418	Canada	708440
Myanmar	508805	Switzerland	639562	Malaysia	649388
Switzerland	381155	Malaysia	604818	Germany	548130
United Kingdom	310804	Myanmar	604531	Thailand	495294
Italy	264133	Thailand	600851	United Kingdom	491699
Japan	253148	United Kingdom	566247	Vietnam	473900

Source: Authors' calculation using UN Comtrade.

4.7 India's pattern of trade in capital goods

Figure 6.5 displays imports and exports of India's capital goods over the period 2008 to 2017. Like intermediate goods, India imported more capital goods than it exported over the period. The fall in imports during 2008–9 could be due to the financial crises. By comparison, exports of capital goods have consistently been lower than imports for ten years.

Table 6.6 shows the top ten exporting partners of India's capital goods. In 2008, the United States, Singapore, and the United Arab Emirates were the top three countries to which capital goods were exported, followed by the Netherlands and Brazil. In 2017, the United States was the top exporting partner of India with 12.17% of the total exports in that year, followed by the United Arab Emirates (11.55%) and Singapore (5.15%). The compound annual growth rate of imports of capital goods from 2008 to 2017 is negative (-1.36%), but the CAGR of exports of capital goods is 2.08%.

Table 6.7 shows India's top ten importing partners of capital goods for the years 2008, 2012, and 2017. In 2017, 38.3% of imports in capital goods originated from China, followed by Germany (8.03%), France (7.05%), USA (6.95%), and Korea (5.07%).

To sum up this section, it was found that imports of intermediate goods accounted for 83% of total merchandise imports in 2017 while imports of final and capital goods made up 6% and 11% in 2017. Also, in 2017 60% of export value was in exports of intermediate goods. By comparison, the share of final and capital goods reached 33% and 6% respectively in 2017. India has consistently been a net importer of intermediate goods over the period 2008–17, and a net exporter of final goods and a net importer of capital goods for the period of 2008–17.

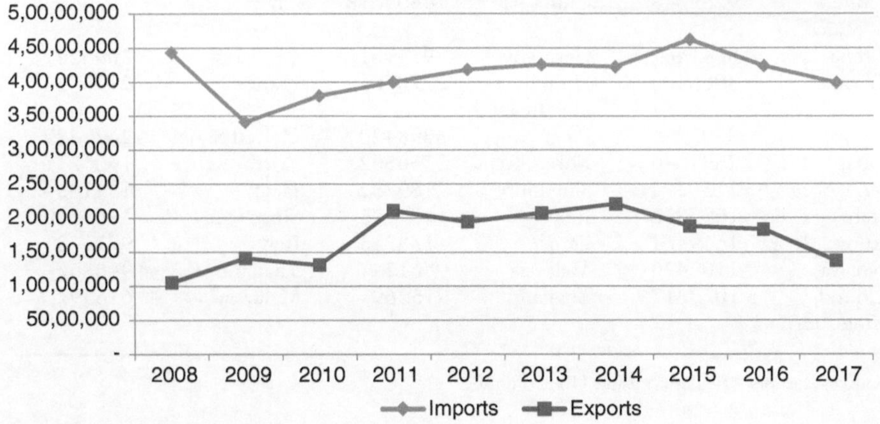

Figure 6.5 India's imports and exports of capital goods.
Source: Authors' illustration using UN Comtrade data.

Table 6.6 India's top ten exporting partners of capital goods

2008		*2012*		*2017*	
Country	*Trade Value (1000 US$)*	*Country*	*Trade Value (1000 US$)*	*Country*	*Trade Value (1000 US$)*
United States	1205517	Singapore	2132177	United States	1636240
Singapore	1099806	United Arab Emirates	1871943	United Arab Emirates	1552644
United Arab Emirates	451472	United States	1397674	Singapore	692418
Netherlands	305659	Indonesia	931322	Bangladesh	687467
Brazil	295154	Sri Lanka	656703	Nepal	518588
Saudi Arabia	285400	Saudi Arabia	521106	China	498915
United Kingdom	257311	South Africa	486401	Sri Lanka	445965
Germany	241826	Nigeria	484618	United Kingdom	410612
Nigeria	238699	Netherlands	477354	Germany	374890
Australia	202943	Germany	454774	Indonesia	362003

Source: Authors' calculation using UN Comtrade.

Table 6.7 India's top ten importing partners of capital goods

2008		*2012*		*2017*	
Country	*Trade Value (1000 US$)*	*Country*	*Trade Value (1000 US$)*	*Country*	*Trade Value (1000 US$)*
United States	9259848	China	14404613	China	14766622
China	8541467	Germany	3914961	Germany	3096281
Germany	3986400	United States	3770761	France	2715323
France	3707786	Japan	3298420	United States	2678389
Japan	2591646	Korea, Rep.	2750552	Korea, Rep.	1956211
Singapore	2130394	Singapore	2189752	Japan	1841054
Italy	1697356	Italy	1437175	Singapore	1368140
Korea, Rep.	1669451	France	1138715	Italy	971173
Norway	1102420	Malaysia	986124	Thailand	946867
United Kingdom	1073317	Thailand	915269	Malaysia	616597

Source: Authors' calculation using UN Comtrade.

While the USA is an important destination for Indian exports, China is the most important source of Indian imports.

According to data from UN Comtrade database, India's top imported items from China were capital goods (except transport equipment) (BEC 4) (about 50% of total imports from China), industrial supplies (BEC 2) (45% of total), and consumption goods n.e.s. (BEC 6) (8.2% of total) in 2018. At the two-digit level, the top imported items were processed industrial goods (BEC 22), capital goods (except transport equipment) (BEC 41), and parts and accessories of capital goods (BEC 42) (except transport equipment). India's top exported items to China in 2018 were industrial supplies n.e.s. (BEC 2) (about 64% of total exports to China), goods n.e.s. (BEC 7) (20% of total) and fuels and lubricants (BEC 3) (18% of total). At the two-digit level, the top categories were processed industrial goods (BEC 22), processed or refined fuels and lubricants (BEC 32), and primary industrial supplies n.e.s. (BEC 21).

5 Implications of US–China trade war for India

Part of the fallout of the recent use of tariffs and counter-tariffs by the different countries is a disruption in the world trading process. Due to the nature of globalised production, disruption in the trading system and the higher cost of trade could have two or three effects. First, the costs of certain products may go up in most countries imposing these tariffs at least temporarily. Second, production (and jobs) may shift from the countries in which these costs have gone up to other lower-cost countries. Third, escalation in tariffs may lead to lower volumes of trade worldwide. Hence, the implications of the trade war may be felt for some time to come. Analysis by the IMF shows that the trade wars could wipe US$455 billion off the world's gross domestic product in 2020. A consequence of the US–China trade war has been the realignment of global value chains. However, the effect will be uneven: certain countries will benefit. In order to examine the impact of the trade war, it is important to examine what the countries export and import from each other.

The USA exported products worth US$2.35 trillion in 2017.[8] It had an exporter rank of 2nd (among 133 countries). Exports grew by an annual average of 1.3% over the five years to 2017, while non-oil exports grew at the same rate. Imports to the country totalled US$2.84 trillion, with a trade deficit in goods and services. The top destinations for US exports in 2017 were Canada, Mexico, and China. The top US exports in goods to China were soybeans, electronic integrated motor vehicles, and civilian aircraft. Its imports from China include electrical machinery, machinery, furniture and bedding, toys and sports equipment, and plastics. China exported US$2.73 trillion in 2017, with a 1st rank among 133 countries. Exports in China grew by an annual average of 2.1% in the five years to 2017, while non-oil exports increased at the same rate. China's imports in 2017 were US$2.03 trillion, leaving China with a trade surplus in goods and services.

India exported US$483 billion of goods and services (with services approximately 36% of the total) with a rank of 13th (among 133 countries). India's exports have grown at an annual average of 1.6% while non-oil exports have grown at 2.8%. Imports in 2017 were equal to US$524 billion, indicating the deficit in goods and services. The top Indian exports were to USA, UAE and Hong Kong in 2017. Barring motor vehicles, machinery, and plastics, India is not competitive in the other products that the USA and China export to each other. India's own exports to China consist of organic chemicals, cotton, plastics, etc. and to the USA diamonds, pharmaceuticals, machinery, mineral fuels, and vehicles.

Increasing India's share in global exports remains the main thrust of the Government of India's trade policy objectives. The objective of the Foreign Trade Policy of the Ministry of Commerce and Industry for 2015–20 was to make India a significant participant in international trade and raise its share of global exports from 2% in 2015 to 3.5% by 2020. This was to be achieved, among other initiatives, by promoting export diversification and assisting key sectors to become more competitive. The acceleration in exports was expected to be achieved through exemption and remission of indirect taxes on inputs for producing final export products and imports of capital goods at concessional duties.

The WTO Trade Policy Review 2015 for India noted that, despite the focus on increasing exports, India continues to use trade policy as a means to regulate domestic supply and to address short-term objectives such as containing inflation and fluctuations in commodity prices. A wide range of end-user exemptions for industrial use has been made in successive annual tariffs, indicating the government's general policy of encouraging the manufacturing sector. Measures to reduce the cost of raw materials as well as correct 'inverted' duty structures (tariffs for primary and intermediate products are higher than for final products) have been part of the government's policy initiatives in the last few years. The proposed custom duty increase should be implemented with caution in light of these policy goals.

The increase in customs duties announced by the Finance Minister in 2019 is indicative of the Government's efforts to protect its domestic industries. While import substitution has been used by many developing countries in the past, since the 1990s most countries have significantly lowered tariffs. Most East Asian countries have also successfully integrated with global and regional value chains. In recognition of the importance of infrastructure and logistics in enabling GVC integration, India has undertaken a slew of measures including the *Bharatmala Pariyojana* project for roads, investor facilitation cells, reducing the number of documents for exporting and importing. The recent move to raise import tariffs is contrary to the reform process undertaken in India to improve its GVC integration. India, while it has been very successful in GVC integration (Ray and Miglani, 2018), could, through such policy changes, destroy its chances further. Moreover, the 'Make in India' programme could also be affected by the higher costs of intermediate goods. The important point to note here is that, if intermediate goods are made expensive, then the other enabling factors must also ensure the manufacturing of competitively priced and final quality goods to enhance overall exports. Unless this happens, the country may only end up adding more costs.

In the last couple of years, the USA has become unconventionally protectionist, denying market access to several countries on the grounds of national security using the GATT Article XXI clause. This has included additional tariff duties on manufactured goods imported from countries like China, India, and South Korea. Additionally, it declared withdrawal of the Generalised System of Preferences (GSP) status for India with effect from 5 June 2019. India has been discussing various issues with the US such as GSP restoration, and withdrawal of their Section 232 tariffs and India's retaliatory duties.[9] An analysis of the implications of the withdrawal of GSP by Mukhopadhyay and Sarma (2020) suggests that there will be sizeable negative impact on Indian exports, particularly articles of leather (HS 42), chemicals (HS 29), iron and steel (HS 73), electrical machinery (HS 85), plastics (HS 39), articles of stone (HS 68), and miscellaneous articles of base metals (HS 83).

An analysis by Bown (2019) reveals that, since the beginning of 2018, the US administration increased duties on 14% of India's exports to the country, while India retaliated by imposing new tariffs on about 6% of US exports to India.[10] The US tariffs have hit trade in goods like appliances, mechanical and electrical machinery, chemicals, steel, and auto parts. India's retaliation list has included products like chickpeas, lentils, steel, and chemicals exported from the US. The analysis also reveals that, first, the tariff increase likely violates MFN treatment, since it only applies to the United States. Second, the increase in tariffs on almonds, walnuts, and apples pushes India's tariff to levels exceeding its WTO legally binding rates. Such decisions have repercussions for the strategic relations between the two countries.[11]

Maurya (2017) analyses India's trade with its biggest trade partners, the US and China, to find out opportunities for India amid the trade differences between two economic giants. There could be opportunities for India to increase its market access in China if the government comes up with appropriate strategies. There are several market access issues with China, which need to be negotiated and addressed. India should also keep a watch to ensure that China does not dump the goods meant for the US into the Indian market. Authors like Ayyub and Nag (2018) have explored the context of the impact of tariff increases in India. They contend that the decision on the current trade wars in the WTO would decide the future of multilateral trade arrangements and trade policies of individual countries around the world. In the short run, some trade diversion is expected to happen due to sudden import restrictions in the USA and the Chinese market and countries with an exportable surplus like India have the chance to exploit the opportunity. However, dumping is more likely once the Regional Comprehensive Economic Partnership (RCEP) Agreement comes into force. Further, they state that markets where India has competition with China and the USA would become comparatively tougher for Indian exporters post-trade war as the two countries would play more aggressively in those markets to sell out their surplus.

6 Conclusions

The objective of this chapter was to analyse the implications of the US–China trade war on India. Trade data were analysed using the BEC. This classification allowed us to examine the three classes of goods in the system of national accounts: intermediate goods, final goods, and capital goods. This was used to analyse Indian trade patterns over the period 2008–17. It was found that imports of intermediate goods accounted for 83% of total merchandise imports in 2017, while imports of final and capital goods made up 6% and 11% in 2017. Also, in 2017 60% of export value was in exports of intermediate goods. By comparison, the share of final and capital goods reached 33% and 6% respectively in 2017. India has consistently been a net importer of intermediate goods over the period 2008–17. Also, it is a net exporter of final goods and net importer of capital goods for the period of 2008–17.

The implications of a trade war for a country like India will be very different than for a country like the People's Republic of China. India's imports are dominated by petroleum, crude oil, and products, and its exports consist of engineering goods. PRC is the factory of the world, and India is hoping to increase its exports to the world. One of the reasons that India has been unable to increase its exports is that it is uncompetitive, especially in comparison with countries like Bangladesh or Vietnam. Hence India's response should have been different from China. The United States is a very important export destination for India. Perhaps India, having considered this point, has agreed to give some concessions in the limited trade deal.

Appendix

The figures have been generated from the Growth Lab at Harvard University in the Atlas of Economic Complexity: www.atlas.cid.harvard.edu.

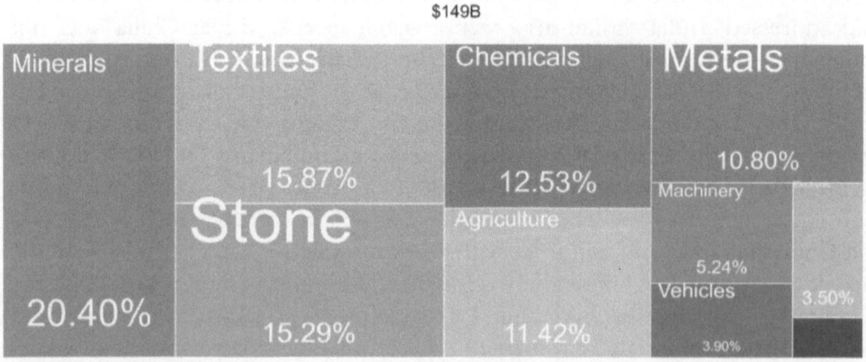

Figure 6.A1 Gross exports of India, sectors, 2007 (goods).

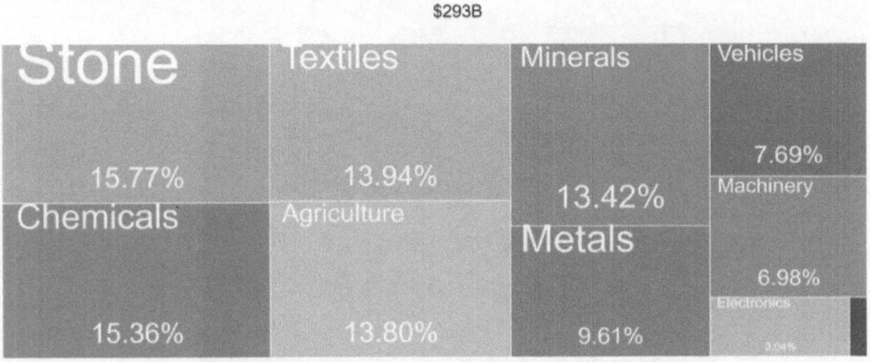

Figure 6.A2 Gross exports of India, 2017 (goods).

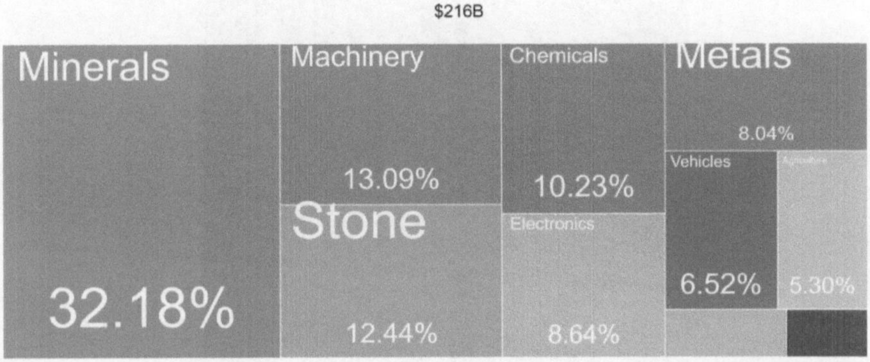

Figure 6.A3 Gross imports of India, 2007 (goods).

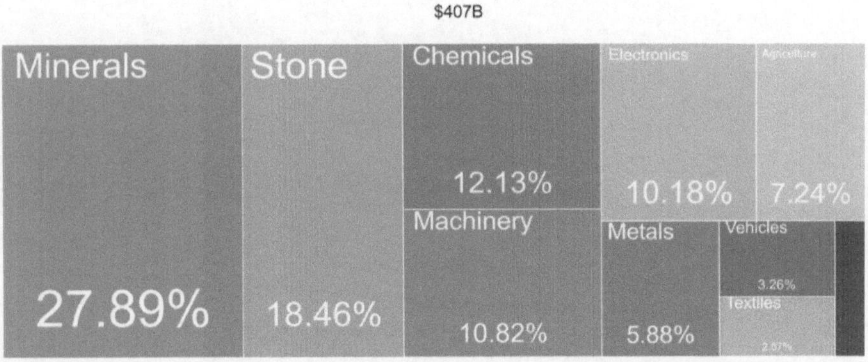

Figure 6.A4 Gross imports of India, 2017 (goods).

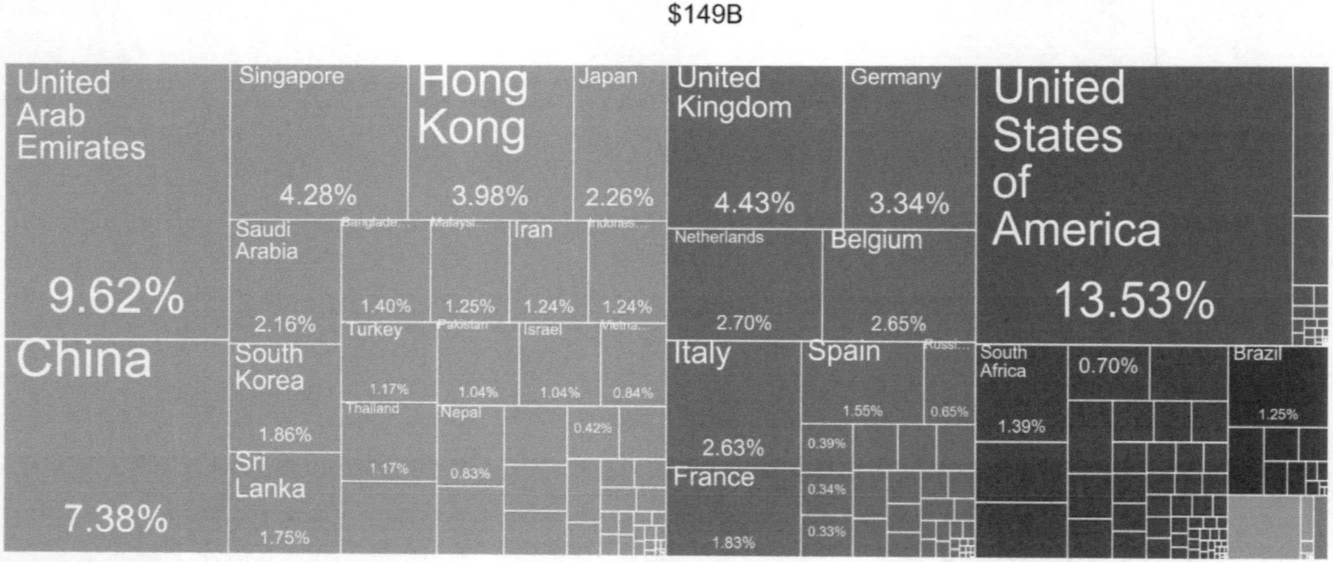

Figure 6.A5 Gross exports of India, countries, 2007.

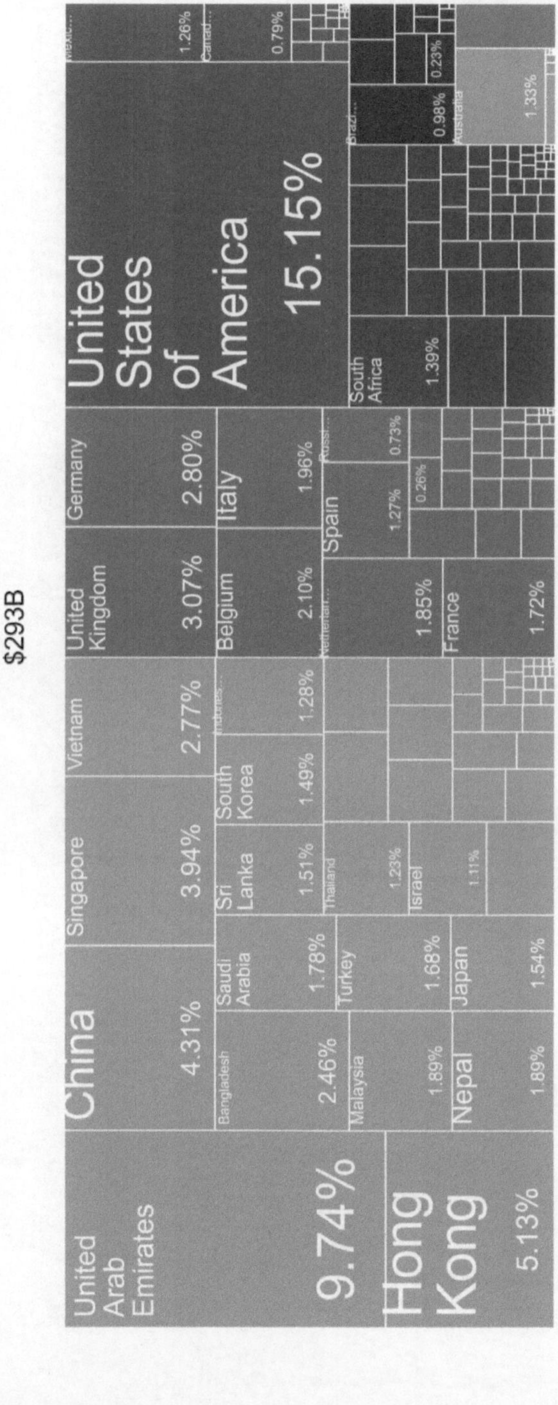

Figure 6.A6 Gross exports of India, countries, 2017.

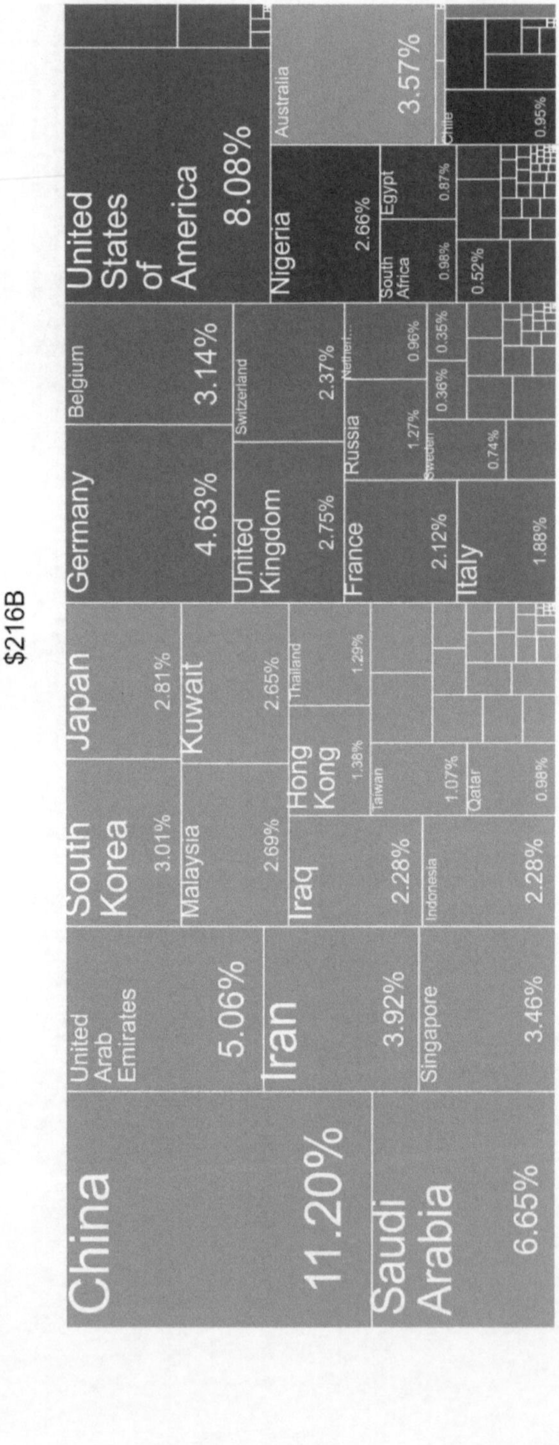

Figure 6.A7 Gross imports of India, countries, 2007.

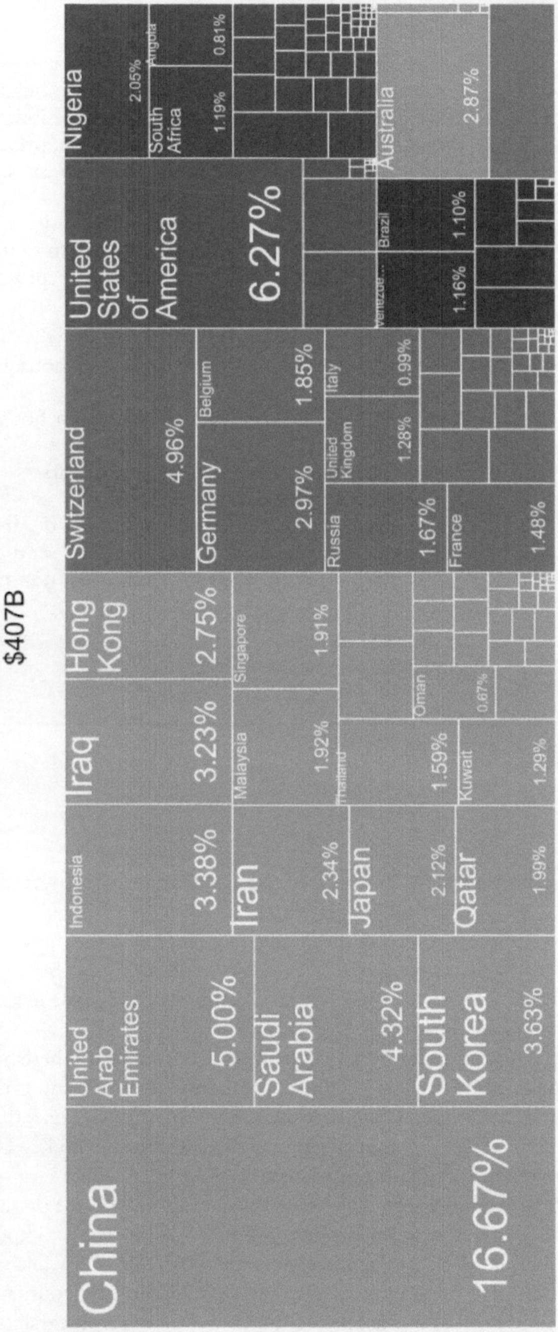

Figure 6.A8 Gross imports of India, countries, 2017.

Table 6.A1 Correspondence between SNA Classes of goods and BEC classification

Classes of goods	*BEC Codes*	*BEC Categories*
Intermediate Goods	111	Food and beverages, primary, mainly for industry
	121	Food and beverages, processed, mainly for industry
	21	Industrial supplies not elsewhere specified, primary
	22	Industrial supplies not elsewhere specified, processed
	31	Fuels and lubricants, primary
	321	Food and beverages, processed, motor spirit
	322	Fuels and lubricants, processed (other than motor spirit)
	42	Parts and accessories of capital goods (except transport equipment)
	53	Parts and accessories of transport equipment
Final Goods	112	Food and beverages, primary, mainly for household Consumption
	122	Food and beverages, processed, mainly for household Consumption
	51	Transport equipment, passenger motor cars
	522	Transport equipment, non-industrial
	61	Consumer goods not elsewhere specified, durable
	62	Consumer goods not elsewhere specified, semi-durable
	63	Consumer goods not elsewhere specified, non-durable
Capital Goods	41	Capital goods, except transport equipment
	521	Transport equipment, industrial
Not elsewhere Specified	7	Goods not elsewhere specified.

Source: UNSD (2003).

Notes

1 www.piie.com/blogs/trade-investment-policy-watch/trump-trade-war-china-date-guide
2 Only the Indian responses or countermeasures are listed here. Many other countries including the EU and China retaliated – however, these responses have not been documented. Readers may refer to www.piie.com/blogs/trade-investment-policy-watch/trump-trade-war-china-date-guide.
3 President Trump is reportedly considering raising tariffs to 25% on these products, which a PIIE analysis finds could cost 195,000 American jobs, assuming no exemptions. That number could more than triple if other countries retaliate in kind. The tariffs would affect US$208 billion of imports, not counting auto parts, nearly all from key US allies.
4 Commerce Department submits National Security Report to White House, 17 February 2019 and President Trump has 90 days (until 18 May 2019) to agree or disagree with the findings. He has 15 days after accepting findings of a threat to restrict imports, or he may pursue negotiations and defer new trade actions for up to 180 days while talks proceed.
5 The trade in value added initiative measures the value added by a country (labour compensation, taxes, and profits) in the production of a good or service that is exported and eliminates the double counting in current gross flows of trade (www.oecd.org/sti/ind/measuring-trade-in-value-added.htm).

6 See http://atlas.cid.harvard.edu/

7 The BEC groups goods into 19 categories. Of these, 16 basic categories make up the three broad end use categories. The Broad Economic Categories classification was introduced by the UN statistical Commission in 1961. There have been four revisions to BEC since 1961, mainly coinciding with revisions to Standard International Trade Classification (SITC). The fifth revision of BEC was endorsed for international use by UN Statistical Commission in March 2016 (BEC5), but the trade data t and concordances between BEC and HS were not available . Therefore, BEC4 is used to analyse Indian trade patterns. This chapter uses data for ten years 2008–17. Data are extracted from the UNCOMTRADE website using HS2007 and BEC4 Concordance for the years 2009–17 while the data for the year 2008 are extracted using HS2002 and BEC4 concordance. See also www150.statcan.gc.ca/n1/pub/13-605-x/2017001/article/54883-eng.htm

8 See http://atlas.cid.harvard.edu/

9 On 8 March 2018, US President Donald Trump signed two proclamations placing tariffs on imports of steel and aluminum. The tariffs are authorised under Section 232 of the US Trade Expansion Act of 1962 on the grounds of national security.

10 US tariffs on India increased from an average level of 3% in January 2018 to 3.9% in July 2019.

11 The US and India are negotiating a limited trade agreement which will cover 15% of the bilateral shipment between the countries and could have an early harvest trade agreement on 50–100 items. Both sides are agreeing to greater market access in certain goods (India may open up its dairy sector in return for greater access in garments). Also they may agree on reducing tariffs on certain items (India on Harley Davidsons and 29 other products and US to roll back tariffs on steel and aluminium). GSP will be reinstated for India, giving greater market access to the US. www.financialexpress.com/economy/india-us-limited-deal-to-cover-just-15-of-trade-details/2035829/

References

Ayyub, S., & Nag, B. (2018). China US trade war: Opportunities and challenges for India. *The Chartered Accountant Student*, *22*(5), 34–35.

Bown, C. P. (2019). Trump's mini-trade war with India. *PIIE Trade and Investment Watch*, VOX-CEPR Policy Portal, 8 July.

Dean, J. M., Fung, K. C., & Wang, Z. (2011). Measuring vertical specialization: The case of China. *Review of International Economics*, *19*(4), 609–625.

De Backer, K., & Miroudot, S. (2013). *Mapping Global Value Chains.* OECD Trade Policy Papers, 159. Paris: OECD Publishing.

Feenstra, R. C., & Hanson, G. H. (2003). Global production sharing and rising inequality: A survey of trade and wages. *Handbook of International Trade*, *1*, 146–185.

Grunwald, J., and Flamm, K. (1985). *The Global Factory: Foreign Assembly in International Trade.* Washington, DC: Brookings Institution Press.

Gereffi, G., Humphrey, J., & Sturgeon, T. (2005). The governance of global value chains. *Review of International Political Economy*, *12*(1), 78–104.

Hanson, G. H., Mataloni Jr, R. J., & Slaughter, M. J. (2005). Vertical production networks in multinational firms. *Review of Economics and Statistics*, *87*(4), 664–678.

Helleiner, G. K. (1973). Manufactured exports from less-developed countries and multinational firms. *The Economic Journal*, *83*(329), 21–47.

Helpman, E. (2011). *Understanding Global Trade*. Cambridge, MA: Harvard University Press.

Hummels, D., Ishii, J., & Yi, K. M. (2001). The nature and growth of vertical specialization in world trade. *Journal of International Economics, 54*(1), 75–96.

Johnson, R. C., & Noguera, G. (2012). Accounting for intermediates: Production sharing and trade in value added. *Journal of international Economics, 86*(2), 224–236.

Jones, R. W., & Domeij, D. (2000). *Globalization and the Theory of Input Trade,* vol. 8. Cambridge, MA: MIT Press.

Jones, R. W., & Kierzkowski, H. (2001). A framework for fragmentation. In S. Arndt and H. Kierzkowksi (eds), *Fragmentation: New Production Patterns in the World Economy* (pp. 17–34). Oxford: Oxford University Press.

Jones, R. W., & Kierzkowski H. (2004). Globalization and the consequences of international fragmentation. In R. Dornbusch, G. Calvo, and M. Obstfeld (eds), Money, *Factor Mobility and Trade: The Festschrift in Honor of Robert A. Mundell* (pp. 365–381). Cambridge, MA: MIT Press.

Jones, R., Kierzkowski, H., & Lurong, C. (2005). What does evidence tell us about fragmentation and outsourcing? *International Review of Economics and Finance, 14*(3), 305–316.

Koopman, R., Powers, W., Wang, Z., & Wei, S. J. (2010). *Give Credit Where Credit is Due: Tracing Value Added in Global Production Chains.* No. w16426. Cambridge, MA: National Bureau of Economic Research.

Krugman, P. R. (2008). Trade and wages, reconsidered. *Brookings Papers on Economic Activity, 2008*(1), 103–154.

Maurya, A. (2017). US China trade war: Opportunities for India. Available at SSRN 3043699.

Mukhopadhyay, A., & Sarma, N. (2020). US trade ‘realignment’: The impact of GSP withdrawal on India’s top exports to the United States. Occasional Paper, 233. Observer Research Foundation. www.orfonline.org/research/us-trade-realignment-the-impact-of-gsp-withdrawal-on-indias-top-exports-to-the-united-states-60997/

OECD (2015). *The Participation of Developing Countries in Global Value Chains: Implications for Trade and Trade-Related Policies.* OECD Trade Policy Paper, 179. Paris: OECD Publishing.

Ray, S., & Miglani, S. (2018). *Global Value Chains and the Missing Links: Cases from Indian Industry.* New Delhi: Taylor & Francis.

Sturgeon, T. J. (2002). Modular production networks: A new American model of industrial organization. *Industrial and Corporate Change, 11*(3), 451–496.

Sturgeon, T., & Memedovic, O. (2010). Mapping Global Value Chains: Intermediate Goods Trade and Structural, Development Policy and Strategic Research Branch. Working Paper 05/2010. Vienna: UNIDO.

Taglioni, D., & Winkler, D. (2016). Making Global Value Chains Work for Development. Washington, DC: World Bank.

The Growth Lab at Harvard University. The Atlas of Economic Complexity. www.atlas.cid.harvard.edu.

The Hindu Business Line (2019). The trade war: India and USA must address issues as early as possible, says Indian envoy. July 17.

United Nations Conference on Trade and Development (UNCTAD) (2013). *World Investment Report 2013, Global Value Chains: Investment and Trade for Development* New York and Geneva: United Nations.

UNSD (2003). *Classification by Broad Economic Categories*. Statistical Papers, 53/4. New York: United Nations.

WTO (2015). Trade policy review: Report by the Secretariat. WT/TPR/S/313, 28 April. www.wto.org/english/tratop_e/tpr_e/s313_e.pdf (last accessed 27 August 2020)

WTO (1996). Ministerial declaration on trade in information technology products, Singapore, 13 December 1996. www.wto.org/english/news_e/pres97_e/inftech.htm (last accessed 27 August 2020)

Yi, K. M. (2003). Can vertical specialization explain the growth of world trade? *Journal of Political Economy*, *111*(1), 52–102.

7 US–China trade war

The potential impact on Bangladesh

Anu Anwar

1 Introduction

Since the second half of the twentieth century, global growth and prosperity have largely been driven by manufacturing and international trade. The trade conflict that broke out between the US and China in early 2018 presents a major stumbling block to global trade and economic integration. The US and China, the two main protagonists, are among the world's largest economies and traders, together accounting for two-fifths of global gross domestic product (GDP) and about a quarter of global trade (Abiad et al., 2018). However, the trade conflict is not just bilateral but global, with many countries hit by the waves of tariffs imposed by the US and China on each other's goods. The contentious US–China trade conflict, however, does not seem to bring any benefit for either country's economy; rather, indicators show that other nations may benefit to a large extent. Developing countries like Bangladesh, Vietnam, and Chile may reap the most benefits from a widening trade dispute between the world's two biggest economies.

This trade war is the latest instance of existing geopolitical rivalry between the United States and China that has alarmed many countries who have trade stakes with these two nations – though it does raise hope for Bangladesh. The effect of the trade war on supply chain dynamics and investment patterns could help Bangladesh to emerge as a potential winner. Despite the different nature of trade, both the US and China have been stable trading partners in Bangladesh for decades. While China is Bangladesh's top import partner, the United States is the second-largest destination for Bangladesh's exports.[1] Therefore, any changes in these two economies will impact Bangladesh's pattern of trade and investment.

Against this backdrop, the current chapter attempts to estimate the possible impact of the trade war on Bangladesh's economy. It first describes the unfolding of the US–China trade war and its background. Then this study sheds light on the impact of this ongoing trade tussle on Bangladesh's economic and geopolitical landscape. It goes on to make some recommendations for Bangladesh on how to reap the benefit from it.

2 US–China trade war unfolds

There have been five major tariff-related trade wars across the world in different centuries. There were the Opium Wars between 1839 and 1842 between the UK and China. In 1930 US President Herbert Hoover signed the Smoot-Hawley Tariff Act to protect the falling stock market and domestic industry, leading to a 61% dip in US exports by 1933 and to the Great Depression. In the Chicken War in the early 1960s France and Germany imposed high tariffs on American chickens and the US retaliated by imposing higher tariffs on a bunch of commodities, including light trucks. The US-imposed tariffs affected auto industries' supplies coming from Japan, Turkey, and Thailand – resulting vehicles emerge as locally manufactured, free from the tariff. In 1985 there was the Pasta War – the Reagan administration of US raised tariffs on pasta from Europe as its complaints of discrimination against its citrus products failed. Europe retaliated in kind with higher tariffs on American lemons and walnuts. In August 1986, both sides signed an agreement ending the citrus dispute, and in October 1987 ended the pasta dispute. The Banana War saw Europe trying to limit its import of bananas to its colonies in Africa and the Caribbean. Europe imposed heavy tariffs on the import of Latin American bananas in 1993. Since US companies own most of the banana farms in Latin America, the US filed eight separate complaints in the WTO. However, only in 2012 did the EU and ten Latin American countries sign an agreement to formally end all the eight WTO cases, ending the 20-year-long dispute (Kennedy, 2018).

The US was involved in four of the five historic trade wars. The US is also involved in the ongoing trade war. However, those trade wars were different from the current one in three ways. First, none of those trade wars were between the US and China. Second, those trade wars were largely driven by economic consideration but in the current trade war – in addition to economic aspects – the geopolitical calculations between the world's two largest economies are playing a dominating role. Further, the earlier wars were limited to a few items or a particular sector, whereas the current war affects a large number of items of several sectors. Third, the world economy is way much more interconnected and interdependent now than at any time before. So, this trade dispute will bring substantial consequences not only to the US and China but also countries around the globe.

Since the triumph of Donald Trump in the US election, the world economy has encountered various instabilities, challenges rather than unity. The so-called 'America First' nationalistic ideology of President Trump questions the traditional US leading role in global governance and international organisation. Since President Trump's early days in office, he has been critical of the US trade deficit with countries, especially China's unfair trade practices that undermine WTO standards. In the first quarter of 2018, the US imposed additional tariffs on imports of steel, aluminum, washing machines, and solar panels (Cavallo et al., 2019). The economies of China, Canada, the EU, Mexico, the Russian

Federation, Turkey, and, in developing Asia, India and China retaliated with their own tariffs affecting exports from the USA (Abiad et al., 2018). The conflict escalated and became more bilateral in the second and third quarters of 2018. While the US was able to settle the trade tussles with most of these countries, China's issue remains unsolved.

The Trump administration acted because of the persistent increase of the trade deficit with the whole world, and especially a significant amount with China. Because of this trade war, the world trading system and economy have been hampered, and more or less every country is affected by this ongoing war. Despite the Phase-1 trade deal, the ultimate result of this ongoing trade spat is still uncertain. The recent struggle to control the narrative of the ongoing pandemic of COVID-19 inflamed the widening rivalry between these two great powers. This new dimension could couple with an already existing trade war and ultimately kill the Phase-1 trade deal. Meanwhile, besides the US and China, the rest of the world is weighing the impact of a potential full-blown trade war between these two giants in their own economy. Each country is calculating how to protect their economy from this trade war. Some labour-intensive manufacturer countries such as Bangladesh, Vietnam, Thailand, and Chile are in the lead. The war has changed supply chains and investment patterns that could set these developing countries up as potential winners.

3 Impact on Bangladesh

According to the World Bank report (2018), trade represented 38.2% of Bangladeshi Gross Domestic Product (GDP).[2] Bangladesh's main export products are apparels, raw jute, tobacco, leather, fish, and frozen seafood, and it mainly imports electrical machinery and equipment, chemical products, steel and metals, cotton, cement, food, and oil-derived products (Nordeo, 2020). Bangladesh's main trade partners are the United States, China, and the European Union. The United States is the largest export partner at $6 billion, and China is the largest import partner at $10 billion (Anwar, 2019). The trade war between the US–China has alarmed many trading countries, but maybe gives hope for Bangladesh. As Yasuyuki Sawada argued, Bangladesh's exports can be expected to 'increase by $400 million' amid the trade war (*Dhaka Tribune*, 2019). The following discussion centres on how the trade war may impact Bangladesh's economy.

4 Relocating factories from China to Bangladesh

China, one of the world's oldest civilisations, has been a prosperous country over centuries. However, when it comes to the modernisation, the country legs behind many Western countries. The industrial revolution – a foundation of modernisation and economic prosperity – did not come to China until the mid-twentieth century, two centuries later than Europe. China's paramount leader Deng Xiaoping introduced reform and an opening-up policy in the 1980s, and since then the country has been thriving. It is today known as the world's factory.

In 2018, China accounted for 28% of global manufacturing output (Richter, 2020). As one-fifth of the world's population live in China, and most of them are skilled workers, companies flooded into China for their manufacturing and access to the Chinese market. Apple, Tesla, and many other leading companies opened manufacturing bases in China. Thanks to the US–China trade war, this rosy picture seems to be changing.

The US–China trade war forced a significant number of companies to move from China to other countries. The companies that are leaving, however, are not all foreign; some Chinese companies are also looking for offshore production bases. For example, Huizhou-based electronics maker TCL and the Zhejiang-based yarn producer Zhejiang Hailide New Material are among the Chinese companies that are relocating factories to Vietnam (Garber, 2019). Last year, *Washington Post* reported that more than 50 leading companies pulled production from China, including Dell, Nintendo, and many others (Telford, 2019). Due to the additional tariffs that the United States imposed on Chinese products, the price of goods has increased. As a result, the overall sale of Chinese goods in the US market has reduced dramatically. The United States is the single largest market for Chinese companies – over $500 billion annual value. To avoid the newly imposed tariffs, US retailers are looking for alternative markets elsewhere in Asia and beyond. China-based manufacturing companies are experiencing a decreasing volume of orders that to some extent threaten the existence of some companies. Therefore, they need to find alternative countries where they can produce products and sell to the US market without paying those additional tariffs.

The relocation process of China's low-tech manufacturing companies was under way even before this trade war. As China aimed at becoming a developed country by 2050, the country was gradually phasing out labour-intensive industries in favour of a higher value-added, high-tech, capital-intensive manufacturing sector. China's industrial sector was also under pressure from mounting compliances, social insurance commitments, stringent environmental checks. The Sino-US trade war seems to have accelerated the relocation of companies from China to other countries. As companies seek new countries to relocate their production lines, Bangladesh is in a competitively advantageous position.

Compared with other potential countries, Bangladesh has advantages for a number of reasons. First, the availability of a huge workforce and lower wages make Bangladesh a unique place in Asia for investors. According to the United Nations Population Fund (UNFPA) report, Bangladesh's population reached 168.1 million in 2019.[3] Bangladesh is the seventh most populous country in the world. A country's economic demeanour can often be influenced by the population it has. An increasing population means an increase in the labour force that can participate directly in the development process and economic growth, and a growing population leads to an increase in total output. In addition, an increasing population can provide cheap labour for industry and produce goods at a low cost. Bangladesh can supply a huge workforce and cheap labour to relocated companies, unparalleled in most of the other potential countries in Asia.

Second, Bangladesh's current economy is on an upward trend – one of the fast-growing in Asia. Since 2009, Bangladesh's economy has grown by 188% in size. In the last couple of decades, Bangladesh has experienced annual GDP growth of more than 6.5%. Over a few decades, millions of Bangladeshis have left poverty, and in 2019, 30 million people entered into middle-income status. The urbanisation process in Bangladesh is at its peak – estimates suggest that by 2030, 48% of its population will live in the towns and cities (Hasina, 2019). Bangladesh is now the fourth-largest rice producer, second largest producer of jute and garments. Two-thirds of its 168 million populations is young – mostly under 25 – and they are quickly skill-able, adaptive to technologies. This large young population contributed to Bangladesh's position as the fifth-largest internet user in Asia-Pacific. In 2018, e-commerce transactions reached $260 million. Bangladesh is establishing 100 Special Economic Zones with a one-stop service across Bangladesh. Twelve of the zones are already functioning. Located to the east and north-east of India, west of China and South-East Asia, Bangladesh merits the attention of global and Indian business as a seamless economic space. Bangladesh can serve as the economic hub for the sub-region. Beyond its 168 million people, Bangladesh can be the connecting landmass to a combined market of nearly 3 billion people. Last year, HSBC predicted that Bangladesh would be the 26th-largest economy in the world by 2030 (Henry & Pomeroy, 2018).

Third, despite the tremendous potential for growth and prosperity, the country has suffered due to a legacy of political turmoil. Civil unrest, partisanship, and lack of national unity have been the key to social instability. This social instability led to an economic downturn. For example, according to the World Bank, political unrest in Bangladesh in the first part of 2015 resulted in a loss of 1% of GDP (Bdnews24, 2015). Considering this severe interruption in the supply chain, foreign companies have been hesitant to invest in Bangladesh in the past. However, in recent years, that trend seems to be declining, and if current circumstances prevail, the country can offer a conducive environment for investors.

5 Exporting apparels

As the trade war ratcheted up in mid-2019, the USA imposed additional 15% punitive tariffs on Chinese apparel and textile imports (Wong & Koty, 2020). According to the American Apparel and Footwear Association, these additional tariffs hit 91.6% of apparel, 68.4% of home textiles, and 52.5% of footwear imports from China (Wu, 2019). China is the largest supplier of apparel to the US market, accounting for 38% of the total supply, with Vietnam, Mexico, and India consecutively the second-, third-, and fourth-largest supplier of the total apparel market.[4] Bangladesh is the fifth-largest apparel supplier but accounts for only 4% of total US imports. However, newly imposed tariffs severely disrupted the supply chain from China; thus, US buyers are redirecting their orders from China to other countries such as Vietnam, Cambodia, and Bangladesh. Bangladesh, as the world's second-largest apparel producer, can fill the China vacuum in the

US market. American retailers are placing more work orders in Bangladesh in an effort to offset increasing tariffs on goods manufactured in China. According to the Bangladesh Foreign Trade Institute, Bangladesh enjoyed a 6.46% growth in market share in the US market during the first three quarters of 2018 (Light Castle, 2018).

In 2012, a report by McKinsey forecasted that, as ready-made garment exports from China declined, Bangladesh would be the next hot spot, and the market would triple in value by 2020, up from $15 billion in 2010 (Berg, Hedrich, & Tochtermann, 2012). This forecast was about China's gradual phase-out from labour-intensive industries to the higher value-added, high-tech, capital-intensive manufacturing sector, but it seems that the trade war is accelerating the growth of Bangladesh to achieve just that. The garments sector is Bangladesh's leading exporting industry, accounting for 80% of total export revenue.[5] 3.6 million Bangladeshis work in the garment industry[6] – mostly women. With a workforce of 70 million,[7] Bangladesh has tremendous potential to expand and increase the production line substantially.

When it comes to competition with other leading apparel producer countries such as Cambodia and Vietnam Bangladesh has a competitive advantages. Due to the presence of strong labour unions, setting up factories in Cambodia is more challenging. Moreover, in contrast to the 168 million Bangladeshis, Cambodia has a population of just 16 million. Due to higher wages and production costs, Vietnam also looks less attractive to investors. The minimum wage in Bangladesh is currently $95 per month, which is almost half the $182 per month it is in Cambodia and $180 per month in Hanoi and Ho Chi Minh City (Kathuria & Malouche, 2016).

Bangladesh also has the potential to export apparel to the Chinese market. China is a country of 1.5 billion people – a huge market. China is leapfrogging for high-tech and capital-intensive industries, aiming to dominate the future industrial sector, such as artificial intelligence, machine learning, 5G technology, Quantum computers, robotics, and so on. Therefore, in the long run, China may rely on imports for low-tech goods such as garment products. Bangladeshi apparel could be a potential option for China in that regard. Moreover, due to the demographic dividend and increasing per capita income, labour costs are increasing in China. Low-tech, labour-intensive industries are considered in China as sunset industries. When it comes to investment and factory relocation, China consider seriously the bilateral relations of that particular country with China. Bangladesh wins out from this perspective.

In addition to competitive advantages that Bangladesh has in terms of workforce, low wages, and geographical proximity to China, China-Bangladesh bilateral relations are on an upward trend, especially since the visit by Chinese President Xi Jinping in 2016. Since then, Bangladesh has received a significant volume of Chinese investment in various sectors, from industry to culture. Even though this type of relocation and offshore investment was under way prior to this trade war, the process has now accelerated.

6 Importing agricultural products at lower cost

In August 2018, the Chinese government retaliated with 25% tariffs on US soybeans, wheat, cotton, along with other agricultural goods and food products (Li, 2019). Over the following months of retaliatory tariffs, US export of soybeans, wheat, cotton to China decreased significantly. Consequently, the price of those products has sharply declined in the US domestic market. China is the single largest agricultural product importer from the USA (Light Castle, 2019), so the consequences were drastic and obvious. For example, the price of soybeans declined 91.7% in the US local market as China used to buy 60% of US soybean exports but purchased none for months at the height of trade war (*South China Morning Post*, 2018). This declining price could offer an opportunity for Bangladesh. At the moment, Bangladesh annually imports 2 million tons of crude vegetable oil, of which 600,000 tons is from soybeans (*South China Morning Post*, 2018, p. 8). Bangladesh mainly imports crude soybean oil from Brazil and Argentina. However, the prices of soybeans have jumped in the Brazilian market due to China's increasing demand as China substituted its US supply chain with Brazil. Bangladesh has a robust trading relationship with the US. Bangladesh can easily take advantage of the declining price of the US soybeans by redirecting its supply chain from Brazil and Argentina to the US market and save millions of dollars.

Bangladesh is the world's fifth-largest wheat importer (A. Mahmud, 2019) – with an annual import volume of around 6 million tons. According to the Food and Agriculture Organisation (FAO) report, Bangladesh's imports of grain increased by 36% over the past five years (I. Mahmud, 2019) and this was expected to continue to increase. The ongoing trade war has also affected the US wheat exports to China, and the US domestic market is unable to consume the excessive supply. The resulting declining price could be an opportunity for Bangladesh. Bangladesh relies on Brazilian wheat, but in recent years there have been some questions about the quality of that wheat, reported in the Bangladeshi news media (*The Daily Star*, 2015). The ongoing trade war thus has created an opportunity for Bangladesh to import high-quality wheat at a lower price from the USA instead of the Brazilian market.

China was also the major destination for US cotton, but this too has been affected by the ongoing trade war. The Chinese government imposed 25% tariffs on US cotton that significantly reduced US cotton exports to China. The Bangladeshi economy is mainly dependent on ready-made garment (RMG) exports, and RMG depend on the uninterrupted supply of cotton. However, Bangladesh's domestic production is inadequate to fulfil the demand so Bangladesh has to depend on importing cotton. Bangladesh is the second-largest cotton importer in the world, worth $6.6 billion per year (Anam, 2015). In the past, India was the primary source of cotton for Bangladesh, but now African nations are most important for Bangladeshi importers. However, relying on African markets for the industrial raw material could be a bit risky due to the prevailing instability and political turmoil on the African continent. Bangladesh could benefit by importing cotton from the US, guaranteeing essential supplies.

Moreover, as the 51st largest trading partner of the United States, Bangladesh enjoys a $4 billion trade surplus.[8] The current US administration has been going after trade surplus countries. By importing soybeans, wheat, and cotton from the United States, Bangladesh can benefit by both importing those goods at a cheaper rate and reducing the trade deficit with the US. A robust and more balanced trade may ultimately contribute to stronger bilateral relations. Furthermore, Bangladesh and other low-income countries in South Asia face US duties of 15.2% of the total value of exports, which might ease if the United States wants to increase imports from these countries to minimise gaps from China.

7 Steel and iron

Steel and iron are considered the backbone of America's manufacturing sector and national security. The US military industries use steel extensively, ranging from aircraft carriers and nuclear submarines to missiles, armour plate for tanks, and every major military aircraft in production. But, today, the American steel industry is at risk from record amounts of foreign-produced steel flooding into the United States. Cheap, subsidised foreign imports are taking steel jobs away. In 2015, almost one in three tons of steel sold in the United States was produced outside the country. During the 2016 US presidential election, candidates campaigned on this issue, especially current president Donald J. Trump.

After taking office, he imposed additional tariffs on imported steel and aluminum. Therefore, US scrap suppliers are storing their scrap reserves and postponing their scrap exports. According to the United Nations COMTRADE database, in 2015, Bangladesh imported US$2.41 billion of iron and steel. Bangladesh mainly meets its demand for iron from its domestic ship-breaking industry and importing scrap from the US market.[9] However, the ongoing trade war hampered Bangladesh in importing scrap from the USA. As a result, the price of steel in the Bangladeshi domestic market has seen a significant rise. So, for iron, Bangladesh is being disadvantaged by the trade war between the US–China. Bangladesh has to develop its ship-breaking industry and import scrap from alternative sources.

8 Attracting Chinese investment to Bangladesh

China is one of the largest investors in the US financial and property market. The economic engagement of the two countries is robust and deep-rooted. However, amid this trade war, the majority of both countries' policymakers are emphasising economic decoupling. It is an extension of existing geopolitical rivalry between the world's two largest economies. Therefore, Chinese investors have already started diverting their investment from the US to other countries, especially to the Belt and Road Initiative (BRI) countries. As a BRI country, Bangladesh already has the advantage of attracting Chinese investment. Since the establishment of diplomatic relations with Bangladesh in 1974, China has maintained friendly relations. As time passes, the bilateral relations between these two countries have improved significantly, and today, they are at a peak. As a result of the trade war, Chinese policymakers are seeking to tighten capital flows in hopes of preventing a depreciation of the yuan. However, China's increasing involvement in various projects in Bangladesh may mean constraints will not be as effective. Bangladesh has seen an increase in foreign direct investment (FDI) from China higher than forecasted, through factory relocations, especially in the growing export processing zones (EPZs) (Siu, 2019).

Furthermore, as a member of China's BRI, it is more meaningful for China to increase investment in Bangladesh in those sectors which are affected in China by the trade war. Beijing's support of Bangladesh was evident in the 27 agreements for investments and loans signed by the two countries – for $24 billion – when President Xi Jinping visited in 2016 (Ruma Paul, 2016). Along with an earlier $13.6 billion investment in joint ventures, those deals brought Chinese investment in Bangladesh to a total of $38 billion, the largest sum ever pledged to Bangladesh by a single country (Hossein, 2016). Bangladesh is the second-largest recipient of Chinese FDI behind Pakistan in the South Asian region. In the fiscal year of 2017–18, FDI from China reached $506 million, about one-fifth of total foreign capital flow in Bangladesh. Currently, about 400 Chinese companies do business in Bangladesh, of these 200 are large and 200 are small and medium enterprises (Siddique, 2019). According to Commerce Minister Tipu Munshi, Bangladesh is expected to get more than $50 billion FDI in the next 10 to 15 years in the energy and power, transport, and communications sector (Siddique, 2019, p. 8). So, these increasing investment trends indicate that, in the height of a full-fledged trade war, Chinese investors may consider Bangladesh as a good alternative. Such an investment could help to revamp Bangladesh's overall economic development.

9 Policy recommendation

The above discussions reveal that, despite some pitfalls, the US–China trade war opened for Bangladesh a window of opportunity. However, whether the country can reap the benefits will depend on a host of factors.

First of all, Bangladesh would need to display that the country's infrastructure is capable of handling additional industrial investment. With quality infrastructure, Bangladesh could also attract Western investment. However, for Bangladesh companies, there is a roadblock to winning more orders from Western firms. With its infrastructure ranked at 114 in the World Economic Forum's Global Competitiveness Index,[10] compared with 36 for China, Bangladesh needs to improve its supply chain, modernise its garment factories, build highways, and reduce red tape at ports to lure more buyers. As a part of revitalising infrastructure, the incumbent government recently opened two four-lane bridges on the highway to the Chittagong Port facilities, cutting travel time to the nation's main port by almost half. The government has also been accelerating the construction of highways. Still, it takes 168 hours for exporters in the country to ship from Dhaka, while it takes just 23 hours in Shanghai, according to the World

Bank's latest 'Doing Business' report.[11] Meanwhile, despite Bangladesh's efforts to reduce corruption and red tape, they remain enduring problems for foreign investors. For example, Bangladesh ranked 168 among 190 economies in the World Bank's 'Doing Business' 2020 report. It also ranked only 146 among 183 countries surveyed in Transparency International's 2019 Corruption Perception Index.[12] Therefore, Bangladesh requires an urgent and rapid transformation in its physical infrastructure and to ensure good governance if it is aiming to attract significant FDI.

For the RMG sector, it will be crucial to improve productivity by upgrading technologies and automation. There is a trend towards automation among Bangladeshi garment factory owners, but it is now at a low level. To make this sector competitive globally, automation is needed widely across the sector. For example, due to China's technical superiority, it has price dominance over other nations. China exports garments at about $2.3 a piece, compared with $2.79 for Bangladesh and $2.52 in Cambodia. However, with a foresighted policy and adequate investment, Bangladesh can use the technology, and with the large garment workforce, it can edge the competition in its favour. The US has started limiting the supply of critical parts that are the lifeline for Chineses hi-tech companies such as Huawei. However, Bangladesh's lack of skilled workforce, with technical and scientific knowledge, wouldn't be able to benefit much in this aspect. Those tech firms may rather prefer Vietnam or other North Asian countries, should they relocate.

Political instability has always been a great challenge for Bangladesh's development and prosperity. Partisanship and vested interests divide the nation, which ultimately slows the overall development process and paralyses society. A confrontational political culture is also the opposite of a conducive environment for business. In the past, the country experienced a lower amount of FDI and limited expansion of multinational companies due to this unstable political culture. In addition, due to the colonial legacy, the bureaucracy is inefficient and overly procedure-oriented. Bangladeshi administration focuses more on vested interests than being citizen-centric. These are the underlying challenges that the country would need to overcome in order to bring substantial reforms and a conducive business environment that can compete on a global scale. This is particularly true in the era of great power competition, when countries are finding their way to protect their own interests. Bangladesh has the potential to gain, but that would require a foresighted policy and institutional reforms.

10 Conclusion

The current trade conflict between the world's two biggest economies clearly has an uneven impact on Asia and the world. Analysis shows that, under a worst-case scenario, where the Phase-1 deal does not follow through, and all documented threats and retaliations are carried out, China's GDP would fall by over 1% and GDP for the US would decline by 0.2% over a period of two to three years (Abiad et al., 2018). In developing Asia, the effects of the trade conflict are mildly positive, as the region benefits from trade redirection in investment and industries. The impact, however, will largely depend on how countries are prepared and deal with great powers. In South Asia, because of the trade war, changing supply chain dynamics and investment patterns could help Bangladesh emerge as a potential winner from the conflict. However, to materialise such potential will require prompt policy action and rapid infrastructure modernisation. The competition is intense, and many countries are working round to the clock to fill the vacuum of China's supply, notably South-East Asian countries. Even though Bangladesh has tremendous potential to emerge as a desired destination for the investor, it will largely depend on the policy regime, whether it can offer a conducive business environment and the readiness of its institutions to tackle the additional industries.

Notes

1 The Observatory Economic Complexity. https://oec.world/en/profile/country/bgd/
2 https://data.worldbank.org/indicator/NE.TRD.GNFS.ZS?locations=BD
3 World Population Dashboard Bangladesh, UNFPA, www.unfpa.org/data/world-population/BD
4 United States Trade Commissions, www.usitc.gov/research_and_analysis/trade_shifts_2017/textiles.htm
5 Bangladesh Exports, *Trading Economics,* November 2019, https://tradingeconomics.com/bangladesh/exports
6 Bangladesh's Garments Workers, Asia Foundation https://asiafoundation.org/slideshow/bangladeshs-garment-workers/
7 Ibid., p. 7. https://tradingeconomics.com/bangladesh/exports
8 Office of the United States Trade Representatives, https://ustr.gov/countries-regions/south-central-asia/bangladesh
9 Ibid., p. 9.
10 World Economic Forum's Global Competitiveness Index-2019, World Economic Forum. http://reports.weforum.org/global-competitiveness-report-2019/competitiveness-rankings/#series=GCI4.A.02
11 Doing Business, The World Bank. www.doingbusiness.org/en/data/explore economies/bangladesh#DB_tab
12 Corruption Perception Index – 2019, Transparency International. www.transparency.org/en/cpi/2019/results/bgd

References

Abiad, A., Baris, K., Bernabe, J. A., Bertulfo, D. J., Camingue, S., Feliciano, P. N., … & Mercer-Blackman, V. (2018). The impact of trade conflict on developing Asia. Economics Working Paper Series, 566. Washington, DC: Asian Development Bank.

Anam, M. (2015). Bangladesh poised to be biggest cotton importer. The Daily Star, 20 December. www.thedailystar.net/business/bangladesh-poised-be-biggest-cotton-importer-189913

Anwar, A. (2019). Is Bangladesh winning in the US-China trade war? *The Diplomat* https://thediplomat.com/2019/06/is-bangladesh-winning-in-the-us-china-trade-war/

Bdnews24 (2015). Political turmoil cost Bangladesh $2.2 billion in three months of 2015: World Bank. 12 April. https://bdnews24.com/economy/2015/04/12/political-turmoil-cost-bangladesh-2.2-billion-in-three-months-of-2015-world-bank

Berg, A., Hedrich, S., & Tochtermann, T. (2012). Bangladesh: The next hot spot in apparel sourcing? McKinsey & Co., 1 March. www.mckinsey.com/industries/consumer-packaged-goods/our-insights/bangladesh-the-next-hot-spot-in-apparel-sourcing

Cavallo, A., Gopinath, G., Neiman, B., & Tang, J. (2019). *Tariff Passthrough at the Border and at the Store: Evidence from US Trade Policy.* No. w26396. Cambridge, MA: National Bureau of Economic Research.

Dhaka Tribune (2019). ADB: Trade war to generate additional $400m for Bangladesh. 6 March. www.dhakatribune.com/business/2019/03/06/adb-trade-war-to-generate-additional-400m-exports-for-bangladesh" www.dhakatribune.com/business/2019/03/06/adb-trade-war-to-generate-additional-400m-exports-for-bangladesh

Garber, J. (2019). Trade war causing companies to flee China. 5 September. www.foxbusiness.com/economy/trade-war-companies-fleeing-china

Hasina, S. (2019). Bangladesh is booming – and here is why, says prime minister. World Economic Forum, 4 October. www.weforum.org/agenda/2019/10/bangladesh-is-booming/

Henry, J., & Pomeroy, J. (2018). The world in 2030: Our long-term projections for 75 countries. *HSBC Global Research,* September. https://enterprise.press/wp-content/uploads/2018/10/HSBC-The-World-in-2030-Report.pdf

Hossain, M. (2016). How huge China investment in Bangladesh affect region. Anadolu Agency, 10 November. www.aa.com.tr/en/analysis-news/opinion-how-huge-china-investment-in-bangladesh-affects-region/683065

Kathuria, S., & Malouche, M. M. (2016). Attracting investment in Bangladesh – sectoral analyses: A diagnostic trade integration. World Bank Group. http://documents.banquemondiale.org/curated/fr/270381476694893059/pdf/109156-PUB-PUBLIC-PUBDATE-10-13-16.pdf

Kennedy, L. (2018) 7 contentious trade wars in the US history. *History,* 2 October. www.history.com/news/7-trade-wars-boston-tea-party-smoot-hawley

Li, Y. (2019). China could remove extra tariffs on US farm goods to boost imports, says trade association chief. *CNBC*, 3 October. www.cnbc.com/2019/10/31/china-could-axe-tariffs-on-us-agriculture-to-boost-imports-trade-association-chief.html

Light Castle (2018). US-China trade war: Bangladesh's golden goose. 23 December. https://databd.co/stories/us-china-trade-war-bangladeshs-golden-goose-1238

Light Castle (2019). US-China trade war: Bangladesh's golden goose. 10 April. www.lightcastlebd.com/insights/2019/04/10/us-china-trade-war-bangladeshs-golden-goose

Mahmud, A. (2019). Chinese investment in Bangladesh comes with risks, *Asia Times,* 17 July. www.asiatimes.com/2019/07/article/chinese-investment-in-bangladesh-has-sometimes-violent-implications/

Mahmud, I. (2019). Bangladesh fifth largest wheat importer. *Prothom Alo,* 6 January. https://en.prothomalo.com/bangladesh/news/189251/Bangladesh-fifth-largest-wheat-importer

Nordeo (2020). Foreign trade figures of Bangladesh. May. www.nordeatrade.com/en/explore-new-market/bangladesh/trade-profile

Richter, F. (2020). China is the world's manufacturing superpower. *Statista,* 18 February. www.statista.com/chart/20858/top-10-countries-by-share-of-global-manufacturing-output/"www.statista.com/chart/20858/top-10-countries-by-share-of-global-manufacturing-output/

Ruma Paul, B. B. (2016). China to sign some $24 billion in loans to Bangladesh as Xi visits. 14 October. https://uk.reuters.com/article/uk-bangladesh-china/china-to-sign-some-24-billion-in-loans-to-bangladesh-as-xi-visits-idUKKCN12D33Z

Siddique, A. (2019). Infrastructure and energy bind Bangladesh to China. 13 May. www.thethirdpole.net/en/2019/05/13/infrastructure-and-energy-bind-bangladesh-to-china/

Siu, P. (2019). Move over, 'Made in China'. It is the 'Made in Bangladesh' era now. *South China Morning Post*, 8 June. www.scmp.com/week-asia/economics/article/3013632/move-over-made-china-its-made-bangladesh-era-now

South China Morning Post (2018). As trade war batters Chinese demand for soybeans, US farmers turn back to grains. 3 November. www.scmp.com/news/china/diplomacy/article/2171525/trade-war-batters-chinese-demand-soybeans-us-farmers-turn-back

Telford, T. (2019). More than 50 major companies, from Google to Nintendo, pull production from China because of the trade war. *Washington Post*, 19 July. www.washingtonpost.com/business/2019/07/18/more-than-major-companies-apple-nintendo-pull-production-china-because-trade-war/

The Daily Star (2015). No more imports of Brazilian wheat. 21 June. www.thedailystar.net/city/no-more-import-brazilian-wheat-100543

Wong, D., & Koty, A. C. (2020). The US-China trade war: A timeline. *China Briefing,* 11 May. www.china-briefing.com/news/the-us-china-trade-war-a-timeline/

Wu, J. (2019) 92% of apparel imports from China will be hit with tariffs on Sunday – here's how companies are coping. CNBC, 30 August. www.cnbc.com/2019/08/30/92percent-of-apparel-from-china-will-be-hit-with-tariffs-sundayhow-retailers-are-coping.html

8 US–China trade war

Trade and investment implications for Sri Lanka

Janaka Wijayasiri and Anushka Wijesinha

1 Introduction

The US and China are engaged in a trade war, with both countries imposing tariffs on hundreds of billions of dollars' worth of goods. The US imposed four rounds of tariffs since July 2018 'to counter unfair trade practices' by China, after months of threats to impose sweeping tariffs, while China has responded by hitting back with tariffs on American imports. Among the alleged unfair trade practices by China and their effects are the growing trade deficit of the US vis-a-vis China, the theft of intellectual property, and the forced transfer of American technology to China. So far (as of February 2020), the US has imposed tariffs on US$550 billion worth of Chinese products while China has placed tariffs on US$185 billion goods from the US (Wong & Koty, 2020).

The economic impact of the US–China trade war has been a great concern among politicians, policymakers, and business leaders. Given the size of the US and Chinese economies and their share of world trade, the impacts of the trade war on each other as well as the spillover effects to the rest of the world are likely to be significant. China is the world's largest exporter, and the US is the world's largest importer. In the US, the trade war has affected farmers, manufacturers, and consumers. In other countries, it has also disrupted supply chains and slowed down investments while some countries have benefited from the trade war. China's export losses in the US have resulted in trade diversion effects to the advantage of other countries in Asia, the Americas, and Europe. However, even these countries may not benefit in the long term if the trade dispute continues.

As a small and relatively open-market economy, Sri Lanka is particularly sensitive to trends in global trade. According to some observers in Sri Lanka, the US–China trade war will hit Sri Lanka indirectly through a slowdown of the global economy (Fernandopulle, 2019), whilst presenting trading and investment opportunities in the short term, as both countries search for alternative source markets and production bases (Wijesinha, 2019). The tariffs imposed on China raise the possibility of trade and investment diversion to Sri Lanka.

The objective of the chapter is to examine the impact of the US–China trade war on Sri Lanka's exports to the US and investment inflows. Section 2 provides a brief background to the US–China trade war, focusing on developments up to February 2020, while Section 3 briefly reviews some of the literature on the topic. Section 4 examines Sri Lanka's trade and investment regime to highlight the prospects of Sri Lanka benefiting from the trade/investment diversion from the trade war. Sections 5–7 provide *ex ante* and *ex post* analysis of the trade war on Sri Lanka's exports to US and investment flows to the country based on primary and secondary information (up to December 2019), while Section 8 concludes on how Sri Lanka can make use of the opportunity by enacting necessary reforms.

2 Brief background to the US–China trade war

Since the mid-2018s, the US and China have been locked in a trade confrontation that has resulted in several rounds of retaliatory tariffs. In the early summer of 2018, the US and China raised tariffs on about US$50 billion worth of goods – first applying 25% tariffs on US$34 billion in July (List 1) and then an additional US$16billion in August (List 2) – see appendix Table 8.A1. This escalated further in September 2018 when the US introduced an additional 10% tariff to cover US$200 billion worth of Chinese imports (List 3), to which China retaliated by imposing tariffs on imports from the US worth an additional US$60 billion. In May 2019, the US increased tariffs further from 10% to 25%. China responded by raising the tariffs on a subset of products that were already subject to tariffs.

In September 2019, the US imposed 15% tariffs on a large subset of the remaining US$300 billion worth of imports from China not yet subject to tariffs (List 4A), while China retaliated on some US products (a subset of US$75 billion). Tariffs of 15% on approximately US$160 billion worth of goods (List 4B) were scheduled to take effect on 15 December 2019, but it was postponed indefinitely. Instead, there was an announcement to decrease the 15% tariff on $120 billion worth of goods from China to 7.5%. China took corresponding measures and cancelled its scheduled tariff increase (York, 2020).

In January 2020, the two sides signed a preliminary deal, easing the trade war. Under the so-called "Phase One" deal, China pledged to boost US imports by $200 billion above 2017 levels and address issues long disputed such as intellectual property, technology transfer, and currency. In exchange, the US suspended some tariff increases (List 4B) and will roll back others (List 4A) (Sandler & Rosenberg, 2020). This chapter will focus on the implications of the four lists (1–4A) for Sri Lanka.

3 Literature review

Conventional trade models provide a framework for understanding the impact of tariffs on trade: tariffs raise the prices of foreign goods with the result of reducing demand for imports. Moreover, in the case of tariffs applied only to specific countries, as in the US–China trade war, tariffs can lead to trade diversion effects as importers avoid the higher tariffs by sourcing the goods from elsewhere. Trade diversion effects do not necessarily happen, and generally are not complete, meaning that third countries are only able to capture part of the trade, while the rest can be lost or internalised by the country imposing the tariff. The existing literature on the ongoing US–China trade war looks at the economic effects on both countries as well as on the rest of the world, often using computable general equilibrium (CGE) models to provide an *ex ante* analysis.

The trade war between the US and China is hurting both consumers and producers, lowering their economic well-being. Consumers in the US and China face significantly higher prices due to tariffs while producers are affected by lower foreign sales (Freund, Maliszewska, & Constantinescu, 2019), resulting in lower income, reduced employment, and output.

Li, He, and Lin (2018) find that trade conflict between China and the US will manifest more prominently in the case of China, which will see a decline in GDP by 1.15 % when tariffs are raised to 30%. On the other hand, the US gains by a small margin: 0.04% of GDP. Although the trade conflict hurts China more than any other economy, they find the effects are still manageable. However, the impact for both countries is more severe the higher the tariff rate.

Similarly, Bollen and Rojas-Romagosa (2018) find that the economic effects of current measures are limited, but some specifically targeted sectors in China and the US suffer more. Over time, amid more tariffs, China's economic loss is equivalent to 1.3% of GDP, whereas the decline in the US is limited to 0.3% of GDP due to its lower total share of exports in GDP, and in particular, its relatively low exports to China. Other economies benefit via the trade diversion channel, but this quickly fades with a full-blown escalation of the trade conflict, when a much larger number of products are targeted.

Itakura (2019) also finds that the escalation of the trade war reduces GDP in China and the USA by 1.41% and 1.35%, respectively. The trade war reduces nearly all sectoral imports and outputs in both countries. He also finds, when global value chains are accounted for, that the negative impacts on bilateral trade are more widespread, and world GDP is reduced by US$450 billion.

There have been a number of studies that have looked specifically at trade diversion effects at the country/sectoral level due to the trade war. The loss of the US and China has benefited exports of competing countries – both large and small exporters. Rosyadi and Widodo (2018) and Freund, Maliszewska, and Constantinescu (2019) observe a trade diversion effect due to the trade war, with shrinking bilateral trade between China and the US, and increasing exports from third-country trading partners.

Similarly, UNCTAD (2019) finds that the ongoing US–China trade war will lead to a sharp decline in bilateral trade, higher prices for consumers, and trade diversion effects due to increased imports from countries not directly involved in the trade war. According to the study, US tariffs on China have made other countries more competitive in the US market, and this will have trade diversion effects. Of the US$35 billion Chinese export losses in the US market, about US$21 billion (or 63%) will be diverted to other countries, while the remainder of US$14 billion will either be lost or captured by US producers. US tariffs on China result in Taiwan gaining US$4.2 billion in additional exports to the US in the first half of 2019 by selling more office machinery and communication equipment.

Mexico increases its exports to the US by US$3.5 billion, mostly in the agri-food, transport equipment, and electrical machinery sectors. The European Union gains about US$2.7 billion due to an increase in exports, largely in the machinery sector. Vietnam's exports to the US swell by US$2.6 billion, driven by trade in communication equipment and furniture. Trade diversion benefits to South Korea, Canada, and India are smaller but still substantial, ranging from US$0.9 billion to US$1.5 billion. The remainder of the benefits is largely distributed amongst other South-East Asian countries. Office machinery is the hardest hit sector in the trade war. In this category, the imports of products subject to additional tariffs dropped by 65%. For other sectors, such as agri-food, communication equipment, and precision instruments, trade in the tariffed goods falls by more than 30%.

Abiad et al. (2018) look at the effects of the trade war specifically on developing Asia. Results from the study show that the negative effects are small for all the implemented and proposed tariff measures up to mid-October 2018, reducing China's GDP by 0.5% and US GDP by 0.1% over two to three years. A full escalation of the bilateral trade conflict would shave 1% and 0.2% off the GDP of China and the US, respectively. The rest of developing Asia could see small net gains thanks to trade redirection, particularly in the electronics sector. A number of developing Asian economies that are dependent on textile and garment exports such as Cambodia, Bangladesh, Sri Lanka, and Pakistan would see an increase in exports ranging from 1.3 to 3.4%.

While some studies note that countries, including those in the developing world, will benefit from the trade diversion in the short-medium run, others indicate that there will be a loss in the long run across countries and regions. Freund, Maliszewska, and Constantinescu (2019) find that a full-blown trade war could reduce global exports by 3% and income by 1.7%; roughly between one-third and a half of the decline in global exports and income would be accounted for by developing countries (excluding China). In their analysis of India, Misra and Choudhry (2020) find that the trade war may provide some opportunities in the short to medium run for India as gains from trade diversion would be higher than the losses due to trade reduction. However, in the long run, further escalation of tariffs will have a negative impact at the global level and, in turn, on India.

In the case of Sri Lanka, there has been some general discussion on how the country could benefit from the US–China war. According to Economic Intelligence Unit (2018), for example, Sri Lanka is expected to gain in at least one sector – the garment industry. The US garment industry is expected to be greatly disrupted by tariffs on Chinese goods and 'this will benefit major garment-exporting countries in Asia', creating a worldwide opportunity worth US$50 billion for other major players in the garment industry to make greater inroads in the US market and expand their market share (EIU, 2018). The article cited Sri Lanka in particular as a potential gainer, behind Bangladesh and Vietnam, and the following factors as reasons: 'wages are still competitive (though not as low as in Bangladesh)'; 'the business environment is favourable compared with those of regional peers'; and 'it is easier to set up new businesses' (EIU, 2018). However, there has not been any in-depth study to date on the implications of the trade war for Sri Lanka, a gap in the literature that is addressed by this chapter.

4 Sri Lanka's trade and FDI performance

International trade plays an important role in the Sri Lankan economy, given the small size of the country, although its importance has fallen in recent times; trade in goods and services accounts for 50% of GDP in 2017. While exports and imports grew between 2010 and 2017, the trade deficit (the difference between exports and imports) widened as imports increased more rapidly, from US$12.4 billion to nearly US$21.4 billion, and exports from US$8.3 billion to US$11.7 billion during this period (Figure 8.A1 in Appendix). Services trade exhibited strong growth, both in imports and exports; receipts more than doubled due to large increases in transport and travel services, reflecting a significant increase in tourism.

Sri Lanka's exports remain heavily concentrated on agriculture, and textiles and clothing, accounting for over 65% of 2017 total exports, while imports remain more diversified (Figure 8.A2). The textiles and clothing subsector is particularly important to trade and accounted for over 45% of total exports in 2017, ranked second in terms of foreign exchange earnings after worker remittances. Sri Lanka's agricultural sector is also an important contributor to trade, making up about a quarter of the total exports. Agricultural exports are dominated by a few commodities (i.e. tea, coconuts, cinnamon, and pepper). Sri Lanka's largest export markets continued to be the EU-28 (33%), followed by the US (23%), India (11%), CIS (3%), and China (3%). While Sri Lanka's exports are most directed to the West, its main sources of imports are from Asia, namely India (23%) and China (21%), followed by the EU-28 (9%). Imports were dominated by intermediate (38%), consumer (31%), capital (21%) goods, and raw materials (10%) in respective order.

Sri Lanka recognises the importance of attracting foreign direct investment (FDI), in particular, to rebuild the country after the internal conflict, as FDI levels remain relatively low. Despite a general increase over the period, FDI inflows reached the highest historical level of US$1611 million in 2018, which is about 2% of GDP, below the government's target of 3% of GDP (Table 8.A2). The top five source countries of FDI in 2018 were China, Hong Kong, India, Malaysia, and the US. Infrastructure, namely ports and telecommunications, were the largest recipient of FDI, followed by services and manufacturing (Table 8.A3).

5 Implications of trade war for Sri Lanka's exports to the US

One of the positive impacts of the trade war is that countries like Sri Lanka have been presented with an opportunity to increase exports to the US and China, particularly to the former due to trade diversion.

It is worth noting here that Sri Lanka has two mechanisms to support this: the US Generalised System of Preferences (GSP) programme and the Trade and Investment Framework Agreement (TIFA). Nearly 3,500 export products from Sri Lanka are eligible to enter under the GSP programme, including most manufactured items and inputs used in manufacturing, except most textiles and apparel. Meanwhile, the US–Sri Lanka bilateral TIFA provides a framework for the two governments to discuss and resolve trade and investment issues and economic cooperation opportunities on an ongoing basis. The most recent TIFA discussions took place in Washington, DC, in June 2019, with high-level ministerial participation from the Sri Lanka side. The US market is Sri Lanka's largest single export destination, and Sri Lankan exports to the US totalled US$2.8 billion (of which US$193.4 million were under the GSP scheme).

In order to examine whether Sri Lanka has an opportunity in the US market, one can examine the similarity in the exports of China and Sri Lanka in a particular commodity to the US to find out the potential for substitutability.

5.1 Finger–Kreinin Index (FKI) and Relative Export Competitive Pressure Index (RECPI)

One widely used measure of the similarity of export structures of countries is the Finger–Kreinin Index (FKI), which facilitates an analysis of the pattern of Chinese exports to the US and how similar these are to Sri Lanka's exports to the US. This indicator varies between 0 and 1. In the case where FKI is equal to 1, it implies that a pair of countries (Sri Lanka and China) export exactly the same goods in exactly the same proportions to a market (US). When the indicator is equal to zero, it implies that the exports of these countries do not share any similarities. For instance, if FKI is 0.50, then this may be interpreted as representing a 50% overlap in the export structures of the two countries.

The similarity index is low (0.123) in the case of exports of Sri Lanka and China to the US, implying dissimilarity in the composition of exports to the US. In other words, about 12% of goods exported by Sri Lanka and China to the US are similar in kind. This is not surprising given that the exports of China to the US are more diverse compared to that of Sri Lanka, which exports mainly of textiles and clothing (75%), and plastics and rubber (10%); see Figures 8.A3 and 8.A4. It is noteworthy that the figure is much lower between the US and Sri Lanka in relation to exports to China (0.062); indicating that there will be little or no trade diversion in the Chinese market for Sri Lanka due to retaliatory tariffs against US goods by China, because of highly dissimilar exports of Sri Lanka and US to the Chinese market.

Sri Lanka nonetheless does face some competition from China in the US market as indicated by the Relative Export Competitive Pressure Index (RECPI) of 10.899. RECPI provides a summary measure of the degree of competition one country faces from another country in a particular market. It is, therefore, useful for consideration along with FKI for trade similarity. However, these indices provide *only* an aggregate view regarding the potential benefits which might accrue to Sri Lanka due to the trade war. A more disaggregated analysis would provide further insights as to whether Sri Lanka might gain from the tariffs imposed on China by the US.

5.2 Bilateral Revealed Comparative Advantage (RCA)

One way to obtain an in-depth analysis would be an examination of Sri Lanka's presence in the US market by computing the ratio of 'Sri Lanka's exports to US' vis-a-vis 'China's exports to US' for various sectors where tariffs have been imposed. The sectors in which the exports of Sri Lanka as a proportion of China's exports to the US are high are indicative of the potential gains that Sri Lanka may derive due to the higher tariffs imposed on goods imported from China by the US (Table 8.A4). Articles of apparel and clothing (HS61&62), rubber and plastic articles (HS40), etc. which are already major exports to the US are few sectors where Sri Lanka enjoys a comparative advantage over China in the US market. Most of these items are in the tariff List 4A, which came into effect in the autumn of 2019.

5.3 SMART model

The extent of trade 'diversion' can be gauged by using the SMART model, which is hosted on the World Integrated Trade Solution (WITS) portal developed by the World Bank, UNCTAD, ITC, UNSD, and WTO. SMART model is a single-market partial equilibrium simulation tool, which focuses on an importing market and its exporting partners and assesses the impact of tariff change (an increase or decrease) on a set of variables (trade creation/diversion effects, net trade effect, tariff revenue variations, change in consumer surplus). Using the SMART model, a number of simulations were run (a tariff increase of 15% and 25% on Chinese imports by the US as per the Lists) to find out the trade diversion effects on third countries, including Sri Lanka.

Table 8.A5 shows the top imports by the US from Sri Lanka in 2018 (at HS six-digit level) and an increase in imports due to trade diversion caused by the US imposing a tariff increase on China. For example, the main import by the US from Sri Lanka is HS621210 (brassieres), and the US imported US$248mn worth of this in 2018. The imposition of an additional 15% tariff on the item under List 4A by the US on China would result in trade diversion from China to other competing countries in the US market, including Sri Lanka. As a result of trade diversion, Sri Lanka could potentially increase its exports of brassieres to the US by US$2 million, or almost by 1% over and above the 2018 (baseline) figure. Other countries that are likely to reap the benefits from the US–China trade conflict include Vietnam, Indonesia, Honduras, Dominican Republic, which are major suppliers of brassieres to the US market together with Sri Lanka. The apparel exports from Sri Lanka, which accounts for the largest share of exports to the US, stand to gain from the US–China trade war, as reflected by Table 8.A5.

5.4 Trend analysis

The effect of the trade war on Sri Lanka can also be assessed from comparing pre-tariff and post-tariff export performance using data of US imports from Sri Lanka. On aggregate, Sri Lankan exports to the US (of both tariff-affected and non-tariff-affected products) fell in 2018 (US$2801 million) compared to 2017 (US$2996 million). While the export figure for 2019 (US$2868 million) was higher compared to 2018, it was still lower than in 2017, indicating limited benefit from trade diversion.

More specifically, we also matched the tariff-affected products under the four lists (Lists 1, 2, 3, and 4A; 4B was not considered as the list was suspended before its implementation) with the list of products that US imports from Sri Lanka (at a disaggregate HS six-digit product level) to find out the extent of trade diversion. Following the various tariff announcements, exports of tariff-affected products from China to the US have declined under all four lists (Figures 8.A6, 8.A8, 8.A10, 8.A12). Data from the initial round of US$50 billion in tariffs (Lists 1 and 2), which have been in place since summer 2018, show that Sri Lanka was able to take some advantage of the current price difference created by the tariffs (Figures 8.A5 and 8.A7), especially in machinery (HS84–5) but the results are mixed for the next two rounds of tariffs (Lists 3 and 4A), recording an overall fall of exports to the US. The performance of two main exports of Sri Lanka to the US (HS50–63 textiles and clothing, and HS39–40 plastics and rubber) is also mixed, indicating Sri Lanka has not significantly benefited from the trade war or 'trade diversion' for these two important products. For example, exports of textiles and clothing in List 3 rose by almost US$3 million over the previous year while plastics and rubber under List 3 fell by US$15 million (Figure 8.A9) despite exports from China to the US being negatively affected by the tariffs (Figure 8.A10). However, the export of both products by Sri Lanka, which is contained in List 4A, fell (Figure 8.A11). In the case of apparel, exports fell by US$11 million between October to December 2019 after 15% tariffs came into effect in September 2019.

It has been reported that exports to the US decreased in November 2019 due to the continued slowdown in sales of Victoria's Secret, which is a large customer of Sri Lanka (Mahadiya, 2020). Consequently, other countries that are competing with Sri Lanka in the US market (e.g. Vietnam, Bangladesh, Indonesia, India, Cambodia) may have reaped some of the benefits from the US–China trade conflict (C. Cheng, 2019). In fact, there is evidence to show that Vietnam's exports to the US have increased at a rate much higher than other exporting countries (Ha and Phuc, 2019). In 2019, US imports from Vietnam were 35% higher than in 2018, compared to 2% in the case of Sri Lanka. In fact, other countries in Asia enjoyed faster growth rates in their market share than Sri Lanka; these included: Mongolia, Myanmar, Taiwan, Pakistan, India, Thailand, Laos, South Korea, Bangladesh, Malaysia during 2018. While the trade war has led to a diversion of trade to other countries in the region and reduced US companies from China, it has not shaken China's role as a dominant textiles and apparel supplier (Weijia et al., 2020).

Another reason why there might not have been a substantial trade diversion to Sri Lanka since the trade war began in mid-2018 can be attributed to the fact that most of the tariffs on apparel imports in the US from China (over 91%) were backloaded and only hit with tariffs in September 2019 (Wu, 2019) under the List 4A. For example, while the Combined List (1, 2, 3, 4) contains tariff lines relevant to 95% of Sri Lanka's exports to the US, List 4A alone contains tariffs which cover 75% of exports of interest of Sri Lanka to the US including much of Sri Lanka's textile and apparel exports (Table 8.A6).

Nevertheless, there have been reports in the media that, because of the US–China trade war, some of the US clothing importers which source their products from China are interested in coming to Sri Lanka (Wettasinghe, 2018). According to the Chairman of Sri Lanka Apparel Exporters Association (SLAEA): 'The US–China trade war to some extent helped with orders diverted to Sri Lanka, so it was in our favour' (Mahadiya, 2020). At the same time, there is a concern whether Sri Lanka will be able to manufacture the volume of orders currently being serviced by China since the local industry does not have the economies of scale of China or the required manpower. For example, the US currently sources approximately one-third of its apparel imports from China, while Sri Lanka supplies about 2% of the US market (ITC, 2020).

Large diversion of trade in textiles and clothing may only become visible with certain time lags. The industry in Sri Lanka is yet to fully capitalise on the benefit of the trade war despite the initial interests of buyers in the US (Y. Lawrence, personal communication, 22 June 2020). However, these benefits from the trade war are likely to be dissipated by the outbreak of COVID-19. The apparel industry has been adversely affected by the COVID-19, first on the supply side, and then on the demand side as the epicentre of the outbreak shifted from China to the rest of the world, including to Sri Lanka's main export markets in the US and EU. Sri Lanka's US$5 billion apparel export business is expected to lose US$1.5 billion between March to June 2020 (Economynext, 2020). In order to mitigate the situation, apparel exporters are currently looking to reposition its exports to the production of personal protective equipment (PPE), which has seen a surge in worldwide demand. Apparel exporters have already received US$500 million worth export orders to supply PPE (*Daily Mirror*, 2020).

6 Implications for investment diversion to Sri Lanka

To sidestep the higher tariffs imposed by the US and uncertainty, some companies are choosing to move out of China. A recent survey by the American Chambers of Commerce in China and Shanghai found a quarter of respondents had redirected investments originally planned for China to other countries or were considering doing so in light of the trade dispute, mostly to South-East Asia (E. Cheng, 2019). In fact, there is anecdotal evidence of firms (both foreign and Chinese) moving out of China or planning to do so. These include Nintendo, Panasonic, Samsung, Foxconn, to name a few who are now setting up dual supply chains: one to service the huge consumer market in China and the other for the US/other markets (Hoshi, Nakafuji, & Cho, 2019).

One country which has benefited most from the trade war is Vietnam due to its relatively stable government, low wages (64% lower than China), proximity to China/ASEAN, steady economic growth, and ease of doing business, which has provided the right conditions for businesses to relocate from China (Harrison, 2019). In fact, companies have been moving their production out of China because of the rising cost of production over the years and moving up the value chain; the trade war only sped up the shift to South-East Asia (Twigg, 2019). In turn, Vietnam is becoming home to many manufacturers of electrical and electronic equipment.

According to the data by the US Census Bureau in mid-2019, US imports from China in the first quarter of 2019 shrank by 13.9% year-on-year, while imports from Vietnam grew by a staggering 40.2%. Vietnam had begun an aggressive investment promotion campaign to attract small and medium-sized factories that make everything from electronics, to shoes, to furniture, to textiles in China's Pearl River Delta and Yangtze River Delta regions, which are the main export production hubs in the country. Data from Vietnam's Foreign Investment Agency (FIA) showed that FDI to Vietnam in the first five months of 2019 reached a four-year high of US$16.74 billion. This inflow represents a sharp 69.1% year-on-year increase. Around 1,363 new projects were licensed with a total registered capital of US$6.46 billion during the January–May 2019 period, up 38.7% against that same period the previous year. Out of 19 sectors receiving capital, the manufacturing and processing sector came on top with US$10.5 billion, accounting for 72% of total FDI (Samuel, 2019).

Table 8.A7 in the appendix ranks countries in Asia that could stand to benefit from international companies moving their production out of China, based on a composite index which takes into account a number of factors including export similarity to China; low wages; attractive investment climate in terms of ease of doing business; and sound institutional quality. Apart from Vietnam, other top contenders that are likely to benefit because of production relocation include Thailand, Malaysia, Taiwan, and India. Outside of Asia, Mexico is likely to attract FDI meant for China (Hayat, 2019). Sri Lanka ranks poorly in the list due to dissimilarity to China's export basket (low FKI), political instability and policy uncertainty, despite low manufacturing wages compared with some other countries in the region and recent improvements in the World Bank's ease of doing business rankings. Nonetheless, countries at the bottom of the list, such as Sri Lanka, Bangladesh, and Pakistan, might still be able to benefit from the relocation of production from China in specific sectors such as textiles and clothing (Hayat, 2019).

In fact, Sri Lanka's Joint Apparel Association (JAAF), an industry body, is working with the country's Board of Investment (BOI) to set up a fabric processing park in Eravur, in the eastern part of the island, to draw investors from countries like China and India (*Daily Mirror*, 2020). Sri Lanka is targeting

Chinese textile and apparel exporters, who are looking to relocate their production due to the trade war with the US. According to the BOI, there has been a positive foreign investor response to the setting up of the fabric processing park in Sri Lanka.

At the same time, countries which are likely to gain disproportionately from these developments run the risk of getting slapped with tariffs by the US if their exports grow rapidly in relation to imports from the US, widening the US trade deficit which the Trump administration views as 'unfair trade' (Hayat, 2019). Already Trump has threatened Vietnam with tariffs and called it the 'single worst abuser of everyone'. In May 2019, the US Treasury added Vietnam to its list of countries being monitored for 'possible currency manipulation'. The US has also taken action on the so-called 'round-tripping' of steel exports from Vietnam, which originated in South Korea and Taiwan (Boudreau and Chau, 2019). In this context, the benefits of the relocation would be more spread out across the Asian region. Also, with the outbreak of the novel coronavirus in China and its disruption to global supply chains, companies are likely to accelerate their diversification of production in Asia, with governments in countries such as Japan providing an impetus to this process by offering financing for companies to shift their production back to Japan or other countries in South-East Asia. Japan has reportedly earmarked US$2.2 billion of a stimulus package towards reducing its dependence on China as a manufacturing hub (Reynolds and Urabe, 2020).

In the case of Sri Lanka, the trend from 2014 to 2018 shows an increasing share of China in total inflows of FDI (Table 8.A2), with China becoming the largest source of FDI to the country (nearly half). In terms of sub-sectors, much of the increase in investments (over 70% in 2018), particularly from China, has gone into infrastructure development in Sri Lanka under China's ambitious Belt and Road Initiative (BRI). Investments in infrastructure included ports, telecommunications, housing, and property development, and hotels. FDI inflows in 2018 were mainly received by the Hambantota International Port, amounting to US$828 million, of which US$ 682 million was received by the government as proceeds of the long lease of Hambantota port during the year (Central Bank of Sri Lanka, 2018). FDI inflows to the manufacturing sector remained moderate in 2018; manufacturing accounted for about 12% of the FDI in 2018 (Table 8.A3). In this context, Sri Lanka could be a contender for investments relocating out of China to circumvent the tariffs that the US has imposed on China. In fact, the Sri Lankan government has been trying to attract Chinese investments to set up manufacturing plants in the country for the purpose of export to offset the trade war (Zhou, 2019).

7 Efforts to attract FDI from China

By 2019, high government officials had begun canvassing China-based manufacturers affected by the trade war to consider Sri Lanka as an investment location. At an investor forum in Beijing in June 2019, Sri Lanka's Minister of

Development Strategies and International Trade remarked to a gathering of Chinese investors:

> *China has invested heavily in infrastructure and assisting us to invest in ports, roads, railways, water supplies, and so on. Now we would like China to get involved in setting up their manufacturing plants in Sri Lanka, primarily for the purpose of exports. (you) can make use of the preferential market access we have – we have duty-free access to European Union countries and we have free-trade agreements with Pakistan, Singapore and India. And, since the cost of manufacturing in China is going up, we would like the Chinese to look at Sri Lanka for their manufacturing … We are even willing to look at providing special economic zones for Chinese investors.*
>
> (Zhou, 2019)

Senior Sri Lankan officials also participated in China's Belt and Road Forum for International Cooperation in Beijing, the China International Import Expo (CIIE) in Shanghai, and the Annual Meeting of New Champions in Dalian, and held bilateral meetings with senior Chinese officials as well as high-level private sector meetings, all aimed at drumming up investor interest. The government was also in talks with Chinese banks with representation in Sri Lanka (like the Bank of China) and foreign banks with a prominent presence in China (HSBC and Standard Chartered), to explore leveraging their networks to approach China-based firms who may be interested in investing in the country.

During 2019, several investors from China had begun explorations as well as negotiations to invest in Sri Lanka, according to an official at the Board of Investment (P. Wijayathilake, personal communication, 30 January 2020). In rubber tyres, steel, and petroleum and chemical products, in particular, discussions with potential investors for around US$200–500 million size of projects had reached an advanced stage by late 2019, but the actual investment was yet to materialise. The Chinese parties' insistence on retaining a majority controlling stake (at least 60%), discouraged local joint venture partners in the rubber products sector. Meanwhile, the prospective investments in steel manufacturing (primarily aimed at selling into the domestic market first, before export orientation) were discouraged by Sri Lanka's high cost of energy. Additionally, some limited investor interest was seen in assembly of electrical vehicles, white goods, and metal recycling, but again primarily aimed at the growing local market and perhaps unrelated to the US–China trade war effects. Investor interest in petroleum and petrochemicals were linked to China's port investments in Hambantota. According to a former senior government official, 'China was mainly looking at Sri Lanka for selling into the domestic market, manufacturing of some commodity items to sell to other countries, but not so much value-added export-oriented manufacturing' (M. Yapa, personal communication, June 2020).

Yet there has been a media report of a leading wall and floor tile manufacturer in Sri Lanka, Lanka Tiles, entering into a strategic partnership with a Chinese

Company (Foshan Shiwan Yulong Ceramic Co. Ltd) to obtain the technical know-how, and with an American counterpart (Benjamin Malloy of Texas) to export mosaic tiles to the USA in light of the trade barriers on Chinese exports to the US (AdaDerana, 2020). Lanka Tiles is said to have invested LKR 200 million (US$1 million) in the venture to manufacture porcelain mosaic tiles for export to the US, with shipping to start in mid-2020 (Economynext, 2019).

Discussions with several investor groups during mid to late 2019 revealed that many non-Chinese firms based in China had also begun looking for an alternative or additional locations to invest in, as part of a determined risk-diversification exercise. Several of these investors observed that a primary motivating factor was the desire to deconcentrate their supply chains, and Sri Lanka was a destination of interest for them in choosing a South Asian location – given its geographical location and balanced foreign policy. The government at the time was considering approaching US firms in particular, considering 60% of China's exports to the US are produced at factories owned by non-Chinese companies. Many of them produce customised inputs for American manufacturers, and so tariffs imposed by President Trump would affect many American companies that have factories in China.

However, pre-existing weaknesses in the investor facilitation framework, and the lack of an informed and focused investment promotion effort, meant that this interest did not materialise into actual investments. Sri Lanka, as an investment destination, was not well known to Chinese investors and the Chinese business community, beyond knowing about historical political and cultural ties. A senior government official noted that 'Sri Lanka was not ready, and we were not doing what was necessary. There were some familiarisation tours for Chinese business groups, and we did a few investment missions, but there was nothing concrete. China is such a huge place; you need to do promotion frequently' (M. Yapa, personal communication, June 2020).

On the investor facilitation front, the most critical constraint appears to be the dilution of the once-powerful BOI Act and the agency's lack of ability to make sweeping administrative facilitation efforts, in a timely and transparent manner, to help prospective investors. Over half of total FDI from 2009–18 was approved not under the BOI Act but under the more powerful and discretionary Special Development Projects Act No. 14 of 2008. Projects registered under the SDP Act are eligible for exceptional tax and other incentives, unlike those registered under the BOI Act. Even under the SDP Act, nearly all FDI projects were real estate and mixed property development projects, and none were related to export-oriented manufacturing or services.

Additionally, the lack of land (and related facilities) for new industrial establishments was a constraint. Existing BOI zones are fully occupied, and difficulties in accessing commercial water, labour, and energy were unfavourable to Chinese investors who expected these to be readily available (M. Yapa, personal communication, June 2020).

Domestic political, security, and economic issues held back any meaningful progress in attracting investors from China to Sri Lanka. First, the October

2018 'constitutional coup' caused several months of disruption to governance and government operations. Subsequently, the Easter Sunday terrorist attacks caused political and economic distress, distracting from trade and investment liberalisation efforts. The deterioration of economic conditions during the rest of 2019 and the political fallout of the terrorist bombings, led to a government change at the November 2019 Presidential Elections. The new president has not articulated a vision of trade and investment liberalisation, but has reaffirmed commitment to close economic engagement with China. Any substantive efforts for trade and investment reforms that help catalyse FDI looking for new locations are unlikely to be considered until after Parliamentary General Elections due in mid to late 2020.

8 Conclusion

Increases in bilateral trade costs such as those resulting from the ongoing trade war between the US and China have resulted in lower trade, higher prices for consumers, and trade diversion effects. While government officials and businessmen in Sri Lanka have highlighted the trade and investment opportunities for Sri Lanka to benefit from the US–China trade war (*Daily FT*, 2018), the outcome has been mixed so far. Various trade indicators (FKI, RCEPI, RCA) and simulations (SMART) conducted show that the trade war could benefit the leading exports from Sri Lanka to the US – namely textiles and clothing and plastics/rubber sectors. While the trade war started in the summer of 2018, tariffs on textiles and apparel, which are important exports to the US from Sri Lanka, were back loaded in the trade war and came into effect in the autumn of 2019. Thus, one cannot see significant benefits to the sector based on available data up to December 2019. The performance of rubber exports from Sri Lanka has been inconsistent at best. Similarly, signs of 'investment diversion' to Sri Lanka are limited up to December 2019. Although the government had commenced several initiatives aimed at attracting Chinese-based investors looking for alternative locations to invest in Sri Lanka, Sri Lanka's lack of readiness to promote the destination and provide conducive facilitation, as well as the domestic political, security, and economic conditions, hampered the success of these efforts.

In reaping the most benefits from the trade tensions, Sri Lanka needs to continue reforms to the trade, investment, and ease of doing business regime, accelerate trade liberalisation/integration efforts, attract FDI, and diversify its product basket, given that apparel still accounts for a sizeable share of Sri Lanka's exports. A World Bank (Devarajan et al., 2018) study found that the best response to the trade war is for developing countries to pursue deeper trade and investment integration among themselves whilst liberalising tariffs to increase the competitiveness of the countries to capitalise on the opportunities, but this is likely to be challenging with disruptions caused by COVID-19.

Appendix

Table 8.A1 US tariffs imposed on China

List	*Total Import Value*	*Goods Covered Include*	*Subject to an Additional Tariff*	*Effective Date*
1	$34 billion	818 products including machinery, manufacturing inputs, elevators, aircraft parts	25% tariff	19 Jul 2018
2	$16 billion	279 products including soybeans, automobiles and chemicals	25% tariff	23 Aug. 2018
3	$200 billion	5745 products: food, beverages, chemicals, wood, fabrics	10% tariff increased to 25%	24 Sept. 2018 & 18 May 2019
4A	$112 billion	3805 products: electronics, sports equipment, clothes, wooden hangers, food, beverages, chemicals, glasses, blinds, clothing	15% tariff reduced to 7.5%	1 Sept. 2019 & 15 January 2020
4B	$160 billion		15% tariffs	Scheduled for Dec 2019 but suspended until further notice

Sources: USTR (2020); Shapiro (2020).

Table 8.A2 Foreign direct investments (FDI) in Sri Lanka, top ten country wise breakdown, US$ mn

Country	*FDI Flows*					*Stock Position*				
	2014	*2015*	*2016*	*2017*	*2018*	*2014*	*2015*	*2016*	*2017*	*2018*
China	21	147	103	456	872	627	657	742	1,191	2,128
Netherlands	95	118	113	45	56	1,985	1,749	1,472	1,600	1,774
India	60	72	126	180	177	1,320	1,181	1,112	1,179	1,737
Singapore	120	27	48	203	138	538	676	720	903	1,023
Malaysia	48	-8	204	-1	23	1,433	1,143	1,107	1,103	967
Hong Kong	77	36	18	125	19	608	658	666	544	951
UK	75	29	39	76	64	550	492	573	662	666
Switzerland	5	21	3	17	22	841	757	708	589	543
Mauritius	38	21	-6	20	109	301	302	296	335	443
UAE	24	69	64	34	50	545	581	621	615	368
Total FDI	894	680	879	1373	1611	10572	10022	9845	10755	12757

Source: Central Bank of Sri Lanka (2018).

Table 8.A3 Foreign direct investment of BOI enterprises by sector, US$ mn

Sector	*2014*	*2015*	*2016*	*2017*	*2018*
1. Manufacturing	333.9	257	247.7	347.6	291.5
- Food, beverages, and tobacco products	44.7	42.7	49.5	62.6	22.3
- Textile, wearing apparel, and leather products	83.1	45.4	21.3	78.2	90.6
- Wood and wood products	2.5	2.8	3.1	2.3	4.9
- Paper, paper products, printing, and publishing	36.3	2.2	3.1	7.9	9
- Chemicals, petroleum, coal, and rubber products	91.9	75.4	99.5	105	97.3
- Non-metallic mineral products	29.7	13.7	31.2	28.1	21
- Fabricated metal, machinery, and transport equipment	7	46.1	11.9	9	7.8
- Manufactured products (n.e.s.)	38.7	28.7	28.2	54.5	38.6
2. Agriculture	5.7	3.9	1.9	1.4	0.5
3. Services	506.3	255.4	211.9	317.8	301.3
- Hotels and Restaurants	68.4	181.9	141.3	252.6	223.4
- IT and BPO	24.7	13.6	23	25	58.7
- Other services	413.3	59.9	47.6	40.1	19.2
5. Infrastructure	682.5	453.4	339.5	1,043.50	1,773.70
- Housing, property development, and shop office	339.2	212.1	79.5	540.6	397.8
- Telephone and telecommunication network	152.5	138.8	243.6	209	522.2
- Power generation, fuel, gas, petroleum and other	12.5	51.3	14.8	1.1	3.7
- Port container terminals	178.2	51.2	1.6	292.8	850
6. Total	1,528.40	969.7	801	1,710.30	2,366.90

Source: Central Bank of Sri Lanka (2018).

Table 8.A4 Products in which Sri Lanka has a comparative advantage over China in US (HS6 level)

HS Code	*Description*	*China's Exports to the US (US$ mn)*	*Sri Lanka's Exports to the US (US$ mn)*	*Ratio of Sri Lanka's Exports to US/China's Exports to US*	*List*
121190	Plants, parts of plants, incl. seeds and fruits, used primarily in perfumery, in pharmacy	27.34	1.28	4.68	3
200819	Nuts and other seeds, incl. mixtures, prepared or preserved (excl. . . .)	54.19	22.29	41.13	3
210120	Extracts, essences, and concentrates, of tea or mate, and preparations with a basis of these …	16.71	1.25	7.50	4A
330190	Extracted oleoresins; concentrates of essential oils in fats, fixed oils, waxes, and the like	2.72	17.69	650.35	4A
380210	Activated carbon (excluding medicaments or deodorant products for fridges, vehicles etc.)	20.07	24.58	122.44	3
400811	Plates, sheets, and strips of cellular rubber	11.10	9.52	85.74	3
401290	Solid or cushion tyres, interchangeable tyre treads and tyre flaps, of rubber	51.72	112.21	216.94	3
401519	Gloves, mittens and mitts, of vulcanised rubber (excluding surgical gloves)	117.28	23.34	19.90	4A
401691	Floor coverings and mats, of vulcanised rubber (excluding hard rubber), with chamfered sides, …	22.32	2.58	11.55	3
401699	Articles of vulcanised rubber (excluding hard rubber), n.e.s.	208.25	30.47	14.63	3
441700	Tools, tool bodies, tool handles, broom or brush bodies and handles, of wood; boot or shoe …	1.43	1.79	125.24	4A
482020	Exercise books of paper or paperboard	2.85	1.01	35.33	3

Table 8.A4 Cont.

HS Code	*Description*	*China's Exports to the US (US$ mn)*	*Sri Lanka's Exports to the US (US$ mn)*	*Ratio of Sri Lanka's Exports to US/China's Exports to US*	*List*
531100	Woven fabrics of other vegetable textile fibres; woven fabrics of paper yarn (excluding those …)	1.22	1.03	84.88	3
560790	Twine, cordage, ropes and cables, whether or not plaited or braided and whether or not impregnated, …	12.60	5.35	42.45	3
560819	Knotted netting of twine, cordage, ropes, or cables, by the piece or metre; made-up nets, …	43.41	6.39	14.71	3
591000	Transmission or conveyor belts or belting, of textile material, whether or not impregnated, …	9.63	1.20	12.47	3
610220	Women's or girls' overcoats, car coats, capes, cloaks, anoraks, incl. ski jackets, windcheaters, …	18.69	1.57	8.38	4A
610332	Men's or boys' jackets and blazers of cotton, knitted or crocheted (excluding wind-jackets …)	106.17	7.38	6.95	4A
610333	Men's or boys' jackets and blazers of synthetic fibres, knitted or crocheted (excluding wind-jackets …)	83.18	6.18	7.43	4A
610339	Men's or boys' jackets and blazers of textile materials (excluding of wool, fine animal hair, …)	2.35	3.96	168.41	4A
610343	Men's or boys' trousers, bib and brace overalls, breeches and shorts of synthetic fibres, knitted …	244.81	16.70	6.82	4A
610349	Men's or boys' trousers, bib and brace overalls, breeches and shorts of textile materials, …	6.45	1.57	24.39	4A

(*continued*)

Table 8.A4 Cont.

HS Code	*Description*	*China's Exports to the US (US$ mn)*	*Sri Lanka's Exports to the US (US$ mn)*	*Ratio of Sri Lanka's Exports to US/China's Exports to US*	*List*
610443	Women's or girls' dresses of synthetic fibres, knitted or crocheted (excluding petticoats)	633.95	36.29	5.72	4A
610449	Women's or girls' dresses of textile materials, knitted or crocheted (excluding of wool, fine …)	7.38	13.80	186.91	4A
610462	Women's or girls' trousers, bib and brace overalls, breeches and shorts of cotton, knitted …	440. 01	66.92	15.21	4A
610463	Women's or girls' trousers, bib and brace overalls, breeches and shorts of synthetic fibres, …	627.01	114.29	18.23	4A
610469	Women's or girls' trousers, bib and brace overalls, breeches and shorts of textile materials, …	105.80	6.74	6.37	4A
610510	Men's or boys' shirts of cotton, knitted or crocheted (excluding nightshirts, T-shirts, singlets …	117.37	43.35	36.93	4A
610610	Women's or girls' blouses, shirts and shirt-blouses of cotton, knitted or crocheted (excluding …)	20.46	5.72	27.98	4A
610711	Men's or boys' underpants and briefs, knitted or crocheted, of cotton	56.12	42.63	75.97	4A
610719	Men's or boys' underpants and briefs, of textile materials (ex cotton or mmf), containing 70% or more wt of silk or silk waste, k/c	2.10	1.48	70.50	4B
610811	Women's or girls' slips and petticoats, knitted or crocheted, of man-made fibres	1.96	1.73	88.32	4A

Table 8.A4 Cont.

HS Code	*Description*	*China's Exports to the US (US$ mn)*	*Sri Lanka's Exports to the US (US$ mn)*	*Ratio of Sri Lanka's Exports to US/China's Exports to US*	*List*
610821	Women's or girls' briefs and panties, knitted or crocheted, of cotton	67.24	114.27	169.95	4A
610822	Women's or girls' disposable briefs and panties designed for one-time use, of man-made fibres, k/cr	197.13	114.48	58.07	4A
610829	Women's or girls' briefs and panties (other than disposable), of textile materials (other than cotton or mmf) contining 70% or more wt of silk, k/c	1.06	66.38	6,280.88	4B
610839	Women's or girls' nightdresses and pyjamas, knitted or crocheted, of wool or fine animal hair	4.58	3.21	70.02	4B
610990	T-shirts, singlets, tank tops and similar garments, knitted or crocheted, of man-made fibres	966.03	122.75	12.71	4A
611090	Sweaters, pullovers, sweatshirts, vests and similar articles, of text mat (except wool, cotton, or mmf), containing 70% or more by wt of silk, k/c	66.44	6.60	9.94	4B
611120	Babies' blouses and shirts, except those imported as parts of sets, knitted or crocheted, of cotton	649.93	50.26	7.73	4A
611190	Babies' garments and clothing accessories, knitted or crocheted, of wool or fine animal hair	6.31	2.37	37.61	4A
611231	Men's or boys' swimwear, knitted or crocheted, of synthetic fibres	12.66	1.27	10.06	4A
611241	Women's or girls' knitted or crocheted swimwear of synthetic fibres	403.59	58.82	14.57	4A

(*continued*)

Table 8.A4 Cont.

HS Code	*Description*	*China's Exports to the US (US$ mn)*	*Sri Lanka's Exports to the US (US$ mn)*	*Ratio of Sri Lanka's Exports to US/China's Exports to US*	*List*
611610	Gloves, mittens & mitts impregnated, coated, or covered with plastics or rubber, knitted or crocheted	242.16	95.18	39.30	4A
620342	Rec perf outwear, men's/ boys' trousers, overalls & shorts, not knit/crochet, of cotton, containing 10 to 15% or more by wt of down	1071.72	118.87	11.09	4A
620349	Rec perf outwear, men's/ boys' bib and brace overalls, not knitted or crocheted, of artificial fibres	24.65	23.58	95.65	4A
620449	Women's or girls' dresses, not knitted or crocheted, containing 70% or more by weight of silk or silk waste	78.66	6.61	8.40	4A
620463	Rec perf outwear, women's/girls' trousers, bib/brace overalls, breeches & shorts, not knit/crochet, syn. fibres, containing 15% or more down, etc.	252.54	11.43	4.52	4A
620469	Rec perf outwear, women's or girls' bib and brace overalls, not knitted or crocheted, of artificial fibres	299.75	84.86	28.31	4A
620520	Men's or boys' shirts, not knitted or crocheted, of cotton, certified hand-loomed and folklore products	538.10	123.83	23.01	4A
620530	Men's or boys' shirts, not knitted or crocheted, of manmade fibres, certified hand-loomed and folklore products	81.81	5.33	6.51	4A

Table 8.A4 Cont.

HS Code	*Description*	*China's Exports to the US (US$ mn)*	*Sri Lanka's Exports to the US (US$ mn)*	*Ratio of Sri Lanka's Exports to US/China's Exports to US*	*List*
620590	Men's or boys' shirts, not knitted or crocheted, of wool or fine animal hair, certified handloomed and folklore products	67.23	14.10	20.97	4A
620630	Women's or girls' blouses and shirts, not knitted or crocheted, of cotton, certified handloomed and folklore products	180.14	32.36	17.97	4A
620640	Women's or girls' blouses and shirts, not knitted or crocheted, of manmade fibres, certified handloomed and folklore products	180.85	8.86	4.90	4A
620690	Women's or girls' blouses, shirts, and shirt-blouses, not knitted or crocheted, of textile materials n.e.s.	23.60	12.71	53.85	4A
620711	Men's or boys' underpants and briefs, not knitted or crocheted, of cotton	11.57	5.03	43.44	4A
620721	Men's or boys' nightshirts and pyjamas, not knitted or crocheted, of cotton	20.74	3.24	15.62	4A
620821	Women's or girls' nightdresses and pyjamas, not knitted or crocheted, of cotton	45.93	15.43	33.60	4A
620920	Babies' dresses, not knitted or crocheted, of cotton	85.25	5.66	6.64	4A
620990	Babies' garments and clothing accessories, not knitted or crocheted, of wool or fine animal hair	4.56	1.18	25.83	4A
621111	Men's or boys' swimwear, of textile materials (except mmf), containing 70% or more by wt of silk or silk waste, not knit or crocheted	27.33	3.91	14.31	4A

(*continued*)

Table 8.A4 Cont.

HS Code	*Description*	*China's Exports to the US (US$ mn)*	*Sri Lanka's Exports to the US (US$ mn)*	*Ratio of Sri Lanka's Exports to US/China's Exports to US*	*List*
621210	Brassieres containing lace, net, or embroidery, containing under 70% by weight of silk or silk waste, whether or not knitted or crocheted	776.97	306.94	39.50	4A
621220	Girdles and panty-girdles	8.67	1.77	20.42	4A
621290	Braces, suspenders, garters, and similar articles and parts thereof	7.08	1.50	21.16	4A
710490	Synthetic or reconstructed precious or semiprecious stones, cut but not set and suitable for use in the manufacture of jewelry	11.30	1.03	9.13	4A
842390	Parts of weighing machinery using electronic means for gauging, except parts for weighing motor vehicles	28.12	9.04	32.16	1
843120	Parts suitable for use solely or principally with the machinery of heading 8427	272.29	23.44	8.61	1
950720	Fish hooks, snelled	9.73	1.68	17.27	4A
960310	Whiskbrooms, wholly or pt. of broom corn, over $0.96 each	1.826787	10.79	590.43	4A

Source: Compiled from WITS Database; Note: 1) Sectors with export value greater than US$1 million are listed above; 2) In order to work out comparative advantage, all the sectors where Sri Lanka's share is higher than 4 % as a proportion of China's exports to the US have been taken as the ones where Sri Lanka enjoys comparative advantage vis a vis other country.

Table 8.A5 Trade diversion to Sri Lanka due to US imposing additional tariffs on China (US$1000)

HS Code	*List (Tariff Increase)*	*Exports in 2018 Before*	*Exports After Tariff Increase*	*Trade Diversion*	*Top Beneficiaries*
621210	List 4A (15% tariff)	247,985.45	250,103.23	2,117.78	Vietnam, Sri Lanka, Indonesia, Honduras, Dominican Rep,
401290	List 3 (25% tariff)	128,785.83	128,950.48	164.66	Sri Lanka, Mexico, Taiwan, Brazil, Vietnam
620462	List 4A (15% tariff)	126,379.91	127,204.58	824.67	Bangladesh, Vietnam, Pakistan, Indonesia, Cambodia
620520	List 4A (15% tariff)	116,333.11	116,998.83	665.72	Bangladesh, Vietnam, India, Indonesia, Sri Lanka
620342	List 4A (15% tariff)	112,920.49	113,239.73	319.23	Bangladesh, Mexico, Vietnam, Nicaragua, Pakistan
611610	List 4A (15% tariff)	97,425.43	98,519.46	1,094.04	Sri Lanka, S. Korea, Pakistan, Vietnam, Malaysia

Source: Calculated using WITS Database.

Table 8.A6 Tariff lists under Section 301 and relevance to Sri Lanka's exports, 2019

	List 1	*List 2*	*List 3*	*List 4A*	*List 4B*	*Combined List*
01–05 Animal Products						
06–15 Vegetable Products			7.9%	17.3%		25.2%
16–24 Foodstuffs			61.2%	38.8%		100.0%
25–26_Minerals			18.6%			18.6%
27–27 Fuels						
28–38 Chemicals and Allied Industries			70.3%	8.4%	21.3%	100.0%
39–40 Plastics/Rubbers		0.9%	80.5%	10.3%	0.7%	92.4%
41–43 Raw Hides, Skins, Leather and Furs			100.0%			100.0%
44–49 Wood and Wood Products			64.6%	28.0%	3.9%	96.5%
50–63 Textiles			1.4%	**97.2%**	1.3%	100.0%
64–67 Footwear/Headgear			10.0%	88.4%	1.6%	100.0%
68–71 Stone/Glass			4.4%	94.6%	0.3%	99.3%
72–83 Metals			14.9%	85.1%		100.0%
84–85 Machinery	87.0%	0.9%	8.7%	3.1%		99.8%
86–89 Transportation	7.0%		93.0%			100.0%
90–97 Miscellaneous	3.0%	0.2%	11.7%	30.0%	22.5%	67.4%
Total	3.2%	0.1%	13.7%	**74.5%**	1.9%	93.5%

Source: Compiled from TradeMap Database and USTR (2020).

Table 8.A7 Where might production capacity in China move to?

Country	*Where will they go (WWTG) index*
Thailand	0.62
Malaysia	0.61
Vietnam	0.60
Taiwan	0.55
India	0.31
Singapore	0.30
Philippines	0.18
South Korea	0.17
Indonesia	0.17
Japan	-0.03
Sri Lanka	-0.07
Mongolia	-0.27
Cambodia	-0.36
Laos	-0.39
Pakistan	-0.43
Myanmar	-0.59
Bangladesh	-0.67

Source: Hayat (2019).

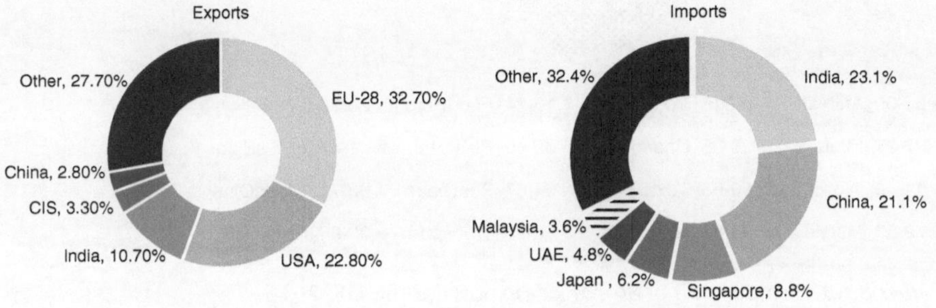

Figure 8.A1 Direction of trade – Sri Lanka, 2017.
Source: WITS Database.

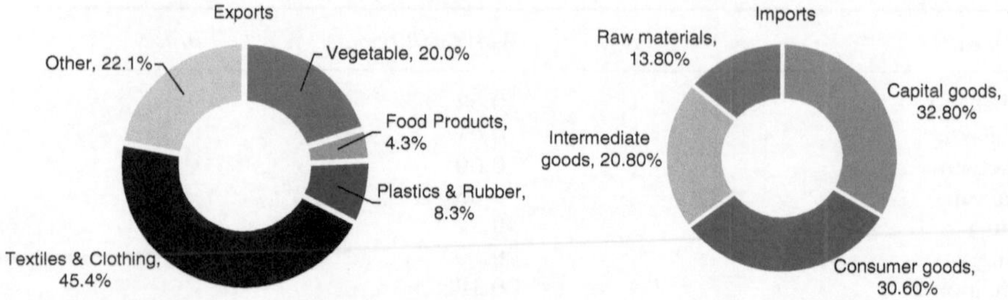

Figure 8.A2 Product composition of trade – Sri Lanka, 2017.
Source: WITS Database.

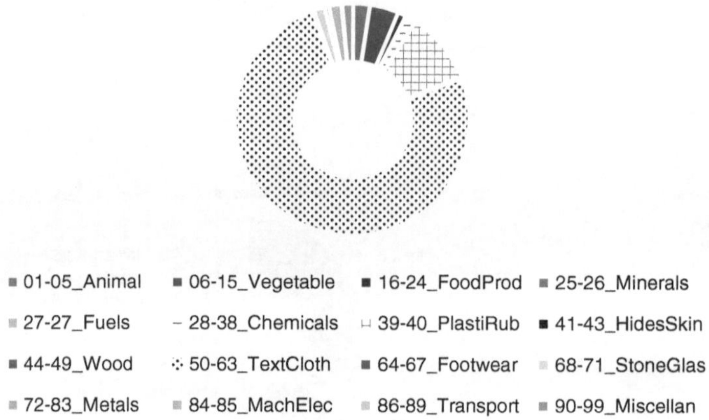

Figure 8.A3 Composition of Sri Lanka's exports to the US, 2017.
Source: Compiled from TradeMap database.

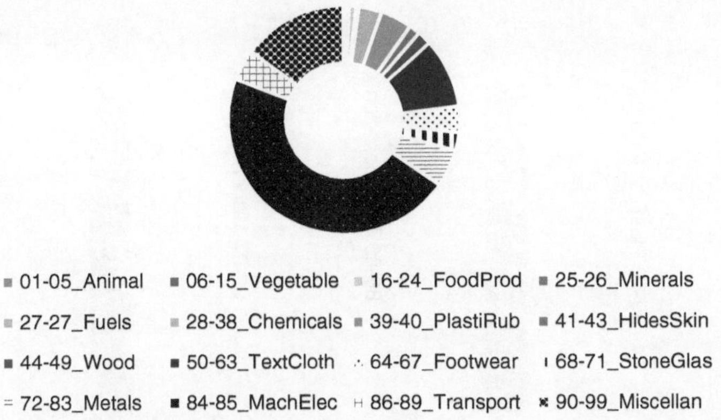

Figure 8.A4 Composition of Chinese exports to the US, 2017.

Source: Compiled from TradeMap database.

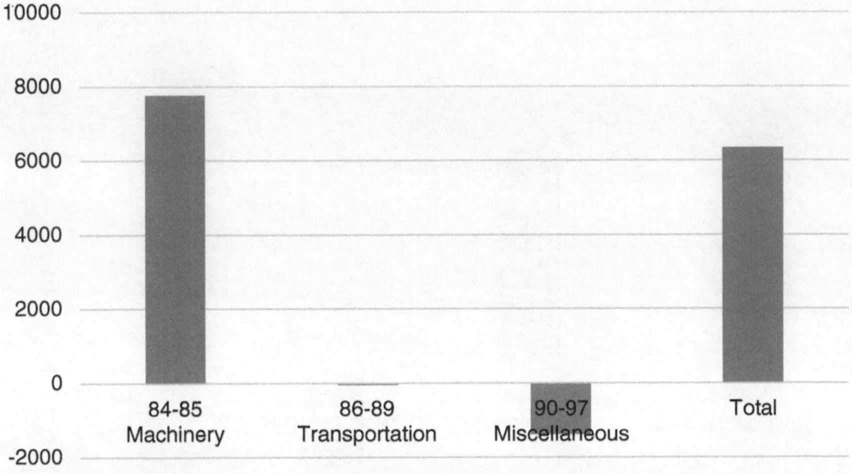

Figure 8.A5 Changes in Sri Lanka's exports to the US of tariff-affected products on List 1 (One year).

Note: * Difference between 08/2018–07/2019 vs. 08/2017–07/2018.

Source: Compiled from TradeMap database.

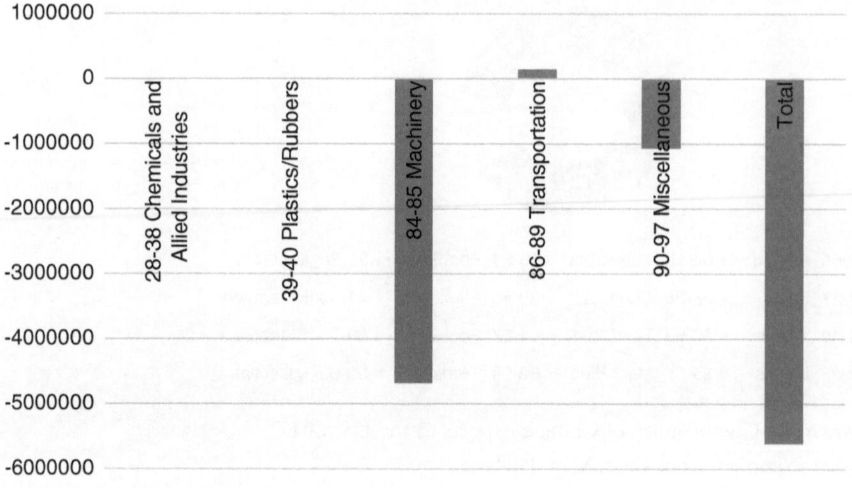

Figure 8.A6 Changes in China's exports to the US after tariff imposition List 1.
Note: * Difference between 08/2018–07/2019 vs. 08/2017–07/2018.
Source: Compiled from TradeMap database.

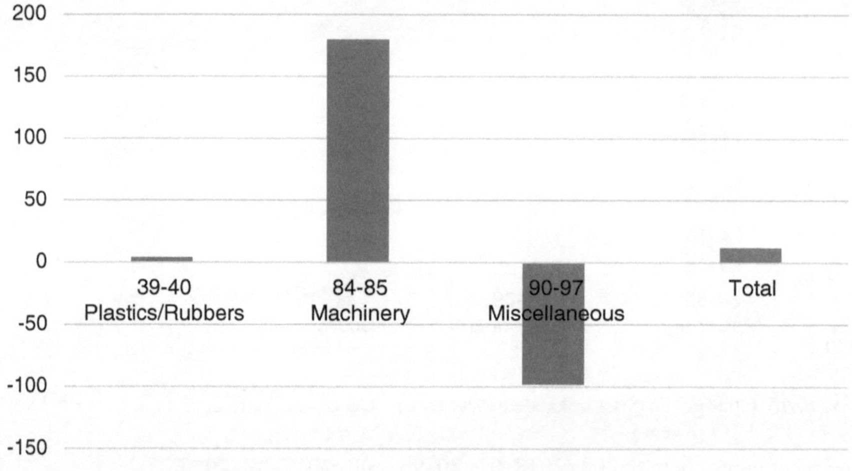

Figure 8.A7 Changes in Sri Lanka's exports to the US of tariff-affected products on List 2 (One year).
Note: *Difference between 09/2018–08/2017 vs. 09/2017–08/2018.
Source: Compiled from TradeMap database.

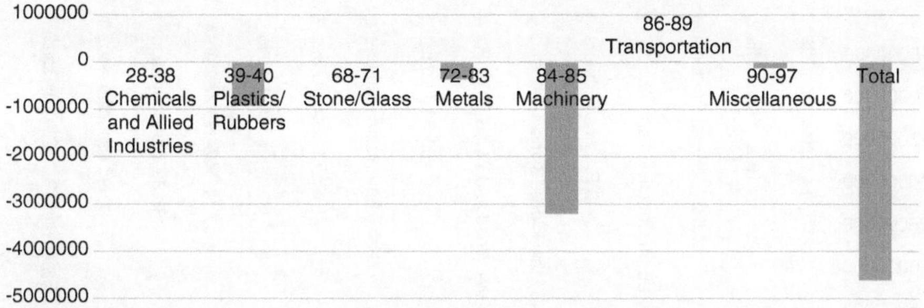

Figure 8.A8 Changes in export from China to US of tariff-affected products under List 2 – one year.

Note: *Difference between 09/2018–08/2017 vs. 09/2017–08/2018.

Source: Compiled from TradeMap database.

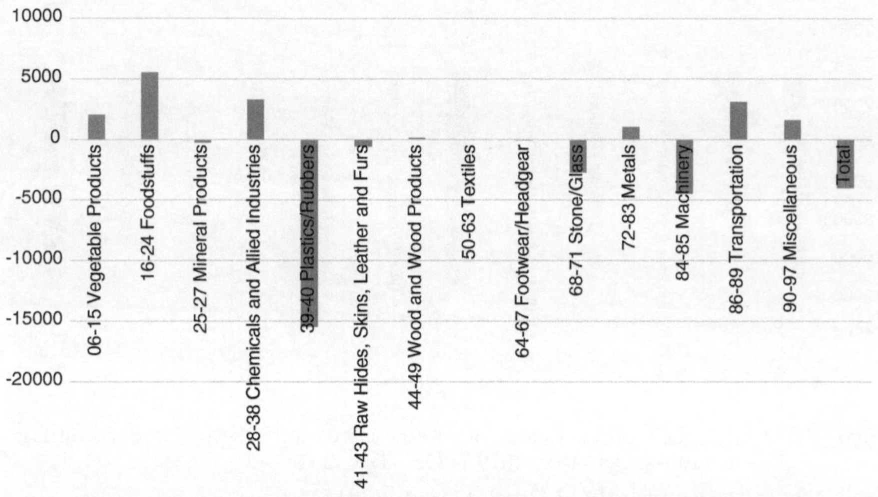

Figure 8.A9 Changes in Sri Lanka's exports to the US of tariff-affected products on List 3.

Note: *Difference between 10/2018–09/2017 vs. 10/2017–09/2018.

Source: Compiled from TradeMap database.

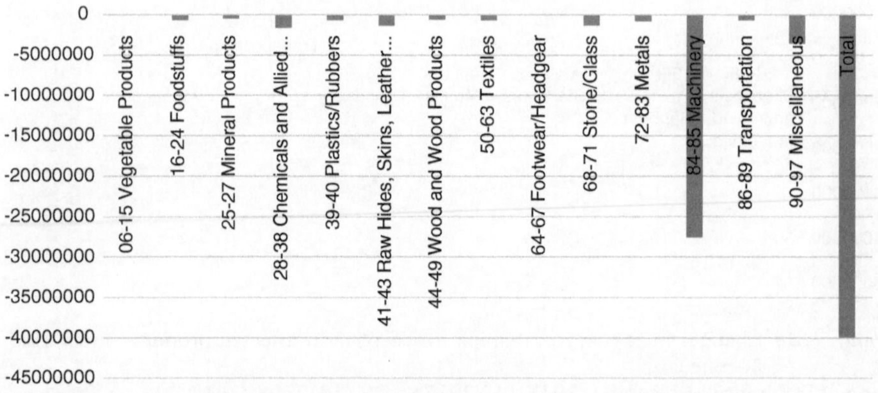

Figure 8.A10 Changes in export from China to the US of the tariff-affected products under List 3.

Note: *Difference between 10/2018–09/2017 vs. 10/2017–09/2018.

Source: Compiled from TradeMap database.

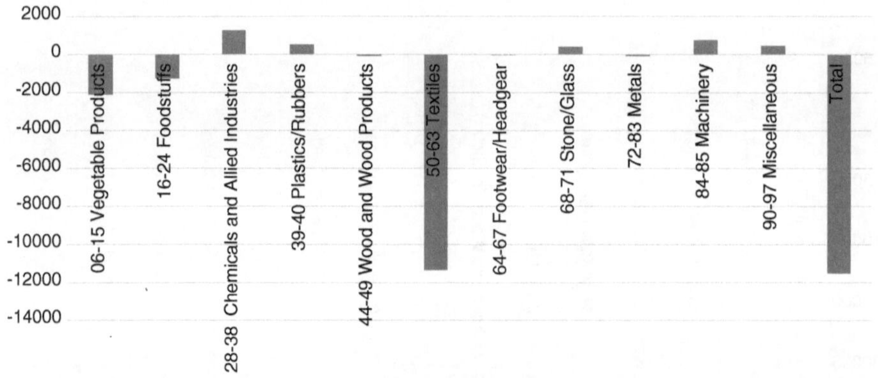

Figure 8.A11 Changes in Sri Lanka's exports to the US of tariff-affected products on List 4a (List 4a: Oct.–Dec. 2019 vs Oct.–Dec. 2018).

Note: *Difference between 10–12/2019 vs. 10–12/2018.

Source: Compiled from TradeMap database.

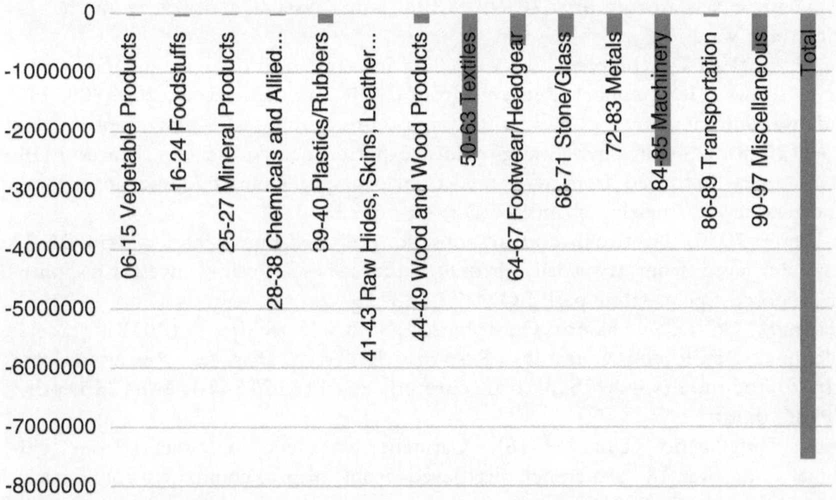

Figure 8.A12 Changes in export from China to the US of tariff-affected products in List 4a.

Note: *Difference between 10–12/2019 vs. 10–12/2018.
Source: Compiled from TradeMap database.

Acknowledgement

The authors would like to thank Nuwanthi Senaratne, Institute of Policy Studies of Sri Lanka, for the research assistance.

References

Abiad, A., Baris, K., Arvin, J., Bertulfo, D. J., Camingue-Romance, S., Neilmer Feliciano, P., … Mercer-Blackman, V. (2018). *The Impact of Trade Conflict on Developing Asia.* Retrieved from www.adb.org/sites/default/files/publication/471496/ewp-566-impact-trade-conflict-asia.pdf

AdaDerana (2020). LANKATILES collaborates with a Chinese Company & an American counterpart for exporting mosaic tiles to USA. 7 January. Retrieved from AdaDerana: bizenglish.adaderana.lk/lankatiles-collaborates-with-a-chinese-company-an-american-counterpart-for-exporting-mosaic-tiles-to-usa/

Bollen, J., & Rojas-Romagosa, H. (2018). *Trade Wars: Economic Impacts of US Tariff Increases and Retaliations. An International Perspective.* 19 November. Retrieved from www.cpb.nl/sites/default/files/omnidownload/CPB-Background-Document-November2018-Trade-Wars-update.pdf

Boudreau, J. and Chau, M. N. (2019). Vietnam goes from trade war winner to Trump target, 11 July. Retrieved from www.bloomberg.com/news/articles/2019-07-11/from-trade-war-winner-to-trump-target-vietnam-braces-for-shocks

Central Bank of Sri Lanka (2018). *Annual Report.* Colombo: CBSL.

Cheng, C. (2019). Is Malaysia benefitting from the US–China trade war? 5 August. Retrieved from www.eastasiaforum.org/2019/08/05/is-malaysia-benefitting-from-the-us-china-trade-war/

Cheng, E. (2019). US companies are cancelling investment into China at a faster clip, survey shows. 11 September. Retrieved from CNBC: www.cnbc.com/2019/09/11/trade-war-amcham-survey-shows-tariffs-weigh-on-us-businesses-in-china.html

Daily FT (2018). US-China trade war gives local exporters new partnership chances: EDB. 22 October. Retrieved from www.ft.lk/front-page/US-China-trade-war-gives-local-exporters-new-partnership-chances--EDB/44-665235

Daily Mirror (2020). Positive investor response for proposed Eravur fabric park: BOI. 22 May. Retrieved from www.dailymirror.lk/business-news/Positive-investor-response-for-proposed-Eravur-fabric-park-BOI/273-188713

Deverajan, S., Go, D. S., Lakatos, C., Robinson, S., & Thierfelder, K. (2018). Traders' Dilemma: Developing Countries' Response to Trade Disputes. Retrieved from http://documents.worldbank.org/curated/en/115171541615454756/pdf/WPS8640.pdf

Economic Intelligence Unit (2018). Garment exporters to benefit from US-China trade war. 8 September. Retrieved from http://country.eiu.com/article.aspx?articleid=1847103368

economynext (2019). Lanka Tiles partners China firm to export tiles to the US amid trade war. 16 December. https://economynext.com/lanka-tiles-partners-china-firm-to-export-tiles-to-the-us-amid-trade-war-35990/

economynext (2020). Brandix apparel plants in Sri Lanka, India making PPE in Covid-19 battle. 4 May. Retrieved from https://economynext.com/brandix-apparel-plants-in-sri-lanka-india-making-ppe-in-covid-19-battle-69553/

Fernandopulle, L. (2019). US-China trade war will hit Sri Lanka, say economists. 1 September. Retrieved from www.sundayobserver.lk/2019/09/01/business/us-china-trade-war-will-hit-sri-lanka-say-economists

Freund, C., Maliszewska, M., & Constantinescu, C. (2019). How are trade tensions affecting developing countries? 18 March. Retrieved from https://blogs.worldbank.org/trade/how-are-trade-tensions-affecting-developing-countries

Ha, L., & Phuc, N. (2019). *The US-China Trade War: Impact on Vietnam*. Singapore: ISEAS.

Harrison, V. (2019). US-China trade war: 'We're all paying for this'. 1 August. Retrieved from www.bbc.com/news/business-49122849

Hayat, R. (2019). Leaving China: Which countries might benefit from a relocation of production? 8 August. Retrieved from https://economics.rabobank.com/publications/2019/august/leaving-china-countries-might-benefit-from-relocation-production/#3fd039ef-e3d6-4b8e-b63f-fe15ef3610ad

Hoshi, M., Nakafuji, R., & Cho, Y. 2019). China scrambles to stem manufacturing exodus as 50 companies leave. 18 July. Retrieved from https://asia.nikkei.com/Economy/Trade-war/China-scrambles-to-stem-manufacturing-exodus-as-50-companies-leave

Itakura, K. (2019). Evaluating the impact of the US–China trade war. *Asian Economic Policy Review*, 30 August. https://onlinelibrary.wiley.com/doi/abs/10.1111/aepr.12286

ITC (2020). Trade map. 4 April. Retrieved from www.trademap.org/Index.aspx

Mahadiya, H. (2020). Sri Lanka apparel exports up 2.8-pct in Nov with investments in production. 13 January. Retrieved from https://economynext.com/sri-lanka-apparel-exports-up-2-8-pct-in-nov-with-investments-in-production-40018/

Minghao, L., Balistreri, E., & Zhang, W. (2018). The 2018 trade war: Data and nascent general equilibrium analysis. Retrieved from Iowa State University: https://lib.dr.iastate.edu/card_workingpapers/605/

Misra, R., & Choudhry, M. (2020). Trade war: Likely impact on India. *Foreign Trade Review*, *55*(1), 93–118.

Parker, P. (2019). Will a trade deal end US-China rivalry? 9 May. Retrieved from www.bbc.com/news/av/business-48205665/will-a-trade-deal-end-us-china-rivalry

Rosyadi, S. A., & Widodo, T. (2018). Impact of Donald Trump's tariff increase against Chinese imports on global economy: Global Trade Analysis Project (GTAP) model. *Journal of Chinese Economic and Business Studies*, 125–145.

Reynolds, L., & Urabe, E. (2020). Japan to fund firms to shift production out of China. 8 April. Retrieved from www.bloomberg.com/news/articles/2020-04-08/japan-to-fund-firms-to-shift-production-out-of-china?fbclid=IwAR0gQvrFGgkB3vjfvHuqaayTxlASNfCrmL8Us1H5tWwDpFbYPUfbiBdCdXI

Samuel, P. (2019). FDI in Vietnam – where is the investment going? 7 June. Retrieved from www.vietnam-briefing.com/news/fdi-in-vietnam-investment-by-sector.html/

Sandler, T., & Rosenberg, P. A. (2020). Tariff actions resource page. Retrieved from www.strtrade.com/f-tariff-actions-resources.html#china301

Shapiro (2020). The Section 301 tariffs: U.S. timeline. Retrieved from www.shapiro.com/tariffs/tariff-news/

Sunday Observer (2019). Benefits of US-China trade war: 'Lanka should explore export opportunities'. 21 July. Retrieved from www.sundayobserver.lk/2019/07/21/benefits-us-china-trade-war-'lanka-should-explore-export-opportunities'

Twigg, M. (2019). US-China trade war accelerates apparel factories' shift from China to Southeast Asia and Bangladesh. *South China Morning Post*, 4 November. www.scmp.com/lifestyle/fashion-beauty/article/3035927/us-china-trade-war-accelerates-apparel-factories-shift

UNCTAD (2019). Trade and trade diversion effects of United States tariffs on China. Retrieved from https://unctad.org/en/pages/newsdetails.aspx?OriginalVersionID=2226

United States Trade Representative (2020). China Section 301 – tariff actions and exclusion process. Retrieved from https://ustr.gov/issue-areas/enforcement/section-301-investigations/tariff-actions

Weijia, L., Mo, H., Hou, L., & Jing, L. (2020). Crunching numbers: U.S. apparel trade deficit grows wider during trade war with China. 9 March. Retrieved from https://news.cgtn.com/news/2020-03-09/U-S-apparel-trade-deficit-grows-wider-during-trade-war-with-China-OISdnUhKZG/index.html

Wettasinghe, C. (2018). Sri Lankan apparel stands to gain from US-China trade spat. 18 April. Retrieved from www.dailymirror.lk/article/Sri-Lankan-apparel-stands-to-gain-from-US-China-trade-spat-148760.html

Wijesinha, A. (2019). Slow trade growth, America's tariff fallout, and implications for Sri Lanka. 26 April. Retrieved from www.lki.lk/blog/slow-trade-growth-americas-tariff-fallout-and-implications-for-sri-lanka/

Wong, D., & Koty, A. C. (May 13, 2020). The US-China trade war: A timeline. 13 May. Retrieved from www.china-briefing.com/news/the-us-china-trade-war-a-timeline/

Wu, J. (2019) 92% of apparel imports from China will be hit with tariffs on Sunday – here's how companies are coping, CNBC, 20 August. Retrieved from www.cnbc.com/2019/08/30/92percent-of-apparel-from-china-will-be-hit-with-tariffs-sundayhow-retailers-are-coping.html

York, E. (2020). Tracking the economic impact of U.S. tariffs and retaliatory actions. 14 February. Retrieved from https://taxfoundation.org/tariffs-trump-trade-war/#timeline

Zhou, L. (2019). Sri Lanka could help Chinese manufacturers offset trade war impact. *South China Morning Post*, 4 July. www.scmp.com/news/china/diplomacy/article/3017294/sri-lanka-could-help-chinese-manufacturers-offset-trade-war

Part III

Decoding the benefit of preferential trading partners

9 US–China trade war and the RCEP negotiations

An analysis

Sanchita Chatterjee

1 Introduction

In 2018, the United States of America (US) began imposing unilateral tariff and non-tariff measures against Chinese imports and technology companies. China responded with its own retaliatory measures. This led to a build-up of tit-for-tat unilateral measures between the two countries, popularly known as the US–China trade war. Respite came in the form of an economic and trade agreement between the countries ('US–China Agreement') in January 2020.

In recent years, China has been involved in another major economic event with the potential to significantly impact at least the regional, if not the global, trading system. This is the negotiation to conclude a mega-regional trade agreement between China, and the ten member countries of the Association of East Asian Nation (ASEAN), Australia, New Zealand, Japan, Republic of Korea (South Korea) and India, formally known as the Regional Comprehensive Economic Partnership (RCEP). The RCEP negotiations concluded in November 2019, when the RECP negotiating parties (except India) announced they had reached an 'agreement on text-based negotiations' (ASEAN, 2019).

China's presence in the trade war and the RCEP agreement creates a conundrum: could there be a form of spillover or some impact of one on another? The current chapter will focus its attention on the possible impact of and linkages between the US–China Agreement and the RCEP agreement on two strands. The analysis of this chapter will mostly focus on the impact of the US–China Agreement on the economies of the RCEP, rather than the agreement itself. However, in a few places, the chapter does analyse the possible impact on the RCEP agreement itself (considering whether provisions can be added to the agreement for the benefit of its negotiating parties).

The chapter will look at implications for regional and global value chains and, intellectual property rights and innovation environments in the countries involved in the RCEP negotiations. The rationale is as follows:

- The US–China Agreement may outweigh the trade liberalisation effects of the RCEP agreement by creating trade diversion and have an adverse impact on regional value chains that involve the RCEP negotiating parties ('RCEP countries'). Such trade diversion effects may be created by the US–China Agreement because of, for example, China's commitment in the agreement to purchase additional goods and services from the US.

- The US–China Agreement seeks to strengthen China's IPR regime by asking China to undertake a range of commitments in the intellectual property rights (IPR) chapter of the agreement. A changed IPR environment in China may impact all the RCEP countries, even benefiting some of them. Further, this scenario presents an opportunity for the RCEP countries, depending on interests and negotiating dynamics, to lock in commitments which China made in the US–China Agreement, in the RCEP agreement.

The chapter is organised as follows. Section 2 provides a brief description of the US–China Agreement and the RCEP timeline so far. Sections 3 and 4 give a brief overview of engagement of the FTAs of the US and the RCEP countries and a comparison of the broad provisions of the RCEP agreement with free trade agreements (FTAs) between the RCEP negotiating parties. Sections 5–7 look at relationships and linkages between the US, China, and the other RCEP countries from various angles – trade, investment, regional and global value chains, and IPR. Section 8 contains a discussion on the impact of unexpected events such as COVID-19 on the linkages between the US–China Agreement and the RCEP. In section 9, conclusions are drawn and recommendations made on the basis of the findings of the earlier sections.

2 US–China economic and trade agreement and RCEP timeline

2.1 US–China economic and trade agreement

The US–China economic and trade agreement signed in January 2020 (US–China Agreement) has sections on IP, technology transfer, trade in food and agricultural products, macroeconomic policies, exchange rate matters, transparency, and expanding trade (Table 9.1). The agreement is seen as the first phase of an agreement between the US and China to resolve the issues that led to the US–China trade war; in particular, issues that arose in investigations carried out by the US (USTR, n.d. b).

The US–China Agreement would probably benefit the US more than it would China. In any case, for China, the issues covered by the agreement itself did not seem to be high on the priority list, or signing such an agreement itself was not imperative.[1] While the US hailed the agreement as a major victory, China has apparently said the agreement would help the country to meet market and World Trade Organisation (WTO) requirements.[2] The two countries were expected to begin work on phase two of the agreement soon after signing the first phase agreement.

There is a degree of uncertainty, however, whether phase one of the agreement will be implemented in the current situation (elaborated in section 8). The fate of the US–China Agreement has been questioned, as the US elections were

Table 9.1 Summary of substantive provisions of the US–China Agreement

Intellectual property	Protection for trade secrets & confidential business information; provisions on pharma-related IPR e.g. protection of supplemental data		Effective patent term extension, piracy and counterfeiting on E-commerce platforms etc	Transparency and procedural fairness wrt protection of GIs, respect for prior trademark rights, and clear procedures
Technology transfer	Enhance mutual trust and cooperation wrt tech issues	No pressure to persons of other party to transfer technology	No administrative and licensing requirements and processes that require or pressure tech transfer	Due process and transparency
Trade in Food and Agricultural Products	Ensure safe and reliable supplies, science- and risk- based sanitary and phytosanitary (SPS) measures			Further commitments in Annexes 1–7
Financial Services	Provide fair, effective, and non-discriminatory market access for each other's services and services suppliers		Provisions on Banking, Credit Rating, Electronic Payment, Financial Asset Management (Distress and Debt), Insurance, Securities, Fund management, Future services	
Macroeconomic Policies and Exchange Rate Matters and Transparency	Avoid manipulating exchange rates	Transparency	Enforcement mechanism	
Expanding trade	China to increase the importation of quality and affordable goods and services'	From January 1, 2020 through December 31, 2021, China to import the US of manu & agri goods, energy products, and services more than corresponding 2017 amount by no less than $200 billion		China is entitled to request consultations with the United States of they cannot meet this obligation

Source: Office of the United States Trade Representative.

by the end 2020, and may lead to a change in nature and/or degree of the relationship between the US and China.[3]

2.2 *Regional Comprehensive Economic Partnership (RCEP) agreement*

The negotiation for the RCEP agreement was launched by the ASEAN along with its six dialogue partners (ASEAN plus one) in 2012. The group of countries that participated in the RCEP agreement is a disparate group with a membership of high-income economies (Brunei Darussalam, Singapore, Japan, Australia, New Zealand, and South Korea), upper-middle-income economies (Malaysia and Thailand), and lower-middle-income economies (India, Indonesia, Vietnam, the Philippines, Laos, Myanmar, and Cambodia) (UN, 2019). While most of the analysis carried out in this chapter would take the RCEP negotiating parties as one group, for some parts of the analysis, individual countries, in particular from the ASEAN, will be separately mentioned. The conclusions in this chapter may not be applicable to all the countries evenly.

In November 2019, the leaders of the RCEP countries announced the negotiating parties, except India, had reached an agreement on market access issues and would sign the agreement after completing 'legal scrubbing of the texts'. Since India is not included in the RCEP agreement as of now, the present analysis excludes India. The present chapter refers to the RCEP negotiating parties as the RCEP countries minus India or the RCEP-I. In November 2020, the RCEP-I signed the agreement while options are open for India to join at a later date.

Table 9.2 provides a timeline and description on guiding principles agreed upon at the time of the launch of the negotiations for the RCEP. The headings of the chapters and issues on which agreement has been reached among RCEP-I are available. The guiding principles indicate that RCEP would take forward much of the progress made in ASEAN+1 agreement.

The guiding principles indicate the RCEP is intended to be a comprehensive agreement with special provisions for the less developed countries within the negotiating parties. Since the RCEP is expected to take forward the progress made in the ASEAN+1 FTAs, the level of ambition for the 'comprehensiveness' (i.e. level of liberalisation achieved in the agreement) of the RCEP is linked to the level of comprehensiveness achieved in the ASEAN+1 FTAs. In this sense, if the ASEAN+1 FTAs score low in relative comprehensiveness – as section 4 demonstrates that they do – the level of ambition on comprehensiveness for the RCEP is likely to be low.

The US–China Agreement may impact the RCEP through both trade diversion and trade creation effects. Evidence suggests the US–China trade war has led to trade diversion effects, which brought substantial benefits for Taiwan, Mexico, the EU, and Vietnam (Nicita, 2019). Such trade diversion effects are likely to be sustained, accentuated, or brought about in a different way by the US–China Trade Agreement, in particular since it has commitments for China to import US\$200 billion worth of goods from the US by December 2021. However, the US–China Agreement does not include any commitment to tariffs, and both the US and China still apply discriminatory tariffs on each other's' goods (Wong

Table 9.2 Timeline and summary of provisions of the RCEP

Negotiations	*Launched - Nov 2012*			*Concluded – Nov 2019*	
Guiding principles	Facilitate trade and investment, special & differential treatment, plus flexibility to least-developed ASEAN Member States (LDC AMS), other ASEAN FTA Partner can join later subject to t&c, tariff elimination on a high percentage of tariff lines and trade value, early tariff elimination for LDC AMS, services commitments building on RCEP members' commitments under the GATS and the ASEAN+1 FTAs, investment to cover four pillars of promotion, protection, facilitation and liberalisation, economic and technical cooperation provisions building upon existing ASEAN and its FTA partners, reduce IP-related barriers to trade and investment, competition, dispute settlement & other issues				
Meetings	3 ministerial summits, last in Nov 2019	28 rounds of negotiations, last round Sep 2019; 29th round Mar 2020	9 intersessional ministerial meetings, last one Oct 2019	7 intersessional meeting of trade negotiating committee, last one Oct 2019	3 special meetings of trade negotiating committee, last meeting Feb 2020
Current status	Concluded text-based negotiations, agreement reached on all market access issues				
Chapters agreed	20 Chapters incl. annexes on financial services, telecommunication services and financial services (the chapters agreed have been described in Table 9.1)				

Source: Department for Foreign Affairs and Trade, Australian Government.

et al., 2020). This presents a particular paradox because, while China has committed to purchasing additional products, it has discriminatory tariffs on certain products and reduced most favoured nation tariffs on the import of certain other products from the US.[4]

The US–China Agreement should also lead to trade creation as it includes substantive provisions on non-tariff issues such as IPR, technology goods, various categories of services, etc. The overall impact of the US–China Agreement will result from an interplay of the two effects (Bhagwati & Panagariya, 1996; Mattoo, Mulabdic, & Ruta, 2019).

3 Current engagements in FTAs of US and RCEP-I

The US and the RCEP-I are involved in various kinds of free trade agreements (FTAs) with disparate levels and degrees of liberalisations.

The data in Figure 9.1 illustrate current engagement in FTAs of the RCEP-I. Figure 9.1 contains data on FTAs entered into individually by the ASEAN countries and the remaining RCEP-I. Among the RCEP-I, Singapore has the highest engagement in FTAs – under negotiation, signed and not yet in effect, or signed and in effect. Outside the ASEAN, South Korea is engaged in the most FTAs, under negotiations, signed and in effect/not yet in effect.

The US has 14 FTAs in force with 20 countries. Among the RCEP-I, the US has FTAs in force with Australia, Singapore, and South Korea (ITA, n.d.). The ASEAN has FTAs with its dialogue partners (known as ASEAN+1 FTAs): Australia and New Zealand, China, India, South Korea and Hong Kong, China (ASEAN, n.d.). All the ASEAN members are party to ASEAN FTAs.

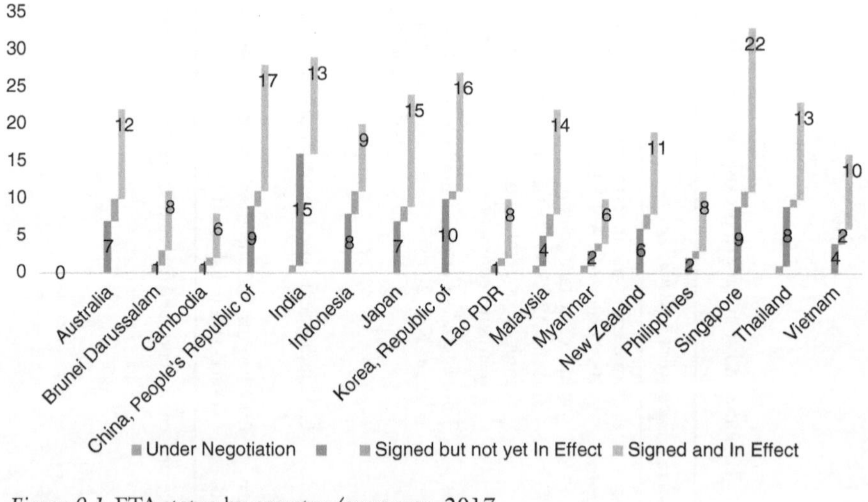

Figure 9.1 FTA status by country/economy, 2017.
Source: Asian Development Bank 2019.

Table 9.3 is a matrix explaining the engagement of the RCEP countries and the US with each other through FTAs (the RCEP agreement is not included). It is clear most of the countries are already engaged with each other in FTAs, which are in force or are being negotiated. Apart from bilateral FTAs, there are trilateral FTAs between the ASEAN, Australia, and New Zealand in force and between China, South Korea, and Japan under negotiation. Further, Australia, Japan, New Zealand, and four ASEAN countries (Brunei, Malaysia, Singapore, and Vietnam) are parties to another mega-regional trade agreement, Comprehensive and Progressive Agreement for Trans-Pacific Partnership (CPTPP) (Government of Canada, 2020).

Evidently, there is a maze of FTAs already in force or under negotiation in the region, potentially creating the effect of a 'spaghetti bowl' or a 'noodle bowl' situation, with multiple rules of origin and other requirements (Chatterjee, 2014). The region is also unique in that two of the three mega-regional trade agreements under negotiation or in effect (i.e. the RCEP and the CPTPP) overlap in many countries.[5] Further, some of the RCEP-I have FTAs in effect with the US. Therefore, there are or will be in future a number of effects at play in the region because of the existence of various agreements involving the RCEP-I, including the US–China Agreement.

4 Comparing other FTAs with RCEP

This section provides a comparison between the overall provisions of the RCEP agreement and the FTAs in force between RCEP-I. The objective is to assess the 'comprehensiveness' of the RCEP agreement. Since detailed provisions of the RCEP were not available at the time of writing this analysis, chapters and provisions in the FTAs between the RCEP-I are compared with the chapter headings of the RCEP. Chapter headings provide an idea of the substantive issues covered by the RCEP agreement as usually the issues of importance are covered in standalone chapters in trade agreements.

Comparing in this manner, the AANZFTA appears to have the highest number of common chapters with the RCEP agreement among the ASEAN+1 agreement (Table 9.4). The common chapters between the FTAs have not been listed in the table. Trade in goods, investment, trade in services (except annexes and chapters on particular category or modes of services), economic and technical cooperation are the common chapters between these FTAs.

Compared to ASEAN+1 FTAs, non-ASEAN RCEP-I FTAs appear to be relatively more comprehensive. Table 9.5 illustrates FTAs among the non-ASEAN RCEP-I and CPTPP. There are more common chapters between these FTAs than the ASEAN+1 FTAs: trade in goods, rules of origin, SPS and TBT, trade in services, investment, IP, and dispute settlement are the common chapters. Some of these non-ASEAN RCEP-I FTAs number more additional chapters and annexes than the RCEP agreement, indicating these FTAs possibly cover more subject areas than the RCEP.

Table 9.3 Engagement of RCEP-I and the US with each other through FTAs

	USA	*China*	*Japan*	*Republic of Korea*	*Australia*	*New Zealand*	*ASEAN*
USA		No FTA *US-China agreement, Jan 2020*	No FTA	In force	In force	No FTA	No FTA
China	No FTA *US-China agreement, Jan 2020*		Under negotiation *Tri FTA Chn-Jap-Kor*	In force *China-ROK FTA* Under negotiation *Tri FTA Chn-Jap-Kor*	In force	In force *Upgraded*	In force
Japan	No FTA	Under negotiation *Tri FTA Chn-Jap-Kor*		Under negotiation *FTA Chn-Jap-Kor*	In force *Jap-Aus FTA* In force *CPTPP*	In force *CPTPP*	In force
Republic of Korea	In force	In force *China-ROK FTA* Under negotiation *Tri FTA Chn-Jap-Kor*	Under negotiation *Tri FTA Chn-Jap-Kor*		In force	In force	In force
Australia	In force	In force	In force *Jap-Aus FTA* In force *CPTPP*	In force		In force *One of most compr agreements* In force *CPTPP*	In force *ASEAN-Aus-NZL Tri FTA*
New Zealand	No FTA	In force	In force *CPTPP*	In force	In force *One of most compr agreements* In force *CPTPP*		In force *ASEAN-AUS-NZL Tri FTA*
ASEAN	No FTA	In force	In force	In force	In force *ASEAN-AUS-NZL Tri FTA*	In force *ASEAN-AUS-NZL Tri FTA*	

Source: Author's compilation from various websites of governments and the ASEAN.

Table 9.4 Comparing RCEP provisions with ASEAN+1 FTAs

Technical chapters in RCEP/Corresponding chapters and provisions in ASEAN+1 FTAs	*ASEAN-Aus-NZ-FTA (AANZFTA)*	*ASEAN-China FTA*	*ASEAN-Korea FTA*	*ASEAN-Japan Comprehensive Economic Partnership*
Rules of Origin	☐	☐ *Not separate chapter*	☐ *Not separate chapter*	☐
Customs Procedures and Trade Facilitation	☐ *(excl TF)*			
Sanitary & phytosanitary Measures	☐	☐	☐ *Not separate chapter*	☐
Standards, Technical Regulations and Conformity Assessment Procedures	☐	☐	☐ *Not separate chapter*	☐
Trade Remedies				
Trade in Services	☐	☐	☐	☐
Annexes on Financial Services, Telecommunication Services & Professional Services	*Ann on financial and telecom*		*Ann on financial*	
Movement of Natural persons	☐			
Intellectual Property	☐			
Electronic Commerce	☐			
Competition	☐			
Small and Medium Enterprises				
Government Procurement				
Dispute Settlement	☐		☐	☐
Additional	*Safeguards Measures*		*Safeguards Measures Not separate chapter*	*Annex on information technology products*

Source: Author's compilation from various websites of governments and the ASEAN.

Among the FTAs of the non-ASEAN RCEP-I, Australia-New Zealand Closer Economic Relations (ANZCER) Trade Agreement (not included in Table 9.5) is one the world's most comprehensive, effective, and mutually compatible FTAs and would definitely be more comprehensive than the RCEP.[6] Further, the CPTPP has even more numbers of additional chapters than the RCEP and thus has a considerably higher level of 'comprehensiveness'.

In terms of comprehensiveness, the RCEP agreement lies somewhere between ASEAN+1 agreements and non-ASEAN RCEP-I agreements. The fact that some of the countries have more comprehensive agreements in place between them or are part of the CPTPP accentuates the 'spaghetti/noodle bowl' scenario by adding to issues for businesses in terms of understanding the various tariff and non-tariff regimes under the different FTAs, and escalation of costs of understanding and utilising provisions of various FTAs. This may affect the utilisation of the RCEP agreement, in particular if rules of origin of the other RCEP-I FTAs and the CPTPP are more favourable than that in the RCEP (ECORYS, 2018; Yi, 2015). A relatively less utilised RCEP agreement, in turn, may strengthen the importance of the US–China Agreement for the RCEP-I.

5 Trade and investment relationship of US and China with RCEP-I

The US and China are important players in the RCEP countries. This is evidenced by the trade and investment relationships between the US and China with the remaining 14 countries of the RCEP. For the analysis in this section, data for the ASEAN economies are grouped together either under the ASEAN or South-East Asia headings.

5.1 Imports

Imports of all the other RCEP-I from China have grown since 2000 (Figure 9.2). The growth is especially remarkable for ASEAN between 2010 and 2018. ASEAN's imports from China more than doubled between 2010 and 2018.

Imports of the RCEP-I from the USA present a mixed picture. Imports by Japan saw a dip between 2000 and 2010 before growing again in 2018. Imports by Australia and New Zealand were more or less steady between 2000 and 2010. Imports by the ASEAN from the US increased between 2010 and 2018, though by not as much as its imports from China.

5.2 Exports

Exports by the other RCEP-I to China between 2000 and 2018 present a mixed picture (Figure 9.3). Japan increased its exports by almost five times between 2000 and 2010 but decreased its exports slightly between 2010 and 2018. South Korea, too, experienced a huge jump in exports between 2000 and 2010 (by almost five times) and maintained its increase between 2010 and 2018, though at

Table 9.5 Comparing RCEP provisions with non-ASEAN RCEP-I FTAs

Technical chapters in RCEP/ Corresponding chapters and provisions in ASEAN+1 FTAs	*China-Aus FTA*	*China-NZ FTA (upgraded)*	*Korea-Aus FTA*	*Jap-Aus FTA*	*Kor-NZ FTA*	*China-ROK FTA*	*CPTPP*
Customs Procedures and Trade Facilitation	☐	☐ *Customs procedures and cooperation*	☐ *Customs administration and TF*	☐	☐	☐	☐ *Competitiveness & business facilitation*
Trade Remedies	☐	☐	☐		☐	☐	☐
Trade in Services	☐	☐	☐	☐	☐	☐	☐
Annexes on Financial Services, Telecommunication Services & Professional Services	*Ann on financial*		*Ann on professional services; Audiovisual Coproduction Agreement*		*Ann on professional services; WTO basic telecom ref paper*		
Movement of Natural persons	☐	☐	☐	☐	☐ *Temp entry of business persons*	☐	☐
Electronic Commerce	☐		☐	☐		☐	☐
Competition				☐	☐	☐	☐
Small and Medium Enterprises							☐

(*continued*)

Table 9.5 Cont.

Technical chapters in RCEP/ Corresponding chapters and provisions in ASEAN+1 FTAs	*China-Aus FTA*	*China-NZ FTA (upgraded)*	*Korea-Aus FTA*	*Jap-Aus FTA*	*Kor-NZ FTA*	*China-ROK FTA*	*CPTPP*
Economic and Technical Cooperation		☐ *Specifies only cooperation*	☐	☐	☐ *Agri, forestry & fisheries cooperation*	☐	☐
Government Procurement		*Side letter*	☐	☐	☐		☐
Additional	*Chapter on Transparency*	*Chapter on Transparency Electrical and Electronic Equipment Mutual Recognition Agreement*	*Chapters on Fin Services, telecom, labour, environment*	*Chapters on food supply, energy and mineral resources, Fin Services, telecom,*	*Chapters on transparency, labour, environment; Audiovisual Coproduction Agreement*	*Chapters on Fin Services, telecom, environment & trade, transparency*	*Chapters on textile & apparel, Fin Services, Telecom, state-owned enterprise & designated monopolies, labour, environment, labour, environment, development, regulatory coherence, transparency & enti-corruption,*

Source: Author's compilation from various websites of governments and the ASEAN.

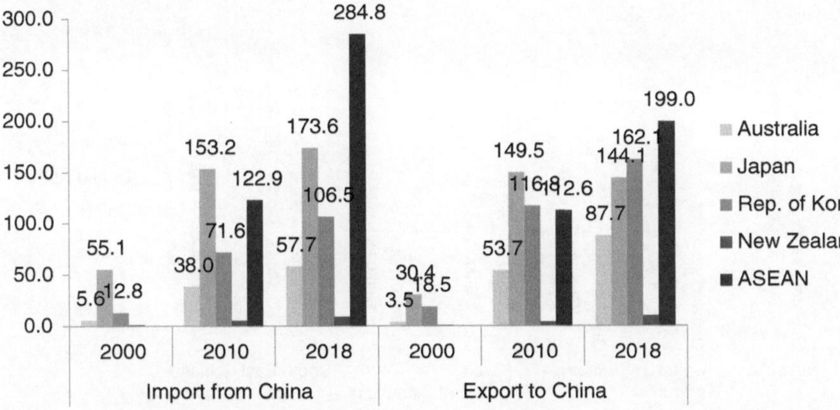

Figure 9.2 Growth in import from and export to China of the other RCEP countries.
Source: UNCOMTRADE.

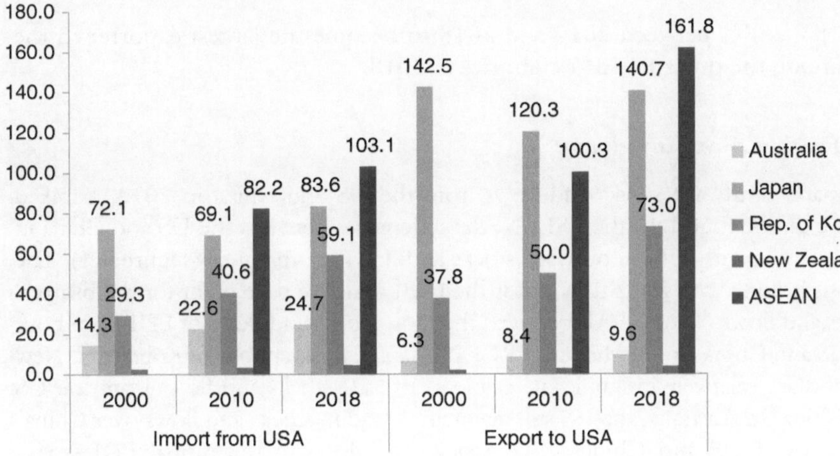

Figure 9.3 Growth in import from and export to USA of RCEP countries.
Source: UN COMTRADE.

a lesser rate than that in the period before. The ASEAN, too, saw a sharp rise in exports between 2010 and 2018 and became the biggest exporter from the other RCEP-I countries to China in 2018.

Exports by the other RCEP-I to the US present a mixed picture too. Japan has been among the largest exporters from these countries to the US, but its exports fluctuated between 2000, 2010, and 2018. Exports from Australia and New Zealand have been steady but relatively low in this period. South Korea increased its exports steadily between 2000, 2010, and 2018. The ASEAN increased its

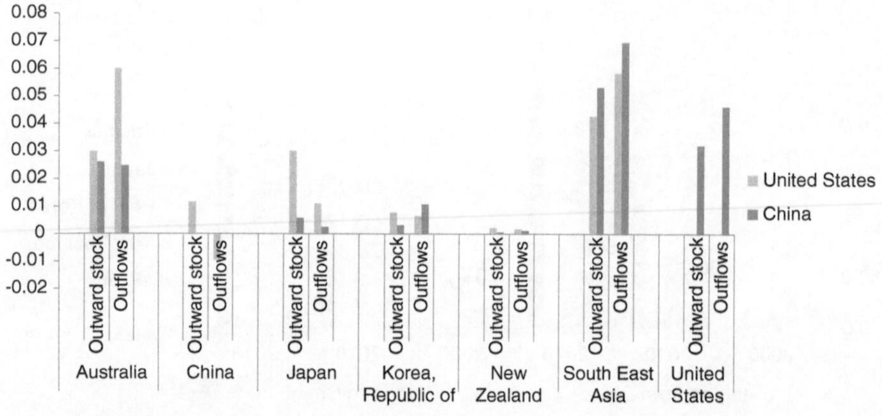

Figure 9.4 Outward FDI stock and flows as % of world stocks and flows from the US and China to RCEP Countries in 2012.

Source: UNCTAD 2014.

exports by 60% between 2010 and 2018 to become the largest exporter to the US among the other RCEP-I countries in 2018.

5.3 Foreign direct investment

Comparing outward stocks and flows from the US and China in 2012, a mixed picture can be found. In the ASEAN, the differences between the US and China in terms of amounts of both outward stocks and flows are marginal (Figure 9.4). The analysis is done with 2012 data as it is the latest available time point for the bilateral stocks and flows. The ASEAN received the most stocks and flows of FDI from both the US and China among the other RCEP-I. Japan, the Republic of Korea, and New Zealand are relatively insignificant recipients of FDI stocks and flows from the US and China. In Australia, the US still maintains a lead in stocks and flows over China.

Shares of US and Chinese FDI stocks and flows in the global FDI stocks and flows are examined in Figure 9.5 to understand the latest trends. China has doubled its share in outward FDI stock between 2014 and 2018, and marginally increased its share in inward FDI stock. In terms of both inflows and outflows too China has experienced an increase in its shares. In contrast, the US experienced a fall in its shares in both outflows and outward stocks. Its share in inflows and inward stocks rose in this period.

Broadly the trends seen in this section can be summarised as following:

1) The growing relative importance of the ASEAN as a trade partner and investment destination for the US and China.
2) The growing relative importance of South Korea in trade with the US and China.

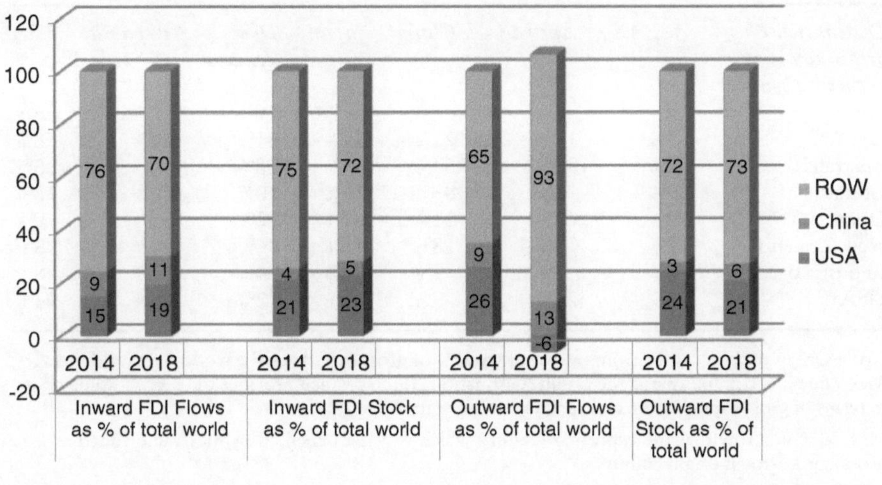

Figure 9.5 Shares of inward and outward FDI flows and stocks of US and China in total FDI values.

Source: UNCTAD, 2014.

3) The growing importance of China – relative to the US – as a trading and investment partner for the other RCEP-I between 2000 and 2018.
4) The US–China Agreement is likely to have a differential impact on the RCEP-I as these countries have varying degrees and levels of exposure to China and the US through trade and investment.
5) The export and import trends also give an indication of the extent of participation of the different countries in regional and global value chains (more on this in section 6).

6 Integration into regional and global value chains

Regional and global value chains (R-GVCs) have emerged due to the fragmentation of the production process across countries and regions and globalisation/regionalisation of supply chains. R-GVCs-related trade has different dimensions in terms of trade in parts and components, trade in value-added, employment, investment, services, intangibles, and intellectual property. A manner of understanding R-GVCs-related trade is to look at trade in value-added of goods and services for assessing the extent of integration among the RCEP-I and the US to R-GVCs.

Table 9.6 shows the percentage of value-added from a country in terms of gross exports to the same country, which is an indicator of backward linkages. From the table, it appears South Korea has the most backward linkages with the other RCEP-I countries followed by the ASEAN. Conversely a lesser percentage of value-added of gross exports of South Korea and the ASEAN to the world

Table 9.6 Origin country of value-added as % of gross exports to the country in 2015

Destination & origin country/ exporting country	*ASEAN*	*Australia*	*China*	*Japan*	*New Zealand*	*Republic of Korea*	*USA*
ASEAN	71%	14%	21%	12%	21%	26%	8%
Australia	22%	88%	34%	37%	13%	60%	5%
China	29%	5%	83%	11%	10%	21%	15%
Japan	32%	7%	21%	87%	12%	58%	9%
New Zealand	12%	11%	13%	15%	86%	21%	5%
Rep of Korea	35%	7%	39%	8%	14%	67%	8%
USA	24%	24%	9%	8%	12%	25%	91%

Note: Origin of value added from own country as % of gross exports to the world – forward linkages. Max value in a column that is the origin/destination country which provides the highest value added in terms of gross exports from an exporting country to it.

Max value in a row that the exporting country which is being benefited by max value added as % of gross exports to an origin country.

Source: Adapted from OECD TIVA.

had forward linkages. Considering this indicator, the US had the least backward linkages with the RCEP countries and the highest forward linkage among the countries under consideration here. This suggests the US is less integrated with R-GVCs, especially those involving the RCEP-I countries.

Another measure of R-GVCs is to look at value-added from a country in imports from the country. For all countries, imports from the US had the highest value-added originating from their own country, confirming the finding of the earlier table that the US is relatively less integrated with R-GVCs (in this respect) than the RCEP-I. Table 9.7 confirms the earlier finding South Korea and the ASEAN are relatively more integrated with regional value chains than the other countries as percentages of value-added originating from South Korea and the ASEAN in imports originating in these two are the lowest.

Tables 9.6 and 9.7 illustrate that there are variations in the degree of integration among RCEP-I.

- For example, while about 79% of Japan's imports from the ASEAN originated in the ASEAN itself, about 68% of imports from South Korea originated in South Korea itself.
- While 58% of imports of New Zealand from South Korea originated in South Korea itself, 70% of imports of the US from South Korea originated in South Korea.

Some of these differences may be attributed to the presence (or absence) of FTAs between the countries and the comprehensiveness of these agreements. However, the percentage of value-added in Australian imports from South Korea is even

Table 9.7 Origin of value-added from a country as % of gross imports from the country in 2015

Country of origin of value-added & import/ Country which is importing	*ASEAN*	*Australia*	*China*	*Japan*	*New Zealand*	*Republic of Korea*	*USA*
ASEAN	0.48%	68.15%	69.45%	78.85%	68.82%	34.72%	69.62%
Australia	87.79%	0.62%	89.07%	89.19%	86.55%	88.70%	87.23%
China	82.62%	82.38%	3.56%	84.09%	83.44%	81.85%	82.49%
Japan	86.91%	80.52%	85.84%	1.25%	85.48%	85.36%	87.68%
New Zealand	86.15%	86.37%	85.75%	85.04%	0.08%	85.75%	86.54%
Republic of Korea	66.60%	58.17%	65.92%	68.13%	58.39%	0.90%	70.13%
USA	91.96%	90.86%	90.08%	92.05%	89.89%	91.64%	4.62%

Source: Adapted from OECD TIVA.

less than that of Japan (and Australia and South Korea do have an FTA between them). A detailed analysis of trade in value-added at product levels and comparing these with provisions of corresponding FTAs would give a better explanation of the differences between the countries in integration with R-GVCs.

Economic theory indicates there is a link between FTAs and a country's integration in global value chains. Furthermore, evidence suggests the 'depth' or comprehensiveness of FTAs has a positive effect on integration in global value chains (Ruta, 2017). Interestingly, regional trade agreements are more effective when their membership is consistent with regional production networks (OECD, 2013).

As explained in section 2, the US–China Agreement contains provisions on trade in goods and services, IPR, technology goods, and so on. Though it will have trade diversion and creation effects, the US–China Agreement cannot be termed as a comprehensive or deep trade agreement. The RCEP agreement is expected to promote or enhance the participating countries' integration to R-GVCs – even though, as the earlier sections demonstrate, it is not as comprehensive as some other FTAs between the RCEP-I. The existing 'spaghetti bowl' situation in the RCEP-I adds layers to the assessment of the impact on R-GVCs.

From the current analysis, it appears the RCEP-I has different degrees of integration with the R-GVCs. The findings of sections 5 and 6 indicate the ASEAN and South Korea are relatively more integrated with R-GVCs of the RCEP-I. The US and China seem to be comparatively less integrated with R-GVCs of the RCEP-I, which may imply the US–China Agreement will not have a substantial impact on R-GVCs involving the RCEP-I. Further, neither the US–China Agreement nor the RCEP agreement is 'comprehensive' enough to exert significant influence on the R-GVCs.

7 Intellectual property and innovation

RCEP-I and the US are among the leading economies in the world in terms of innovation performance and intellectual property creation. In recent years China has topped or has been near the top spot in patent applications, scientific publications, and other indicators, which suggest its domination in creating intellectual property. Data from the top five patent offices demonstrate China experienced an 11.6% growth in applications in 2018 over 2017, whereas the US and Japan experienced declines. China's share in total patent applications in 2018 was about 46% (Table 9.8).

Considering the filing of total patent applications in 1980–2018, Japan is the leader, closely followed by the US and China. South Korea is trailing the top three countries. The other RCEP-I are far behind these four countries (Figure 9.6).

Table 9.8 Data on the top five patent offices

Office	*% growth in applications in 2018 over 2017*	*Share in total patent applications in 2018*
China	11.6%	*46.4%*
U.S.	-1.6%	*18.0%*
Japan	-1.5%	*9.4%*
Republic of Korea	2.5%	*6.3%*
EPO	4.7%	*5.2%*
Other offices		*14.7%*
WORLD patent applications		*3,326,300*

Source: WIPO 2019a.

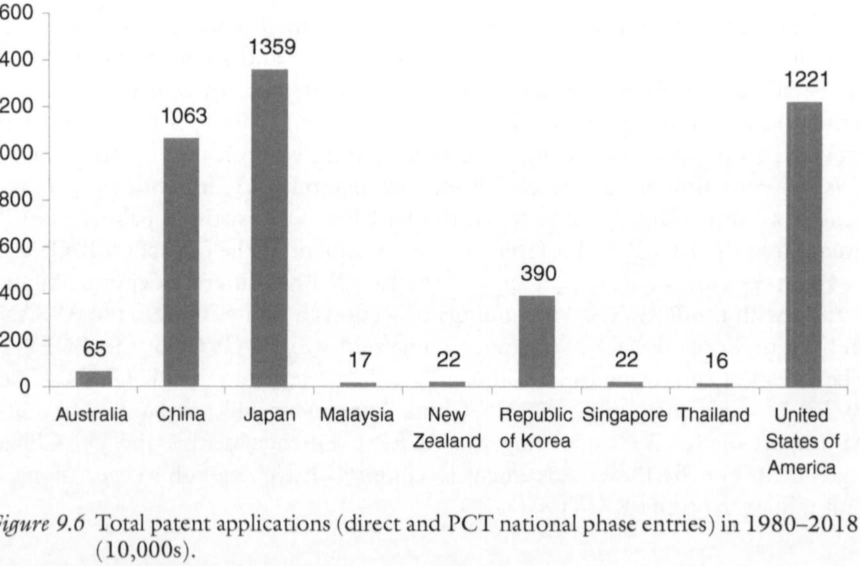

Figure 9.6 Total patent applications (direct and PCT national phase entries) in 1980–2018 (10,000s).

Source: WIPO 2019a.

Table 9.9 Global Innovation Index 2019 rankings

Country	*Overall rank in 2019*	*Income group*	*Rank in income group*
US	3	*Hi*	3
Singapore	8	*Hi*	8
Republic of Korea	11	*Hi*	11
China	14	*UM*	1
Japan	15	*Hi*	14
Australia	22	*Hi*	21
New Zealand	25	*Hi*	24
Malaysia	35	*UM*	2
Vietnam	42	*LM*	1
Thailand	43	*UM*	4

Source: WIPO 2019b.

Looking at the innovation performance of the economies, the US is the leader among the countries under consideration in this chapter, followed by Singapore and South Korea. China, which is the leader in its income group, is followed by Japan and Australia (Table 9.9). Ten of the 16 countries under consideration here are in the top 50 out of 130 countries (WIPO, 2019b).

China and the US have been locked into frictions over IPR for quite some time, within the WTO and bilaterally. The US initiated investigations under Section 301 of the US Trade Act of 1974 and the 337 Survey under the US Tariff Act to establish intellectual property barriers in China several times in the last few years. A majority of the companies implicated in these investigations are Chinese companies (Yang, 2018). Japan and the European Union (EU) too have drawn attention to China's 'high level of infringement, ineffective criminal prosecutions, local protectionism, institutional deficiencies, and non-transparent administration' in various meetings and forums at the WTO. In general China and other WTO members have 'clashed' repeatedly over 'procedural and substantive matters', and online piracy, IPR theft, 'technology transfer requirement of discriminatory nature', and a 'complicated and expensive IPR regime', as well as China's manner of handling these complaints at the WTO (Liu & Lu, 2019).

The latest investigation instituted by the USTR under Section 301 of the US Trade Act was conducted in 2017–18, and the report was published in March 2018 and updated in November 2018. The report details IP infringements by China, including 'Cyber-Enabled Theft of Intellectual Property and Sensitive Commercial Information.'

Set against this background, the US–China Agreement of January 2020 aims to address many of these specific complaints on IPR which the US had against China. While the US has undertaken a few commitments beyond its current sets of regulations, policies, and practices (such as investigating additional means of combating the sale of counterfeit and pirated goods, cooperating with China in the global fight to end the manufacture of counterfeit products), most of the provisions of the agreement are already compliant with existing US regulations.

Therefore the 'burden' of implementation of IPR provisions of the agreement is mostly on China (Greenberg Traurig, 2020).

Table 9.10 looks at IPR provisions in the FTAs of RCEP-I and compares these with the provisions on IPR in the US–China Agreement of January 2020. Four FTAs have no IPR chapter, provisions in the China-New Zealand FTA are relatively basic, and most other FTAs affirm the Agreement on Trade-Related Intellectual Property Rights (TRIPS) of the WTO. The Japan-Australia FTA has the most comprehensive IPR chapter among the RCEP-I FTAs. Compared to these, IPR provisions in the US–China Agreement of January 2020 go further with a few TRIPS-plus provisions and with significant stress on enforcement measures.

Table 9.10 does not include a comparison of provisions of the RCEP agreement as its provisions were not known at the time of writing this analysis. However given the earlier findings that the RCEP agreement is moderate in terms of comprehensiveness within RCEP-I FTAs and especially given that none of the other FTAs that included China has provisions that go as far as the US–China Agreement, it can be concluded the IPR chapter of the RCEP too does not go as far as the US–China Agreement.

China has been playing a leading role in intellectual property creation and innovativeness in recent years. Any change brought in China's intellectual property environment is likely to also have a significant effect on the other countries under consideration. China's commitment to the substantial provisions in the US–China Agreement could be an opportunity for the RCEP members to upgrade the IPR provisions in the RCEP agreement. This depends on whether the RCEP

Table 9.10 IPR provisions in different FTAs of RCEP-I and US–China Agreement

No IPR Chapter	*IPR Chapter with Basic Provisions*	*Affirmation to the TRIPS Agreement*	*Relative more comprehensive than IPR chapters in the other RCEP minus I agreements*	*Further ahead*
ACFTA, AKFTA, AJCEP, ANZCER	China–New Zealand	AANZFTA, China–Australia, Korea-Australia, Korea–New Zealand, China-Korea	Japan-Australia- it reaffirms to TRIPS; Had additional provisions such as Copyright infringement by users of online services	US–China Economic & Trade Agreement; contains TRIPS plus provisions such as patent term extension;* mostly measures are for strengthening enforcement

Sources: Author's compilation; * WTO 2006.

agreement includes provisions for an upgrade of its chapters as well as negotiating power and influence of the other RCEP-I countries vis-à-vis China. Further, given the RCEP-I contains several lower-middle-income economies as members, caution needs to be adopted while considering any measures to strengthen or make IPR stricter than they are in these countries.

Rather, it is likely the RCEP agreement would have a less stringent IPR chapter than other comprehensive FTAs of the region, notably the CPTPP, given the presence of the LDC AMS in the RCEP.[7]

8 The impact of unexpected events

COVID-19 pandemic has shown the possible worldwide impact that an unexpected and unprecedented event can bring about within a very short time. As per the forecast made by the WTO on 8 April, global trade may shrink between 13% and 32% in 2020 and that 'trade is likely to fall more steeply in sectors characterised by complex value chain linkages, particularly in electronics and automotive products' (WTO, 2020). COVID-19 seems to have hit trade negotiations and discussions hard as well.[8]

Further, COVID-19 made linkages between US–China Agreement and the RCEP more complicated in the following manner.

- Since the RCEP agreement, like other FTAs, would create losers (as well as winners), for many of the RCEP-I, it would be difficult to sign and implement an agreement when their economies have been hard hit.[9] Further, the priority of most countries is managing the pandemic for the moment and is likely to remain so for the next few months.
- In a similar vein, the US and China may find it difficult to implement their commitments under the US–China Agreement. Article 7.6(2) of the US–China Agreement says the following 'In the event that a natural disaster or other unforeseeable event outside the control of the Parties delays a Party from timely complying with its obligations under this Agreement, the Parties shall consult with each other.' The US–China Agreement, therefore, has incorporated the impact of possible unforeseeable events. Given this particular fact, it is not clear whether China or even the US would implement their commitments under the agreement any time soon. The two countries have not resumed their talks on the second phase of the agreement yet. There may even be an escalation of tensions between the two countries following the US allegations of China's handling of the crisis in the initial stages.[10]
- The RCEP and US–China agreements, by offering secure markets, in fact, may contribute to the recovery of exports and domestic economies of the countries involved. In particular, the Chinese import of an additional US$200 billion of goods from the US may help the US economy, which, like other economies, has been hard-hit. The RCEP countries may also benefit by locking in their in-principle agreement, which they had reached in November 2019. Signals from some of the RCEP-I indicated that they may

push forward with the signing of the RCEP as scheduled as they resolved to keep their markets open for trade and maintain supply chains.[11]

- R-GVCs have demonstrated a certain degree of resilience in the face of the current collapse of both supply and demand. There are signs that adjustments are being made in supply chains, and in many cases, agriculture, food, and other essential industries have seen an increase in demand (Lee, 2020). For now, it appears the domestic economy in China is on the rebound, and China is looking more inwards than to the external environment for its economic recovery (Kung & Hongxu, 2020). In this sense, China is ahead of major economies of the world (including the US and other RCEP-I) which are experiencing increasing shutdown of their economies.
- COVID-19 may bring about changes in the innovation environment as well – perhaps to start with on health-related innovation and its spillover in other areas. There are also developments that suggest innovations of various kinds are being used to tackle the impact of the pandemic, in particular, to identify low-cost and easy-to-produce innovative solutions in developing countries.[12] Such developments may have a significant impact on the RCEP-I as it includes both countries which are leaders in innovation and countries that require low-cost, easy-to-produce innovations.

Apart from direct fallout of COVID-19, there may be other events – which could not be fully predicted – exerting influence on both the US–China Agreement and signing and implementation of the RCEP. Most notably, political economy such as the outcome of the US elections or the willingness of the RCEP-I to sign and implement the RCEP agreement in the current situation (such as Japan's unwillingness to sign an agreement without India as a party to it, and ongoing dispute between China and Australia over COVID-19) will be determining factors for the fate of the two agreements.[13]

9 Conclusions and recommendations

The RCEP-I are linked with the US through various channels, though it appears the importance of the US has fallen vis-à-vis China over the years in terms of exports, imports, foreign direct investment flows, and intellectual property creation. In terms of certain indicators of GVCs too, it appears the US, except with the ASEAN and South Korea, is relatively less connected with the RCEP-I. China has increased its influence on the RCEP-I in the last two to three decades in terms of all the indicators under consideration. In comparison, China does not appear to be highly integrated with R-GVCs of the RCEP- I on the indicators presented in this analysis.

The RCEP agreement lies somewhere in the middle among the FTAs of the RCEP-I in terms of comprehensiveness. This probably means it will have less impact on R-GVCs and IPR than the more comprehensive FTAs, notably the CPTPP. This may also imply that the utilisation of the RCEP by businesses will not be too high. Further, the 'noodle bowl' situation in the RCEP-I may hurt the effectiveness of the RCEP.

The US–China Agreement may create trade diversion, but there could be trade creation effects on the RCEP-I as well. The US–China Agreement may have a differential impact on the individual RCEP-I countries through various modes and routes. Though its impact on R-GVCs may not be significant given the relatively weaker links of the US and China in the R-GVCs involving the other RCEP-I countries, it may in fact, have a positive impact on the IPR and innovation environment of the RCEP-I.

A detailed analysis of trade in value-added at product levels and comparing these with provisions of corresponding FTAs may help to determine the extent and the ways in the US–China Agreement may impact R-GVCs of the RCEP-I. For the RCEP agreement to have a positive impact on R-GVCs, the agreement should take into account differences between the RCEP-I in their integration in regional value chains. One way to do this is to analyse R-GVCs of the RCEP-I at product levels. Efforts to harmonise different rules of origin in different FTAs would also be helpful.

It is unlikely the RCEP countries will bind China's commitments in the US–China Agreement in the RCEP agreement for various reasons.

Lastly, the impact of COVID-19 pandemic on these two agreements is uncertain, but for sure, it is likely to make the linkages more complicated. The RCEP-I countries could consider including suitable provisions in the RCEP agreement to protect their economies from impacts of unexpected and rapid changes such as due to COVID-19 (or even the US–China trade war, if it resumes).

Currently, there are signs that the countries would honour/move forward with their commitments on trade agreements, and supply chains are more resilient than previously anticipated. This situation provides a unique opportunity for the RCEP countries to lead the way in balancing the economic situation and interests of its disparate group of negotiating parties. The US–China Agreement, too, may contribute to revival and recovery of the hard-hit economies of the RCEP and the US. It remains to be seen though whether the countries will rise up to the challenge and undertake coordinated measures for revival and recovery of their economies – many of which could be taken within the frameworks of the trade agreements. For now, it is clear the countries are implementing measures independently, leaving the fates of the two agreements, and several other commitments and initiatives at the international level, hanging.

Notes

1 E.g. see Wang (2019).
2 E.g. see Wong, Cyril, & Zhang (2020).
3 Based on the author's group discussion with trade experts.
4 From the author's group discussion with trade experts.
5 The third mega-regional trade agreement – currently under negotiation – is the Trans-Atlantic Trade and Investment Partnership (TTIP); see Bown (2017).
6 E.g. see DFAT, n.d. b.
7 Based on the author's conversation with trade experts.

8 E.g. see Delaney (2020) and Date (2020).
9 E.g. see Tachikawa (2020).
10 E.g. see Wang (2020).
11 On 14 April 2020 the ASEAN held two special summits on COVID-19 with ASEAN heads of states and ASEAN plus three (China, Japan, and South Korea) heads of states. The leaders of the countries affirmed they will keep trade channels open and make efforts to maintain connectivity and supply chains, see https://asean.org/category/asean-statement-communiques/; Aravindan (2020).
12 E.g. see Beach (2020), Handforth (2020).
13 E.g. see Tachikawa (2020); Smyth (2020).

References

Aravindan, A. (2020). Singapore minister says RCEP trade deal on track for year-end signing. 3 May. Retrieved from https://in.reuters.com/article/singapore-trade-rcep/singapore-minister-says-rcep-trade-deal-on-track-for-year-end-signing-idINKBN22F09T

Association of South East Asian Nations (2019). Joint leaders' statement on the Regional Comprehensive Economic Partnership. 4 November. https://asean.org/joint-leaders-statement-regional-comprehensive-economic-partnership-rcep/

Association of South East Asian Nations. (n.d.). Free trade agreements with dialogue partners. https://asean.org/asean-economic-community/free-trade-agreements-with-dialogue-partners/

Beach, P. (2020). These new gadgets were designed to fight COVID-19. World Economic Forum, 5 April. www.weforum.org/agenda/2020/04/coronavirus-covid19-pandemic-gadgets-innovation-technology/

Bhagwati, J., & Panagariya, A. (1996). The theory of preferential trade agreements: Historical evolution and current trends. *American Economic Review*, *86*(2), 82–87.

Bown, C. P. (2017). Mega-regional trade agreements and the future of the WTO. *Global Policy*, *8*(1). Retrieved from https://doi.org/10.1111/1758-5899.12391

Chatterjee, S. (2014). Regional comprehensive economic partnership: Implication for India's rules of origin. *Economic and Political Weekly*, *49* (45), 27–29.

Date, S. V. (2020). China demand for 'other unforeseeable event' out in trade deal was possible red flag. 15 April. www.huffpost.com/entry/trump-china-red-flag_n_5e976c52c5b65eae709e736a

Delaney, R. (2020). Economic havoc wreaked by Coronavirus has likely throttled US-China trade deal, experts say. South China Morning Post, 15 April. www.scmp.com/news/china/politics/article/3079925/economic-havoc-wreaked-coronavirus-likely-has-throttled-us

Department for Foreign Affairs and Trade, Australian Government (n.d.). RCEP news. www.dfat.gov.au/trade/agreements/negotiations/rcep/news/Pages/rcep-news

Department for Foreign Affairs and Trade, Australian Government (n.d.). Australia-New Zealand closer economic relations trade agreement. www.dfat.gov.au/trade/agreements/in-force/anzcerta/Pages/australia-new-zealand-closer-economic-relations-trade-agreement

ECORYS (2018). *Study on the Use of Trade Agreements: Final Report.* 22 June. Rotterdam: Ministry of Foreign Affairs,

Government of Canada (2020). Comprehensive and progressive agreement for Trans-Pacific Partnership. 21 February. www.international.gc.ca/trade-commerce/trade-agreements-accords-commerciaux/agr-acc/cptpp-ptpgp/index.aspx?lang=eng

Greenberg Traurig (2020). Impact of the China-U.S. trade deal on intellectual property protection. GT Alert, 21 January. www.gtlaw.com/en/insights/2020/1/impact-of-the-china-us-trade-deal-on-intellectual-property-protection

Handforth, C. (2020). *Bringing the Power of Global Innovation to Tackle COVID-19.* New York: United Nations Development Programme. www.undp.org/content/undp/en/home/blog/2020/bringing-the-power-of-global-innovation-to-tackle-covid-19.html

International Trade Administration, Department of Commerce, US (n.d.). Free Trade Agreements. www.trade.gov/free-trade-agreements

Kung, C., & Hongxu. W. (2020). Would Covid 19 halt China's going out economic strategy? https://thediplomat.com/2020/03/will-covid-19-halt-chinas-goi

Laget, E., Osnago, A., Rocha, N., & Ruta, M. (2018). Deep trade agreements and global value chains. Policy Research Working Paper, 8491. Washington, DC: World Bank Group, Macroeconomics, Trade and Investment Global Practice.

Lee, A. (2020). Coronavirus: global logistics show glimmer of recovery, but Chinese exporters still struggling with delays. *South China Morning Post*, 18 April. www.scmp.com/economy/global-economy/article/3080343/coronavirus-global-logistics-show-glimmer-recovery-chinese

Liu, H., & Lu, S. (2019). The future of China's trade pact and intellectual property rights. In K.-C. Liu & J. Chaisse (eds), *The Future of Asian Trade Deals and IP*, 61–84. London: Bloomsbury.

Mattoo, A., Mulabdic, A., & Ruta, M. (2019). *Trade Creation and Trade Diversion in Deep Agreements.* Washington, DC: World Bank. Retrieved from http://pubdocs.worldbank.org/en/328491559591517896/Trade-Creation-anf-Trade-Diversion.pdf

Nicita, A. (2019). *Trade and Trade Diversion Effects of United States Tariffs on China.* Geneva: UNCTAD, UNCTAD/SER.RP/2019/9.

Organisation of Economic Cooperation & Development (2013). *Trade Policy Implications of Global Value Chains.* Paris: OECD.

Ruta, M. (2017). Preferential trade agreements and global value chains: Theory, evidence, and open questions. gvcs_report_2017_chapter8_appendix.pdf

Smyth, J. (2020). Business feels the fear in Australia-China trade dispute. *Financial Times,* 5 May. Retrieved from www.ft.com/content/d3ebba4d-3a1a-4bc0-88a0-ff49945fe2f9

Tachikawa, T. (2020). Virus pandemic may force Japan to give up RCEP agreement in 2020. *Kyodo News*, 14 April. https://english.kyodonews.net/news/2020/04/9655ed670d0c-focus-virus-pandemic-may-force-japan-to-give-up-rcep-agreement-in-2020.html

United Nations (2019). *World Economic Situation and Prospects*, Statistical Annex. New York: United Nations.

United Nations Conference on Trade and Development (2014). *Bilateral FDI Statistics.* https://unctad.org/en/Pages/DIAE/FDI%20Statistics/FDI-Statistics-Bilateral.aspx

United Nations Conference on Trade and Development. (2019). *World Investment Report.* https://unctad.org/en/Pages/DIAE/World%20Investment%20Report/World_Investment_Report.aspx

United States Trade Representative (n.d. a). *Economic and Trade Agreement between the government of the United States of America and the Government of the People's Republic of China.* https://ustr.gov/countries-regions/china-mongolia-taiwan/peoples-republic-china/phase-one-trade-agreement

United States Trade Representative (n.d. b). *Section 301 China.* https://ustr.gov/issue-areas/enforcement/section-301-investigations/section-301-china

Wang, O. (2019). Trade war: China's trade ministry fails to mention phase one deal as a priority for 2020. South China Morning Post, 18 December. www.scmp.com/economy/china-economy/article/3042657/trade-war-chinas-trade-ministry-fails-mention-phase-one-deal

Wang, O. (2020). Coronavirus: Can China and the US uphold the phase one trade deal amid Covid-19? South China Morning Post, 5 May. www.scmp.com/economy/china-economy/article/3082998/coronavirus-can-china-and-us-uphold-phase-one-trade-deal-amid

Wong, D., Cyril, M., & Zhang, Z. (2020). US, China sign phase one trade deal: How to read the agreement. 2 March. www.china-briefing.com/news/us-china-phase-one-trade-deal-takeaways-businesses-global-trade/

World Intellectual Property Organisation (2019a). *Intellectual Property Statistics.* www3.wipo.int/ipstats/

World Intellectual Property Organisation (2019b). *Global Innovation Index 2019.* www.wipo.int/publications/en/details.jsp?id=4434

World Trade Organisation (2006). Pharmaceutical patents and the TRIPS agreement. www.wto.org/english/tratop_e/trips_e/pharma_ato186_e.htm

World Trade Organisation (2020). Frequently asked questions: The WTO and COVID-19. www.wto.org/english/tratop_e/covid19_e/faqcovid19_e.htm

Yang, Y. (2018). Analysis of China-US intellectual property trade friction. *Advances in Economics, Business and Management Research, 68*, International Symposium on Social Science and Management Innovation (SSMI 2018), Law School of Silk Road, Gansu Political Science and Law Institute, Gansu 730070, China.

Yi, J. (2015). Rules of origin and the use of free trade agreements: A literature review. *World Customs Journal*, 9(1), 43–58.

Source: Author's compilation from various websites of governments and the ASEAN.

10 US–China trade war

Impact on potential trade of their FTA partners

Swati Singh and Sachin Sisodiya

1 Introduction

The idea of trade war between the United States (US) and China did not start with Donald Trump but at the time of Obama administration. It began with a vision of creating higher economic growth, support for American jobs, and to strengthen the middle class. During second tenure of the Obama administration there were anxieties about globalisation and trade, and his team were in favour of an anti-trade liberalisation platform. The Obama administration agenda focused on removing foreign barriers to the US exports, levelling the playing field by raising global standards, and enforcing US trade rights, aiming to support American jobs and to have balanced trade with the world.

The United States was concerned about its growing trade deficit, and it identified China as a prime reason. Some of the major problems of the US with China were China's diverse record on executing its World Trade Organisation (WTO) obligations; contravention of the US intellectual property rights (such as through cyber-theft of the US trade secrets and forced technology requirements placed on foreign firms). China used its industrial policies to promote and protect Chinese firms, giving unfair treatment to foreign firms while practising lack of transparency in trade rules and regulations (USTR, 2018). The US believes all these factors led to its huge trade deficit with China. Therefore, the US took remedial measures and imposed higher tariffs on Chinese import to reduce its trade deficit. The retaliatory measures adopted by China took the shape of the ongoing trade war.

The trade war has affected a large number of countries who are in the global production and supply chain connecting these two superpowers (Huang & Jeremy, 2019; Witada & Lobo, 2019). One such network is created through trade agreements. So far, both China and the US have signed trade agreements with many of their trading partners. It is interesting to see how these trading partners have been affected by the trade tussle. After digging into the existing literature, and reviews available on US–China trade war, we found that there is hardly any study exploring the impact of trade war on their free trade agreement (FTA) partners. Therefore, this chapter aims to explore the impact of the US–China trade war on its FTA partners. In addition, it seeks to understand whether the trade war has benefited the FTA partners or affected them adversely. The sectors selected for the study are automobiles, electrical machinery, and iron and steel. The selection of these sectors is primarily because major actions were taken by both US and China against these sectors under the trade war.

The study considers two time periods. The period between 2013 to 2017 is the pre-tariff escalation period and 2018 is the period of post-tariff escalation. The study kept 2013 as the reference point to understand the trade patterns in selected sectors at the time of Obama administration. The study used a simple gravity model to assess the potential gains/losses to their FTA partners. The potential gains/losses suggest some important policy implications in future relations between the US and China with their FTA partners at the time of a trade war.

2 Research methodology and data sources

The empirical analysis concerns bilateral trade between China and the USA's FTA partners.[1] The data on exports are taken from WITS (UN COMTRADE). The data on partners' GDP have been taken from World Bank publication, *World Development Indicators*, for 2012, 2014, and 2016. The CEPII Database provided the statistics for the distance variable.

The study focused on three sectors, i.e. iron and iron products, electrical machinery, and automobiles. It covers HS chapter levels 72, 73, 84, 85, and 87 for the analysis. We take the year as the panel identifier. For the sectoral analysis, chapter 87 represents automobiles and we combine chapters 72 and 73 to represent iron and iron products, and chapters 84 and 85 for the electrical machinery sector.

3 Data analysis and interpretations

The data suggest that the US exports to the world are higher than China exports to the world in the automobile sector but the electrical machinery and iron and steel sectors are dominated by China having more exports to the world. During 2018, the USA exported US$121 billion worth of automobiles to the world while the figure was US$75 billion for China. During the same time China exported electric machinery worth US$1094 billion and the USA exported only US$251 billion to the world. In case of iron and steel the figures were US$33 and 112 billion for the USA and China respectively (see Table 10.1). The data further reveal that the electrical machinery imports of China and the US are equally high. China imports a lot of sub-parts of electrical machinery and finishes them in its assemblies and sends them back to the world.

Since 2018, in post-tariff escalation, the US imports from the world have increased in all three sectors. The exports marginally declined for automobiles but increased for the other two sectors. On the other hand, China's exports and imports of all three sectors have shown a rising trend in trade values with the

Table 10.1 USA's and China's trade with the world (2013–18) in US$ billion

Year	*USA-World*	*China-World*	*USA-World*	*China-World*
	Exports		*Imports*	
Automobiles (87)				
2013	123.02	58.55	249.02	74.06
2014	125.4	64.19	265.32	89.4
2015	118.17	62.6	284.38	69.54
2016	115.69	60.15	284.71	71.51
2017	121.09	67.26	294.28	79.14
2018	120.91	75.09	306.53	81.49
Electrical Machinery (84 and 85)				
2013	269.52	943.46	599.84	478.45
2014	275.79	970.58	645.22	480.84
2015	259.84	957.41	660.01	462.68
2016	236.96	895.64	647.71	552.92
2017	243.11	981.03	700.79	511.16
2018	250.84	1094.38	748.71	723.86
Iron and Steel with Articles (72 and 73)				
2013	38.91	95.97	59.65	30.94
2014	38.06	116.12	75.71	32.15
2015	31.4	109.72	66.59	27.52
2016	27.8	95.14	56.07	26.49
2017	31.48	99.71	67.94	30.81
2018	32.62	112.48	74.35	33.14

Source: ITC Trade Map extracted in 2019.

world. Therefore, many studies show that China has not curtailed the demand and supply from the world in the post-tariff escalation period.

It is equally important to understand the bilateral trend of exports and imports of the US and China in all three sectors. Tables 10.2 and 10.3 depict the dependency of exports and imports on each other in all three sectors. The rise in tariffs would have an impact on the trade values of China and the US. US imports from China are more dependent on electrical machinery, followed by automobiles and iron and steel. If data are compared between 2013 and 2018 then, even after tariff escalation, there is a 2% hike in imports from China in the automobile sector. But the US has curtailed its imports from China in electrical machinery and the iron and steel sector.

Table 10.3 shows that China's imports in the automobile sector declined in 2018 but trade increased for electrical machinery and iron and steel from the US. The share of each sector is very low for China as compared with the US. A large body of literature also suggested there would be more impact of tariff escalation on the US than China (Robinson and Thierfelder, 2019; Stewart 2020). It is clear from the share of trade exposure of each country and trade dependency of each country in the three sectors. In this case, too, the impact of tariff escalation is high for the US in all three sectors.

Table 10.2 USA imports from China in three selected sectors (2013–18) in US$ billion

	USA imports from China			*China's exports to world*			*Share in %*		
Years	*Automobile*	*Electrical Machinery*	*Iron and Steel*	*Automobile*	*Electrical Machinery*	*Iron and Steel*	*Automobile*	*Electrical Machinery*	*Iron and Steel*
2013	10.48	223.26	11.33	58.5	944.4	96.0	18%	24%	12%
2014	12.19	237.97	13.35	64.2	971.8	116.1	19%	24%	11%
2015	13.89	242.99	13.36	62.7	964.8	109.9	22%	25%	12%
2016	14.32	231.74	12.03	60.4	901.9	96.5	24%	26%	12%
2017	15.54	262.22	13.16	67.4	981.9	100.4	23%	27%	13%
2018	18.73	275.52	14.88	75.1	1094.4	112.5	25%	25%	13%

Source: ITC Trade Map extracted in 2019.

Table 10.3 China imports from USA in three selected sectors (2013–18) in US$ billion

China imports from USA				*USA exports to world*			*Share in %*		
Years	*Automobile*	*Electrical Machinery*	*Iron and Steel*	*Automobile*	*Electrical Machinery*	*Iron and Steel*	*Automobile*	*Electrical Machinery*	*Iron and Steel*
2013	10.76	38.40	1.88	134.08	379.3	41.7	8%	10%	4%
2014	14.18	38.32	1.66	135.97	392.1	41.2	10%	10%	4%
2015	13.20	35.66	1.48	127.39	376.2	34.2	10%	9%	4%
2016	13.98	30.44	1.27	124.70	357.9	30.4	11%	9%	4%
2017	15.09	33.91	1.54	130.39	376.4	34.5	12%	9%	4%
2018	12.63	38.02	1.67	130.73	389.7	35.8	10%	10%	5%

Source: ITC Trade Map extracted in 2019.

After understanding the bilateral trade pattern of the US and China, let us understand how the trade of these three sectors might move towards their FTA partners. Here we follow Jacob Viner's theory of trade creation in the case of FTA partners (Viner, 1951). Data collected from the USTR and China FTA Network show that in 2019 the US had 20 FTA partners and China had 14 FTA partners.

Tables 10.4–10.9 show the US and China's exports, imports, and trade balance of selected sectors to its FTA partners. These tables indicate pre-tariff and post-tariff escalation changes in the US and China with its FTA partners in all selected sectors. The discussion of trade balance has an important connotation with FTAs, as measuring the success of the agreements of these selected sectors shows the substitution effect of Chinese goods in the US and vice versa.

The maximum exports and imports of the auto sector of the US to its FTA partners are with Canada and Mexico. This represents the United States-Mexico-Canada Agreement (USMCA) deal in which the US auto sector is largely reliant on the Mexico's exports to the US. In fact, the USMCA negotiations focused mainly on auto exports and steel and aluminium tariffs in the agreement. In the post-tariff escalation and under the Trump administration, it is quite evident that the trade balance of the US with Mexico has increased. The US has substituted its Chinese auto imports in the post-tariff period with ones from Mexico. The trade balance of the US is very large with Mexico in auto sectors and the trade balance of the US improved with Canada from 2016 to 2018.

Reliance on Asian exports to the US has declined since 2016. After Canada and Mexico, the US is reliant on South Korea and Chinese imports in the auto sector. But it is apparent from data that with the Trump administration, the trade balance of the US has improved with South Korea (see Table 10.4). Although the Trump administration has imposed tariffs on auto sectors after 2017, still the trade balance of the US has not improved with China in 2018, which means reliance on China's imports is still visible in the US imports in the auto sector. The US has a trade surplus with all its FTA partners in the auto sector except Canada, Mexico, and South Korea. Largely in the post-tariff period, the US trade balance has improved marginally with major FTA partners and this indicates the US inclination of trade direction towards its FTA partners. The US is also revisiting its signed negotiations, especially with North America Free Trade Agreement (NAFTA), now new negotiations as 'USMCA', and the US–South Korea FTA (KORUS).

Table 10.5 shows the US negative trade balance in electrical machinery with Mexico, South Korea, Israel, Honduras, and Nicaragua. The US electrical machinery sector is largely reliant on China's imports and US has huge dependency even after the post-tariff escalation period. Otherwise, the US has a positive trade balance with Canada and all other FTA partners. US imports of electrical machinery have increased in the post-escalation period from Mexico, Canada, South Korea, and Singapore.

The main sector of iron and steel presents variation in US trade balance with its FTA partners. Table 10.6 indicates that the US is reliant on many FTA partners in this sector. The US has a negative trade balance with many FTA partners

Table 10.4 United States' exports, imports, and trade balance of automobile sector to FTA partners (2013–18) in US$ billion

FTA Partners/ Year	*US Exports*						*US Imports*						*US Trade Balance*					
	Automobile						*Automobile*						*Automobile*					
	2013	*2014*	*2015*	*2016*	*2017*	*2018*	*2013*	*2014*	*2015*	*2016*	*2017*	*2018*	*2013*	*2014*	*2015*	*2016*	*2017*	*2018*
Australia	3.35	3.54	3.25	2.59	3.12	3.37	0.3	0.35	0.33	0.31	0.31	0.18	3.05	3.19	2.92	2.28	2.81	3.19
Bahrain	0.25	0.26	0.25	0.18	0.11	0.13	0	0	0	0	0	0	0.25	0.26	0.25	0.18	0.11	0.13
Canada	***48.29***	***48.1***	***44.85***	***45.5***	***48.83***	***48.93***	***55.7***	***56.25***	***55.85***	***58.26***	***56.18***	***53.55***	***-7.41***	***-8.15***	***-11***	***-12.76***	***-7.35***	***-4.62***
Chile	1.4	1.08	0.87	0.64	0.86	1.05	0.02	0.02	0.02	0.01	0.01	0.02	1.38	1.06	0.85	0.63	0.85	1.03
Colombia	0.72	0.58	0.39	0.29	0.37	0.47	0.01	0.02	0.02	0.02	0.02	0.02	0.71	0.56	0.37	0.27	0.35	0.45
Costa Rica	0.12	0.14	0.17	0.16	0.17	0.15	0.04	0.03	0.03	0.03	0.03	0.03	0.08	0.11	0.14	0.13	0.14	0.12
Dominican Republic	0.32	0.35	0.42	0.48	0.47	0.54	0.01	0.01	0.01	0.02	0.02	0.02	0.31	0.34	0.41	0.46	0.45	0.52
El Salvador	0.07	0.06	0.07	0.08	0.07	0.07	0	0	0	0	0	0	0.07	0.06	0.07	0.08	0.07	0.07
Guatemala	0.17	0.18	0.22	0.23	0.25	0.25	0	0	0	0	0	0	0.17	0.18	0.22	0.23	0.25	0.25
Honduras	0.09	0.08	0.09	0.11	0.13	0.13	0.06	0.05	0.06	0.07	0.07	0.08	0.03	0.03	0.03	0.04	0.06	0.05
Israel	0.33	0.41	0.44	0.45	0.38	0.35	0.07	0.04	0.07	0.08	0.11	0.07	0.26	0.37	0.37	0.37	0.27	0.28
Jordan	0.59	0.39	0.33	0.32	0.45	0.52	0	0	0.001	0.001	0.001	0.004	0.59	0.39	0.329	0.319	0.449	0.516
Rep. of Korea	***1.19***	***1.49***	***1.76***	***2.1***	***2.03***	***2.16***	***16.62***	***19.93***	***22.81***	***21.52***	***20.57***	***18.9***	***-15.43***	***-18.44***	***-21.05***	***-19.42***	***-18.54***	***-16.74***
Mexico	***18.62***	***18.37***	***19.79***	***18.89***	***18.35***	***19.05***	***59.6***	***68.27***	***75.12***	***75.15***	***84.02***	***93.77***	***-40.98***	***-49.9***	***-55.33***	***-56.26***	***-65.67***	***-74.72***
Morocco	0.06	0.04	0.08	0.09	0.05	0.09	0	0.004	0.001	0.002	0.002	0.002	0.06	0.036	0.079	0.088	0.048	0.088
Nicaragua	0.04	0.04	0.05	0.05	0.04	0.03	0	0	0	0	0.001	0.001	0.04	0.04	0.05	0.05	0.039	0.029
Oman	0.41	0.37	0.39	0.42	0.28	0.31	0.007	0.006	0.003	0	0	0.001	0.403	0.364	0.387	0.42	0.28	0.309
Panama	0.27	0.23	0.22	0.2	0.25	0.29	0.001	0	0	0	0	0	0.269	0.23	0.22	0.2	0.25	0.29
Peru	0.52	0.42	0.35	0.33	0.31	0.36	0.001	0.001	0.005	0.041	0.063	0.067	0.519	0.419	0.345	0.289	0.247	0.293
Singapore	0.26	0.24	0.18	0.16	0.18	0.28	0.04	0.04	0.04	0.05	0.04	0.04	0.22	0.2	0.14	0.11	0.14	0.24
China (Non-FTA partner)	***10.76***	***14.18***	***13.2***	***13.98***	***15.09***	***12.63***	***10.48***	***12.19***	***13.89***	***14.32***	***15.54***	***18.73***	***0.28***	***1.99***	***-0.69***	***-0.34***	***-0.45***	***-6.1***

Source: WITS database.

Note: Rows with italic font show trade balance deficit with US FTA partners.

*China is not an FTA partner but for comparison it has been included.

Table 10.5 United States' exports, imports and trade balance of electrical machinery sector to FTA partners (2013–18) in US$ billion

FTA Partners/ Year	*US Exports*						*US Imports*						*US Trade Balance*					
	Electrical Machinery						*Electrical Machinery*						*Electrical Machinery*					
	2013	*2014*	*2015*	*2016*	*2017*	*2018*	*2013*	*2014*	*2015*	*2016*	*2017*	*2018*	*2013*	*2014*	*2015*	*2016*	*2017*	*2018*
Australia	6.81	6.3	5.76	4.63	5.23	5.54	0.72	0.72	0.71	0.66	0.72	0.75	6.09	5.58	5.05	3.97	4.51	4.79
Bahrain	0.21	0.17	0.26	0.14	0.23	0.31	0.006	0.008	0.005	0.001	0.002	0.003	0.204	0.162	0.255	0.139	0.228	0.307
Canada	49.19	50.26	45.75	42.45	44.63	46.85	27.79	29.19	27.7	26.72	29.08	31.46	21.4	21.07	18.05	15.73	15.55	15.39
Chile	2.77	2.2	2.3	1.82	1.83	1.94	0.11	0.13	0.08	0.06	0.08	0.09	2.66	2.07	2.22	1.76	1.75	1.85
Colombia	2.89	2.88	2.11	1.46	1.6	1.8	0.08	0.11	0.1	0.12	0.11	0.12	2.81	2.77	2.01	1.34	1.49	1.68
Costa Rica	*1.68*	*1.17*	*0.84*	*0.92*	*0.88*	*0.82*	*8.15*	*5.85*	*0.7*	*0.39*	*0.3*	*0.34*	*-6.47*	*-4.68*	*0.14*	*0.53*	*0.58*	*0.48*
Dominican Republic	0.93	0.92	0.93	1.11	1.02	1.13	0.5	0.5	0.52	0.52	0.54	0.81	0.43	0.42	0.41	0.59	0.48	0.32
El Salvador	0.28	0.26	0.29	0.26	0.24	0.25	0.03	0.06	0.06	0.07	0.07	0.09	0.25	0.2	0.23	0.19	0.17	0.16
Guatemala	0.62	0.57	0.57	0.51	0.47	0.44	0.01	0.01	0.02	0.01	0.01	0.01	0.61	0.56	0.55	0.5	0.46	0.43
Honduras	*0.52*	*0.56*	*0.54*	*0.49*	*0.52*	*0.5*	*0.62*	*0.58*	*0.63*	*0.59*	*0.57*	*0.6*	*-0.1*	*-0.02*	*-0.09*	*-0.1*	*-0.05*	*-0.1*
Israel	*2.35*	*2.49*	*2.7*	*2.4*	*1.69*	*1.87*	*2.78*	*2.98*	*3.81*	*3.47*	*3.1*	*2.8*	*-0.43*	*-0.49*	*-1.11*	*-1.07*	*-1.41*	*-0.93*
Jordan	0.19	0.21	0.2	0.12	0.12	0.15	0.004	0.009	0.018	0.029	0.028	0.048	0.186	0.201	0.182	0.091	0.092	0.102
Rep. of Korea	*10.19*	*10.06*	*9.94*	*8.32*	*8.6*	*8.78*	*25.28*	*27.12*	*26.78*	*26.33*	*27.81*	*29.67*	*-15.09*	*-17.06*	*-16.84*	*-18.01*	*-19.21*	*-20.89*
Mexico	*43.07*	*47.2*	*46.94*	*43.72*	*43.65*	*44.87*	*100.03*	*103.53*	*112.58*	*112.65*	*115.64*	*127.52*	*-56.96*	*-56.33*	*-65.64*	*-68.93*	*-71.99*	*-82.65*
Morocco	0.18	0.17	0.11	0.14	0.14	0.19	0.12	0.14	0.16	0.15	0.14	0.16	0.06	0.03	-0.05	-0.01	0	0.03
Nicaragua	*0.2*	*0.17*	*0.2*	*0.25*	*0.19*	*0.13*	*0.48*	*0.48*	*0.52*	*0.58*	*0.53*	*0.51*	*-0.28*	*-0.31*	*-0.32*	*-0.33*	*-0.34*	*-0.38*
Oman	0.48	0.46	0.52	0.34	0.38	0.45	0.001	0.002	0.002	0.005	0.008	0.01	0.479	0.458	0.518	0.335	0.372	0.44
Panama	0.98	0.87	0.99	0.68	0.68	0.8	0.02	0.01	0.02	0.02	0.03	0.03	0.96	0.86	0.97	0.66	0.65	0.77
Peru	1.94	1.82	1.65	1.25	1.12	1.2	0.03	0.03	0.03	0.03	0.02	0.03	1.91	1.79	1.62	1.22	1.1	1.17
Singapore	7.12	7.09	6.29	5.74	6.75	6.77	5.7	4.82	5.69	5.82	6.09	6.95	1.42	2.27	0.6	-0.08	0.66	-0.18
China (Non-FTA partner)	*38.4*	*38.32*	*35.66*	*30.44*	*33.91*	*38.02*	*223.26*	*237.97*	*242.99*	*231.74*	*262.22*	*275.52*	*-184.86*	*-199.65*	*-207.33*	*-201.3*	*-228.31*	*-237.5*

Source: WITS database.

Note: Rows with Italic font show trade balance deficit with US FTA partners.

Table 10.6 United States' exports, imports, and trade balance of iron and steel sector to FTA partners (2013–18) in US$ billion

FTA Partners/ Year	*US Exports*						*US Imports*						*US Trade Balance*					
	Iron and Steel						***Iron and Steel***						***Iron and Steel***					
	2013	*2014*	*2015*	*2016*	*2017*	*2018*	*2013*	*2014*	*2015*	*2016*	*2017*	*2018*	*2013*	*2014*	*2015*	*2016*	*2017*	*2018*
Australia	0.31	0.31	0.28	0.23	0.25	0.26	0.22	0.33	0.3	0.27	0.42	0.5	0.09	-0.02	-0.02	-0.04	-0.17	-0.24
Bahrain	0.01	0.01	0.01	0.01	0.01	0.01	0.002	0.005	0.002	0	0.041	0.011	0.008	0.005	0.008	0.01	-0.031	-0.001
Canada	12.65	12.58	9.76	8.82	9.9	9.77	8.95	9.99	8.46	7.71	9.24	10.34	3.7	2.59	1.3	1.11	0.66	-0.57
Chile	0.15	0.11	0.11	0.09	0.09	0.11	0.1	0.13	0.02	0.03	0.05	0.15	0.05	-0.02	0.09	0.06	0.04	-0.04
Colombia	0.33	0.25	0.16	0.08	0.09	0.11	0.1	0.2	0.09	0.06	0.1	0.12	0.23	0.05	0.07	0.02	-0.01	-0.01
Costa Rica	0.1	0.09	0.08	0.09	0.09	0.08	0.01	0.01	0.01	0.01	0.04	0.04	0.09	0.08	0.07	0.08	0.05	0.04
Dominican Republic	0.15	0.12	0.12	0.09	0.09	0.09	0.07	0.02	0.02	0.02	0.08	0.14	0.08	0.1	0.1	0.07	0.01	-0.05
El Salvador	0.01	0.01	0.01	0.01	0.01	0.01	0	0.001	0.002	0.001	0.002	0.003	0.01	0.009	0.008	0.009	0.008	0.007
Guatemala	0.06	0.04	0.03	0.03	0.03	0.02	0.01	0.02	0.02	0.02	0.09	0.08	0.05	0.02	0.01	0.01	-0.06	-0.06
Honduras	0.06	0.06	0.03	0.02	0.05	0.02	0.002	0.004	0.004	0.004	0.007	0.008	0.058	0.056	0.026	0.016	0.043	0.012
Israel	0.08	0.08	0.09	0.1	0.08	0.1	0.06	0.08	0.08	0.08	0.09	0.1	0.02	0	0.01	0.02	-0.01	0
Jordan	0.004	0.01	0.004	0.003	0.003	0.005	0	0	0.001	0.001	0.001	0.003	0.004	0.01	0.003	0.002	0.002	0.002
Rep. of Korea	1.46	1.18	0.83	0.6	0.54	0.67	3.98	5.81	5.03	3.61	4.01	3.76	-2.52	-4.63	-4.2	-3.01	-3.47	-3.09
Mexico	8.16	9.04	8.47	7.84	8.64	9.02	5.56	6.7	5.76	5.46	6.29	7.52	2.6	2.34	2.71	2.38	2.35	1.5
Morocco	0.05	0.02	0.02	0.005	0.01	0.01	0	0	0	0	0.016	0.021	0.05	0.02	0.02	0.005	-0.006	-0.011
Nicaragua	0.02	0.01	0.02	0.01	0.01	0.01	0	0	0	0	0	0	0.02	0.01	0.02	0.01	0.01	0.01
Oman	0.04	0.03	0.03	0.02	0.02	0.03	0.09	0.14	0.11	0.07	0.1	0.15	-0.05	-0.11	-0.08	-0.05	-0.08	-0.12
Panama	0.39	0.19	0.05	0.08	0.12	0.08	0.002	0.002	0.003	0.001	0.001	0.002	0.388	0.188	0.047	0.079	0.119	0.078
Peru	0.3	0.32	0.23	0.16	0.22	0.2	0.01	0.03	0.01	0.01	0.03	0.02	0.29	0.29	0.22	0.15	0.19	0.18
Singapore	0.38	0.37	0.29	0.22	0.23	0.26	0.03	0.05	0.04	0.04	0.03	0.03	0.35	0.32	0.25	0.18	0.2	0.23
China (Non-FTA partner)	1.88	1.66	1.48	1.27	1.54	1.67	11.33	13.35	13.36	12.03	13.16	14.88	-9.45	-11.69	-11.88	-10.76	-11.62	-13.21

Source: WITS database.

Note: Rows with Italic font show trade balance deficit with US FTA partners.

but the highest is with South Korea. In 2018, US imports of iron and steel from South Korea declined marginally. There are two countries,as the Dominican Republic and Guatemala, with whom the US trade balance became negative in the Trump administration even though the figures are very low.

Table 10.7 shows China's trade balance with its 14 FTA partners. Unlike the US, China has negative trade balance with South Korea and Switzerland. China has only two important FTA partners: ASEAN and South Korea. With ASEAN members, China has a positive trade balance. In the post-tariff period, imports of the auto sector of China have declined with all its FTA partners. This is an impact of tariff escalation on China. The analysis is at HS two-digit level, but the imports of tariff lines must have been affected due to the US–China trade war.

Table 10.8 analyses China's electrical machinery sector. China's trade balance is negative with ASEAN countries, South Korea, and Switzerland. It was negative with Costa Rica also but became positive in 2018. China's imports of electrical machinery are largely from ASEAN and South Korea. On the other hand, Hong Kong is the largest export market for China's electrical machinery followed by Singapore and Australia. In the post-tariff period the sudden rise of China's exports to Australia, ASEAN, and Hong Kong is significant, reflecting the inclination of China's dependency on its FTA partners than the US. From Table 10.9 it is evident that China has a negative trade balance with Switzerland but with rest of the partners it has maintained a surplus balance. It is noticed that, after the tariff escalation, China's exports to ASEAN nations, South Korea, and Australia have increased significantly.

4 Conclusion

The so-called 'trade war' between US and China has had huge impact globally. Putting restrictions and using protectionist policies not only restrain the production of the two countries but affect other countries as well. The economic restraints can affect many other dimensions of trade such as disruption to global value chains and product cycles. The changes in these dimensions have made FTA or trade integration even more important.

The study clearly shows the changes in the post-tariff period, the moves of China's trade in the direction of its FTA partners are greater in all selected sectors than those of the US to its FTA partners. It has been evident that the reliance of the US on China has not reduced in the post-tariff period, but China has reduced its dependency on the US marginally and diverted trade towards its FTA partners.

Another important observation is that the trade war has not benefited all the FTA partners of the two respective countries but that the closer countries with high GDPs felt the positive impact of the trade war. In the case of the US, automobile sectors exports in post-tariff period with FTA partners will increase substantially, as compared to the electrical machinery and iron and steel sectors. China's exports of automobiles, electrical machinery,and iron and steel have more significant results a few FTA partners. In the case of the US, Canada, Mexico, and South Korea are the countries who have benefited more as compared to other

Table 10.7 China's exports, imports, and trade balance of automobile sector to FTA partners (2013–18) in US$ billion

Year	*China Exports*						*China Imports*						*China Trade Balance*					
	Automobile						*Automobile*						*Automobile*					
	2013	*2014*	*2015*	*2016*	*2017*	*2018*	*2013*	*2014*	*2015*	*2016*	*2017*	*2018*	*2013*	*2014*	*2015*	*2016*	*2017*	*2018*
ASEAN	6.74	7.62	8.59	7.42	7.53	7.4	0.57	0.82	0.97	1.36	1.83	1.91	6.17	6.8	7.62	6.06	5.7	5.49
Australia	0.99	0.97	0.96	0.9	1	1.21	0.02	0.02	0.02	0.04	0.04	0.03	0.97	0.95	0.94	0.86	0.96	1.18
Chile	0.98	0.64	0.61	0.57	0.76	1.02	NA	NA	NA	NA	NA	NA	0.98	0.64	0.61	0.57	0.76	1.02
Costa Rica	0.09	0.09	0.12	0.13	0.1	0.1	NA	NA	NA	NA	NA	NA	0.09	0.09	0.12	0.13	0.1	0.1
Georgia	0.02	0.02	0.02	0.02	0.03	0.04	NA	NA	NA	NA	NA	NA	0.02	0.02	0.02	0.02	0.03	0.04
Hong Kong	0.67	0.72	0.94	0.84	0.71	0.69	0.004	0.004	0.003	0.003	0.006	0.002	0.666	0.716	0.937	0.837	0.704	0.688
Rep. of Korea	*1.49*	*1.43*	*1.47*	*1.52*	*1.57*	*1.67*	*5.2*	*5.71*	*5.03*	*4.46*	*2.85*	*2.33*	*-3.71*	*-4.28*	*-3.56*	*-2.94*	*-1.28*	*-0.66*
Macao	0.03	0.02	0.04	0.05	0.02	0.03	NA	NA	NA	NA	NA	NA	0.03	0.02	0.04	0.05	0.02	0.03
Maldives	0.002	0.006	0.004	0.009	0.009	0.016	NA	NA	NA	NA	NA	NA	0.002	0.006	0.004	0.009	0.009	0.016
New Zealand	0.1	0.12	0.12	0.14	0.17	0.24	0.002	0	0.001	0.001	0	0	0.098	0.12	0.119	0.139	0.17	0.24
Pakistan	0.18	0.2	0.3	0.47	0.51	0.47	NA	NA	NA	NA	NA	NA	0.18	0.2	0.3	0.47	0.51	0.47
Peru	0.69	0.52	0.5	0.49	0.57	0.62	NA	NA	NA	NA	NA	NA	0.69	0.52	0.5	0.49	0.57	0.62
Singapore	0.25	0.32	0.28	0.19	0.22	0.18	0.142	0.043	0.011	0.008	0.006	0.003	0.108	0.277	0.269	0.182	0.214	0.177
Switzerland	*0.06*	*0.05*	*0.05*	*0.05*	*0.05*	*0.06*	*0.09*	*0.1*	*0.09*	*0.1*	*0.1*	*0.1*	*-0.03*	*-0.05*	*-0.04*	*-0.05*	*-0.05*	*-0.04*

Source: WITS database.

Note: Rows with Italic font show trade balance deficit with China's FTA partners.

Table 10.8 China's exports, imports, and trade balance of electrical machinery sector to FTA partners (2013–18) in US$ billion

Year	*China Exports*						*China Imports*						*China Trade Balance*					
	Electrical Machinery						*Electrical Machinery*						*Electrical Machinery*					
	2013	*2014*	*2015*	*2016*	*2017*	*2018*	*2013*	*2014*	*2015*	*2016*	*2017*	*2018*	*2013*	*2014*	*2015*	*2016*	*2017*	*2018*
ASEAN	***81.65***	***90.05***	***93.21***	***86.74***	***100.84***	***118.46***	***89***	***88.11***	***90.82***	***90.42***	***103.92***	***123.29***	***-7.35***	***1.94***	***2.39***	***-3.68***	***-3.08***	***-4.83***
Australia	12.79	13.41	13.68	12.32	14.8	16.97	0.54	0.47	0.33	0.35	0.44	0.44	12.25	12.94	13.35	11.97	14.36	16.53
Chile	3.28	3.16	3.46	3.26	3.47	3.76	0.012	0.007	0.013	0.008	0.003	0.003	3.268	3.153	3.447	3.252	3.467	3.757
Costa Rica	***0.28***	***0.35***	***0.35***	***0.42***	***0.44***	***0.51***	***4.66***	***4.04***	***0.62***	***0.54***	***0.48***	***0.32***	***-4.38***	***-3.69***	***-0.27***	***-0.12***	***-0.04***	***0.19***
Georgia	0.24	0.28	0.25	0.22	0.28	0.34	0.001	0.001	0.001	0.001	0	0.002	0.239	0.279	0.249	0.219	0.28	0.338
Hong Kong	239.53	210.6	218.74	190.59	185.08	205.49	1.94	1.8	1.85	1.1	1.07	0.91	237.59	208.8	216.89	189.49	184.01	204.58
Rep. of Korea	***43.01***	***45.93***	***48.04***	***43.52***	***47.16***	***50.62***	***92.07***	***93.09***	***97.82***	***88.19***	***103.87***	***123.74***	***-49.06***	***-47.16***	***-49.78***	***-44.67***	***-56.71***	***-73.12***
Macao	0.46	0.57	0.71	0.34	0.36	0.38	0.002	0.001	0.001	0.001	0	0.001	0.458	0.569	0.709	0.339	0.36	0.379
Maldives	0.03	0.03	0.05	0.07	0.08	0.13	NA	NA	NA	NA	NA	0	0.03	0.03	0.05	0.07	0.08	0.13
New Zealand	1.12	1.24	1.24	1.25	1.4	1.57	0.102	0.096	0.097	0.073	0.054	0.112	1.018	1.144	1.143	1.177	1.346	1.458
Pakistan	3.46	4.03	5.12	6.45	6.78	5.81	0	0	0.001	0	0	0.001	3.46	4.03	5.119	6.45	6.78	5.809
Peru	1.76	1.84	1.83	1.75	2.12	2.34	0	0.001	0.001	0.001	0.001	0.001	1.76	1.839	1.829	1.749	2.119	2.339
Singapore	18.4	19.83	21.82	18.68	19.35	20.74	13.07	12.5	12.09	10.86	13.04	14.44	5.33	7.33	9.73	7.82	6.31	6.3
Switzerland	***1.08***	***1.21***	***1.05***	***0.97***	***1.11***	***1.45***	***3.36***	***3.47***	***2.9***	***2.78***	***3.07***	***3.54***	***-2.28***	***-2.26***	***-1.85***	***-1.81***	***-1.96***	***-2.09***

Source: WITS database.

Table 10.9 China's exports, imports, and trade balance of iron and steel sector to FTA partners (2013–18) in US$ billion

Year	*China Exports*						*China Imports*						*China Trade Balance*					
	Iron and Steel						*Iron and Steel*						*Iron and Steel*					
	2013	*2014*	*2015*	*2016*	*2017*	*2018*	*2013*	*2014*	*2015*	*2016*	*2017*	*2018*	*2013*	*2014*	*2015*	*2016*	*2017*	*2018*
ASEAN	17.84	22.76	22.71	21.66	20.8	25.78	0.69	1.38	1.25	1.51	2.83	3.72	17.15	21.38	21.46	20.15	17.97	22.06
Australia	2.47	2.25	2.06	1.82	2.16	2.6	0.13	0.05	0.04	0.03	0.03	0.05	2.34	2.2	2.02	1.79	2.13	2.55
Chile	1.12	1.35	1.17	1.09	1.33	1.7	0.005	0.004	0.003	0	0	0.001	1.115	1.346	1.167	1.09	1.33	1.699
Costa Rica	0.06	0.1	0.13	0.19	0.23	0.25	NA	NA	NA	NA	NA	NA	0.06	0.1	0.13	0.19	0.23	0.25
Georgia	0.12	0.13	0.09	0.08	0.13	0.16	NA	NA	NA	NA	NA	NA	0.12	0.13	0.09	0.08	0.13	0.16
Hong Kong	2.72	2.83	2.55	2.33	2.5	2.05	0.11	0.05	0.02	0.02	0.03	0.02	2.61	2.78	2.53	2.31	2.47	2.03
Rep. of Korea	9.31	11.16	9.33	8.68	9.35	7.89	5.24	5.55	4.71	4.51	4.75	4.82	4.07	5.61	4.62	4.17	4.6	3.07
Macao	0.33	0.4	0.56	0.28	0.37	0.16	0.002	0.001	0.001	NA	NA	NA	0.328	0.399	0.559	0.28	0.37	0.16
Maldives	0.01	0.01	0.02	0.05	0.05	0.08	NA	NA	NA	NA	NA	NA	0.01	0.01	0.02	0.05	0.05	0.08
New Zealand	0.23	0.28	0.29	0.25	0.29	0.32	0.002	0.003	0.002	0.002	0.003	0.004	0.228	0.277	0.288	0.248	0.287	0.316
Pakistan	0.83	1.21	1.64	1.82	1.93	1.72	NA	NA	NA	NA	NA	NA	0.83	1.21	1.64	1.82	1.93	1.72
Peru	0.66	0.82	0.71	0.64	0.78	1.03	0	0.02	NA	NA	NA	NA	0.66	0.8	0.71	0.64	0.78	1.03
Singapore	2.92	3.12	2.57	2.04	1.8	2.07	0.22	0.62	0.35	0.08	0.07	0.08	2.7	2.5	2.22	1.96	1.73	1.99
Switzerland	***0.04***	***0.05***	***0.05***	***0.05***	***0.05***	***0.1***	***0.12***	***0.13***	***0.12***	***0.12***	***0.14***	***0.14***	***-0.08***	***-0.08***	***-0.07***	***-0.07***	***-0.09***	***-0.04***

Source: WITS database.

Note: Rows with Italic font show trade balance deficit with China's FTA partners.

FTA partners. In the case of China, potential exports are rising in all selected sectors to ASEAN countries, Australia, and South Korea.

Lastly, the results of tariff impositions on potential exports in the three selected sectors varied across two countries. The countries which are good at the production of a commodity got a positive impact from the tariff escalation. For example, the automobile sector of the US has its comparative advantage in the world and the export potential of this sector is more promising than the two other sectors. On the other hand, China is the hub of automobile parts, known for electrical machinery, and the iron and steel sector. Therefore, China's export potential in the three selected sectors is very significant and promising for its FTA partners. This also points towards China being a hub of global value chains.

Note

1 China's FTA partners are ASEAN, Australia, Chile, Costa Rica, Georgia, Hong Kong, South Korea, Macao, Maldives, New Zealand, Pakistan, Peru, Singapore, and Switzerland.

The US's FTA partners are Australia, Bahrain, Canada, Chile, Colombia, Costa Rica, Dominican Republic, El Salvador, Guatemala, Honduras, Israel, Jordan, South Korea, Mexico, Morocco, Nicaragua, Oman, Panama, Peru, and Singapore.

References

Huang Y., & Jeremy S. (2019). *In U.S.-China Trade War, New Supply Chains Rattle Markets.* Washington, DC: Carnegie Endowment for International Peace. Retrieved from https://carnegieendowment.org/2020/06/24/in-u.s.-china-trade-war-new-supply-chains-rattle-markets-pub-82145

Robinson, S., & Thierfelder, K. (2019). *US–China Trade War: Both Countries Lose, World Markets Adjust, Others Gain.* Policy Brief 19–17. Washington, DC: Peterson Institute for International Economics.

Stewart, P. (2020). Trade war impacts and why a US–China trade deal won't boost the economy. Hinrich Foundation. Retrieved from www.hinrichfoundation.com/research/article/us-china-trade/trade-war-impacts-on-economy/

United States Trade Representative (2018). *Report to Congress on China's WTO Compliance.* February. Washington, DC: Office of the United States Trade Representative.

Viner, J. (1951). *International Economics.* Glencoe, IL: Free Press.

Witada, A., & Lobo, R. S. (2019). Trade wars: Risks and opportunities for Asia-Pacific economies from US tariffs. *Trade, Investment and Innovation Working Paper* (01). Bangkok: UN ESCAP.

World Bank (2014). *World Development Indicator*, Washington DC: World Bank,

World Bank (2016). *World Development Indicator*, Washington DC: World Bank.

World Bank (2018). *World Development Indicator*, Washington DC: World Bank.

Part IV

Is it for the establishment of technological supremacy?

11 The US–China technology conflict
The causes

Daniel Gros

1 Introduction

For a long time, the US has been the largest economy, and has dominated the global trading system, mainly with exports of high technology products. This supremacy is now under threat. The Chinese economy is, in purchasing power parity terms, roughly the same size as that of the US, and China is also rapidly catching up in key technology sectors. These rivals also trade intensively with each other (Qin, 2019).

Since 2018/19, this trading relationship has been increasingly disrupted by a series of unilateral US actions to impose tariffs on an increasing proportion of its imports from China. The internal basis for these tariffs was the US allegation of unfair trade practices in technology transfer and intellectual property by China under Section 301 of the Trade Act of 1974. The US further accused China of using administrative processes and ownership restrictions to impel US firms to transfer technology to Chinese businesses (USTR, 2018). Subsequent to this, the USA launched an investigation into Chinese tech firms, and the US Department of Commerce blacklisted' Chinese tech giant Huawei.[1] This officially triggered the technology war between the US and China. Thus the trade war has evolved into a technology war.

Given this backdrop, the current chapter attempts to investigate the factors that led to the trade war and the further escalation to the technology war. The chapter also tries to explore how justified US allegations are against China around the issue of forced technology transfer. The chapter provides empirical evidence to justify the argument.

The chapter is arranged as follows. Section 2 investigates the factors that led to the trade war covering the US–China trade in goods and services. Section 3 scrutinises whether China protects its imports while section 4 describes the Chinese treatment of its state-owned enterprises. Section 5 examines the FDI inflows in China. Sections 6 and 7 look at US allegations of forced technology transfers against China and how these benefit Chinese entities. The final section concludes the study.

2 Is there a *casus belli* for a trade war?

In many advanced countries, the attitude towards US trade measures against China seems to be: Trump is wrong in using blunt tools, but he is right in pointing to a real problem. But what exactly is the problem? Is there a *casus belli*?

US complaints are often based on the large (bilateral) US external deficit. The office of the United States Trade Representative (USTR) reports that US goods and services trade with China totalled an estimated $737.1 billion in 2018. The (bilateral) US goods and services trade deficit with China was $378.6 billion in 2018, resulting from US exports of only $179.3 billion and imports of $557.9 billion.

The balances in the goods and services trade are very different. Goods exports totalled $120.3 billion; goods imports totalled $539.5 billion. The US goods trade deficit with China was $419.2 billion in 2018. Trade in services with China (exports and imports) totalled an estimated $77.3 billion in 2018. Services exports were $58.9 billion; services imports were $18.4 billion. The US thus had a services trade surplus with China of $40.5 billion in 2018.

However, economists like to point out that trade balances have little to do with trade policy because a current account deficit is just the mirror image of an excess of domestic investment over domestic savings (Ansari, 2004). As long as trade measures do not have an impact on savings or investment, they will not affect the current account balance. But even abstracting from these considerations, it is difficult to find a rationale for a US–China trade war, given that the current account surplus of China has disappeared, as shown in the last column of Table 11.1.

US President Donald Trump's actions are often motivated by trade (rather than current account) balances. Looking at trade imbalances yields a somewhat different picture than current accounts, especially if one focuses on trade in goods, which seems to be the metric preferred by the US president himself. For example, on goods (first two columns in Table 11.1) one finds that the US deficit is very large, at $750 billion (4% of US GDP), while both the euro area and China have very large surpluses, worth more than 4% of GDP (and Japan does not figure anymore). This implies that, even viewed from this angle, there is no reason for the United States to focus on China.

Analysing the trade in services (columns 3 and 4 in Table 11.1) we find the relative strength of the United States in this sector. The United States has a huge surplus of $250 billion, while China is running a deficit on services (primarily in the tourism sector) of the same magnitude. However, the United States receives only a part of Chinese tourism, which leaves the bilateral balance on goods and services deeply negative. Economists tend to focus on the current account (last columns in Table 11.1), which besides goods and services also includes capital income. On this measure, China is no longer a part of the problem, as its current account surplus has essentially disappeared. Global imbalances have become a transatlantic issue, as the deficit of the United States is mirrored in a surplus of the same size for the euro area.

Table 11.1 Trade and current account imbalances

	Net balances 2016				*Current account 2018*
	Goods		*Services*		
	USD billion	*% GDP*	*USD billion*	*% GDP*	*% GDP*
USA	- 753	- 4.0	248	1.3	- 2.5
China	494	4.4	- 244	- 2.2	0.3
Euro area	487	4.1	65	0.5	3.5
Japan	51	1.0	- 11	- 0.2	3.7

Source: World Bank.

In terms of trade 'imbalances' it is thus difficult to find a *casus belli* against China unless one focuses on bilateral balances in goods. But in this case, the transatlantic dimension is equally important.

3 Does China protect against imports?

One argument for the United States to focus on China could be that the euro area is running a large trade surplus, but at least has open markets, whereas the trade surplus of China could be due to protectionism. But even this argument does not stand up to scrutiny. The standard tool of protectionism is tariffs. On this front, the problem seems very limited. The average tariff rate applied by China has continued to fall even after its entry into the WTO in 2001, which had already forced the country to reduce tariff protection by one-half. Indeed, the average applied tariff now seems to have fallen to less than 4%, and there are few complaints about tariffs, even though China maintains an unusually high number of tariff peaks, i.e. high tariffs for very limited product categories[2] as highlighted in a CEPS study. But these high tariffs affect only products of limited relevance. Moreover, tariff peaks are not on the list of complaints of either the United States or the EU (Pelkmans et al., 2018).

Tariffs were, in any case, yesterday's problem (until Trump dusted them off as a weapon for his trade war). But they provide one clear numerical indicator of obstacles that traders (in goods) might encounter at the border. There are many other ways to create obstacles to trade. (Hornok and Koren, 2015). It is difficult to measure the overall importance of these 'non-tariff' barriers to trade because they can consist of so many different measures, including licensing, conformity assessment, etc. These non-tariff measures are difficult to keep track of because they usually concern only a specific sector or product.

However, the website of the Global Trade Alert[3] Observatory has since 2008 provided an excellent running observatory of new measures (called state interventions) introduced by major trading nations. For China, this independent body finds only around 25 new measures that might restrict trade with the

United States (annual average since 2008). Interestingly, China also enacted about the same number of new measures that have the effect of liberalising trade with the United States. China has thus not become more protectionist against the United States. The other way around the situation looks very different: the United States has enacted between 80 and 100, or about four times more, restrictive measures against China, which far outstrip the much less numerous liberalising measures. Analysing market-distorting measures for Germany vs US and Germany vs China, Gros (2019) finds a similar asymmetry between Germany and China: in recent years, China has introduced about as many liberalising as protectionist measures. But Germany has taken mostly protectionist measures vis-à-vis China.

This means that, in terms of trade measures, China is more sinned against than sinning. One could, of course, argue that protection against Chinese exports is needed because exporters there receive subsidies. This is one point on which the complaints seem justified. When China joined the WTO, it took on the obligation of notifying the phase-out of a number of existing subsidies and notifying all those that continue (Annex 5a and 5b to the Accession Protocol[4]). However, this 'soft' commitment was not honoured. In late 2018, China suddenly sent a notification to the WTO for all the missing prior years (Hu, 2019; WTO, 2019b). However, it seems that these notifications were incomplete, as found in the latest WTO Trade Policy Review (WTO, 2019a). In principle, the United States and Europe could offset the advantages that these more or less hidden subsidies give Chinese exporters by introducing countervailing duties. In practice, this is difficult because the opaque nature of the subsidies makes it difficult to prove their impact in specific cases.

4 State-owned enterprises

The case for countervailing action would be justified, in particular in the case of exports by state-owned enterprises (SOEs). This might have been a problem in the past when SOEs accounted for one-half of exports. But now their shares of overall Chinese exports have fallen to less than 10%.[5] Despite their now very limited importance for trade, SOEs constitute another bone of contention between China and the 'West'. This has of course, little to do with 'trade' policy since SOEs are just one element of the economic order in China. As mentioned, SOEs do not play a large part in Chinese exports, and if they practise unfair pricing, the problem can be dealt with by traditional countervailing duties and other measures.

The real complaints about SOEs relate to the structure of the Chinese economy. Complaints from the several Chambers of Commerce in China concern the preferential treatment given to SOEs mostly in non-tradable sectors like financial services, etc. Of course, the dominance of huge state-owned banks creates the temptation to favour SOEs in the allocation of credit. But a lack of access to cheap credit should not be a problem for foreign-owned or invested companies, which usually have a major multinational enterprise with access to global capital markets behind them. Private Chinese enterprises ought to be equally, or perhaps even more, disadvantaged by SOEs having preferential access to capital.

The role of SOEs in the Chinese economy is difficult to document in detail, but most statistics suggest it remains important, albeit having fallen somewhat over the last two decades. For example, SOEs still account for about half of the capital stock of industrial enterprises (down from three-quarters). Moreover, SOEs tend to be large. A number of them, especially the large state-owned banks, now rank among the largest global companies.

But these examples are not representative of the entire sector. SOEs remain an important factor in the Chinese economy, but their importance has declined considerably over the last decade and more recently. For example, SOEs now account for only about one-quarter of (urban) employment and a similar share of profits (and only one-tenth of exports, as mentioned above). Foreign-controlled enterprises make more profits (31% of the total), while the share of profits going to private Chinese enterprises is even higher.

Chinese statistics show that foreign-invested enterprises generally achieve much higher profitability than state-owned ones and that the profitability of foreign-invested enterprises has persisted, not fallen, over time, although it remains slightly lower than that of private Chinese ones. There is thus evidence that, while SOEs are not efficient in their investment, they play only a small role in exports, and their continuing role has not impeded continuing high profitability of foreign investment in China. Some observers have detected a revival of the role of SOEs more recently, but the evidence for this is still tentative.[6]

5 The real problem is FDI

The finding that there is no *casus belli* for a classic trade war is confirmed if one looks carefully at the complaints enumerated by the United States or at the detailed report published by the European Chamber of Commerce in China summarising the complaints from its over 1,600 member companies. This report does make interesting reading because one does not find many complaints about 'trading' practices, at least in the narrow sense (European Chamber, 2019). The main complaint of EU enterprises in China is the perception of unfair treatment by the Chinese authorities. The main complaint of the US government is that US high-tech firms are forced to reveal their technology and trade secrets. An additional common complaint is that, in many sectors, foreign firms are not permitted to hold a majority stake in joint ventures. The core of all these complaints is thus not trade but FDI, and the situation 'behind the border', in the Chinese market.

Measuring barriers to FDI is as difficult as measuring non-tariff barriers to trade. Barriers to cross-border investment can take many forms, such as limits on foreign ownership in certain sectors, different fiscal treatment for foreign-owned enterprises, or outright bureaucratic discrimination. The Organisation for Economic Cooperation and Development (OECD) publishes a composite indicator of restrictiveness towards FDI (OECD, 2018). For China, this indicator shows that, overall, the country is far less open than OECD countries, but that there has been continuous, albeit slow, improvement.

A further subtle distinction one needs to make is between barriers to new inflows of direct investment (i.e. investment with the implication that the foreign investor obtains control over the investment) and the treatment of enterprises that are under foreign control. In most OECD countries, a company incorporated in a different home country is treated in the same way as any other domestically incorporated company (this is called 'national treatment'). But in China, there is a special regime for 'foreign-invested enterprises' (FIE). In the past, the purpose of this special regime might have been to protect foreign investors from an overbearing domestic bureaucracy. But today, there is a widespread perception that 'foreign-invested enterprises' are not treated fairly.

The complaints have come in light of the rapidly changing context in China itself. The real change might simply be that, in the past, the formal handicaps that foreign-owned enterprises faced were compensated by the eagerness of the provincial authorities to attract foreign investment. As long as provincial leaders were also judged on the amount of FDI they attracted, they would provide many incentives to outweigh the formal restrictions on FIEs. Today, there is less emphasis on growth in the evaluation criteria of provincial leaders, which means local authorities have less reason to provide incentives for FDI.

Moreover, the technology gap between Chinese and foreign enterprises is shrinking rapidly in many sectors. Restrictions on majority foreign ownership mattered little in the past when the formally majority Chinese partner (often owning 51%) had an incentive to acquiesce to the de facto control of a foreign investor who had superior technology or market access abroad. With technology on a more level playing field, it is the restrictions on foreign majority ownership that start to matter. This is also the reason why it is more appropriate to speak about a 'technology war' than a 'trade war'.

6 Forced transfer of technology: a *casus belli*?

Forced technology transfer is a central issue in the ongoing US-China trade tussle. For a long time, the US has been complaining about unfair Chinese practices in the form of 'forced transfer of technology'. The term 'forced' suggests a degree of coercion that does not make economic sense. A US company can always choose not to invest in China. If a US or European company chooses to invest in China despite the requirement to transfer technology, it does so because it expects to make a profit. That profit might be smaller than it would have been with no technology transfer requirement, but the choice of going into China anyway reveals that the company sees more opportunities than risks.

Moreover, the Chinese partners (e.g. in a joint venture[7]) know that the foreign investment will come with a technology transfer. This means that the local partners will be ready to accept that the valuation of the foreign investor's contribution to a joint venture includes the value of the transfer of technology. For example, the local partner or the local government can provide cheap land, infrastructure, tax exemptions, or loans on favorable terms. In other words, the transfer of technology, because it is the rule, will be priced into any FDI deal. The continuing high profitability of foreign-invested enterprises suggests that this has indeed been the case.

The United States, in its Section 301 report and in a 2017 USTR Report to Congress on China's WTO Compliance, makes several complaints against China. They allege that China forces foreign companies to transfer technology to Chinese companies, for example, as a condition for granting a joint venture agreement; that the Chinese government gives more favourable treatment to Chinese companies than to foreign companies in certain circumstances; that China is using outbound investment to acquire foreign technology; and that China engages in cyber intrusions to steal intellectual property from US companies in order to benefit Chinese companies (Brum, 2019).

It is only natural that foreign companies will assert in surveys that they would be better off if they had not been 'forced' to transfer technology. However, these statements do not take into account the fact that the terms on which the initial investment was made probably contained advantages that were available to the foreign investors only because of the expectation of technology transfer. It is of course likely that, in many cases, the most efficient investment deal would not have involved a wholesale transfer of technology, but perhaps only a licensing agreement or the payment of royalties. However, that should be only a secondary consideration, since the present value of the foregone licensing fees or royalties would have figured implicitly in any investment deal.

It is often impossible to prove the pressure exerted by Chinese authorities to transfer technology because China made a formal undertaking when it entered the WTO that it would no longer require technology transfers.[8] However, because of this WTO undertaking, it seems that the pressure to make technology transfers has become informal. A large body of experts and market observers acknowledge that China has repeatedly forced foreign multinational corporations (MNCs) to transfer technology to indigenous firms as a condition for market access and that China has persistently failed to protect the intellectual property of foreign firms doing business in China. (See Wei, 2018; Campbell and Ratner, 2018; *The Economist*, 2018).

According to many observers, the Chinese authorities even avoid emails that could be used as proof, instead giving only indirect oral 'hints'. It is thus likely that, in reality, this pressure to transfer technology does persist.

In a report issued on 22 March 2018, USTR cited numerous instances of forced technology transfer and failure to protect US intellectual property from infringement or theft (Lee, 2018). Examples of forced technology transfer abound in industries ranging from autos to information technology (IT). In the auto industry, foreign ownership restrictions (and high tariffs) force foreign firms to serve the booming Chinese auto market – now the world's largest – through joint ventures in which they are prevented from holding a controlling interest. China's well-publicised drive to become a leader in electric vehicles has resulted in complaints by European auto firms that they are being pressured to turn over sensitive technology, including proprietary software code, to joint venture partners who may later compete with them in China and elsewhere (Lee, 2018; Clover, 2017).

7 Has forced technology transfer affected profits?

As argued above, FDI inflows should continue only if it remains in the interest of foreign enterprises to invest in China, knowing in advance that the pressure to transfer technology will exist, but might be offset by other advantages. The confirmation of this reason can be found in the rates of return on FDI in China: these have remained high, as can be seen from different angles. Chinese statistics themselves report the high rate of return on foreign-invested, state-owned, and private domestic enterprises.

Figure 11.1 shows the profit rates of these three groups since China joined the WTO. The rate of return on FDI (as measured by Chinese statistics) has in fact tended to increase slightly over time. It reached a natural peak during the Chinese boom of 2010, but at around 8% it remains much higher than that of SOEs (around 3%). The profitability of private Chinese enterprises is somewhat higher than that of foreign ones, but the difference has narrowed recently to about 2 percentage points.

Another indicator is the profitability as seen from the home country. Figure 11.2 shows the profitability of FDI for the EU. The average rate of return on outgoing FDI is somewhat below 5%: under 3% for EU investment in Canada and the United States, but 10% for investment in China. China seems to offer by far the highest rate of return among all the major destinations for EU direct investment abroad.

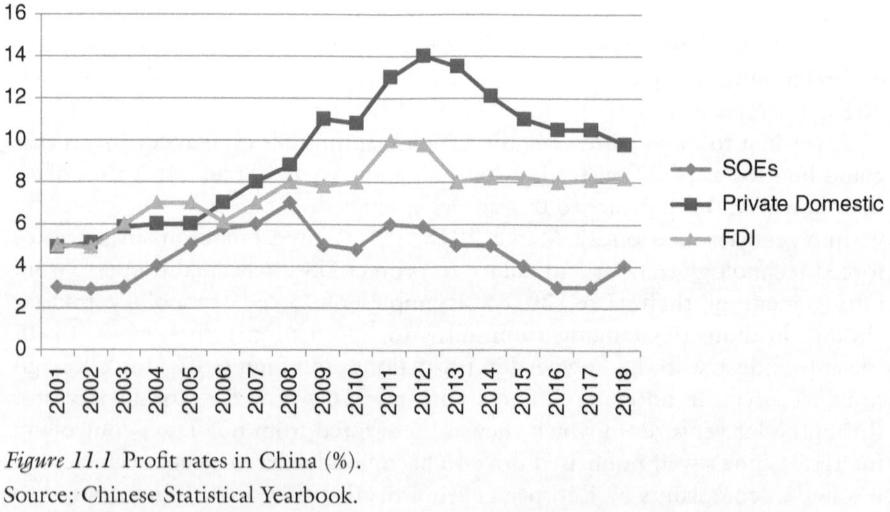

Figure 11.1 Profit rates in China (%).
Source: Chinese Statistical Yearbook.

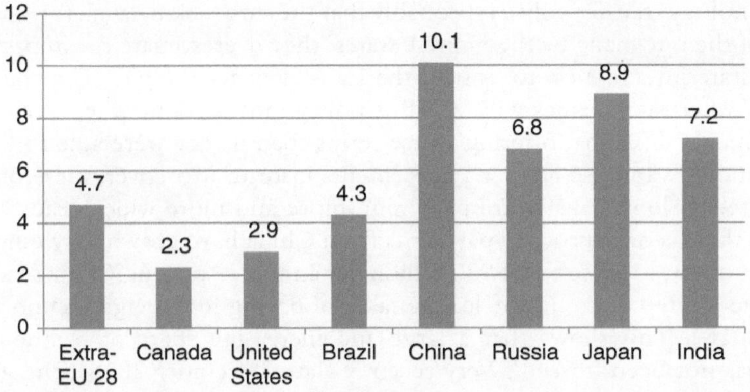

Figure 11.2 Average rate of return on FDI (2014–2017) (%).

Source: Own calculations on the basis of Eurostat data.

The problem with the FDI statistics is that almost none of the FDI from OECD countries to China goes directly into that country. In both the US and the EU statistics, the share of foreign direct investment going to China is less than 4% (less than for Brazil, for example). This is why one has to take the balance-of-payments FDI data with a big pinch of salt.[9]

All these considerations suggest that the cost of 'forced transfer of technology' for the US and other Western high-tech companies might be vastly exaggerated. But the argument also applies the other way around. Why should China continue to insist on this policy of linking market access for foreign investors to a transfer of technology? The key official argument on the Chinese side is that, in a developing country, the local companies are in a weak position vis-à-vis foreign investors whose technology they might not fully understand. This argument is also used in many less developed countries, whose FDI regimes are often as restrictive as that of China.

However, the argument that China is a developing economy that deserves special exemptions from WTO rules becomes less and less tenable as the country develops its own technological expertise. China's indigenous capacities for research and development have exploded over the past few decades. Spending on R&D is now larger as a percentage of GDP and larger in absolute terms than in Europe and many other OECD countries (World Bank, 2019). Today, there is thus little need to protect Chinese 'infant' industries.

Rapidly advancing domestic know-how and the absorption of technology also explain why Western complaints have become more vocal. Many Western firms probably agreed to a transfer of technology under the assumption that Chinese competitors would not be able to adapt and master it. Part of today's complaints stem from the fact that this expectation of superiority has been confounded. China produces more bachelor graduates in science and engineering than the United States and Europe combined.

One reason why the Chinese authorities remain so reluctant to give up on their technology transfer policy is probably that they are making a mirror-image mistake of the one made by the United States: they overestimate the impact of informal state intervention to 'foster' the transfer of technology. They fail to see that Western companies will take this policy into account when deciding on investments in China, offering worse terms than if they were able to keep their technology and use licensing agreements instead. Moreover, these other forms of technology transfer are becoming more and more widespread, with the result that recorded royalty payments from China have grown very quickly and now amount to close to US$30 billion per annum— putting China second only to the United States in the league table of paying for foreign technology (Lardy, 2018). This shows that a large and increasing share of technology transfer has not been 'forced'. Very recently (late December 2018), the government of China announced that it would abolish those administrative measures that result in de facto 'forced technology transfer'. It remains to be seen whether this new policy will actually be implemented across the many different layers of government involved (central, provincial, and local governments, many different ministries, etc.).

8 Conclusion

An outright trade war between the United States and China (in the sense of both sides imposing stiff tariffs on each other's imports) remains unlikely. However, tensions between the two countries are likely to persist. President Trump's tough stance on China remains popular in the United States, not so much due to the bilateral trade deficit or frustration about lost business opportunities, but because of the concern that China is about to outcompete the United States for technological leadership in a number of sectors considered critical for national security (on both sides of the Pacific). The reason Sino-US tensions on FDI and the associated 'forced transfer of technology' are so intense is that they are mostly about income distribution between two monopolists. The Chinese authorities hold the key to a vast and rapidly growing market, whereas Western companies still have a monopoly on the best technology in many sectors.

The United States and China account for a large share of global trade, but they alone do not dominate the global economy. In the coming 'cold economic war', the side that can garner the support of neutral powers will have a strong advantage. Other large trading powers – Europe and Japan, for example – do not share the US desire to keep China down and are thus unlikely to back unreasonable trade measures. However, Europe and Japan share the narrower US concerns about an uneven playing field generated by persistent Chinese state intervention in the economy. It is up to the Chinese authorities to allay legitimate concerns regarding these issues, which go to the heart of a global rules-based trading system. The Chinese economy is now so strong that restrictions on foreign ownership and any form of forced transfer of technology are no longer needed.

Notes

1 US Department of Commerce has 'blacklisted' Huawei and several other Chinese tech companies for export control. See 84 FR 22961 (21 May 2019); 84 FR 29371 (24 June 2019).
2 See TRAINS data in the UN COMTRADE data base.
3 See www.globaltradealert.org/.
4 China accession document, WTO. Retrieved from www.wto.org/english/thewto_e/acc_e/a1_chine_e.htm.
5 There is one exception that proves this rule. The Chinese Railway Corporation, which is of course vastly larger than any other railway company in the world, has spent heavily on R&D, allowing it to become an important exporter of trains and material. China alone now accounts for one half of all global trade in this sector. But this sector is not typical of overall Chinese trade patterns.
6 The data for 2017 show an unusual jump in the profits of SOEs (while those of private Chinese enterprises fell). It is too early to tell whether this is the result of a reclassification or other statistical adjustments.
7 Invest in China (中国投资指南 zhongguo touzi zhinan) website (maintained by the Ministry of Commerce of the People's Republic of China FDI site) [Chinese/English]: www.fdi.gov.cn.
8 See the Chinese WTO Agreement. Also, in Annex 1 of the Protocol, China pledged to abolish technology transfer requirements in order to comply with the WTO Trade-Related Investment Measures (TRIMS) – but that is only with regard to trade in goods.
9 Data on Greenfield (projects) assembled by UNCTAD shows a very different picture regarding the distribution of FDI, but this source has no information on the profitability of these projects.

Acknowledgements

This is an amended version of the paper earlier published as 'This is not a trade war; it is a struggle for technological and geo-strategic dominance', CESifo Forum 1 / 2019 March, vol. 20. Available at www.ifo.de/DocDL/CESifo-Forum-2019-1-gros-us-china%20trade-war-march.pdf.

References

Ansari, M. I. (2004). Sustainability of the US current account deficit: An econometric analysis of the impact of capital inflow on domestic economy. *Journal of Applied Economics*, *7*(2), 249–269.

Brum, J. (2019) Technology transfer and China's WTO commitments. *Georgetown Journal of International Law*, *50*, 709–743.

Campbell, I., & Ratner, D. (2018). America versus China: The battle for digital supremacy. *The Economist*, 17 March.

Clover, C. (2017). Foreign carmakers on edge despite China tech transfer assurances. *Financial Times,* 30 March. www.ft.com/content/adb80896-1462-11e7-80f4-13e067d5072c

Gross, D. (2019). This is not a trade war, it is a struggle for technological and geo-strategic dominance. *CESifo Forum 1,* 20.

David, D., & Ryan, H. (2017). Trump could be on the brink of starting a trade war with China. Order from Chaos blog. 9 August. Brookings Institution.

European Union Chamber of Commerce (2019). *The European Business in China*. Position Paper 2019/2020. Brussels: European Union Chamber.of Commerce in China.

Hornok, C., & Koren, M. (2015). Administrative barriers to trade. *Journal of International Economics, 96*, S110–S122.

Hu, W. (2019). *China as a WTO Developing Member: Is it a Problem?* No. 25627. Brussels: Centre for European Policy Studies.

Lardy, N. R. (2018). China: Forced technology transfer and theft? Peterson Institute for International Economics, blog. Washington, DC. Retrieved from www.piie.com/blogs/china-economic-watch/china-forced-technology-transfer-and-theft

Lee, G. B. (2018). *China's Forced Technology Transfer Problem: And What to Do about it?* Policy Brief (18-13). Washington, DC: Peterson Institute for International Economics.

National Bureau of Statistics in China (2018). *Chinese Statistical Year Book*. Beijing: Government of China.

OECD (2018). *FDI Regulatory Restrictiveness Index*. Paris: OECD.

Pelkmans, J., Hu, W., Mustilli, F., Di Salvo, M., Francois, J., Bekkers, E., Manchin, M., & Tomberger, P. (2018). *Tomorrow's Silk Route: Assessing an EU-China Free Trade Agreement,* 2nd ed. Brussels: CEPS.

Qin, J. Y. (2019). Forced technology transfer and the US–China trade war: Implications for international economic law. *Journal of International Economic Law, 22*(4), 743–762.

The Economist (2018). Technopolitics: The challenger. 17 March.

USTR (2018). *Findings of the Investigation into China's Acts, Policies and Practices Related to Technology Transfer, Intellectual Property and Innovation under Section 301 of the Trade Act of 1974 ('Section 301 Report')*. Washington, DC: USTR.

Wei, S.-J. (2018). How to avoid a U.S.-China trade war. Project Syndicate. 23 March. www.project-syndicate.org/commentary/trump-china-avoiding-trade-war-by-shang-jin-wei-2018-03?barrier=accesspaylog

World Bank (2019). *World Development Indicator*. Washington, DC: World Bank.

WTO (2019). *Trade Policy Review 2019*. Geneva: WTO.

WTO (2019). *Responses to Points Raised by Members under the Review Process. Committee on Agriculture*. Geneva: WTO.

12 Technology rents and the new Great Game

Dan Ciuriak and Maria Ptashkina

1 Introduction

The global economic and political order is being reshaped by an eruption of tensions. By far the most serious of these for the system of global commerce is the multi-dimensional conflict between the United States and China. However, important contributions are being made by the transatlantic frictions between the United States and the European Union, the US undermining of the World Trade Organisation (WTO) – not to mention other multilateral organisations – and the rise of anti-globalisation populism. Most recently, the ultimate wild card – the pandemic – added powerful impetus to the centrifugal forces by highlighting the vulnerabilities of exposure to trade and global supply chains, especially in light of the nationalistic reactions to which nations succumbed when the chips were down.

Many narratives can be and have been advanced to explain particular features of the great disruption that is now under way, including the inevitability of conflict between an established hegemon and a rising power (the so-called 'Thucydides Trap' thesis; Allison, 2017), the excesses of neoliberal globalisation that have unduly constrained domestic policy space (e.g. Rodrik, 2017; Mazzucato, 2011), system friction from the failure of the rules-based system to handle the rise of a large state capitalist economy (Wu, 2019), the rise of 'strongmen' leaders – including Donald Trump and Xi Jinping – driving their economies in new and controversial directions, and others.

Many of these issues are interlaced, and it is of interest whether there is a unifying theme, particularly one that helps explain the scale of the conflict, its timing, and the alignment of the parties. Technological developments arguably provide such a theme. Specifically, the digital transformation puts in play a sufficiently valuable bone of contention to induce strategic trade and investment policies and stoke geostrategic rivalry at the same time. Moreover, the essentially secular progress of technology development provides a coordinating mechanism to cause seemingly unrelated underlying tensions to surface at the same time, giving the impression of a 'perfect storm' arising from an unusual confluence of events. Finally, technological change leaves different countries in different positions – some with primarily offensive interests in terms of commercial capitalisation and others with primarily defensive interests in terms of minimising negative externalities, while seeking to catch up. While technology has hardly been ignored in the narratives, particularly latterly with the US moves to deny China access to critical digital technology, the issues run deep, are pervasive, and have been steadily building with the transition to a data-driven economy (DDE) based on the nexus of artificial intelligence (AI), machine learning (ML), and big data (Ciuriak, 2018a).

We argue that the contest to command these new technology heights explains the new global Great Game that is unfolding. Worldwide, countries are formulating strategies to claim a foothold in the new digital economy, playing the hands that they have been dealt (Ciuriak and Ptashkina, 2018a). The United States is seeking to maintain its technological leadership and the ascendancy of its roster of global digital economy champions (e.g. White House, 2019a, 2019b; also see in respect of the Internet Freedom programme, Hanson, 2012; Farrell, 2016). China is seeking to catch up by leveraging its domestic scale and the enormous amounts of data generated behind its Great Firewall by rapid consumer adoption of digital technologies (Webster et al., 2017); and the European Union is pioneering the regulation of digital space to minimise the negative impacts of technologies that it does not own while seeking to use its Digital Single Market to gain a competitive foothold in this new economy (Viola, 2018). In the case of the United States and China, this contest has become unbridled because of the added geostrategic component.

To the extent that this reading has merit, patchwork solutions that address specific flashpoints (e.g. Huawei's role in the build out of fifth generation, 5G, telecommunications infrastructure or the European Union's move to tax digital companies) will likely fail to restore trade peace and avert an economically and politically costly decoupling dynamic.

While a more comprehensive approach is required, with the multilateral trade and investment system itself under great stress, it is an open question as to whether it will be possible to constrain the strategic behaviour induced by the emerging DDE and to channel the rivalry into constructive technological competition, which would have benefits for all parties. Nonetheless, it helps to have a sense of where a multilateral accord for the digital age would go. The recently signed Digital Economic Partnership Agreement (DEPA) between Chile, New Zealand, and Singapore sets up a potential basis on which to build, although its initial set of commitments largely reiterated those in the Comprehensive and Progressive Agreement for Trans-Pacific Partnership (CPTPP) (Elms, 2020).

Based on the economics of the DDE, there remains substantial work to be done over and beyond what has been addressed in the DEPA or is within the scope of the current WTO negotiations on electronic commerce and the dialogue on taxation of electronic emissions (and the related Organisation for Economic Cooperation and Development, OECD, talks on taxation of multinationals). Areas of additional treatment would include strengthening of competition policy measures, formulation of new international conventions on intellectual property (IP) (including the regulation of AI) and on flow of data across borders (particularly as regards policy space for national security and digital sovereignty), the reframing of disciplines on subsidies and industrial policy, and an updating of the WTO investment agreement (Ciuriak, 2019).

The rest of this chapter is organised as follows. The next section describes how the digital transformation and the emergence of the DDE set the stage for destabilising conflict over technology and the rents that it promises. The third section considers specifically the issues raised in the US–China trade conflict. The fourth section considers the alignments that are emerging in this conflict – the new Great Game. The fifth section scopes out the multilateral response needed to put the contest over rents into a constructive framework.

2 How the data-driven economy sets the stage for conflict

The DDE has several features that individually can induce market failure. These features include large economies of scale and scope – often accompanied by network externalities – and pervasive information asymmetry (Ciuriak, 2018a). Combined, these characteristics result in the 'winner takes most' dynamics that support the emergence of firms that dominate their industry at the global level.

The international rents at stake from having national champions dominating global markets promise to be very large indeed and serve as an inducement for strategic trade and investment policy (Ciuriak, 2018b). The mobilisation of these strategic policies is already well advanced: worldwide, governments are pouring massive sums into the development of technology in the digital space to capture these rents.

The winner-takes-most dynamic is most visible in the major internet areas, such as search and social media, where a handful of US firms largely dominate globally, while within China replicas of these firms dominate the Chinese market. In the absence of China's Great Firewall, the world would likely be a Google-Facebook lake. While digital markets are contestable through new entry, which provides some discipline on abusive practices, competition does not tend to last as the market tips to one or the other firm, and the loser exits. The market capitalisation of the dominant firms testifies to their ability to capture economic rents despite this discipline.

The pace of data growth is beyond imagination. In the past decade, it was so large that, according to an often-quoted estimate from IBM in 2017, 90% of all data ever collected was captured in the preceding several years (Petrov, 2020). To get a sense of the scale at which data is gathered, it may be noted that Facebook alone has 2.5 billion monthly users, which is more than the combined populations of China, the European Union, and the United States. Through its WhatsApp utility, Facebook has 2 billion clients generating 65 billion messages a day. These data can be commercialised, they can be abused, and they can be weaponised for political purposes, including psychological operations (Cadwalladr, 2018). The advantages that accrue to the firms that succeed in attaining market dominance are seemingly overwhelming: firms with data see the market more clearly – in that sense, it can be likened to an industrial-strength sixth sense. It gives rise to a new form of capitalism – 'surveillance capitalism' (Zuboff, 2019) – and to new ways to exercise and expand state power.

Valuable as data is, it is remarkable that, while being gathered almost literally everywhere, it mostly does not show up in the national economic accounts, it is not in the international trade statistics, and it does not even show up directly in firms' financial statements. It is measured at best indirectly as part of the intangible assets of data-rich firms. Currently, about 90% of the market capitalisation of firms in the S&P 500 (which totalled US$25.64 trillion in June 2020; YCharts, 2020) is comprised of intangible assets. A good part of that is attributable to data.

Even on the basis of what we currently know about data, they clearly have extraordinary value. And yet, what has been realised in terms of data applications appears to be only a prologue to what is coming as the Internet-of-Things (IoT) is put in place and as ever more powerful ML engines and techniques learning on exponentially growing stocks of data generate increasingly sophisticated and powerful AI.

Data is the essential and definitive capital asset of this age and just like its predecessors in this role – land in the feudal age, the machinery of mass production in the mercantile era, and IP in the knowledge-based economy – it is worth fighting over. In that sense, the emergence of the DDE promised conflict and it has arrived (Ciuriak, 2020).

3 The US–China dynamics

3.1 A bit of history

The United States and China have had a long and rather checkered political relationship, with overall mostly limited trade in a handful of commodities and no particular bone of contention.

Formal relations got off on a problematic foot when the United States joined European powers in the Opium Wars and imposed the Treaty of Wanghia on the Chinese Qing Dynasty in 1844, granting Americans extra-territorial rights in China, patterned on the British model that also saw the establishment of the British colony of Hong Kong (Ruskola, 2005). This is not insignificant. In US popular culture, to say that something is 'history' is to dismiss it as unimportant. Yet to China, the period of 'unequal treaties' came to represent a mark of shame and remains in China's cultural and political memory and is of relevance to its current international relations (Rappeport, 2019; Wang, 2003).

The United States and China were briefly allies against Japan in the Second World War, which led the United States to terminate the Treaty of Wanghia in 1943 (Wright, 1943). Notably, at this time, China had American-style democratic governance machinery, which it adopted following the 1911 Xinhai Revolution, which overthrew the Imperial system and established the Republic of China (Wen, 2016). But, all too quickly, they became geopolitical enemies on the edge of nuclear war during the Cold War when Mao Zedong's communist forces defeated the US-backed government, which decamped to Taiwan (Chen, 2019).

Relations improved when US President Nixon played the 'China card' in the geostrategic contest with the Soviet Union through his historic visit to Beijing in 1972 (Goh, 2005); the United States and China thus became 'tacit allies' (Chen, 2019). Things further improved with the renewal of trade relations following Deng Xiaoping's visit to Washington in 1979, which set up China's period of 'opening up' and which the United States facilitated by granting China normal trade relations status (which allowed Chinese goods to enter the United States under its 'most favoured nation', MFN, tariff programme) under Title IV of the Trade Act of 1974 (Pregelj, 2001).

Following some bumps in the road (including the chill following the Tiananmen Square incident of 4 June 1989), relations reached a recent apogee in the early 2000s with a series of developments: the Clinton administration extended 'Permanent Normal Trade Relations' (PNTR) to China in 2000, which paved the way for the incoming Bush administration to broker China's accession to the WTO in 2001; two-way trade soared as labour-rich but capital-poor China made a natural trading partner for a US economy with the opposite characteristics; and the subsequent reopening of direct links with Taiwan in 2008 at the direct urging of President Bush in his last year in office (Wei, 2012).

However, this was a prologue to an abrupt shift towards renewed confrontation with the Obama administration's 'pivot to Asia' (Ford, 2017) and then the accelerating slide under the Trump administration down the slippery slope to trade war, decoupling, and the blame game following the breakout of the coronavirus pandemic in 2020. At this writing, in mid-2020, US–China relations are at a post-1972 nadir.

3.2 What changed?

The transformation of China from an exporter of low-tech, labour-intensive products into a leading manufacturer of technological products and provider of digital services has, within one generation, changed the geo-economic situation in the Asia Pacific. By 2010, the share of exports classified as medium- or high-tech in total manufactured exports for China reached 60.5%, largely closing the gap with the United States, which stood at 64.7% (see Figure 12.1).

China had also substantially narrowed the gap in the share of research and development (R&D) expenditure in its gross domestic product (GDP), having raised it from 0.5% in 1996 to 1.7% in 2010; it continues on a steadily rising trajectory towards the US level of 2–3% (see Figure 12.2).

China's patent applications have surged since the early 2000s (see Figure 12.3). By 2010, China had passed Japan for the second spot behind only the United States and was on a steeply rising trajectory that would by mid-decade leave its closest competitors far behind.

These measures of rising technological capability on the input side were reflected on the output side: starting in around 2010, the dawn of the DDE era, China's technology sectors dominated growth, reversing the relationship of previous decades (S&P, 2019).

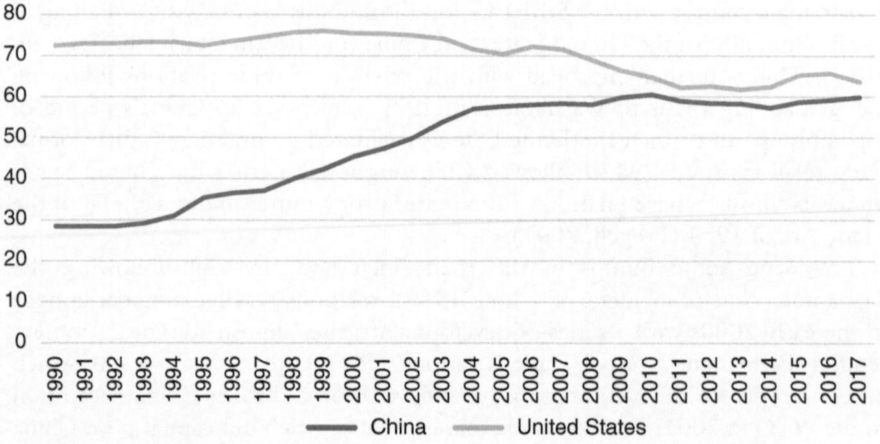

Figure 12.1 Medium and high-tech exports (% manufactured exports), 1990–2017.
Source: World Bank (2020).

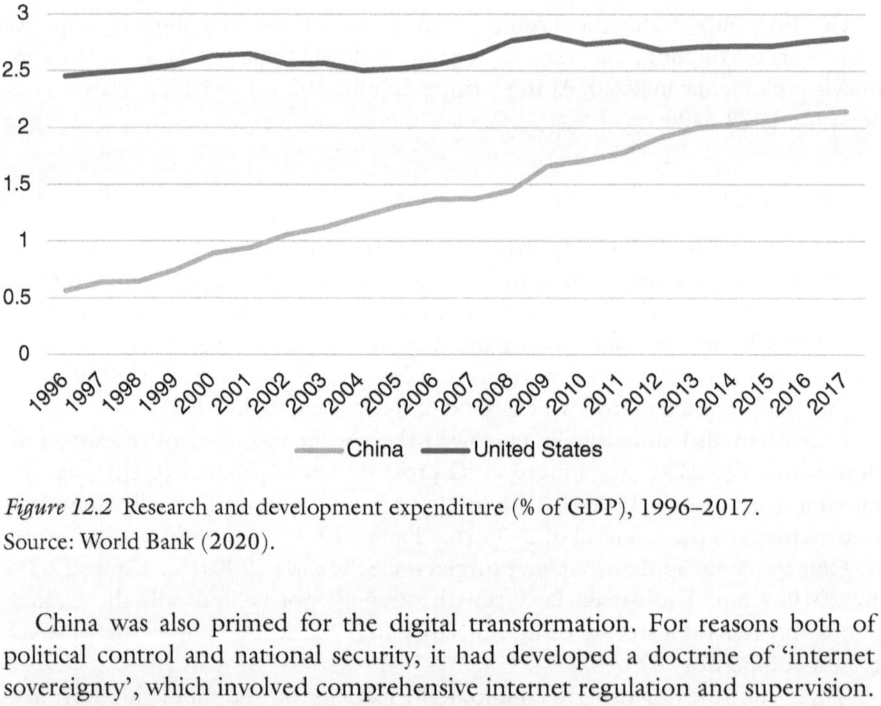

Figure 12.2 Research and development expenditure (% of GDP), 1996–2017.
Source: World Bank (2020).

China was also primed for the digital transformation. For reasons both of political control and national security, it had developed a doctrine of 'internet sovereignty', which involved comprehensive internet regulation and supervision. This was implemented through the Golden Shield Project, which was completed in 2008 and is colloquially referred to as the Great Firewall. Behind this barrier, indigenous Chinese firms were poised to capture what was to become the world's largest and fastest-growing e-commerce market.

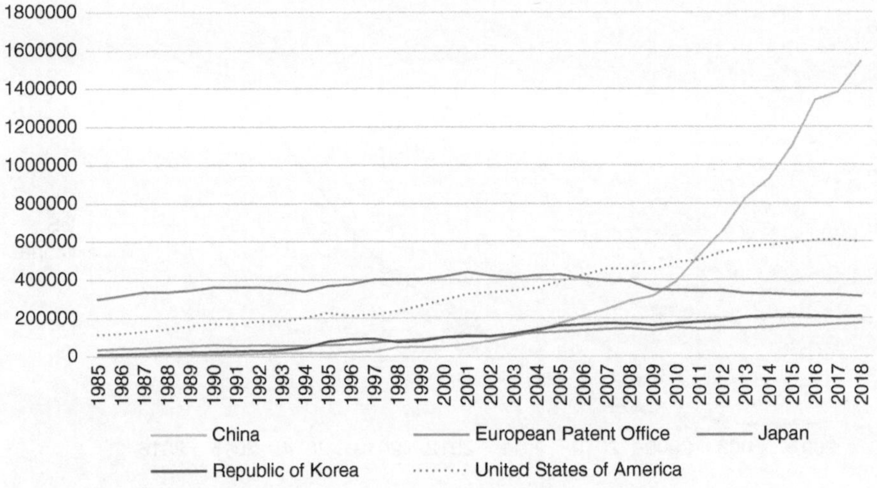

Figure 12.3 Total patent applications of the top-five offices, 1980–2016.
Source: World Intellectual Property Organization (2020).

China also had a technology-using consumer base. When Apple released the iPhone 3 in China in January 2008, China's mobile phone consumers transitioned en masse to smartphones, setting the stage for explosive growth in mobile e-commerce – and the generation of the data that would fuel China's AI development.

The penetration of e-commerce in China's economy soared from a negligible share in 2009 to China's e-commerce as a share of retail sales matching the United States in 2013, to growing 50% larger by 2016, when it surpassed US sales in absolute terms (Figure 12.4).

China started to show up on the technology radar screen – and the United States was watching. However, notwithstanding China's impressive progress, the United States could still rely comfortably on the fact that, at the firm level, it had the dominant players. Its FAANG (Facebook, Apple, Amazon, Netflix, and Google) corporations still dominated the digital world while China's BAT (Baidu, Alibaba, and Tencent) companies were primarily limited to the Chinese market. Moreover, the United States dominated high technology – as late as 2016, China's international earnings on IP were little more than US$1 billion, compared to US earnings of US$125 billion.

That being said, the United States did start to take action.

3.3 The groundwork is laid for confrontation on the battleground of technology

As early as 2008, under the George W. Bush administration, the US Committee on Foreign Investment in the United States (CFIUS) had started to investigate Chinese acquisitions in the United States (Figure 12.5). However, the US

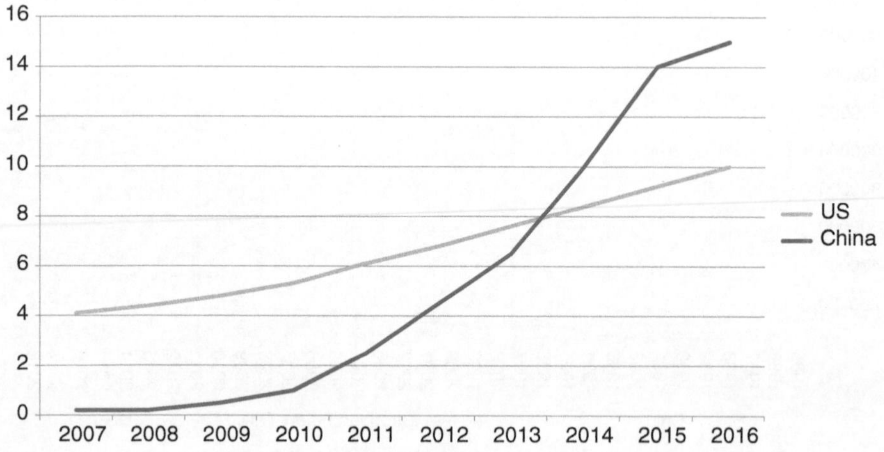

Figure 12.4 E-commerce revenues as share of total retail sales, 2007–2016.
Source: Reproduced from Zhang and Chen (2019), based on Alibaba data.

accommodation of China's self-proclaimed 'peaceful rise' symbolically ended with the US 'pivot to Asia' as the signature foreign policy move of the incoming Obama administration in 2009. This pivot to Asia had both a geopolitical element and a geo-economic element.

As regards the former, Admiral Willard, the incoming US commander in the Pacific in 2009, stated that

> In the past decade or so, China has exceeded most of our intelligence estimates of their military capability and capacity, every year. They've grown at an unprecedented rate in those capabilities. And, they've developed some asymmetric capabilities that are concerning to the region, some anti-access capabilities and so on.
>
> (Cited in Krepinevich, 2010, p. 13, note 20)

The US response was the adoption of a new Air-Sea Battle doctrine to project force in the West Pacific (Krepinevich, 2010; Ford, 2017).

As regards the latter, from the moment the United States joined the Trans-Pacific Partnership (TPP) negotiations in 2009, it made clear that it would be the one 'writing this century's rules for the world economy' (Rodiles, 2019). Notably, those rules were framed for the emerging DDE as they included provisions for the free flow of data across borders, a general prohibition on data localisation requirements, and stronger protection for IP rights, including substantially broadened trade secrets protection, a form of IP of particular importance to data and algorithms built on data that are generally not patented.

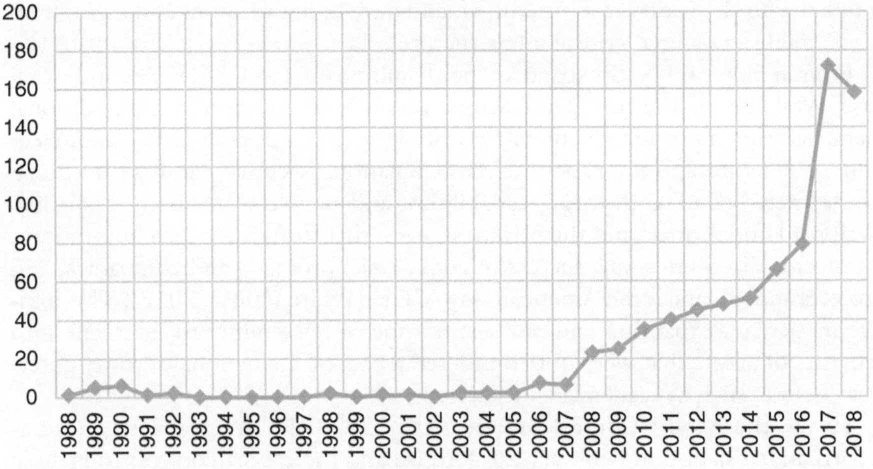

Figure 12.5 Number of CFIUS investigations, 1988–2016.
Sources: For 1988–2005, see Table 2.1 in Graham and Marchick (2006); for 2006–2008, see CFIUS (2009); for 2009–2017, see Congressional Research Service (2020); and for 2018, see CFIUS (2018).

Early on, the Obama administration commissioned a study by the United States International Trade Commission (USITC) on China's IP protection. The USITC report suggested that China observing the US-level of IP protection would raise the returns to US corporations significantly (2011, see table 4.1 at p. 4-4 for point estimates). Moreover, through the Obama years, CFIUS investigations grew steadily in number (Figure 12.5).

In 2017, the first year of the Trump administration, the US Trade Representative (USTR) launched an investigation under Section 301 of the Trade Act of 1974 of China's policies on IP, innovation, and technology, including forced technology transfer, unfair licensing requirements, government-backed cybertheft of US trade secrets, and acquisition of US firms with technology and IP. CFIUS investigations spiked and, in November 2017, the Foreign Investment Risk Review Modernization Act (FIRRMA) was introduced to tighten CFIUS scrutiny of foreign investments in 'critical technologies, critical infrastructure' and businesses that may have access to 'sensitive personal data' (Treasury Department, 2018).

The tone of the Trump administration sharpened as the year drew to a close. The December 2017 National Security Strategy (NSS) accused China of stealing 'US intellectual property valued at hundreds of billions of dollars' yearly and using 'sophisticated means' to weaken businesses and the economy through 'economic warfare and other malicious activities' (White House, 2017). The NSS went even deeper, asserting that even 'largely legitimate, legal transfers and relationships' that gained China access to fields, experts, and trusted foundries 'erode America's long-term competitive advantages'. In addition, the US concerns highlighted in the NSS include the ability of China to collect and control information and data, coupled with the widespread uses of AI, and developing weapons and capabilities which might endanger 'critical infrastructure'.

Prominently, the NSS expanded the definition of the US defence industrial base. While before the considered actors were defence companies and traditional manufacturing inputs, the National Security Innovation Base (NSIB) – the collections of all inputs and actors pertinent to US national security – now is considered as the 'network of knowledge, capabilities, and people – including academia, National Laboratories, and the private sector – that turns ideas into innovations, transforms discoveries into successful commercial products and companies, and protects and enhances the American way of life' (White House, 2017). This massive framework expansion laid out a multitude of possibilities to intervene into activities of actors that were not considered a part of the national security enterprise before, such as academia and start-ups.

Finally, the Export Control Reform Act of 2018 (ECRA) was introduced as bipartisan legislation in February 2018 to expand the export controls to include 'foundational' and 'emerging' technologies. In essence, this means that, instead of targeting specific products, the United States can now manage entire technological areas, in particular technologies relating to robotics, 3D printing, quantum computing, advanced materials, surveillance technologies, synthetic biology, and ML among others. The bill became law in August 2018 shortly after the revised FIRRMA took effect.

3.4 The technological trigger

In tandem with its pursuit of developments on the technological front, the Trump administration launched a broad offensive on conventional trade policy. It withdrew the United States from the TPP immediately upon assuming office; launched a renegotiation of the North American Free Trade Agreement (NAFTA) and the Korea–US Free Trade Agreement (KORUS); refused to affirm new WTO Appellate Body members, which resulted in the Appellate Body ceasing to function in December 2019; dusted off dormant aspects of US tradecraft including self-initiated trade remedy actions on solar panels and washing machines; imposed tariffs on steel and aluminium imports based on Section 232 of the Trade Expansion Act of 1962, which allows a president to act unilaterally if national security is at stake (an implausible framing of these trade restrictions, given that they mainly targeted long-time US military allies); and placed a 25% tariff targeting China pursuant to the Section 301 report findings that US exports and foreign sales were hindered by unfair Chinese trade practices related to technology transfer, IP, and innovation.

The evolution of the conventional trade war in parallel with the building momentum on the technological front blurred the issues. For example, in April 2018, the United States imposed export restrictions on a major Chinese cellphone manufacturer, ZTE, for violating US extra-territorial sanctions regarding sales to Iran. These restrictions were rescinded in July 2018 based on the payment of a fine and agreement to a set of conditions (Ballentine, 2018). Trade actions thus tended to dominate perceptions. At the same time, alarm over the consequences for the rules-based system set in motion various efforts to appease the United States on its demands for reform of WTO rules and also to address issues related to China's so-called 'state capitalism', with a major focus on traditional industrial goods, such as steel, where traditional issues, such as state support, were the basis of complaints.

Another development early in 2018, however, appears to have triggered a shift in US policy that would drive the emergence of a full-fledged technology war. In a leaked memo and slide presentation apparently produced by a National Security Council (NSC) official, the situation in the development of 5G telecommunications networks was described in extraordinarily alarming terms. While 4G networks were described as an evolution of 3G, with the main feature being simply faster speeds, 5G was described as much more than simply a 'faster 4G'. Rather, it represented a change of the consequence of the Gutenberg Press. The NSC memo (cited in Blustein, 2019: 247) stated:

> Whoever leads in technology and market share for 5G deployment will have a tremendous advantage towards commanding the heights of the information domain ... everything from automated cars and aircraft to advanced logistics and manufacturing to true [AI] enhanced network combat.

The United States was described as losing in this race, and failure would mean that: 'China will win politically, economically, militarily.'

This perspective appears to have injected new credibility to the ambitious plans that China had laid out in 2015 in its *Made in China 2025* (MIC2025) programme, which had been formulated to avoid China falling into the middle-income trap (Malkin, 2018), and followed up in 2017 in its *New Generation Artificial Intelligence Development Plan* (AI 2030), which aimed to 'seize the historical opportunity' offered by the emergence of a new technology sector that was not yet dominated by others to 'leapfrog' national technological competitiveness by aiming at these new emerging technologies, to build up 'AI first-mover advantage', and to accelerate 'innovation-driven and globally advanced science and technology' development (MOST, 2017). As late as 2017, for example, the EU Chamber of Commerce in China had fretted about the role of government in MIC2025 and the prospect of over-capacity in industry sectors targeted by MIC2025, but it also noted the opportunity for EU suppliers to take part (EU Chamber of Commerce in China, 2017). That perspective changed sharply as 2018 wore on, with increasingly sharp criticism and counter-measures adopted against China.

China was surprised by the reaction since it had modelled MIC2025 on industrial policies pioneered by the United States in its 2011 Advanced Manufacturing Partnership (White House, 2012), which was designed to take advantage of the so-called 'fourth industrial revolution'. Other countries with similar initiatives included Germany with its Industry 4.0; Japan with its 4.1J (Wu, 2016) and

Connected Industries (METI, 2017) programmes; Korea with its Connected Smart Factory (Park, 2016); and Taiwan with its Smart Machine and Productivity 4.0 (Wu, 2016). By December 2018, China quietly dropped the reference to the MIC2025 programme (although it continued to support the initiative).

Importantly, in assigning cause of the subsequent escalation of the bilateral conflict, it is salient to note that the US tariff policies and renegotiation of trade agreements elicited sharp criticism almost universally, including from the US trade policy community, as they were neither sound in design nor effective in achieving their stated objectives – reducing the US bilateral trade deficit, for example. Partly this was because they triggered trade retaliation. The more significant point, however, is that the stakes at play were modest at best and the actual results were negative for the United States, which settled the renegotiation with Korea quietly and quickly and brought the new NAFTA agreement over the finish line to a reaction that was dominated by relief that the outcome was not worse. But this was not the case with the technology issues, which fuelled the escalation of the conflict over the course of 2018 through the first half of 2020.

4 The Great Game

The 'Great Game' is a concept popularised by Rudyard Kipling in his 1901 novel *Kim* to describe the nineteenth-century Anglo-Russian contest over Central Asia and in particular over Afghanistan (see e.g. Yapp, 2001). The Great Game evokes the sense of a great prize fought over by great powers using the full range of their political, diplomatic, and military assets.

There is now a clear understanding that the conflict between the United States and China is not over trade and tariffs or selected products that harm the interests of US manufacturers, but a strategic move by the United States to slow down China's technological advance, which in a surprisingly short time has positioned China to compete head-to-head in at least some technological market segments for economic rents that, although ill-defined at present, promise to be large – too large to be ignored by national strategists. The headlines proclaim: 'A new world war over technology' (Disis, 2020) – and they are not wrong.

As in the nineteenth century version, the twenty-first century is seeing a sophisticated strategic play emerge, involving the full panoply of policies, short of (to this point) outright kinetic war.

The United States has mounted a relentless, comprehensive programme to push back on China's technological advance and to deny it access to technological markets – in particular to the participation of China's national champion, Huawei, in the build out of 5G networks. These measures include the following:

- Explicit prohibitions on the sale of US technology by US firms to an expanding 'entity' list of Chinese firms, with an increasingly wider definition of what constitutes 'US technology' (with an emphasis on computer chips, especially AI chips, and chip manufacturing technology, such as lithographic machines).

- Curtailment of Chinese investment in the United States and forced unwinding of existing investments.
- A 'China Initiative' established by the Justice Department targeting Chinese researchers and professors working in the United States; this initiative included the use of extradition treaties to reach Chinese nationals abroad (which was the basis for the apprehension of Huawei executive Meng Wanzhou).
- Intense diplomatic efforts to restrict Chinese 5G technology deployment in third countries, including promoting the '5G Clean Network' programme (State Department, 2020).
- Programmes to counter China's Belt and Road Initiative (BRI), including the Indo-Pacific Strategy and a Prosper Africa initiative to challenge China's investment-led rise as an economic partner.
- The inclusion of a new measure in the United States-Mexico-Canada Agreement (USMCA), Section 32.10, which signals risk to partners' trade with the United States if they enter into trade agreements with China.
- Persuasion exercised on US financial firms to limit the flow of US finance to Chinese firms.
- A (failed) attempt to exclude Chinese technology experts from participating in international standards-setting bodies.
- Directives to US universities to review their technology partnerships with Chinese entities and, indeed, to withdraw from them on pain of losing US federal government funding.
- Intensified scrutiny of foreign students applying to US universities in the science, technology, engineering, and mathematics (STEM) fields; in particular, the NSS opened the doors to flag some researchers as 'non-traditional intelligence collectors' (White House, 2017).

China, for its part, has moved to boost its R&D efforts in computer chip development. China's President Xi Jinping announced a US$1.4 trillion investment programme over the period to 2025 to promote China's technological independence (*The Economist*, 2020), particularly in technological capacities in which it still trails the United States (Ernst, 2020). China is also undoubtedly wooing third-country suppliers who have powerful incentives to find workarounds to avoid losing their sales in China (a risk that has raised fears in US technology circles that the export restrictions would undermine them: Swanson and McCabe, 2020; The Economist, 2020).

Ultimately, the war is still over trade – the new forms of digital trade that include the capture and monetisation of data and the future deployment of AI. As noted, this trade war was predicted by the explosive emergence of the DDE based on big data, ML, and AI (Ciuriak and Ptashkina, 2018a) – and it has arrived on cue.

The player board is becoming more complex as the war unfolds. The United States presently dominates the digital world outside China. China claims sovereignty over its cyberspace, which it defends behind its Great Firewall. The European Union has some technology assets, but primarily plays in the technology supply chain rather than capturing market share in the data economy; its situation drives it to develop the regulations to minimise the negative impacts of technologies that it does not own, while it develops its own champions in its Digital Single Market. Russia is retreating into a national digital economy primarily out of national security considerations. India has prospects to develop a national digital economy as well, but is caught between the United States (which has the software assets) and China (which can provide the hardware). For the moment Russia is drifting into China's zone of influence and India into that of the United States. Third countries are caught in the crossfire of the battle for influence.

These cyber zones are becoming differentiated in terms of their rules. Ciuriak and Ptashkina (2018b) highlight the differences with respect to data localisation and privacy, net neutrality and competition, contingent work policies, censorship and digital content, and IP rights that are emerging across these zones. Similarly, Aaronson and Leblond (2018) look in detail at how each of the three 'data realms' has adopted a different approach to developing an enabling environment for data-driven sectors, relying on a mix of tax, transparency, IP protection, competition, and data protection policies.

Strategically, the US approach is rooted in reaping the benefits of the first-mover advantage; it thus naturally seeks maximum openness to lock in the competitive advantage of its big tech firms, as it hosts most of the top-ten internet companies, seven of which have the largest market value in the world (Aaronson and Leblond, 2018). The major features of the US model include a relatively loose approach to data privacy regulations (personal data privacy is considered to be a consumer right, but not a fundamental human right); the denial of the principle of net neutrality; and the prohibition of data localisation and source code disclosure requirements. The United States is increasingly seeking to embed some of these provisions in its new trade deals: after withdrawing from the TPP, the language of the TPP's e-commerce chapter was incorporated (with some strengthening) in the USMCA.

China is currently the world's largest digital market and one of the top-three global locations for venture capital in key types of digital technology, hosting one-third of the world's 262 start-ups valued at over US$1 billion (Aaronson and Leblond, 2018). Deeply innovative in its approach to consumer markets, the Chinese digital sector is also highly regulated, with the government playing an active role in supporting the high-tech as an investor, developer, and consumer. China's position on rules regarding the digital economy is broadly defined in the Cybersecurity Law, which requires all firms to store physical data inside the country, establishes conditions for mandatory security inspections of equipment, and provides for mandatory law enforcement and data retention regulations. China openly blocks cross-border data flows, exercises strict censorship, and does not give priority to the protection of personal data. While not being active in writing digital economy provisions into its trade agreements, China seeks to establish technological dominance through its Digital Silk Road initiative, which aims to construct communications networks across the developing world. China plans to build fibre optic cables, mobile structures, and e-commerce links in countries tied to its BRI initiative in order to supplement the physical infrastructure and introduce common technical standards.

European firms did not play a major role in the development of the internet-based economy, and the EU governments act accordingly to minimise the adjustment costs from the digital transformation. Rooted in its roadmap for the Digital Single Market, the European Union's agenda puts primary focus on personal data protection, maintaining strict rules for net neutrality, and is largely silent on data localisation. The focus on domestic regulation, however, has consequences for companies operating in the EU market, regardless of their origin: the General Data Protection Regulation (GDPR) applies 'ex-territorially' to ensure the personal data of EU residents are collected and treated equally by all service providers.

While the three major players have established the general approach to their respective domestic digital structures, there are multiple issues that cannot be reconciled by any single economy. For example, the regulation of AI, given that its development and applications depend in part on cross-border data flows, needs to be addressed as soon as possible, along with a set of general principles to guide the future regulatory architecture, including technological neutrality, precautionary principle, transparency, and clear separation of personal and non-personal data (Ciuriak & Rodionova, 2021). Alongside data transfer rules and IP protection, regulations related to industrial policy, innovation, and subsidies are becoming increasingly important to support the growth of digital economies, while mediating the affected international trade.

This has major implications for the organisation of global trade going forward. This is not the Thucydides Trap (although there is no guarantee that the United States will fall into this trap) – it is driven by technology and can only be contained by an agreed framework for sharing the economic benefits that channel the state-level competition into constructive forms. While the major powers are unlikely to allow rules to determine the distribution of the economic spoils in the new Great Game, once the contest has been effectively settled, it will be in the interests of all to speedily arrive at a multilateral framework to get on with business in the digitally transformed world.

5 Potential policy responses

Since the trade wars are a manifestation of strategic trade and investment policies, the solutions lie fundamentally in the economic sphere and thus should be addressed through the multilateral trade system through what might be labelled a new 'digital round' of WTO negotiations. Following Ciuriak (2019), an indicative list of issues that should be addressed should include the following:

- **Strengthened competition policy measures**: Competition policy was a minor, if thorny, issue in the Uruguay Round and was hived off as one of the so-called 'Singapore Issues' for later negotiation. Today, in the context of 'winner takes most' economics, it is perhaps the most important economic framework issue to be addressed. For example, three prominent issues are competitive neutrality in technology-intensive sectors, competitive access to proprietary data of companies that provide internet 'platforms' (e.g. Google and Facebook and their Chinese counterparts), and the need to shift regulatory attention on mergers and acquisition activity from implications for current market shares (big companies buying big companies) to pre-emptive take-out strategies of established companies buying out upstart technology firms that pose future competitive challenges.
- **New international conventions on IP**: There is a plethora of issues raised by innovation in the DDE to be addressed, including ownership of IP created by AI and ML; shortened protection terms, given the acceleration of innovation; transparency rules related to secrecy of algorithms; and conditions of access to proprietary data.
- **New conventions for rules on data flows across borders**: These rules must reconcile the need to have free flow of data for commercial services (consistent with the WTO General Agreement on Trade in Services, GATS) with the need for fair international sharing of the asset value of data generated by nations. Further, rules should support full security for data as infrastructure of the digitised economy; establish protocols for use of data to protect sovereignty (e.g. where data are deployed for manipulation of elections and the manufacturing of populism); and set norms to limit state surveillance and so-called 'surveillance capitalism'.
- **Reframed disciplines on subsidies and the economic role of the state**: Huge investments are being underwritten by the state under alternative models of state support – specifically, state-owned or state-directed enterprises (the Chinese model) and state-fed enterprises (the American Defense Advanced Research Projects Agency (DARPA) model). Given the potential for market failure in the DDE, such investments make sense at a transformative moment of economic evolution. There is a much greater need for industrial policy space in this emerging economy, which also demands a rethinking of existing norms and the WTO rules that restrict such policies.
- **An updated Agreement on Trade-Related Investment Measures (TRIMS)**: The new TRIMS should, among other things, distinguish between private investment and state investment; recognise that foreign direct investment (FDI) into the knowledge-based economy aims to extract knowledge assets rather than introduce them; recognise the anti-competitive nature of foreign acquisitions of young technology firms by cash-flush tech giants aiming to prevent the emergence of future competition, and provide for policy leeway for developing countries. It should also broker competitive access to the build out of the digital infrastructure (5G networks, in particular, where national security grounds are being used to exclude China's

participation without adjudication), such that third countries are not caught in the vice of a US–China rivalry.

These negotiations would be premised on the understanding that the issues are larger than the US–China conflict and that a framework must be created in which all countries have a mutual stake in ensuring its integrity – rather than a world of what might be termed 'Digitalpolitik' (the digital version of realpolitik; see McDonald and Xiao Mina, 2018), featuring walled-off and warring realms subject to mutual routine attack, with ruinous prospects for all.

References

Aaronson, S. A., & Leblond, P. (2018). Another digital divide: the rise of data realms and its implications for the WTO. *Journal of International Economic Law*, *21*(2), 245–272.

Allison, G. (2017). *Destined for War: Can America and China Escape Thucydides's Trap?* Boston, MA: Houghton Mifflin Harcourt.

Ballentine, C. (2018). US lifts ban that kept ZTE from doing business with American suppliers. *New York Times*, 13 July.

Blustein, P. (2019). *Schism: China, America, and the Fracturing of the Global Trading System.* Waterloo: Centre for International Governance Innovation.

Cadwalladr, C. (2018). 'I created Steve Bannon's psychological warfare tool': Meet the data war whistleblower. *Guardian*, 18 March. Retrieved from www.theguardian.com/news/2018/mar/17/data-war-whistleblower-christopherwylie-faceook-nix-bannon-trump.

Chen, J. (2019). From Mao to Deng: China's changing relations with the United States. The Cold War International History Project, Working Paper 92, Washington, DC: Woodrow Wilson International Center for Scholars, November.

Ciuriak D. (2018a). The economics of data: Implications for the data-driven economy. In R. Medhora (ed.), *Data Governance in the Digital Age: Special Report.* Waterloo: Centre for International Governance Innovation, 16 May.

Ciuriak, D. (2018b). *Rethinking Industrial Policy for the Data-Driven Economy.* CIGI Paper, 192. Waterloo: Centre for International Governance Innovation.

Ciuriak, D. (2019). *World Trade Organization 2.0: Reforming Multilateral Trade Rules for the Digital Age.* CIGI Policy Brief, 152. Waterloo: CIGI.

Ciuriak, D. (2020). Economic rents and the contours of conflict in the data-driven economy. CIGI Paper 245. Waterloo: Centre for International Governance Innovation, 27 July. www.cigionline.org/publications/economic-rents-and-contours-conflict-data-driven-economy

Ciuriak, D., & Ptashkina, M. (2018a). Started the digital trade wars have: Delineating the regulatory battlegrounds. RTA Exchange. Geneva: International Centre for Trade and Sustainable Development.

Ciuriak, D., & Ptashkina, M. (2018b). *The Digital Transformation and the Transformation of International Trade.* RTA Exchange. Geneva: International Centre for Trade and Sustainable Development (ICTSD) and the Inter-American Development Bank (IDB).

Ciuriak, D., & Ptashkina, M. (2020) *Towards a Coherent Regulatory Architecture for Artificial Intelligence.* CIGI Paper 240. Waterloo: Centre for International Governance Innovation.

Ciuriak, D., & Rodionova, V. (2021). Trading AI: Economic interests, societal choices and multilateral rules. Chapter 4 in S.-Y. Peng, C.-F. Lin, and T. Streinz (eds), *Reconfiguring International Economic Law in an AI Era*. Cambridge: Cambridge University Press, forthcoming

Committee on Foreign Investment in the United States (2009). *Committee on Foreign Investment in the United States Annual Report to Congress*. Washington, DC: Government Printing Office.

Committee on Foreign Investment in the United States (2018). *Committee on Foreign Investment in the United States Annual Report to Congress*. Washington, DC: Government Printing Office.

Congressional Research Service (2020). The Committee on Foreign *Investment in the United States (CFIUS)*. RL33388. Washington, DC: Government Printing Office.

Disis, J. (2020). A new world war over technology. *CNN*, 10 July. www.cnn.com/2020/07/10/tech/us-china-global-tech-war-intl-hnk/index.html>.

Elms, D. (2020). Unpacking the Digital Economy Partnership Agreement (DEPA). 28 January. Asian Trade Centre, <http://asiantradecentre.org/talkingtrade/unpacking-the-digital-economy-partnership-agreement-depa>.

Ernst, D. (2020). *Competing in Artificial Intelligence Chips: China's Challenge amid Technology War*. Waterloo: Centre for International Governance Innovation, Special Report.

European Union Chamber of Commerce in China (2017). *2025: Putting Industrial Policy Ahead of Market Forces*. Beijing: European Union Chamber of Commerce in China.

European Commission (2018). WTO reform: EU proposes way forward on the functioning of the Appellate Body. Press release. http://europa.eu/rapid/press-release_IP-18-6529_en.htm

Farrell, M. (2016). How the rest of the world feels about U.S. dominance of the internet. Slate, 18 November. https://slate.com/technology/2016/11/the-u-s-should-stop-lecturing-about-internet-values.html

Ford, J. (2017). The pivot to Asia was Obama's biggest mistake. *The Diplomat*, 21 January.

Goh, E. (2005). Nixon, Kissinger, and the 'Soviet card' in the US opening to China, 1971–1974. *Diplomatic History*, *29*(3), 475–502.

Graham, E. M., & Marchick, D. (2006). *US National Security and Foreign Direct Investment*. Washington, DC: Peterson Institute Press.

Hanson, F. (2012). *Baked in and Wired: eDiplomacy@State*. Washington, DC: Foreign Policy at Brookings.

Krepinevich, A. F. (2010). *Why Air Sea Battle?* Washington, DC: Center for Strategic and Budgetary Assessments.

Malkin, A. (2018). *Made in China 2025 as a Challenge in Global Trade Governance: Analysis and Recommendations*. Waterloo: CIGI.

Mazzucato, M. (2011). The entrepreneurial state. *Soundings*, *49*(49), 131–142.

McDonald, S., & An, X. M. (2018). The war-torn web. *Foreign Policy*, 19 December.

METI (2017). Connected Industries. www.meti.go.jp/english/policy/mono_info_service/connected_industries/index.html

MOST (2017). Next generation artificial intelligence development plan issued by State Council. China Science and Technology Newsletter, 17 (15 September).

Park, S. (2016). Development of innovative strategies for the Korean manufacturing industry by use of the connected smart factory (CSF). *Procedia Computer Science, 91*, 744–750.

Petrov, C. (2020). 25+ impressive big data statistics for 2020. *Techjury*, 1 July. https://techjury.net/blog/big-data-statistics/#gref

Pregelj, V. N. (2001). *Most-Favored-Nation Status of the People's Republic of China*. Congressional Research Service Report to Congress, RL30225. Washington, DC: Government Printing Office.

Rappeport, A. (2019). 19th-century 'humiliation' haunts China-U.S. trade talk. *New York Times*, 27 March.

Rodiles, A. (2019). After TPP is before TPP: Mexican politics for economic globalization and the lost chance for reflection. Chapter 28 in B. Kingsbury, D. M. Malone, P. Mertenskötter, R. B. Stewart, T. Streinz, & A. Sunami (eds), *Megaregulation Contested: Global Economic Ordering After TPP*, 606–622. Oxford: Oxford University Press.

Rodrik, D. (2017). *Straight Talk on Trade: Ideas for a Sane World Economy*. Princeton, NJ: Princeton University Press.

Ruskola, T. (2005). Canton is not Boston: The invention of American imperial sovereignty. *American Quarterly*, *57*(3), 859–884.

S&P (2019). A new great game: China, the U.S., and Technology. 14 May. S&P Ratings China Senior Analyst Group. www.spglobal.com/en/research-insights/featured/a-new-great-game-china-the-u-s-and-technology.

State Department (2020). *5G Clean Networks*. www.state.gov/5g-clean-networks/.

Swanson, A., and McCabe, D. (2020). Trump effort to keep U.S. tech out of China alarms American Firms. *New York Times*. 16 February.

The Economist (2020). America's latest salvo against Huawei is aimed at chipmaking in China: It may push the industry out of America, too. 23 May.

Treasury Department (2018). *Summary of the Foreign Investment Risk Review Modernization Act of 2018*. Washington, DC: Treasury Department. www.treasury.gov/resource-center/international/Documents/Summary-of-FIRRMA.pdf

USITC (2011). *China: Effects of Intellectual Property Infringement and Indigenous Innovation Policies on the U.S. Economy*. Investigation No. 332-519, Publication 4226. Washington, DC: United States International Trade Commission, May. Viola, R. (2018). European dimension of the digital economy. 28 September. https://ec.europa.eu/digital-single-market/en/blogposts/european-dimension-digital-economy

Wang, D. (2003). The discourse of unequal treaties in modern China. *Pacific Affairs*, *76*(3), 399–425.

Webster, G., Creemers, R., Triolo, P., and Kania, E. (2017). Full translation: China's 'New Generation Artificial Intelligence Development Plan'. New America, 1 August. www.newamerica.org/cybersecurity-initiative/digichina/blog/full-translation-chinas-new-generation-artificial-intelligence-development-plan-2017/.

Wei, C. N. (2012). Cross-strait relations today: Challenges and opportunities. In Z. Q. Zhu. (ed.), *New Dynamics in East Asian Politics: Security, Political Economy, and Society* (pp. 83–101). New York: Continuum.

Wen, Y. (2016). China's rapid rise. *Federal Reserve Bank of St. Louis The Regional Economist*, *24*(2), 8–14.

White House (2012). White House advanced manufacturing initiatives to drive innovation and encourage companies to invest in the United States. Fact Sheet. https://obamawhitehouse.archives.gov/the-press-office/2012/07/17/fact-sheet-white-house-advanced-manufacturing-initiatives-drive-innovati

White House (2017). National security strategy. www.whitehouse.gov/wp-content/uploads/2017/12/NSS-Final-12-18-2017-0905.pdf.

White House (2019a). Executive order on maintaining American leadership in artificial intelligence. www.whitehouse.gov/presidential-actions/executive-order-maintaining-american-leadership-artificial-intelligence/.

White House (2019b). America will dominate the industries of the future. Fact sheet. www.whitehouse.gov/briefings-statements/america-will-dominate-industries-future/.

World Bank (2020). World Development Indicators. Data Catalog https://datacatalog.worldbank.org/dataset/world-development-indicators

World Intellectual Property Organization (2020). WIPO IP Statistics Data Center. www3.wipo.int/ipstats/.

Wright, Q. (1943). The end of extraterritoriality in China. *American Journal of International Law*, *37*(2), 286–289.

Wu, M. (2019). China's rise and the growing doubts over trade multilateralism. In M. A. Crowley (ed.), *Trade War: The Clash of Economic Systems Endangering Global Prosperity* (pp. 101–110). Vox eBook.

Wu, M. J. (2016). Smart machine and productivity 4.0 in Taiwan: Now and future. Presentation, 30 May. Industrial Development Bureau, MOEA.

Yapp, M. (2001). The legend of the Great Game. Proceedings-British Academy, *111*, 179–198)..

YCharts (2020). *S&P 500 Market Cap*. Retrieved from https://ycharts.com/indicators/sp_500_market_cap.

Zhang, M. L., & Chen, M. S. (2019). China's digital economy: Opportunities and risks. IMF Working Paper, 19/16. Washington, DC: International Monetary Fund..

Zuboff, S. (2019). *The Age of Surveillance Capitalism: The Fight for a Human Future at the New Frontier of Power*. New York: Public Affairs.

Conclusion

Rahul Nath Choudhury

Since the beginning of the trade war between the USA and China, a body of literature has been devoted to the study of this area. The literature has been largely dominated by commentaries or opinion pieces in the popular media. In the academic space, the existing studies have mainly focused on its impact on the bilateral trade between the USA and China, while a few of them have attempted to explore how the trade war is shaping the new world order for trade and diplomacy. There was a notable gap in the literature assessing the impact of this trade conflict on the regional perspective and on the individual countries. There was hardly any study that examines the impact of this war on the South Asian region. This book has attempted to bridge the gap.

China being connected to this region through its vast border has been an old trading partner of almost all the countries in the region. This increases the importance of studying the impact of the trade war from the South Asian perspective. This book will help the policymakers of the region to formulate their trade and foreign policy effectively in the future. This will help them to learn better trade negotiation tools from future trade agreements. For the students of international economics and foreign policy and the practitioners, this book will be a primary source of academic reference.

This book tries to evaluate the impact of the trade war on the global economy with a special focus on the South Asian region. The impact of the trade tussle on the ongoing negotiation of RCEP has been analysed in this book. Further, this book examines the role of the technology companies in this tussle. In our introduction we provided an overview and described how the trade war started between these two world economic powers. In this concluding chapter, we will discuss what we have learned.

1 The impact on the global economy

In the first chapter of this book, exploring the effects of all policy measures in global trade wars, and using the GTAP model, the authors have shown an ambiguity in the overall positive effect on the countries other than those that have increased tariffs and a negative effect that is negligible for some and prominent for others. They forecast a global GDP to fall by 0.16% or nearly $150 billion by

2020. In Asia and the Pacific alone, the decline is 0.12% of GDP, or $43 billion. The United States experienced the largest decline, with an estimated decline of 0.65% of GDP, at more than $120 billion. They commented that countries like Vietnam, Kyrgyzstan, and Mongolia are all expected to benefit from the trade war to the tune of more than 0.5% of their respective GDPs.

The second chapter suggests the trade war has a far-reaching impact on the emerging economies, evaluating the scenario based on the available trade balance data for India–China Trade, India–US Trade and India–ROA (Rest of Asia without China), and India–ROW (without ROA, China, and the US). The chapter reveals that the benefit to economies like Korea, Canada, and India ranges from $0.9 billion to $1.5 billion. The South-East Asian countries have also largely benefited from the trade war. The ongoing US-China trade war has resulted in a sharp decline in their bilateral trade, while higher prices for consumers and increased imports from countries not directly involved in the trade war have been recorded. The trade war ultimately hurt both the countries and consumers in the US bore the fullest burden of tariffs as their associated costs have largely been passed down to them in the form of higher prices. The same is not exactly the case in China.

Next, we find India is the single major exporter to the USA from the South Asian region. Moreover, there exists a structural increase in South Asia's export to the US in 2002, which coincides with a structural increase in India's exports to the US. As far as South-East Asian economies are concerned; Malaysia, Thailand, Singapore, and Vietnam are the major exporters to the US. The US's exports to South Asia reveal that Sri Lanka, India, and Pakistan are the top importers of US goods. However, Thailand's imports from the US exceed those by China and any other South or South-East Asian country. Other than Thailand, Vietnam is a key importer from the South-East Asian bloc.

Chapter 4 reiterated the fact that imports and exports both declined after the commencement of trade war between US and China. US imports from China declined by 16.20%, and US exports to China declined by 11.21% between 2018 and 2019. The chapter warns that the trade war will negatively impact on trust in the WTO by its member nations, and will also reduce the free trade between countries, which is one of the basic principles of the WTO.

2 Impact of South Asian region

The second section of the book analyses the impact of the trade war on the individual countries in the South Asian region. Examining the Indian context, the authors conclude that the US's imposition of higher tariffs to Chinese import may bring trade diversion benefits to India. Their findings indicate that such effects in favour of India have taken place in chemicals, metal ore. India also has an opportunity to export products like vehicles, fibre optical cables, and soybeans to China and commodities like electrical machinery, solar panels, and toys to the USA. The chapter warns that China may divert some of its exports to India in the near future.

Chapter 6 highlighted the importance of the intermediate goods in India's trade basket with China and the USA. We find India's imports of intermediate goods accounted for 83% of its total merchandise imports in 2017, while imports of final and capital goods made up 6% and 11% respectively in 2017. Also, in 2017, 60% of export value was in exports of intermediate goods. By comparison, the share of final and capital goods reached 33% and 6% respectively in 2017. The authors record India has consistently been a net importer of intermediate goods over the period 2008–17. Further, it is a net exporter of final goods and a net importer of capital goods for the period of 2008–17.

In Chapter 7, we explored how a trade war might affect the supply chain dynamics and investment patterns of Bangladesh and how this country might emerge as a potential winner from the continuing trade conflict. However, the author reminds us that, to materialise such a potential, Bangladesh will require prompt policy action and rapid infrastructure modernisation. Bangladesh will face competition from many countries who are working round the clock to fill the vacuum of China's supply, notably in the South-East Asian region. Even though Bangladesh has tremendous potential to emerge as a desired destination for the investor, it will largely depend on the policy regime, whether it can offer a conducive business environment, and the readiness of its institutions.

The next chapter throws light on how Sri Lanka can accrue benefits from the progressing trade tussle. The authors highlighted that Sri Lanka needs to bring investment and related policy reforms to boost exports and create a favourable business environment to attract investment into the country. The authors also warn that prolonged trade war could dampen world trade and economic growth, reducing the gains from the trade dispute.

3 Connecting the dots for the RCEP and other FTAs

The complex relationship between the trade war and RCEP and its impact is studied in the third section of this book. Here, it is recognised that RCEP-I members (excluding India) are linked with the US through various channels, though it appears the importance of the US has fallen vis-à-vis China over the years in terms of exports, imports, foreign direct investment flows, and intellectual property creation. In terms of certain indicators of GVCs too, it appears the US, except with the ASEAN and South Korea, is relatively less connected with the RCEP-I. China has increased its influence on the RCEP-I in the last two to three decades in terms of all the indicators under consideration. The US-China Agreement may create trade diversion but there could be trade creation effects on the RCEP-I as well. The US-China Agreement may have a differential impact on the individual RCEP-I countries through various modes and routes.

Another chapter in this section discussed how the FTA partners of the USA and China will be affected by the trade war. This chapter investigated the potential trade diversion from the USA and China to their FTA partners. Analysing three important sectors (automobile, electrical machinery and iron and steel), the study shows the Chinese direction of trade moves towards its FTA partners and are greater in all selected sectors than those of the US to its FTA partners. It has been observed that the reliance of the US on China has not reduced even after the tariffs were increased but China has reduced its dependency on the US marginally and diverted trade towards its FTA partners.

4 Technology war in the guise of a trade war

In the final section of the book, we discussed how the trade war had taken the shape of a technology war. The US was annoyed with the way China was favouring its domestic tech giants at the cost of the US firms. Within a decade, Chinese firms started challenging US dominance in the technology sector, which has been established over a long period of time. In modern areas like the 5G network, Chinese firms even superseded US giants. However, the US has always maintained that Chinese growth in this area was a result of forged technology, IPR theft, and violation of patents. The main complaint of EU and US-based enterprises (having a joint venture with Chinese firms) in China is that it treats them unfairly and forces them to share their trade and technology secrets with Chinese firms. An additional common complaint is that, in many sectors, foreign firms are not permitted to hold a majority stake in a joint venture.

From the last chapter of the book, we find that, in order to command the new technology heights, a new global Great Game that is unfolding. Worldwide, countries are formulating strategies to claim a foothold in the new digital economy, playing the hands that they have been dealt. The United States is seeking to maintain its technological leadership and the ascendancy of its roster of global digital economy champions. This chapter also highlighted how China becomes a major player in the global technology trade with large expenditures in R&D (percentage of GDP) and registering a higher number of patents. The chapter creditably captures the geopolitics revolving around the technology industry between the USA and China and its responses in the WTO.

Based on the analyses in this book, we may conclude that the trade war between these two nations is resulting in lower trade, higher prices for consumers, and trade diversion effects. Businesses in many countries have been affected severely. The existing evidence reveals the cost of the tariffs has been generally passed down to consumers. If the trade tussle prolongs it will have serious consequences to both the USA and China, and the global economy will also suffer. The world is already facing a global pandemic COVID-19, which is affecting all the countries in the world to varying degrees. And if the trade war continues, it will have a devastating effect all across the world, especially for trading partners who are directly or indirectly connected to them. Hence, it is an urgent need in the interest of the world economy to find an amicable solution to this war through diplomatic discussion.

Index

5G technology 129, 230

America first 19, 125
Asian Infrastructure Investment Bank 24
Association of Southeast Asian Nations 26, 175, 180, **182**, **185**, **191**

Baltic Dry Index 3
Banana war 125
Blacklist 217
Belt and Road Initiative 19, 29, 131, 147
Broad Economic Categories 97, **120**
BRICS 24

Capital goods 109, **110**
Chicken war 125
Chittagong Port 132
Chow Forecast 39, 43, 50, **56**, **63**
Computable General Equilibrium 12, 14, 139
COVID 126, 145, 176, 197, 219
CUSUM 38, **39–54**

Data Driven Economy 231, 236
Deadweight loss 3
Digital economy 230
Digital Economic Partnership Agreement 230
Digital Silk Road initiative 243

Final goods 106, **108**
Finger–Kreinin Index 142
Forced Technology Transfer 222, 224, 226
Foreign Invested Enterprises 222
Free Trade 73

Garment 140
General Agreement on Tariffs and Trade 13, 113
General Data Protection Regulation 243
Generalized System of Preferences 113, 142
Global Trade Alert 219
Global Trade Analysis Project 14
Global Value Chain 20, 27, 28, 97, 99
Gulf Co-operation Council 13

Indigenous firms 223
Infringement 223
Innovation **193**
Internet Freedom 230
Intermediate goods 105, **106**
Intellectual Property 68, 191–2, **194**

MERCOSUR 12
Most Favoured Nation 71, 113
Multinational Corporations 68

North American Free Trade Agreement 99

Official Development Assistance 14
Opium Wars 232

Pasta war 125
Patent **192**
Preferential Trade Agreement 13
Protectionism 219

Ready Made Garments 130
Regional Comprehensive Economic Partnership 175, 178, 181
Regional Value Chain 84, 86, 189
Relative Export Competitive Pressure Index 142

Revealed Comparative Advantage 82–3, 89, 143

Soybeans 130
Spaghetti/noodle bowl 181
State-Owned Enterprises 220

Technological Leadership 230
Technology Transfer 217
Technology war 217
Theory of Protection 32
Trade Diversion 81
Trade and Investment Framework Agreement 142
Trade Secrets 221
Treaty of Wanghia 232

Unfair Trade 147
United Nations Conference on Trade and Development 3
United States International Trade Commission 68
US-China Agreement 175

Value Added Tax 13

World Trade Organisation 73, 75

ZTE 236